Praise for *Cleaning*

"I've always been envious c
who could observe every fac
every back corner, unchaineu ю any ...,...
With Cleaning the Kingdom, I can now step into the
shoes of those who do the dirty work that helps millions
to enjoy the magic. I'm ready for my dustpan!"
— David Koenig, author of *Mouse Tales*

"Ask any Disneyland cast member, Who see's the most, gets
to experience the most, and interacts with the most excitement at the park, and they will point towards the custodian.
In *Cleaning the Kingdom* you'll discover what's both onstage
and backstage, stories of celebrities experiencing Disneyland and what it's like to call The Happiest Place on Earth,
your second home."
— Nate Parrish - Co Host WEDWay Radio Podcast

"Have you ever wondered what it would be like to work
at Disneyland? Have you ever thought, how does Disney
have so many caring Cast Members? This book partially
pulls back the curtains to show you the lives of two former Custodial Cast Members. This is not a "tell all" book,
but they do share their experiences and love for the
Park. You will have a new respect for Disney Cast Members after reading this book."
— Russell Flores, author of *Seen, Un-Seen Disneyland*

(Continued on the next page)

Praise for *Cleaning The Kingdom*

"Talk about Disneyland with a friend, and inevitably the conversation turns to how remarkably clean the place is. Drop something on the ground intentionally or not, and within moments, the evidence of your vandalism will have vanished into thin air, thanks to the incredibly dedicated and observant custodial staff at Walt's original magical kingdom. With this book, Lynn and Ken take those powers of observation and turn them into a microscope through which you can inspect the hidden, little-known aspects of maintaining and putting the polish on the world's most beloved theme park."

— Jeff Baham, author of *The Unauthorized Story of Walt Disney's Haunted Mansion*

CLEANING
THE Kingdom

Insider Tales of Keeping Walt's Dream Spotless

by Ken Pellman and Lynn Barron

Cover and Artwork by AnaKaren Aguirre

Synergy Books Publishing, USA

Cleaning the Kingdom

Synergy Books Publishing
P .O. Box 911232
St. George, Utah 84791
www.synergy-books.com

ISBN: 978-1-936434-75-6

Printed in the United States of America

Cleaning the Kingdom

DISCLAIMER

Except where otherwise noted, this work is based on the personal experiences, and the impressions and recollections thereof, of the authors and may involve subjective opinions with which some may differ. But those other people are wrong if they do.

This work is in no way authorized by, endorsed by, nor affiliated or associated with any member of the extended Disney family, nor Disney Enterprises, Inc., Walt Disney Parks and Resorts, the Disneyland Resort, The Walt Disney Company (or any division, subsidiary, or department thereof), nor the Extremely Secret Royal Eternal Fraternal Order of the Armadillos.

All intellectual property contained herein remains the property of respective owners. Certain registered trademarks are used just as a news report or opinion column would use them. All references to such trademarked properties are used in accordance with the Fair Use Doctrine and are not meant to imply this book is a Disney product for advertising or other commercial purposes.

All images used were chosen from Public Domain Sources or from the authors' personal photographs, except artwork commissioned by the authors and images identified by source permissions.

The publisher and authors assume no responsibility for errors or omissions. Neither is any liability or responsibility assumed for damages resulting, or alleged to result, directly or indirectly from the use of the information contained herein.

Some procedures, policies, locations, and other elements described herein may have subsequently changed, and we may or may not note those changes.

Some names have been redacted or changed to protect the innocent, the not-so-innocent, and the embarrassed.

Dedication

To all who have kept the Kingdom Clean,
especially Walt

Cleaning the Kingdom

Contents

Foreword by Disney Legend Rolly Crump...7
Preface By Author David W. Smith...8
Introduction...9

Chapter 1 Nobody Does it Better...18
Chapter 2 Perks and benefits...33
Chapter 3 A Typical Day...71
Chapter 4 It's Not Such a Dirty Job...102
Chapter 5 Disgusting Things...111
Chapter 6 Bowl Games (Restrooms)...127
Chapter 7 Land By Land – Westside...145
Chapter 8 Land By Land – Eastside...185
Chapter 9 Landless...217
Chapter 10 Business is Always Picking Up...241
Chapter 11 Be Our Guest...261
Chapter 12 We Have Character...293
Chapter 13 Whistle While You Work...317
Chapter 14 Eyewitness to History...343
Chapter 15 Rubbing Elbows...353
Chapter 16 Missions and Colonizations...375
Chapter 17 The Empire Strikes Back...385
Chapter 18 Apart of the Magic...389

Appendix 1 The Magic Mishandled and Restored...405
Appendix 2 How to Be Safe...423

Afterword...437
Glossary...440

About the Authors...451
Acknowledgements...455

Recommending Reading and Listening...457

Cleaning the Kingdom

Foreword

Having worked for 3 years as Supervising Art Director at Disneyland I Had a close working relationship with all the departments in the park, including Custodial. I know everyone, including me, took pride in the park. We were dedicated to preserving the image Walt envisioned.

I can remember there were times I would drive my car through the park in the early morning before the gates opened and so as not to allow even the slightest drop of oil to drip onto the street, I would keep a large piece of cardboard with me to slip under the engine whenever the car was parked.

I've always had tremendous respect for the Cast Members responsible for maintaining the reputation for cleanliness that Disneyland has always had and I know Walt would be proud of to this day.

After reading "Cleaning the Kingdom" I have an even greater appreciation for one of, if not, the most important departments in the park. This book allows us to take an in depth, behind the scenes, journey into the land of Custodial. It's written with humor, attention to detail and a 'No subject too delicate to touch' approach.

So climb aboard and be ready to learn all there is to know about what it takes to make the happiest place on earth to, very possibly, the cleanest place on earth. Be prepared to be impressed with the men and women responsible for keeping it that way.

Rolly Crump
Disney Legend

Preface

As publisher of *Cleaning the Kingdom*, I have a vested interest in the book as many would understand. However, as a former Disneyland Cast Member and author of several books on Disney, I have a deeper interest in this book based on a truly personal level.

My six years working at Disneyland, working such attractions as Pirates of the Caribbean, Keel Boats, Canoes and the Disneyland Monorail, literally put me on center stage, a stage that was kept immaculate by an army of custodial and maintenance Cast Members. Where many of us were limited in experiences based on the ride, show, store or restaurant we worked, the Cast Members who kept the Kingdom spotless were right there, in the trenches, interacting with Disneyland guests in a wide variety of locations and situations.

Cleaning the Kingdom is the first of its kind; a memoir by several of those prominent Cast Members who walked among the masses, sharing stories that are as magical as they are revealing.

It isn't rare to overhear guests comment on the cleanliness of Disneyland. In fact, Disneyland is often referred to as the cleanest Theme Park in the world. But, maintaining this reputation is more than sweeping streets or sidewalks or wiping down tables. Ken Pellman and Lynn Barron are here to take you to a deeper level of clean, so to speak! You will indeed learn NEW things about the Park!

Insider stories of those who work at Disneyland are often as fascinating as learning about Walt Disney himself, or discovering a Park Secret or a "Hidden Mickey". *Cleaning the Kingdom* is full of amazing stories; funny, surprising, and even some that reveal the human side of humanity when it comes to unanticipated things that people do!

Get ready to become enlightened and amused! And, at the same time, discover what it really takes to keep the Kingdom Clean!

David W. Smith, Publisher, Synergy Books Publishing
   Creator, Co-Author: HIDDEN MICKEY Mysteries
   Author, In the Shadow of the Matterhorn

Introduction

The khaki-clad fellow slipped and fell in the noisy, dimly-lit cave as poisonous snakes slithered nearby. My heart skipped a beat.

I started to go to him, but before I could reach him, a machine weighing thousands of pounds rolled over him, crushing him.

I hesitated, shocked.

Everything went silent and overhead lights turned on.

There, in front of me, was a dead ride operator, his body broken by what, in essence, was a giant toy. A complicated toy, a very expensive toy, and now a killer toy.

That's going to be an awful cleanup.

But that hadn't actually happened.

Those were just the thoughts that flashed through my mind as I prepared myself to see another human being squashed like a bug. This was the moment that could turn into Disneyland folklore. I could picture the paperwork, the courtroom testimony.

Heavy pieces of very expensive machinery were thundering by every eighteen seconds.

That can be an eternity. It can seem like a split second. It depends on the circumstances. At the moment, it seemed like an impossibly short span.

The Ride Operator was preparing to dash onto the active track of the Indiana Jones Adventure and grab a guest's backpack and get out of the way before another troop transport thundered over it.

If he were to slip, which was a very real possibility given water bottles, candy wrappers, or hydraulic fluid that may have spilled onto the track, he could be killed or maimed.

Fellow Sweeper Francisco and I were poised to respond if the Ride Op did slip.

I would run out and drag him back. Francisco would call the tower. That was the plan.

A transport passed, the Ride Op darted out to the track, grabbed the backpack, and scurried back to us.

Our task was completed successfully.

We returned the backpack to the guest. Although the contents, including a dental retainer, were somewhat mashed, none of us had been. We even got a small reward from an Attractions manager for going out of our way for a guest.

If we'd done the same thing just a few short years later, we would have been fired and Disneyland would quite likely have been fined.

But this was a different era. Things were a little less formal, a little more free. We often used that freedom to come up with new efficiencies or solve an issue for a guest. We'd help out other Departments if we could - even those popcorn-pushers in Outdoor Vending.

In Disneyland Custodial, we had a can-do attitude.

If you let us know where you'd be, we'd figure out how to meet whatever need was created as a result of your event or venue.

Why We Became "A Part of the Magic"

I (Lynn) hired into Disneyland twice. The first was in 1991 into Foods the second was in 1998 into Custodial. I wanted to work at Disneyland because I loved the atmosphere, the history, and memories. The training when I came through was two days, not including restroom training. The first day we did much classroom training, then the second day was in the area sweeping, and dumping trash. I remember clearly that first day of training; our trainers took us over to the wishing well near Sleeping Beauty Castle to get our pictures taken. I still have that picture today. It's neat to look back on that day, and think I had no idea what kind of journey I was about to begin.

My first Summer season, we were encouraged to work six days per week, so got plenty Disneyland atmosphere!.

Not everyone has had the desire to work at Disneyland. There's no doubt working there wasn't for everyone. Of those who did hire in, some might have applied because they lived close and had friends who worked there. Others might have applied because of the perks. Still others might have because they already had a love for the place, like the authors of this book.

It was good to have certain qualities, which would make one a better Cast Member, and some of those were patience, friendliness, and the abilities to be politely assertive, give and take directions, be pleasant to others even when having a bad day, and to function well in crowds. It helped to have an appreciation for the place that Walt Disney dreamed and built, too.

Both of your authors grew up going to Disneyland and became fans. I (Lynn) remember as a child I had a big wall map of Disneyland near my bed. I would stare at the map and plan out my next visit, which was normally once a year.

Both of us have our own stories of our love for Disneyland, and we both appreciate the fine details and overall environment of the park. We both have big collections of Disneyana and Disney-related books. Our continued enthusiasm comes through on our podcast, The Sweep Spot.

I (Ken) was treated to many Disneyland visits throughout my childhood. I can remember seeing new and classic Disney films in the theaters, catching Disney programs on television, and reading books featuring Disney characters.

We lived close enough to Disneyland to make a day, once or twice a year, driving there in the morning, spending the day there, and driving home at night. It was close, but far enough away that going there felt like a special trip. I don't recall ever going to Anaheim for any other reason. When I was twelve, my parents decided they'd burn through some money set aside for vacations by buying Disneyland Annual Passports for the whole family. There were just two passes for adults: Annual Passports and Seasonal Passports, and the Annual was just $100.00 (with parking included and no blockouts!) However, with two parents and four children, it was still a considerable chunk of change.

My parents figured we'd all get sick of Disneyland by visiting once every week or two for that year, and then Disneyland might be something we'd return to if we were hosting family from out of state.

Little did they suspect!

I tried to learn everything I could about the place: the history, what was happening, how it was happening, why it was happening, and what was planned for the next several years.

After renewing our passes four times, I was 17, thoroughly enthusiastic about Disneyland, and old enough to be a Disneyland Cast Member – with the age requirement having been lowered from 18.

I grew up in a city referred to affectionately, and derisively, as Mayberry. It was an upper middle-class childhood, with my parents both being transplants from the Midwest to the Los Angeles area, like Walt Disney himself. We lived there for my entire childhood, almost all of it on a street you've probably seen in a movie or television commercial. There always seemed to be some sort of filming going on in the neighborhood. Marty McFly roamed those very streets in the same days that I did, as did Teen Wolf. Movies and television were inseparably tied to Disneyland in my mind, and Disneyland had always existed, as far as I was concerned. I was collecting Disneyana, I was hungry for information about Walt Disney and the Company, I had been a student filmmaker for years, I contemplated the principles of theme park design and had even been given a private, individual tour of the largest independent theme park design firm in the world, and I liked to use props and special effects makeup to put on a show for trick-or-treaters every Halloween. I was setting my sights on theme park design (Imagineering) as career.

Yet, this privileged boy applied to be an hourly, front-line Disneyland Cast Member and was willing to take on *any* assignment, no matter how humble.

In June of 1990, I was assigned to Disneyland Day Custodial Sweeping at $5.05 per hour. The previous summer, my friends and I had collected armloads of trash, left behind by other guests, to throw away as we waited over and over again to ride the newly opened Splash Mountain. Now I was going to get paid to do that.

And that's how I began my fifteen years and two days as a Disneyland Cast Member.

I could have found comparable monetary compensation close to home, but not a comparable experience.

Friendship

Your authors met each other while working together in Disneyland Day Custodial Sweeping. We quickly realized we had much in common, especially our interest in Disneyland, and became friends. We'd take breaks and lunches together whenever we were able to.

Sometimes, we'd help each other out because we were Leads in neighboring areas. We could shoot the breeze and consult with each other about handling people on our crew.

We both became fathers around the same time.

After we went from being "A Part of the Magic" to being "Apart of the Magic", Ken quitting Disneyland in 2005 and Lynn in 2007, the friendship continued. Lynn started a podcast called "The Sweep Spot" and Ken was a frequent guest co-host, and then became the regular co-host.

The time was right to co-author a book about our experiences working at "The Happiest Place on Earth".

Cleaning the Kingdom

Why We Wrote This Book

Working in Disneyland Custodial was an experience like no other. The well-deserved reputation of effectively keeping Disneyland spotless wasn't always easy to honor, but it was a lot of fun at times. It could also be dreadfully monotonous at other times. And still other times it was grueling. It was everything about working a service industry job and an office job rolled in together, set in a world-famous fantasy environment.

Walt Disney died before we were born, so we only know him through what he left behind. While we were not able to work under Walt, we worked with people who did.

My (Lynn's) love and respect for Disneyland grew over the years working there. Learning what it was really like behind-the-scenes didn't ruin it for me, but enhanced the magic. It was a job, yes, and not every day was hunky dory. There were days I didn't want to be there, or days I was frustrated, but there were also great days. For the most part it was a great job.

I (Ken) realized it was impossible to see Disneyland the same way again. Something was lost in that, but much more was gained.

We were there through a time of tremendous change, with some serious growing pains along the way. Disneyland went from being a theme park with a hotel to a Resort with two theme parks, three hotels, and a shopping and dining district. That was why I was able to stand in the middle of a closed West Street in the middle of the day, which was very strange. The street had been taken over and traffic had been shifted west to a new street. It one of many unusual experiences collected in my memory.

Things changed because of technology, expansion, changes in Disneyland leadership that brought a different culture, periods of high Cast turnover, responses to terrorism, and increased safety regulations.

We have stories to tell that we think you'll appreciate.

How to Read This Book

It is very important to read this book where other people will see you reading it and ask about it, so we can sell more.

You might want to familiarize yourself with the terms in the Glossary, or flip back to the Glossary if there's a word or phrase you don't understand.

This book is full of personal experiences and opinions, and since there are two authors, we distinguish ourselves by writing something like:

I (Ken) was addicted to cotton candy.

Now, I wasn't really addicted to cotton candy. That stuff makes an awful mess and I was glad it wasn't sold at Disneyland when I started.

Most of this is written in the past-tense, because these are the things we experien*ced* and how things *were*. They aren't all necessarily the same now.

For the most part, the chapters are stand-alone and you should feel free to skip or save for later any chapter that doesn't interest you at the moment (although we can't imagine you won't find each and every chapter intensely fascinating and entertaining) or that you think may gross you out. We've tried to keep everything that might disgust you in Chapter 5. The title and introductions to the chapter should make it easy for you to know what to expect in any given chapter.

In describing how the various areas of the park were kept clean, we start with Main Street, then go on to Adventure/Frontier. If we described a process in detail there, we don't repeat it for every area, so reading the earlier parts of Chapter 7 can help you better understand the rest of Chapter 7 and Chapter 8.

"Disneyland," depending on context, might mean the entire Resort or specifically the original theme park that is part of that resort. The second theme park that is a part of that resort is referred to as "DCA".

Let's Clock In

We hope you'll enjoy reading the stories in this book and that you'll learn something along the way, and that our love for Disneyland and Disneyland Custodial will be seen behind our words.

Clock in, grab your pan & broom, remain seated, and keep your hands, arms, and legs inside, because this here's the wildest ride in the wilderness. Let's get started!

-Lynn Barron and Ken Pellman

Cleaning the Kingdom

Chapter 1

Nobody Does It Better

How did it all start? How does it run?

Introduction

"Nobody Does It Better" was a motto of Disneyland Custodial, and we strived to live up to that.

One of the things someone will notice when they take even a cursory interest in the history of Disneyland is that Walt Disney wanted a **clean** place for families to enjoy together.

Disneyland was, and is, scheduled to be open each and every day of the year, year after year, except for the rare special event, usually from between ten to sixteen hours per day. Fifteen million people might pour into and through the park in a year, from the average Joe from middle-America to royalty and celebrities, and they are joined by a diversity of other species, all the while people are sold popcorn and other snacks, candy, drinks, frozen treats, and meals. Trees and bushes abound, shedding leaves, pine needles, and berries. Despite all of this, the Disneyland Custodial team is known around the world for keeping the intricately themed grounds, buildings, trash cans, benches, drinking fountains, lampposts, and ride vehicles clean.

Longtime Day Custodial Sweeping Foreman Vern Hoiland told us that the man who created Disneyland Custodial, Chuck Boyajian, had a saying, "If it's dirty, clean it, if it is clean, polish it, if it is polished keep it that way."

Bob Cobb, a contemporary of ours, told us he had a strong desire to live up to Walt Disney's quote. "If we keep it clean the people will respect it."

That's the way we felt. We, too, worked hard to keep the park clean, not just because that was what we were paid to do, but because we believed in Walt Disney's vision. We wanted to keep it clean so that guests would recognize Disneyland was different and special because it was clean, along with the other reasons it was special. We wanted to keep it clean because we had enjoyed a clean Disneyland and we wanted others to have that experience, too.

While not every Disney Custodial Cast Member sincerely carried the same attitude, each one had been trained and equipped to work as though they did. We were all part of an ongoing tradition, a famous legacy, of providing a clean place for people of all ages to enjoy together.

Sixty years after it was built, with hundreds of millions of visitors, the cleanliness of Disneyland remains legendary.

It All Started With Chuck

Chuck Boyajian was the first person to run Disneyland Custodial.

He "built that." He was born on August 15, 1917, and grew up in Akron, Ohio with three siblings. During World War II, he served for three years with the United States Navy as a mechanic on an aircraft carrier. Three years later, he married Alice Wallace, and moved "out west" to California. He eventually had three children and many grandchildren, but he also "raised" a Custodial family.

Chuck started his career at Disneyland in 1955 when Walt Disney put him in charge of janitorial matters. The way Chuck figured, cleanliness breeds cleanliness.

The team he built included Tom Roppa, Roy Young, Ray Sidejas, Wayne Culver, and Mike Sweeney. He was involved in the Disney presence at the 1964 New York World's Fair. He helped create the Custodial teams for Walt Disney World and Tokyo Disneyland.

He retired in 1981, got a window on Main Street, and passed away in 2004, and was named a Disney Legend in 2005.

A Ray of Sunshine

Chuck's protégé Ray Sidejas was the next person to run Disneyland Custodial. At Chuck's retirement party in the old Grand Hotel (now the Pumbaa parking lot), Chuck announced his hand-picked successor was Ray. The legendary Dick Nunis approached Ray and told him not to try to fill Chuck's shoes, but to fill his own. That was the challenge Ray passed along to everyone – fill your own shoes.

In 1965, Ray took the suggestion of his lifelong best friend John Behrendt, and applied to be a Disneyland cast member. Thus, Ray began his Disney career on May 1 of that year, and was able to personally observe Walt Disney enjoying and scrutinizing the fruits of his vision. And just sixteen short years later, Ray assumed leadership of the Disneyland Custodial team. Ray had helped with the opening of Walt Disney World Resort, and would go on to help with the opening of Tokyo Disneyland, and Disneyland Paris.

Ray Sidejas talked about Walt Disney and his vision as though Walt had just retired. It was people like Ray who perpetuated the core vision of Walt and continued the standards set by Chuck.

Ray and Bruce Kimbrell were the men who had put together a class called "Walt Disney and You" in 2001 to help infuse the heritage and legacy of Disney into the ongoing innovation and growth of the resorts. That was not a Custodial program, but rather an outreach to leaders across all lines of business. The class connected "less tenured" leaders to a man they'd never met. It instilled understanding of the legacy into thousands of leaders directly, leaders who had positions in all levels at Disney's first four Resorts.

In 2002, Ray handed leadership of Disneyland Park Custodial to longtime Custodial manager Mike Sweeney, who had been concentrating on opening and establishing the Custodial operations at DCA. Mike's time also reached back to the Boyajian era. Ray turned his concentration to DCA. Thus, Mike became the third person to lead Disneyland Custodial.

Ray retired on September 30th, 2011 after 46 years at Disneyland.

Mike retired while we were writing this book, and Mary Cobb became the fourth person, and the first woman, to lead Disneyland Custodial. Mary was good to me (Ken) during my time, and she's a great choice for the job. She's one of those people who sticks out in my mind as a quintessential model of the pleasant demeanor of a Disneyland Cast Member. Other women who have long been great pillars within Custodial operations at the Resort are Marci and Charlene.

Leading the Way

Since shift time and days off could vary, and Disneyland Custodial was active 24 hours per day, 365 days per year, various Custodial managers and hourly Custodial cast members would interact, and Leads could have entirely different crews from day to day. A sweeper could be reporting to a different Lead, and they were both reporting to a different Assistant Manager, from one day to the next. While there was one overall Manager leading a park's Custodial operation, to whom Night Custodial, Day Custodial Sweeping, and back in history, Custodial Bussing all reported, there were managers under him (now her) specifically overseeing each of those three parts of Custodial. If we remember right, Bussing and Sweeping both shared the same managers for a given operating day. There were also Assistant Managers, but they were known as Supervisors when I hired in, and while they were more likely to be the people with whom the hourlies interacted with throughout our shift, the managers were very much present, too.

Cleaning the Kingdom

Given all of that, just as no one Lead was the one and only boss of sweepers, no one Assistant Manager was the one-and-only boss of any given hourly. No doubt, people had their favorites, the people they clicked with better, but whichever Manager or Assistant Manager was present was boss. If we were working the Westside and had something we needed to run by management immediately, we'd get in contact with whoever was "Custodial West One" during our shift.

Now that being said, most of us had our preferences about which assignments and shifts we worked, and the more seniority we had, the more likely we were to get what we wanted, and so especially with the opening shifts, a specific day of the week would mean the same Lead would be there and have many of the same crew members. There were more new hires and rookies and more turnover for later shifts. Someone might take a different shift for an extra day. When we were there, Summer season was the only time of year "everyone" had a schedule that somewhat repeated from week to week, but we understand now that more of the Sweeping Department has more of a set schedule year-round.

While a "third shift" job, such as Night Custodial, could be tough on the human body, at least it was usually the same hours, night after night. For Day Custodial Sweeping and Bussing, the managers and the hourlies might need to come in early in the morning one day, and late in the afternoon the next. Or, circumstances may have been such that they started early in the morning and stayed late into the night.

For hourlies like us, management usually avoided having us work a closing shift and then bringing us in for an opening shift the next day if it would give us less than eight hours between shifts. Not only would that be tough on someone, but it put a premium on the pay rate. Still, eight hours of turnaround, which wasn't unheard of, was not much, especially for people who didn't live close to the property.

Leads were hourlies, and all hourlies were union, or, if they objected to obligations of membership, were "agency fee payers". On shorter days, the closing Lead would often work a few hours as a non-Lead, then take over as Closing Lead when the Opening Lead's shift ended.

Seniority meant a whole lot, because it would usually be how schedules were filled and it would determine who got offered what in which order, whether it was a specific shift, or overtime, or an early release, or time off.

As with any other workplace with a large number of people, there were personality clashes and antagonism here and there, but overall, most of us supported and encouraged each other, and we were dedicated to guest service.

All newly hired cast members would go through Disney University orientation, then would be handed over to their respective Departments for job-specific training.

It used to take years, literally, for someone to make Lead. Custodial needed a certain number of Leads, and if that need was filled, there was no reason to make another person a Lead. Turnover was very slow at times. New Leads would be needed if someone "lost their radio" (removed from Lead status) or voluntarily gave it up, or, obviously, if they no longer worked in the Department or at Disneyland.

Because it took so long to make Lead, Lead Training hadn't been developed, because anyone getting a radio should have known whatever there was to know. If they needed advice about something, they would consult another Lead or a Manager. Also, because it took so long for someone to make Lead, people weren't Leads unless their word was good. This meant that when a Lead wanted someone on their crew disciplined, management took that very seriously. If your Lead turned you in or wrote you up, you were screwed, because their version of the issues in question were going to carry much more weight than yours.

I (Ken) was in either the first or second crop of new Leads who got Lead Training. One of the trainers was Gary Garrison. He used an existing Lead as an example, noting that this Lead always said people were working *with* him, not *for* him. It was a good way to look at things. We never asked people to do things we weren't willing to do ourselves. We could show them how to do it, and work alongside them doing it to make sure they got the hang of it.

Setting the Stage

It was a team effort to have a Disneyland Custodian working effectively. Casting would recruit and screen applicants. Disney University leaders and Departmental trainers would impart the knowledge and point to the mindset that would aid the cast member in doing their job. Having the right costume and supplies was a crucial matter. Scheduling was an art form, making sure that the assignments had the cast members they needed. Dispatch clerks were the air traffic controllers of Custodial. Without them, things would quickly fall apart.

Hire the right people, train them, equip them, coach them, give them an area or a task, hold them accountable, reward them. It doesn't sound that complicated, but the challenges were in the details. Writing this book was confirmation of what we already knew: it wasn't so simple.

As far as Day Custodial Sweeping, somebody needed to keep the restrooms cleaned and stocked, someone needed to sweep the grounds, and someone needed to dump the trash, and this needed to be done throughout all guest areas as well as many backstage areas where cast members are like guests. This all had to be done in a way that the restrooms would be cleaned at least once an hour and every guest area inside the park would be passed through by a Sweeper every fifteen minutes, while Bussers would be ready to clean off tables in restaurants as soon as they were left.

To accomplish this, in addition to every restroom having its own stock closet nearby (very small restrooms would rely on a nearby large restroom's stock closet), and each Area in the park needed an Area Locker. This would be the supply closet and meeting place, often with a picnic-style table. This Locker would be filled with pro towels (high-quality paper towels), small cloth towels, pushbrooms, mop buckets, mop handles, mop heads, spray cans and squirt bottles of chemicals, flashlights, pickers, and many different small tools, many rolls of trash bags (two or more sizes), complimentary park maps, and important information. Back in the day, there would also be an ample supply of Sani Sorb Bits, which, despite being packaged in multiple thick bags, would fill the Locker with their aroma.

Other than a pan & broom, there was a time when sweepers went out to the area with some pro towels in a back pocket, maybe a flashlight as well, and that was it. Then we added "sidepacks". They started out as black fanny packs, but then switched to teal sidepacks before settling in to burgundy. We'd have park maps in there, pro towels, and anything else we could fit, such as putty knives, gum scrapers, moist towelettes, the plans to the Death Star; whatever would help. I liked to keep a book with me, too.

While Sweepers did not wear themed costumes for most assignments, most of our trash cans were themed, our ash trays were themed, our 8- 6- and 3-liner trash carts were themed, and we often decorated our Events pushbrooms and industrial vacuum cleaners to the season.

Our day included breaks; a four-hour shift required a fifteen minute break. A six-hour shift required two such breaks. Anything a minute over seven hours required a 30-minute unpaid lunch. Ideally, someone would be ready to work at the start of their eight-hour shift, would get a fifteen minute break about a couple of hours in, get a half-hour unpaid lunch about another two hours in, then another fifteen minute break, and then would "walk" 20 minutes before their off time. It used to be 15 minutes, and many people would walk earlier than 20 minutes because the day would be over or their replacement would be there. Or they were stiffs.

Cleaning the Kingdom

Out and About

Sweepers did a lot of walking. The first week of work, we'd be so sore and tired, before getting used to it, similar to any rigorous exercise workout. The good thing about this, aside from the exercise, was the freedom of movement. We were supposed to be on the move, and to move all throughout our assigned section or split, getting to spend most of our shift outside.

We got to see the entire park. One day we might be scheduled for Tomorrowland, the next day it would be New Orleans/Critter Country.

During the Summer season, we had what was called Summer Lines. What that meant was there were schedules preconfigured with shifts to a specific area at a set time with regular days off. By seniority, each Sweeper would pick the "line" they wanted. The higher someone was in seniority, the more lines from which they could pick, because people were brought into the office to pick their line by seniority. The only advantage someone with lower seniority had in this process was knowing who would be working in what area, so if there was someone with whom they wanted to work or didn't want to work, they could be tipped off in advance. Each Sweeper had to decide for themselves what was most important: the area, the days off, or the hours.

Dedication

A shining example of the dedication the cast members of Disneyland Custodial had to the guest experience was one afternoon when guests had mistakenly thrown away a wallet or purse as they'd left a restaurant patio. They had put the trash from their tray in a can, but forgot their personal item was part of what was on that tray. The bussers had dumped the cans, which were bagged, and thrown the bags in the Adventureland packer, which is behind River Belle Terrace, Stage Door Cafe, etc.

Once we were informed, the two guys we had dumping trash, under supervision of Assistant Manager John, started pulling trash out of the packer to methodically go through trash bags. This was no small feat, and it was a disruption of our operations, and anyone bringing trash to that packer had to set it aside until the task was completed. Mind you, the trash in the packer had been compacted. We also had to make sure nobody pushed the button to operate the packer while one of the guys was inside.

John even did the unusual move of bringing the guests just inside the backstage area so they could see their issue was actually being addressed.

The sweepers did find the item and the guests were relieved and very appreciative. It is just one of many examples of going above and beyond.

Another aspect of dedication is the fact that like most other operations cast members, if someone was in Disneyland Custodial, unless they were of the highest level of seniority, they **would** be working on holidays and special occasions.

The Little Tricks of the Trade

Yes, the basic work of cleaning could be simple. Sweep up this trash with a pan & broom, put it into a trash can, empty that trash can before it gets full. It could involve so much more than that, though, and the more experience we got, the more effective we were, because we learned how to better plan our shifts, how to more effectively use our equipment, which chemicals worked best for various situations, and so forth.

Paper objects, like receipts and FastPass machine tickets would often slip right under the lip of pan when we went to sweep them up. There were a couple of possible solutions that didn't involve crouching or bending. We found the most effective one for us was stepping on the edge of the paper with the toe of one foot, and using our other foot to crinkle the paper, which would then no longer slip under the lip of the pan. The other technique involved using the pan like a fan by putting it down quickly, then catching the paper with the broom and moving it into the pan. While we had some set procedures, improvising was frequently necessary.

We also:

- learned how to use the edge of our pan and our foot to scrape gum or candy.
- knew that the free park maps were great to use on some surfaces to pull up gum.
- knew that hotter days were going to mean more people getting sick, and more ice cream and cold drink spills.
- knew that colder or overcast days would mean more popcorn would be falling and more hot drinks spilled.
- learned when to be seen and when to slip away.
- knew how to use Sani Sorb Bits without wasting bags or making a mess.
- knew any puddle allowed to exist would attract cigarette butts.
- knew stepping on a cigarette butt before sweeping it up was a good way to prevent fires.
- learned how to spot and put out fires in a trash can.
- learned to unclog backed up drinking fountains with paper cups.
- learned to use a distinctive whistle, the jostling of keys, and the sounds of a pan to signal to each other.
- learned where to stash supplies throughout an area so they'd be easier to access.
- knew all of the shortcuts to get from here to there.
- learned how to decipher guest body language and movement.

- learned how to prioritize different pressing situations, such as blood spills, human waste, vomit, fluttering napkins, ice cream, candy, gum, popcorn, drink spills
- learned how to carry many items in our hands and arms and to open doors while doing so.
- learned to see what needed to be cleaned up, so that even if a guest thought the area was clean, we might see differently, but not tell the guest that.

Change and Increasing Challenges

There were many changes over the years. What was originally "Janitorial", which was aligned with Facilities, became Custodial (Disneyland Custodial Guest Services) and aligned with Operations. Disneyland went from being closed or a day or two in off-season weeks to being open literally every day of the year. Guest attendance increased and so did park operating hours. Women were hired for all positions, not just to clean women's restrooms.

Custodial has always had to adapt. Here are just some of the other things that changed over the years:
- removal of Bussing from Custodial
- the proliferation of vending carts and the introduction of carts selling cotton candy
- more food, snacks, and drinks being allowed in more waiting areas
- FastPass tickets and notices littering the grounds
- the increasing popularity, deservedly so, of Entertainment Department productions
- the increase in on-property recycling efforts
- which guests were allowed to use which restrooms
- where smoking was allowed

There was one change in particular that Custodial resisted and rejected. It was Operations Departments eliminating Lead positions coinciding with the idea that hourly

Cleaning the Kingdom

cast members interacting with a computer would suffice. Top Jani Ray Sidejas stood up for his Leads, refusing to eliminate the general use of Lead positions in Custodial, and ultimately much of the attempted change in the other Operations Departments was reverted. Ray sure looked like a smart cookie at that moment, and that's because Ray was a very smart guy when it came to understanding the dynamics of Disneyland and how the cast members function.

Deservedly World Famous

Disneyland Custodial has a well-known reputation as being the best of the best. Is that just good marketing on the part of Disneyland? No, it isn't *just* good marketing. The people who tell Disneyland's stories to the news media and guests *have* done a great job in calling attention to the cleanliness of the park. More importantly, Disneyland Custodial lives up to that reputation.

It must be noted that keeping the Kingdom clean is the responsibility of all cast members, to some extent. Walt Disney himself was known to pick up litter as he walked his park, and his example has been followed by many hourly and managerial cast members who aren't in Custodial, and that has always been something we were thankful to see.

If this chapter hasn't done so, maybe other chapters will explain why we enjoyed cleaning the Kingdom, and why we didn't transfer to other Operations roles at the Resort.

Nobody knows Disneyland better than the men and women of Custodial. Day in and day out, night after night, Day Custodial Sweepers and Night Custodial crew members scour every inch of the place. If anything changes, if anything is out of place, if anything breaks, chips, peels, stains, leaks, clogs, or stops working, they're going to see it.

There's hardly a better person to ask questions of than a Sweeper.

Cleaning the Kingdom

We kept everything clean: walkways, landscaped areas (flower beds), building fronts, benches, waiting areas, drinking fountains, decorations, props, ride vehicles, shops,... if it was there, we cleaned it.

Through all of the changes and challenges, the goal remained the same: meet Walt's vision of a safe, clean, friendly place. As such, Disneyland Custodial runs 24 hours per day, 365 days per year and is world famous.

Chapter 2

Perks and Benefits

Membership had its privileges. What exactly were they?

Introduction

Depending on a person's age and their proximity to Disneyland, they might say something like, "You work at Disneyland? That must be so much fun!!!"

Others might ask, "Why would anyone want to be a janitor, even at Disneyland?"

Make no mistake about it. Being a Disneyland Cast Member, especially a Disneyland *Custodial* Cast Member, could mean a lot of hard work, and enduring all kinds of trials and tribulations. It could be very humbling.

But yes, there were a lot of perks to being "Part of the Magic", especially for people like your authors, who were, and remain, quite fond of Disneyland. They were one of the biggest reasons I (Ken) kept my job as long as I could after I ceased to rely on it for income.

The kids who await visits from Santa Claus and the Tooth Fairy are also of the age at which they think working at Disneyland would be the *coolest thing ever!* Actually, there are some adults who think that way, too. If we could have the compensation packages we enjoy at our current jobs while working in Disneyland Custodial, we would. It was often loads of fun being part of that show and bringing happiness to so many people.

Some perks were official, some we made for ourselves. Some were tangible, some were emotional.

Some of the perks we'll cite in this chapter are shared with other cast member roles, but not all. Some of the perks and benefits described are things that might also be found at other workplaces in some form or another, but most of these have that extra Disney touch.

I've Got a Golden Ticket

Perhaps the biggest perk was being able to not only get ourselves, but family and friends into the parks. When last we had our Main Gate Passes, they worked on an annual calendar basis. While our IDs got us into the parks on an unlimited basis and there were only a couple of days we couldn't use them, ur Main Gate Pass provided 16 times per calendar year we could "sign in" other people into the parks for free. These did not carry over from year to year. For those of us who had no spouse and no dependents, we could get three people in addition to ourselves through the gate. When DCA was added, this meant we and our guests could park-hop, meaning we could visit both parks and go back and forth as we wanted. Considering the admission costs, this was an enormous value, and that value has continued to grow.

In addition to those privileges, we'd usually get two tickets twice a year: early in the Summer season and again close to the end-of-the-year holidays. These tickets were also park-hopper tickets after DCA was added. The tickets used to have no expiration dates, and given how fast admission pricing has risen, that made them increase in value faster than a lot of shares of successful companies. Disney did start placing expirations on the tickets that were at least a couple of years after distribution. Unlike sign-in privileges, these tickets could be handed over to someone or mailed to them and we didn't need to be present when they were admitted to the park. Also, these tickets could usually be used on days that Main Gate Passes were blocked due to predicted crowds.

Finally, there were the tickets we were given for special occasions that we didn't want to redeem, because although they were actual tickets, they were also what amounted to limited-edition collectibles with some nice art on them.

Main Gate Passes used to have only twelve uses per year, but they were also only blocked out for use on Independence Day and New Year's Eve, two days that were traditionally extremely busy. The trade-off for getting 16 uses per year was that, like annual passes, there were many days throughout the year that were blocked out for using them, because those days were expected to be the busiest.

As we understood it, cast members with more dependents could get more people in, with the idea being that they could bring their whole family.

The downside of this perk is that even family could take advantage of the fact that a cast member could get them in. One thing that always got to me (Lynn) was that we'd ask someone to meet us at a certain time to get them into the parks, and they wouldn't show up on time. This could mean the risk of being late to our shift or late coming back from a break.

That is exactly why I (Ken) would tell them, once I had mobile communications, to let me know when they were standing at the Main Entrance, and I would get to them as fast as I could to sign them in. I'd give them a window of time I wouldn't be able to do it, because that would be the time I would be at Roll Call, but other than that, as long as it was during my shift, I'd get there upon being summoned unless I had an urgent matter in my area. I certainly was no longer going to go there at an agreed-upon time and wait!

Another downside was that we could be held responsible if they repaid the generosity by breaking rules or the law during their visit. Fortunately, this never became an issue for either of us.

It was not allowed to in any way sell sign-in privileges. That was grounds for termination. Many people would want to be polite and would try to bring us gifts, but we told them we couldn't accept gifts, at least not there at the Gate. Some sweepers would accept lunch as thanks.

Some cast members would make someone's day if they were signing in one person or a couple but not using up the entire available privilege. For example, they could sign in three people but were only signing in a couple. These cast members would pull someone aside who was planning to purchase a ticket and explain they were going to get them in free, no strings attached. This was very risky, because that was literally taking revenue away from their employer.

If we wanted to get more people in than our privileges allowed, we'd team up with another sweeper to do a little log rolling. They'd sign in some of our group that day, and in the future we'd return the favor.

Even if we were too new or our status was Temporary/Seasonal, and thus we didn't have a Main Gate Pass, the same ID we used to clock in and out also would grant us, as individuals, free admission. We were not supposed to enter the park for pleasure through the backstage, such as when we were done with our shift and had changed. We were supposed to go to the Main Entrance like any other guest. I can think of many reasons for this policy, insurance being one.

These privileges were also effective at Walt Disney World Resort, so that we could get ourselves and three other people into the three (and later four) theme parks there - FREE. Even better was that we didn't "use up" the sign-in privileges at WDW, meaning we could be there for a week or two and visit the parks every day and not have lost a single admission for friends or family back at Disneyland. I (Ken) enjoyed this many times over the years, sometimes twice a year, the last time being my honeymoon.

I think one sweeper in particular I know has an in with an airline, because he'll fly to Orlando many times in a year to visit Walt Disney World Resort.

The Disneyland Express Card

Another reason not to ever leave home without our ID (and I, Ken, never was without my Disneyland ID) was that it got us discounts on food, merchandise, and services.

There were certain times of the year we could get about half off on Disney hotel rooms, and yes this was also true of the hotels at Walt Disney World Resort.

The discount on most merchandise at Disney venues (the parks and resorts, Disney Stores, Mickey's of Glendale, etc.) started at 20%, but after three years of seniority it jumped to 35%. As a Disneyana collector, this was a huge savings. There were certain times when the discount would temporarily jump to 40%, like for holiday shopping. For a few things, the discount was limited to 10%, like with the glass artists, who were lessees, rather than a Disney operation.

The discount on food was 20%.

Cleaning the Kingdom

There was also a discount directory available of local businesses that would give discounts to Disneyland cast members.

Taking a Vacation With Your Coworkers

Because of the discounts detailed above, many of us would opt to plan our own trips to WDW.

There were also trips officially organized for cast members, at least some of which were scheduled for January, after the holiday crowds had dissipated.

I (Ken) never opted for the Company-planned trip, but I think some of my trips did coincide with the timing of the official packages. We even hitched a ride from the airport with the group.

There's No Tram on This Studio Tour

Closer to home, there were also Company-organized visits to the Walt Disney Studios (which is also the corporate headquarters) in Burbank and Walt Disney Imagineering headquarters in neighboring Glendale. WDI used to be much less publicized and secretive, so having a tour through there, for someone like me (Ken), meant trying to soak up every little detail in a way I'd never forget.

We were also able to visit on our own, with our Cast Member ID. We had more freedom at the Studios, but at WDI we could ask to shop at Mickey's of Glendale, which wasn't far from where we'd check in. This would also take us through the Figment Cafe, where one could scan the room or patio for familiar Imagineers to harass with fan adoration.

My wife and I (Lynn) went on our own to the Studios one afternoon, and had a great time. We didn't get to go on any tour, but we were able to walk around the campus, go into the studio store, and see Dave Smith in the Disney Archives. I wish I had done that more often, but at least I can say I have done it once.

A Very Merry Christmas

We used to get our very own private party at Disneyland in early December. It was for all West Coast Disney employees, not just park cast members: the Disney Family Holiday Party.

The party would take place on two successive weekday nights, with the park closing at 6:00 p.m. to guests and reopening later for us! Cast members without dependents could bring one guest. If two cast members without dependents were dating this meant they could bring another couple using their combined privilege.

It would be Disneyland Resort cast members, Walt Disney Studios employees, and Imagineering. Everyone was supposed to bring a new toy for charity, which is not much to ask of people who were getting a free private party at Disneyland. It was something started by Walt Disney.

One nice thing about the party was that managers would help with some of the sweeping. Some Imagineers and Studio employees, including top executives, would work Operations positions, such as serving hot dogs or loading people onto rides. For some, it was returning to their Disney roots.

The park was not crowded, and it made for a nice night to get on attractions and enjoy dinner. The food was discounted, which also included the snacks like churros and popcorn. There were character meet-and-greets set up to get our pictures taken with them.

Cast members would often work one night and attend the other.

In 1996, I (Ken) made sure to be there the second night, because I was able to see the very last Disneyland performance of the Main Street Electrical Parade. I watched it disappear through the Small World gate for the final time. Parades were not a normal part of these parties.

Cleaning the Kingdom

There was another year parade floats were brought out during the party. It was for filming the original finale for Soarin' Over California, using a camera mounted on a helicopter, which repeatedly flew northbound over Main Street. Christmas parade floats and costumed performers were in place. We were told not to look up, but I (Lynn) am sure many people did. At the time we had no idea what it was going to be used for except it was for an attraction at the soon-to-open California Adventure Park.

Sweeping this party was usually a lot of fun. Not only would we see friends and their families, including from other parts of the company, the "guests" made much less of a mess than an average day's guests. Management was more relaxed and we had a lot more freedom over things like sticking to our areas. As long as things were covered, our Supervisors were OK with us going on attractions or eating during the party. I remember riding the Matterhorn and getting a call over my radio for a Code V ...at the Matterhorn. Good timing.

As we exited the party, each family was given a Christmas tree ornament with a Disney Character and the year of the party on it.

The Company grew on the West Coast through acquisitions and expansion, and the holiday season expanded and became more popular with guests. This is probably what prompted Resort management, which had changed over the years, to morph this perk into something unrecognizable. The private parties ceased. Instead, cast members were invited to bring their guests into the parks during regular operating hours, with a few places set aside for them to withdraw from the crowds and enjoy discounted snacks.

Cast Blast Passed Fast

For a couple of years, at least, we had something called Cast Blast. No, this wasn't about cleaning out casts around broken limbs. This was kind of a festive convention-like thing. It varied from year to year.

One year, it was at the Disneyland Hotel in the convention area with booths giving away small items, mostly promotional in nature. I (Lynn) think Disney figured the cast members would take anything for free, and we did.

There was also food, characters, contests, and displays showcasing different Departments across the resort.

Another time, it was downgraded and was held in the Parade building back behind Toontown. This was a much smaller event and I think the last one they had. There was always a free t-shirt, too, with the Cast Blast logo on it.

I think it was held to keep morale going and a reward for working hard, and also to distribute information to us. Those kinds of things were nice as it was something different and was fun at times. A few years before I (Lynn) quit, it seemed as though these type of events were no more.

The Dog Days of Summer

It sounds like a simple gesture: One day each summer, Custodial management would grill up hot dogs and the like for a good chunk of the day, and all of the "fixins" would be available, right there in front of Custodial Central. Simple, and yet it was eagerly welcomed by us every year, and created a positive mood.

This one was for Custodial cast members, not the cast in general, and it was free to us, so we'd stuff ourselves like Takeru Kobayashi. I (Ken) suspect Harry Hemhauser, the most senior of sweepers at the time, was fasting for days in advance in order to make room for more dogs.

With Summer season assignments mostly a set schedule, unlike the rest of the year in those days, it was a popular time to have potlucks at the various Area Lockers or we would decide to set up an ice cream sundae bar by each of us bringing different ingredients.

Cleaning the Kingdom

Custodial Games

You may have heard about the Cast Member Canoe Races, which have been an annual tradition for a very long time, but did you hear there have been Custodial Olympics? These would be races to complete tasks loosely based on what Custodial does. It was a great way to have fun and build rapport.

Minnie's Moonlit Madness

This annual event has been going on since before I (Ken) came to work for Disney. It's a trivia test and scavenger hunt, with teams competing at Disneyland at an after-hours event. It is a fundraiser.

Some fan groups started doing similar events during park operating hours.

Flashback

This is another annual fundraiser. It was started in 1998 and features musical productions. There are many talented cast members and so the shows can be quite entertaining.

Practically Perfect in Every Way

Cast members were invited to special presentations from time to time. One that stuck out to me (Lynn) was a Sherman Brothers event in 1999 at the Team Disney Anaheim building. It was a free presentation. I definitely remember getting my books signed by the Shermans and by author Bruce Gordon.

Here are my (Ken's) recollections of the event as written in December 1999:

* * * * *

Cleaning the Kingdom

   Robert and Richard Sherman are the songwriting team who have created some of the most well-recognized Disney music. Their optimistic tunes have been written for films and for attractions.

   When the Disneyland Line -the Disneyland cast member newsletter- announced that there would be a cast-exclusive presentation and book signing with the Shermans on Wednesday, December 8, I was happy to have the time free to go.

   Cast members filed into the Team Disney Anaheim Auditorium, where enlarged pictures of the brothers, some with Walt Disney, were displayed. A Yamaha keyboard was set up on stage with several chairs. Imagineer David Mumford, collector, author, and unofficial Disney historian, played host with co-editor Jeff Kurtti assisting. Their co-editor, Imagineer Bruce Gordon, made an appearance, but had work to attend to and wasn't part of the presentation.

   The session was informal, Richard at the keyboard, Robert sitting down next to Jeff and then David, each taking turns talking. The Shermans would often finish each other's sentences. All David had to do is ask a single question and the Shermans could run with it for several minutes, talking and performing, despite being a little under the weather.

   The brothers talked about working with Walt Disney. They went over how they got hired in the first place, how "Mary Poppins", "The Parent Trap", and "Winnie the Pooh" came together, and played songs that didn't make it into any films.

   At one point, David announced that he had a surprise for the brothers, and invited Pam from WDI up on stage. I first met Pam almost ten years ago, and knew that she could sing, but I hadn't known that she used to perform at Disneyland Park and I was totally unprepared for what was in store.

   Pam ended up singing for and with the Sherman brothers, including "Supercalifragilisticexpialidocious". We were treated to a song what was meant for Mary Poppins called "In the Land of Sand", but it ended up being Kaa's song in "The

Jungle Book", "Trust In Me". Pam is a great singer and it was a real treat to hear her. She works behind the scenes in the upper levels of Walt Disney Imagineering but has contributed her singing voice to park attractions.

When the brothers talked about "It's a Small World" and how the need for the song came about, they solicited audience participation. We all sang and clapped along.

There were two extra special moments. One was when the brothers performed "Feed the Birds" after explaining how Walt would request it and what the song means. Finally, the brothers talked excitedly about the upcoming Tigger movie. They performed two songs from the film; a lonely song about Tigger realizing that perhaps it isn't so good to be "the only one", and a happy song about the meaning of family.

It was an unforgettable experience, and it was topped off by the book signing. Walt's Time - Before and Beyond by Robert B. Sherman & Richard M. Sherman, edited by Bruce Gordon, David Mumford, & Jeff Kurtti is published by Camphor Tree Publishers. It is a must-have book for any fan of Disney music or the Shermans, as it pours over their careers and is loaded with anecdotes and color pictures.

Everyone lined up to have Richard, Robert, David, and Jeff sign their books. Some of us hung around to chat with each other a bit about the upbeat and inspiring music of the Sherman brothers. It really is a great, big, beautiful tomorrow!

* * * *

It's bittersweet to look back on that event, as David died a relatively young man from an illness, Bruce, who was let go from WDI and went to work for the Disney family to help get their museum going, died suddenly of natural causes, and more recently, Robert Sherman passed. We cherish the memories we made that day and we miss those talented people who've passed.

Crash Test Dummies

There's nothing quite like the pleasant smell of fresh Imagineering.

Before a new attraction was about to open, or a significantly renovated attraction was about to reopen to guests, it was typical for cast members to ride it first.

Sometimes, not all the show elements were working, but most of the time they were by this point. Occasionally, we were allowed to bring family and friends, but we had to make reservations to do so, so to speak, by picking the day.

Many times, we would be working and over the radio, or by word of mouth, we would hear that an attraction was being tested and cast members were needed. There were multiple reasons for this. It gave the cast members working that attraction time to get used to running it with people. It would demonstrate how the queue was going to work. It would test the ride system with live people instead of dead weight.

One attraction I (Lynn) remember doing this for was Space Mountain. This was in 2005 when the track was completely gutted out from the building and new track put back in. It was the same track layout, with some additional new show elements and new music. This was just one of those times I happened to be walking by during my shift and asked if I wanted to ride, of course I said "Yes!" Even though it was the same exact layout, the track was much more smooth than it had been before the renovation. It opened soon after that to the public to be a part of the 50th anniversary of Disneyland.

This was also one of the last such perks I (Ken) enjoyed.

* * * *

Sometimes, a few cast members would get to preview something long before the general cast, and not just those being trained on the maintenance or operation of an attraction. Being in Custodial, we had the freedom, access, and plausible deniability to sneak our way into all sorts of situations.

I (Ken) slipped into the Indiana Jones show building while installation of the show and painting was still going on. I had familiarized myself with the floor plans before, so I was able to walk the track and get a look at how things were coming together with a general understanding of what scene was which. Walking that track was a far different perspective than riding one of the vehicles through. It seemed so much bigger walking through.

Speaking of riding one of the vehicles through - I managed to do that a while before general cast member previews as well. A certain Imagineer who was long connected with the project had a very distinct license plate, and was someone who knew me. I saw his vehicle parked by the show building and managed to find an unlocked door. I walked in as though I belonged there, and when I saw this Imagineer, he did something that was entirely predictable based on our past interactions: He offered me a ride. Things weren't finalized, but riding the vehicle for my first time gave me a good idea of what the finished attraction was going to feel like.

After the Indiana Jones Adventure was opened in 1995 and operating, there were times a Countdown to Extinction vehicle was tested and programmed on the track, as that attraction (now named Dinosaur) was opening at Animal Kingdom in April 1998, and used the same ride system and the same track layout. So, it made sense to program it at Indy. One night, we were offered a ride and we took it. That meant we rode Countdown to Extinction, in a way, long before actually going to the attraction!

Escort Service

Another event I (Lynn) was able to participate in was the opening of Tower of Terror at DCA on May 5, 2004 - not to clean up celebratory confetti, but rather to be a Media Host. A Media Host was someone who assisted with making sure all the needs of a media guest were met. For example, they might need a drink, or food, or have questions about some of the things they were seeing or reporting about. We helped them with Disney terminology and standards.

These media guests could be from a television station, newspaper, website, magazine, or as in my case that day, a radio station.

I was still paid my normal Custodial pay, but just had a different role that day. Without the participation of cast members from different Departments, there was no way for the Resort's full-time media relations staff to assist every media guest with such personal attention.

Before the event, we went through some training on what our role was, and how to respond to the different needs of the media guests. We were then given a special shirt to wear that day of the event. Mine was a polo type shirt with the Tower of Terror emblem on it.

The day began with me meeting the media in the park right in front of Tower of Terror. The radio station I was to be with for that day was from Phoenix, Arizona. There were canopies set up for shade, as it was a warm day.

For most of the day it was somewhat boring until they wanted to ride the attraction. There was one ride vehicle setup specifically for the media people. This was equipped with cameras for television, and microphones for radio stations. I had the choice to ride it with them, or at least take them to the vehicle to be sure they got on, but I chose to ride it, of course. It is always nice to get paid to ride something like TOT.

It was broadcast live to their audience back in Phoenix. We didn't just ride it once, but three times in a row without disembarking. That was enough for me. It was fun, but three times? Not for me.

We returned to our spot in front of the attraction and I took a break. As part of being a media host, we were allowed a

Cleaning the Kingdom

$15 food voucher. I took off my name tag and went to eat at Taste Pilots Grill. Tough job, eh?

I returned to my media people for the rest of the afternoon, and it ended about 4 or 5:00 p.m. For some, it went into the night. I guess for this radio show it was only for the day.

It was a great experience that I will never forget - especially riding Tower of Terror three times in a row.

Closing Time

In addition to getting to test and preview attractions, we typically got to experience them last, too.

On November 9, 1994, Disneyland's Skyway, which had run for 38 years, had its last ride. I (Ken) wrote this report immediately after the closing:

* * * * *

The weather forecasts say a storm is headed to southern California. For some people, gloomy skies came early. They were the people sad over the fact that tonight, Wednesday November 9, 1994, The Disneyland Skyway made its final run.

For days, guests who frequent Disneyland have been getting in their last rides of the milestone attraction that Walt Disney himself opened. People were getting emotional tonight - both guests and cast members - because they are going to miss this piece of Disneyland they have grown so fond of and developed memories with.

I suppose I have always taken the Skyway for granted; for some reason it seemed like it was always there and would always be there. I guess my fear of heights (at least while hanging from a cable instead of inside something solid like a 747) always kept me from really noticing and fully enjoying the spectacular and unmatchable view. The view of Fantasyland, Sleeping Beauty Castle, King Arthur Carrousel, Storybook Land

Cleaning the Kingdom

Canal Boats, Dumbo, Small World, Mickey's Toontown, parades, tea cups, Submarine Lagoon, Tomorrowland, Rocket Jets, and especially the Matterhorn. The Skyway provided a unique view of the Matterhorn and what is inside of it. I know I'm going to miss these things.

So, I turned out to get my last rides in, along with several friends and a whole lot of other people. Cast members were even being allowed to ride the attraction in costume, and in the Tomorrowland station, where the cabins were stored, cast members were signing a banner, getting pictures, and sharing memories over chips. It seems like almost every group of guests and even cast members had their own still and video cameras to capture the beauty of the attraction while they still could.

I was able to get in five trips, ending on the Tomorrowland side. There were relatively long lines - Disnoids of all sorts were getting in their last rides. Even a top Imagineer, Tony Baxter (a swell guy), was there to get in his last rides and say goodbye. I'm sure it was an emotional thing for him too - he grew up at the park and was a cast member for a few years.

As my friends and I prepared to take our final trip, we waited to be among the last. There were plenty of other people determined to be in the last cabin, so we didn't even try for that. We dispatched from the Fantasyland station and headed towards the Matterhorn for one last time. Shouts of "long live the Skyway!" and other such sentiments could be heard echoing into the night. I could even see the new Team Disney Anaheim building that is under construction.

As we descended to the Tomorrowland station, we could see folks waiting down by the entrance of the Tomorrowland Autopia. We exited the attraction for the last time and joined the rest of the crowd below. Several groups of cast members departed for their last trips behind empty cabins, and finally Mickey and Minnie climbed into one of their own, the last one. As it left the Tomorrowland station on its final round trip, the people gathered cheered and applauded the attraction we're all going to miss. We all waited, and soon there was a picture flash in the Matterhorn, as the last two cabins approached their final return to the Tomorrowland station. In the first cabin was a photographer, the second carried his subject matter, Mickey and Minnie, in the last Skyway cabin to carry anyone over Disneyland.

The crowd cheered them all the way to the station. They stepped out of the cabin, and the Disneyland Skyway officially closed. As the crowd broke up and headed for Main Street to exit, it appeared that dismantling of the Tomorrowland station began immediately, almost as if they wanted to make sure it would not run again. Most likely it was because they felt it best to get the attraction out of the way.

Soon, the towers will be gone. Eventually, the Matterhorn will be altered, as there is no need for the passages that the Skyway used.

Such was the final night for the Disneyland Skyway. It was an attraction popular with amorous couples, people who wanted to smoke controlled substances at Disneyland without being caught, graffiti vandals, people who wished to expectorate on others below, and an attraction that will also be missed by those of us who behaved ourselves while on it.

Disneyland will always be changing. I know that, and I support that. But some of us will still miss attractions that are no longer there, and be sad to see them go, even if that appears silly to some. I'll miss the Skyway, but I sure do look forward to Indiana Jones!

* * * * *

We cast members had similar experiences for final screenings of "Captain Eo" and "America the Beautiful" in CircleVision 360, as those attractions were closed to make way for the 1998 New Tomorrowland. Having a 360-degree movie at this location was something that went back all the way to the start of Disneyland. Both the theater and the content were updated over the years, and when I (Ken) started, having "Wonders of China" showing in the morning and "American Journeys" in the afternoon was long-established operation. The two-movie package came to and end July 7, 1996, as the mid-1970s revised version of "America the Beautiful" came back for a special nostalgia encore on July 11, and ran through September 7, 1997, marking the end of the CircleVision 360 theater as an attraction at Disneyland..

I can remember seeing the films with other cast members in post-operating hours screenings just for us - the final screenings.

When we got word in 1998 that the Submarine Voyage we grew up with was closing, there was no announced plans for the future. We lined up for our last rides, thinking this could be the last time there was a submarine ride in Disneyland. Cast members that last night were allowed to ride the attraction one last time after park closing.

Here's what I (Ken) wrote about the experience:

* * * * *

I'm writing this message in the wee hours of September 9, 1998. A couple of hours ago, at 11:15 PM on Tuesday, September 8, I was one of the privileged few who took the final Submarine Voyage aboard sub #301, the Nautilus.

This unique attraction was opened by Walt Disney on June 6, 1959 as part of expansion of Disneyland that included such attractions as the Matterhorn and the Monorail. Until 1985, the eight submarines were gray. Then, the attraction was rethemed slightly and some of the subs were renamed.

Before the park opened on Tuesday, a decommissioning ceremony took place. All throughout the day, guests took their last rides of the subs, taking pictures and taking mementos such as cups of water.

Cleaning the Kingdom

There are 38 seats for guests in each sub, and there were more than that many guests trying to get on the last sub after the 9 PM closing of the park. Triton was the last sub to carry guests around the 1365 foot course, which miraculously transported passengers past sea life, under the North Pole, over mermaids, through the sunken ruins of Atlantis, and around a sea serpent, all in about 10 minutes.

Afterwards, cast members were able to take their last rides. Once the line of cast members was cleared out, one last sub was filled with Voyage cast members, a handful of others (including me, Roberta - from Disneyland Facilities, and Tony Baxter - from Walt Disney Imagineering, of course).

Tony had worked the attraction while he was a ride operator at Disneyland, and can recite the spiel of those days by heart. He watched as others preceded him in their last voyages, chatting with cast members and reminiscing. Designing Disney parks is not just a job for this guy. He cares about the guest experience and is very sentimental about historical attractions such as this one.

Most of us sat quietly and reverently as we took our last trip. Tony sat to my left, leaning into the window, soaking up the experience. Roberta sat next to him. We cheered as we went under the falls (turned on for this trip) one last time. We laughed when the recorded captain's voice advised "Mr. Baxter" to check the air pressure. We applauded as the ride came to an end at about 11:25 PM. Most of the people stayed around to chat more and take pictures.

The attraction did show signs of age, and people do have differing reactions to the closing of the ride, from anger to indifference, but just about everyone is in agreement about this: we hope that Walt Disney Imagineering, Walt Disney Attractions, (and maybe Walt Disney Feature Animation, too), work together to bring Disneyland guests a great new experience in the not-too-distant future

* * * * *

52

As you probably know, the Subs eventually did return as Finding Nemo Submarine Voyage in June 2007. "Finding Nemo" wasn't even released until May 2003, so we couldn't have known it was going to play into the fate of the attraction back in 1998. In September 2004, I wrote this:

* * * *

Since September 8, 1998, the Disneyland Submarine Voyage lagoon has been dormant - unused due to decisions by the Disneyland Resorts previous management. Rumors had persisted for a while that it was an attraction being targeted for closure due to the expense to operate in comparison to the capacity and the labor involved. After all, the attraction has been around since 1959 and was decidedly low-tech by the standards of the 1990s.

With the opening of the New Tomorrowland in 1998, there were new attractions open in Tomorrowland, which management reasoned took some of the burden off of the Subs. One of those new attractions, the Rocket Rods, was apparently causing damage to the lagoon.

Thus, the Submarine Voyage closed so that resources could be allocated elsewhere. Hopeful, maverick Imagineers briefly put park guests on notice of their intentions to bring an Atlantis-themed attraction to the location by 2001. Their visual aid, displayed for guests, was quickly removed. When Walt Disney Feature Animation's "Atlantis: The Lost Empire" failed to generate the buzz or box office returns that make executives more open to investing in permanent ride-through adaptations, it looked like the lagoon would sit around as a giant trash collector for the foreseeable future.

Fast-forward six years from the closing of the attraction.

Resort management has changed, the Rocket Rods have gone the way of the Flying Saucers - only they aren't missed as much, and Tomorrowland needs serious help. The overhaul of

Cleaning the Kingdom

the Autopia, which has existed in various incarnations in the same corner of Tomorrowland since the park opened, has kept the land alive as Space Mountain is rebuilt and Buzz Lightyear's new attraction shoots for a 2005 debut. Most importantly, "Finding Nemo", which is about the underwater world of sea creatures, became one the highest grossing films of all time.

The time has come for the lagoon to rise to the occasion.

After six years, the Disneyland Submarines have come out of the watery grave. Well, kinda. Tests are being conducted in preparation for a new attraction that will adapt the existing facilities and vehicles.

When the pictures of a yellow submarine hit the Internet, I knew a part of the magic was coming back. This past Friday, I saw the sub myself, just to make sure it was really happening.

Many Disneyland fans are excited by the return of a classic attraction, even if it will be in a modified form. They are excited that it will restore more kinetic energy to the Tomorrowland landscape, and that one of the few theme park attractions that takes guests on a extended actual underwater ride will be back.

* * * * *

As referenced, in the time since the Submarine Voyage closed and reopened, the Autopia had been closed and completely overhauled. Here's what I wrote about that in September 1999:

.

* * * * *

It was Monday, September 6, 1999. Tens of thousands of people flocked to Disneyland Park for the ceremonial final weekend of summer. It was Labor Day, the final day to experience the park before some attractions, shops, restaurants, and more get closed for refurbishment.

Cleaning the Kingdom

The biggest "refurbishment" in the park this time around will be for the Autopia. It is an attraction with a long and varied history in several forms, being at the park in some form since opening day, when various celebrities got behind the wheel. Now, one of the last vestiges of the 1960's "World on the Move" Tomorrowland will be overhauled.

The Mark VII model cars debuted in 1967. Just think about that - six other models were used from 1955 to 1967, and just this one version of Autopia car has been used in all of the time since.

In a world where new attractions can be budgeted in the nine figure range and feature state-of-the-art technology for ride systems & special effects, the Disneyland Autopia has remained popular even as a simple, no frills attraction featuring individually driven (though track-guided) cars with gas-powered internal combustion engines.

After years of changes, the Disneyland Autopia system gradually settled into two intertwined versions, both featuring the same model of cars. The Fantasyland Autopia's entrance was opposite the Matterhorn Bobsleds entrance, while the entrance for the Tomorrowland version was located between the Submarine Voyage and the Tomorrowland Disneyland Railroad station.

The Fantasyland Autopia has been closed for quite some time, and in recent years had only opened when Tomorrowland's version was closed. The 1998 renovation of Tomorrowland left the Tomorrowland Autopia almost completely untouched - there was new signage and paint applied to the simple waiting area.

Now, the two Autopias will be reworked and turned into a single two-sided attraction, with the entrance at the Tomorrowland side. There will be new sights and sounds, new, longer roadways, a new waiting area, and several models of new vehicles. That's right - while the Mark VII cars had variety in color only, the new Autopia will feature a variety of body styles.

Cleaning the Kingdom

This is all being made possible by Chevron, the new sponsor. It has been a long time since the Disneyland Autopia has had a sponsor, but Chevron has stepped up to the plate. As a result, the new version will be more whimsical, though it will stop short of placing riders in those popular animated cars seen in the Chevron television commercials. They will probably show up, though, as part of the "show".

Well, you can't just close down and overhaul a Disneyland tradition, especially one that has been essentially the same for thirty-two years, without letting the cast members say their good-byes. Many cast members are teenagers and twenty-somethings who grew up visiting Disneyland and riding this version of the Autopia. They can get very sentimental about these kinds of changes.

So, the summer came to a close as Disneyland Park closed to guests at 10 PM, cast members lined up (many in costume) to get their final rides in. They were given two hours to do so. Photo ops were set up with some cars as well.

I arrived at 11:15 and jumped into line, enjoying the voice of the late great Jack Wagner reciting the spiel so many of us have memorized by heart; "To make your car go, press your foot down on the pedal...". Only the "B" (west) side was running. We drove the route, occasionally whooping, hollering, and smashing the cars together as hard as we could. ("Please do not bump the car ahead of you, or stop your car in the middle of the track.")

Passing the old Submarine Voyage entrance and railroad track, snaking under the Rocket Rod track and Monorail beam, I savored the smell of the fuel and exhaust and the simple signs. I really felt like taking one that showed a graphic discouraging bumping. Three rides and a banged-up spine later the stroke of midnight rapidly approached. I managed to slip in line for one more ride as part of the final pack, staying on the curb afterwards as the final car came in to cheer and applaud.

With the Autopias under renovation, the Submarine Voyage sitting closed, the Motor Boats long gone, and the

Monorail closed due to construction work, the northeastern portion of Disneyland Park will essentially be a long walkway for the time being.

* * * * *

Another attraction I (Lynn) remember fondly as a child and an adult was The Country Bear Playhouse. It closed on September 9, 2001. The days leading up to its closure there were the meet-and-greet characters out in front of the attraction. This was a rare thing because, up to that point I had never seen those characters in the park because they hadn't been meeting with guests regularly for many years..

That last day, cast members and guests flowed into the theatre for the last day of shows. Flash photography was allowed for the first time, and many people said their sad goodbyes to a favorite that had been open at Disneyland since 1972.

Here's what I (Ken) wrote about the closure of the Country Bear Playhouse shortly after it happened:

* * * *

It was Sunday, September 9th. Churches across the county were a lot less full than they'd be a few days later. For people like me, the biggest concern of the day was making sure I got my fill of the Country Bear Vacation Hoedown before the doors were shuttered.

During the preceding days, cast members had been invited to come see the show, in costume if that was more convenient, and had one of the two theaters set aside for them. But on that final day, as the line stretched through Critter County, both theaters were open to a mixed group of guests and cast members in and out of costume.

There's nothing like seeing a show during the farewell performances or riding a ride during the final trips. The audience is always so active and fun as the mood grows nostalgic and people say their sometimes emotional goodbyes to a familiar experience.

Unlike with past events, I wasn't able to stay for the very end, but I did get in my multiple final viewings of the show, complete with foot-stomping, hand-clapping, and singing.

The characters had held up very well, able to perform three different shows over the years, a testament to the incredible talent of Marc Davis. The expressions of the eyes, the visible breathing of the band, Teddi Berra on a swing, the layout of the theater... it was an example of a great attraction that didn't need to throw you around, drop you, scare you, or surprise you with physical gag effects to entertain you. It was a show that didn't need to be interrupted with *something going horribly wrong*. The worst thing that happens is an invasion of a skunk who doesn't smell, and maybe Big Al losing his Swiss Army knife.

Max, Buff, and Melvin freaked me out when I was a kid, and I'll sure miss them. The theater was also a nice place for a cast member to take a break after performances were finished for the day, especially in cold or rainy weather.

It would have been nice to have the original show back for a while, but I guess that's what Walt Disney World is for.

Sunday the 9th of September was a day to enjoy the Hoedown at Disneyland Park for one last time. None of us knew that two mornings later, we'd be stunned by the most heinous acts of terrorism we'd ever seen.

Backstage Amenities

Restaurants - Word on the beat was that Company accounting figured the meals sold to cast members were losses, even though they were generally priced high enough to more than cover cost. That was because sale of this food was being compared to prices charged to guests. Mind you, there was never a situation we ever heard of in which guests were unable to buy food because it was instead being sold to cast members.

The Inn Between was the backstage side of the Plaza Inn. It served breakfast as well as having a menu for the rest of the day. For breakfast, cast members could order things like breakfast burritos, pancakes, and eggs. The rest of the day, there would typically be a few different entrees from which to choose or someone could order things like burgers and sandwiches. There were salads, the basic soft drink dispenser, things like that. There was an indoor seating area with televisions as well as an outdoor patio.

The Westside Diner had limited hours and it was under the restaurants of New Orleans Square, adjoining the kitchen. That meant there was no daylight visible in there. When I (Ken) started, it was still the D.E.C. ("Deck"), which I think stood for Disney Employee Cafeteria. Before we were there, it was The Pit, hence the racecar theming that lasted through the DEC days. The Westside Diner took on a 1950s theme. It was later replaced by a new building on the outside the berm, not far from the Monorail track, to make more room for backstage operations to meet the needs of guests.

There was a Cast Member window for Village Haus that kept the hours of the restaurant. If you're ever standing at the counter in Village Haus, look to the right. Even without leaning over, you might be able to see a Village Haus cast member serving someone on the other side of the wall. Cast members could purchase the same food offered to guests, for a lower price.

There was a similar set up at Space Place, which was a fast food restaurant in Tomorrowland where the Space Mountain entrance is now.

The Eat Ticket was too far out of the way most of the time for Custodial cast members, as it was near the Team Disney Anaheim building. It was another one of those counter-service cafeteria type places.

There was a cast member restaurant at the Disneyland Hotel, where the prices seemed relatively low, but Disneyland sweepers rarely had occasion to eat there unless they were working the Parking Structure. I (Ken) ate there once or twice because of handling some special task.

While working Esplanade, we'd often make our way to a cast member restaurant in Disney's Grand Californian. This place was attached to Storyteller's. We'd get to it by going to the end of our coverage area at the loading/unloading of Mickey & Friends parking trams, open a door on the backside of a Downtown Disney building, descend the stairs, traverse part of the vast basement, and go up some other stairs under the hotel. This place had good food at good prices, but it did take us a bit out of our area.

Break Areas - They typically had tables and chairs, drinking fountains, vending machines, televisions, and sometimes a stand-up arcade video game and pay phones. Some of them weren't fully enclosed, so they would be somewhat exposed to weather conditions.

Free Parking - A lot of cast members took this for granted. Management would have loved it if more cast members took mass transit to come to work, but there were many reasons cast members couldn't or wouldn't. The shifts a cast member might work made mass transit an impossible option for some. Also, some cast members lived too far for the mass transit system to be practical. Living closer was not an option for some due to affordability and not being members of the right gangs to be able to live in the places that were affordable.

Before Resort expansion, most cast members could park in the northeast section of the main Disneyland parking lot that was right there in front of the park. One sweeper even wrapped his car around a Monorail pylon, hitting the passenger side so hard that his driver-side door wouldn't open. The section closest to Harbor House had a gate around it that was opened at

Noon so as to allow cast members working later to park closer. Otherwise, we parked beyond that in what looked like it blended in with guest parking.

With Resort expansion came the Katella Cast Member Lot, which was located on the south side of Katella across from Gardenwalk. Shuttles drove cast members from the lot to Harbor Pointe. Some cast members, especially on weekends, used the parking structure near Team Disney Anaheim off of Ball Road. West of there, there was parking north of the Mickey & Friends parking structure.

Having free parking and a free shuttle was definitely a perk.

Costuming - One of the most basic aspects of being an hourly cast member was spending most of our time wearing clothing for which we didn't pay and weren't required to wash. This could save a person a whole lot on clothing expenses. The massive Disneyland Costuming operation provided us with clean costumes. And if we spilled something on our costume, like caviar, or putrid bullet can liquid, or a new hire's blood, we could make our way to Costuming during our shift to get a clean costume.

With an expanding cast, there were changes to the costuming system, including the location and the process. When I (Ken) hired in, Costuming for Custodial and other Operations Departments was on the north side of the old Administration Building. We'd approach dedicated walk-up windows and do a one-for-one exchange of the articles of clothing. The Costuming Cast Member would take our dirty costumes and go get the replacements. Sometimes there could be a line for this, which made it risky to do before our shifts. We were told during training to do it at the end our shifts so we'd have a clean costume waiting for us in our costume locker when we came in for our next shift, but some of us got in the habit of leaving it for doing before our shifts, because we were tired or in a hurry at the end of our shifts.

The location of Costuming moved to a new building that was built on the south side of the berm, just north of the Monorail track, and things changed so that we were supposed to find our own replacement costumes and take them to be scanned out.

Another big change was Fast Track, sold to the cast as "You'll only have to get dressed once! If you want your costume washed as certain way, you can do it yourself." It meant that cast members could wear their costumes home. This was a huge change. In the past, taking a costume piece home was grounds for termination. With Fast Track, it was being encouraged. This is why we started to see cast members in costume all over Orange County. I (Ken) thought it detracted from the show and I never gave up the minor inconvenience of dressing at home only to change again when I got to the park. I kept my costume locker, whereas if I changed to Fast Track I would have lost it.

FastTrack allowed for Disneyland to not provide "permanent" costume lockers (though day lockers were available) and if cast members washed their own costumes, it was that much more in savings for the Company.

Ear Lowering - Part of "The Disney Look" we were required to follow included strict limitations on our hair. Those limitations were loosened up as the years went by. If cast members wanted to have an expert in the Look cut and style their hair, there was Cast Cutters. Now, how many workplaces do you know of that have their own place for haircuts? It wasn't quite like some dot-com playground of an office. This was not a free service. Even so, it was a convenient thing to have backstage. At least, I (Ken) think it was. I'm not sure, because I never used it. Once I found out Lynn's wife was a professional hair stylist in a salon, I became a customer of hers.

Credit Union - While "Partners" might sound like a specific kind of club or bar, it was the name of the credit union for cast members. When I (Ken) hired in, it was near Harbor

House in a mobile building. There was a separate credit union for the Burbank/Glendale-based Company employees (and Florida, I think) called Vista! No, that's not me being excited; the name had an exclamation point. These credit unions merged and became "Partners!"

Cast-Exclusive Shops - If we didn't want to put our money into the Credit Union, nearby in another mobile building was Company D. They had merchandise exclusive to cast members and Company employees, and things they were clearing out from selling in the park.

Many years after I started, TEAM Centers were created. They were partly a store, partly an information center, and a place there various things could be distributed to cast members. We could buy discounted tickets to other parks and attractions in southern California and movie tickets. This was also the place to go if something happened to our name tag, and where new name tags (specialized to certain years, such as the 50th Anniversary) were distributed. While there was only one Company D, which moved to the Katella Cast Member Lot and, if I recall correctly, somewhere off-property after that, there were multiple TEAM Centers. One was at the Team Disney Anaheim and the other wound up near Harbor Point in the same new building as Costuming, after being upstairs at the back of the Opera House building.

From time to time, an author of a Disney-focused book would come to a TEAM Center to do book signings just for the cast. I (Lynn) remember one author, Jason Surrell. He was selling his Haunted Mansion book. He signed it for me, and I still enjoy this book today.

First Aid and **Physical Therapy** - First Aid for cast members used to be on the backside of the guest facility near the Hub in Disneyland, but with Resort expansion, it was moved to the area near Harbor Pointe. It certainly was convenient to have Registered Nurses right there at all times, in case we were feeling ill or got injured. Sometimes, I (Ken) would stop by for a free sore throat lozenge or some other minor treatment. We also had physical therapy on-property, which I needed for a short while after spraining my shoulder on the job. It was the end of my shift and it had been a rainy one, and I slipped going down some stairs inside the old Administration Building. I ended up being taken to St. Joseph's for an x-ray of my shoulder.

Offsite Activities

As with many other workplaces, there were things like softball leagues and various sports activities for cast members.

I (Lynn) had the opportunity to be a part of Team Disney Bike Club. The main event for this club was to participate in the Bay to Bay M.S. Bike Ride. This was a bike ride to raise awareness and money for Multiple Sclerosis.

I had just got into riding bikes more seriously about a year prior to this event, so I was somewhat prepared for the 100-mile ride over two days. The ride started in Irvine, California and ended in San Diego. So, it was about 50 miles each day. There were about ten of us from Custodial. I mostly stayed with my friend Matt S. We talked along the way and helped each other out. We got to know each other pretty well after those two days.

The first day, we rode to Carlsbad. Then that night there was a festival type event in a parking lot of the local mall. There was food, music, and massages!

We stayed in hotels, and the following day got on our bikes to take on the famous Torrey Pines. This was a big hill that I'm guessing was a mile up and a mile down. This was the most challenging part of the ride. I remember how much pain I was in riding up that hill, but then there was the downhill, so much fun!

Later that afternoon, we made it to the finish line at a park at Mission Bay, right near Sea World. I had a huge sigh of relief, but in a way it wasn't as hard as I thought it would be. This was the most I had ever ridden over two days.

Cleaning the Kingdom

There was another festival for the riders their and families and friends. We rode buses back to Irvine. As we rode on the bus back, which was about a two-hour drive, we looked at what we had covered over the past few days and it was an amazing time, and most of all we were able to raise money to fight a terrible disease.

Another event for which I (Lynn) rode my bike was for the first ever Disneyland Half Marathon in 2006. My role, along with a few others, was to sweep and encourage the runners. For this event, the runners needed to stay at a certain pace to be able to finish the race before the parks opened to the public and so that the streets of Anaheim could be opened up to normal traffic.

The race started near Downtown Disney and eventually went through both Disneyland and DCA, then through Angel Stadium.

It ended up being lots of fun. I was not in a hurry on my bike because I was there to monitor the runners and give them encouragement along the route. It was very cool to be able to ride my bike through Disneyland and DCA. A definite highlight was riding my bike inside Angel Stadium. How many people can say they have done that?

Unfortunately, there was the part where we had to tell the runners who came out of Angel Stadium past a certain time that their race was over. Many of them were very disappointed and emotional, as I could understand. The 13 miles didn't seem too bad of a ride for me, and it was lots of fun. An added bonus is that I can now say I rode my bike in the first-ever Disneyland Half Marathon. Running events around Disneyland are becoming very popular.

Marking Time

As with many jobs, just being there for a certain number of years was considered an accomplishment.

Celebrating our time at our job was something that was done well. After a year, we'd get a one-year "service pin" for our name tag. Then there were such pins for five years, ten years, etc. They'd feature a character or an iconic Disney image.

For five years of service, there was a luncheon. I (Lynn) had mine at the Disneyland Hotel. Ken, who had his many years before me, had his at Aladdin's Oasis. These luncheons were nice.

After ten years or more, there was dinner and entertainment in the Grand Ballroom of the Disneyland Hotel, where cast members would pose for group pictures. A plaque was given for ten years, and there were increasingly impressive gifts every fifth year after that, such as small sculptures.

With Resort expansion, we understand that these events have moved to other locations and may have otherwise changed.

Walt Disney Legacy Awards

When we were there, these were called Spirit Awards, and they were for more than simply showing up. They were for being outstanding cast members. In 2011, the Company unified the various awards different parts of the Company had into something called the Walt Disney Legacy Award. You can spot a recipient by their blue name tag.

This is what I (Ken) wrote in March 2001, after attending a Spirit Awards ceremony:

* * * * *

It Takes People

Disney has always noted that key element in the Disneyland experience is the cast. Cast members can make or break the guest experience, including the cast members guests never see.

Cleaning the Kingdom

Last Wednesday, I went to cheer on a buddy at the annual "Golden Spirit of Disneyland Resort Awards Ceremony" held in the Hyperion Theater inside DCA. Out of the thousands of cast members working at the Resort, twenty-eight were selected by their peers to receive Golden Spirit awards. Yes, there are bronze and silver awards, too. This is the highest internal award a cast member can receive, and they wear a pin on their nametags recognizing their achievement. There are three areas that the cast member must achieve in, and they must excel in one. They cover efficiency and cost saving, guest service, and teamwork.

Here are the criteria:

Each is a recognized role model

Each brings a consistent enthusiasm and sparkle to their workplace

Each is committed to Disneyland Cast and Guests

Each leads by example

Each performs his or her job with the utmost integrity and respect for Disney values

Each sees his or her role and attitude in performing it as critical in keeping the Guests coming back for more

Each is able to inspire others to reach beyond themselves to become more than they ever dreamed possible

My friend Dale is a Foreman is DCA Day Custodial. These days he typically oversees the restroom crew taking care of the men's restrooms at DCA, but he's worked all over Disneyland Park. He works hard, goes above and beyond in giving one-on-one guest service, and coaches others to follow suit. He owns a sizable chunk of Disney stock (he's been into investing for a long time) and encourages other cast members to take advantage of the stock purchase program at the Resort, and take an interest in the success of the company. He's been very active in the company's volunteering program, too.

There was a group of us there to cheer on Dale in particular along with our support of all recipients.

I was greeted warmly by Cynthia Harriss, President of The Disneyland Resort. She is fond of hugging, and very good at keeping track of who you are and what you are up to, and I get the impression that she loves being the Disneyland President. It is the kind of job kids dream about, not knowing the stress that must comes along with it, but it is nice to see someone inhabit the role so well.

Cynthia was hosting the ceremony along with her boss, Paul Pressler, Chairman of Walt Disney Parks and Resorts.

Paul, Cynthia, Mickey, Minnie, and the Disneyland Ambassadors did a great job recognizing each of the individuals, who were brought up one by one to be recognized, and to get their handshakes, hugs, and medals.

The ceremony was kept lively during two breaks with a "mathemagician" demonstrating magic squares, and touching readings from actual guest letters. Beautiful singing started and ended the ceremony - "Go the Distance" to start, and "Just One Dream" to end, during which I noticed even Paul Pressler signing along.

Afterwards, those of us there to cheer Dale mingled outside with Dale, his parents, Cynthia, Susan Cowan (Vice-President in charge of Operations Services), Director of Custodial Matt Gray, and other Custodial managers. The park was closing for the day, but the award recipients and their guests were treated to good eats at the ABC Soap Opera Bistro. The rest of us headed home, reminded that there are some real gems working at the Resort.

* * * * *

Collectible Disneyana Exclusive to Cast Members

Not only did Company D and TEAM Centers have cast-exclusive merchandise, which was very much appreciated by a Disneyana collector like me (Ken), but from time to time there was attraction-specific items created by cast members. For example, there was a specially-designed Haunted Mansion watch created for the attraction's 25th Anniversary in 1994. For you youngsters who may be confused, think of an Apple Watch that is NOT connected to any network. And nothing on the screen moves, except for these things called hands that help people determine time. The watch came in a metal coffin with artwork depicting the hitchhiking ghosts and the Mansion exterior. There was also attraction artwork on the face of the watch and when a button was pressed, we could hear Little Leota inviting us to "Hurry baaaaack..." They were limited to 999 and numbered.

I have never worn mine.

Every Christmas, we were given a cloisonné holiday pin with a Disney character, and for the Disneyland Anniversary on July 17, we'd be given a button marking the occasion.

Employment Benefits

In addition to all of the perks we've gone over in this chapter, Disneyland cast members were offered benefits that were nothing to sneeze at.

To get medical benefits, a cast member had to reach a certain status by working a certain number of hours per week for a certain number of weeks in the "off season".

When I (Lynn) was first hired in 1998, I was under the Casual category. That Summer season, I had more then enough hours working six days per week. Once summer ended, though, so did the hours. The goal then was to get to 25 hours consistently so I could collect benefits. Easier said than done!

I would call up every morning I didn't have a shift and see if a shift was available. Most of the time, that was possible. It took me about a year to get benefits. As the years went on it became harder to get benefits. Once I had benefits, I could get medical, dental, eye care, and prescriptions. I got them just in time, seeing as how I got married in October 1999.

We also had to be a certain level to accrue sick pay. Otherwise, when we called in sick, it meant going without pay. There was also a pension program.

One thing I (Ken) liked was the stock purchase program. We could have a certain percentage of our weekly paycheck go to purchasing, without fees, shares of The Walt Disney Company, which was generally well-performing stock.

Conclusion

Working at the Happiest Place on Earth certainly did have perks, especially for those of us who were Disney or theme park enthusiasts. As Custodians of Disneyland, we covered the entire park, both onstage and backstage. We could go virtually anywhere without being questioned, and if we *were* questioned, we could say we'd been called to do a cleanup.

We were part of a legacy of being the best of the best. We were surrounded by one of the most fascinating collections of design and engineering feats. Every day, our job was to create unparalleled experiences for people from all over the world, and sometimes we could make those experiences for each other and ourselves, too.

Before Fantasmic!, the Mark Twain use to ply the quiet Rivers of America on summer nights for a special trip in preparation for Fantasy in the Sky Fireworks. The boat would stop in the northern area of the River so the guests could get a good view. Those trips were ended, but one night, when Fantasmic! was dark, the Twain was docked and empty. As inconspicuously as I could, I (Ken) slipped on board and went to the pilot's position, then walked out onto the deck behind it, and watched a fireworks show from way up there. It was one of a thousand moments like that I treasure.

That was a perk!

Chapter 3

A Typical Day

(circa April 2001)

Have you ever wondered what a day working at Disneyland is like?

Introduction

This isn't a collection of highlights (or lowlights, as the case may be). This is a look at what a typical day of being a Disneyland Day Custodial Sweeping cast member was like. It

71

will not be an expose', and it will not be so thorough as to completely pull back the curtain. However, if you don't want to know what the "actor" is going through to put on the show known as "The Happiest Place on Earth", then what are you doing reading this book? Isn't that *why* you bought this book? For those of you who *are* interested, we hope we succeed in painting a clear enough picture to satisfy your curiosity.

Although only a small percentage of the cast members working at Disneyland Park are Day Custodial Cast Members, many of the cast members working in operations had similar elements to their workdays, as do cast members working at Disney California Adventure park.

What happens during a "typical" day may vary from season to season, and depends on the weather and attendance.

As a Disneyland Park Day Custodial Cast Member, we could be starting as early as 6 a.m. or as late as 7 p.m. for our shift. In this piece, we'll describe what it is like to be an opening Foreman (a.k.a. "Lead") in Disneyland Park Day Custodial on an average Saturday circa early 2001.

On My Way

The alarm clock goes off at 4 a.m. If I (Ken) owned a rooster, I'd go yell at it to wake it up, just for the sadistic fun of it. It is dark outside, and I tell myself I really need to get to bed on time one of these days. Of course, that would mean getting to sleep at 8 p.m. for a full night's rest. The park is opening at 8 a.m., but we start at 6 a.m. because there are opening procedures to do and "Magic Morning", meaning guests will be in parts of the park at 6:30 a.m. I leave the radio on so that I might catch a traffic report that actually mentions freeway closures. My shift will go until 5 p.m. and I'll have a half-hour unpaid lunch. That will give me a total of ten-and-a-half hours for the day, with two and a half hours of that being overtime..

People who start later in the day are often woken up with a phone call to come in earlier if the day is looking busier than expected or if someone has left a "hole" by calling in sick or calling in with transportation trouble (a dead car), or, in rare cases, simply not showing up with no explanation. If they are called in to be opening Foreman, they often are called too late for them to show up at 6 a.m.

Back when I'd be starting my shift later in the day, I'd check out what a fan website like LaughingPlace.com said and be updated on what was going on at the park before I even got there. Especially, if you're coming out of your two or three days off (depending on your schedule), you can learn more about what is happening "at work" from outside sources, before the people who are actually working there will. The Resort's Cast Communications team does a great job getting information out, though.

Anyway, it is time to shave and shower, because Disney resorts have strict grooming standards and I want to be as clean as possible, because chances are I'll be getting dirty and sweaty during the day. I need to be out the door by 4:45 a.m. or so, so it is just a quick hop online to check things out while I'm drying off and making sure I have all that I need for my day.

I get dressed in normal street clothes. Others are on "Fast Track", meaning they have costumes assigned to them that that can take home or wear home. This means that they don't have to dress twice - once to go to work, and again once they are there. I have opted not to use it, because I get to keep my personal locker and because, since I was always told to protect "the show", I don't feel right wearing my costume off-property and off-the-clock..

I might grab breakfast at home, from a drive-through with a cast member discount on the way to work, or at the park.

It is Saturday morning, and the streets are freeways are light on the traffic but heavy on the fog. It is nice to be able to zip southward on the I-5 Santa Ana Freeway without the usual endless crawl. Fortunately, there are no freeway closures for construction to show me the finer areas of Buena Park,

Fullerton, and Anaheim, and I hurry unimpeded towards my exit.

Cast members live all over the area. Some live in apartments that are walking distance from the Resort, sharing a place with other cast members. There are a lot who are students living at home. Some cast members come from as far as L.A. or deep in the Inland Empire. Some of the only places most cast members can afford homes of their own are so far away that their daily commutes are rather long.

Carpooling is encouraged, but can be hard at a place where shifts can vary so much, and can be shortened or extended.

From Exiting the Freeway to Getting Behind the Berm

I exit the freeway and head for the Katella Cast Member Lot (KCML). White shuttles with the distinctive "Disney" logo on their sides come and go. I'll reach the lot anywhere from twenty to thirty minutes after 5 a.m. Fortunately, at this hour, parking isn't a problem. Later, people will search for parking and may end up parking at the far reaches of the lot and walking a ways to the nearest of the three pick-up points. Still later in the day, the lot will be closed and cast members will be redirected to the Pumbaa lot.

On Saturdays and Sundays, I do have the option of parking at Team Disney Anaheim, the administration building that is at the northern end of the property, along I-5.

Even though parking wasn't a problem, getting on the shuttle may not be an easy task. Sometimes the shuttle fills up at the first stop. Cast members nervously check their watches. If there is a problem with the shuttles, management will usually take that into account and not mark someone late.

There's a building in the lot that has water, television, restrooms, vending machines, newspapers, an ATM, and phones.

Cleaning the Kingdom

I climb into the shuttle, which has no more seats left. I'm in a hurry, and standing, holding on to a bar, won't hurt me, at least as long as we're not hit by some errant driver. I might carry on a conversation with someone I see from my department or someone else I know. It is still early, so things might be quiet on the shuttle, quiet enough to hear the hip-hop, classical music, or sermon the shuttle driver is listening to on the radio.

The shuttle rolls down Clementine, and we can get a good look at the freeway. Thank goodness for the light at Harbor Boulevard, or we wouldn't be able to turn left. The shuttle pulls into Harbor Gate, right behind an errant driver who is stopped by a Security Hostess and directed to turn around. On the left is the access tunnel to the backstage of DCA. On the right are roads leading to the backstage of Disneyland Park. The shuttle pulls forward, next to the Monorail beam, and let's us out at Harbor Pointe, the place to get in or out of the fenced-off area.

A Security Host monitors Harbor Pointe and stands between the clock-in and clock-out areas. Before passing through one of the three turnstiles, each of us has to press a button for clock-in or just for clearance, then scan our cast member identification card. It is 5:40 a.m., according to the clock, which means I don't have any time to delay.

The old Administration Building stretches in front of me, the Costuming building is on the left, Harbor House is on the right, and people walk in all different directions. Harbor House used to be the checkpoint, placing the new Costuming building past the checkpoint for a while. That meant a lot of costumes were taken onto the shuttle, never to be seen at Disneyland again. This is one reason Harbor Pointe was built.

Until recently, I used to head into the Administration building, where I'd descend the stairs to the level where my locker room was, change, and then continue along the corridor to Custodial Central, which was on the same level. However, the downstairs locker rooms were recently cleared as part of an ongoing renovation of the building. In fact, looking up to the upper level from Harbor Pointe, I'm looking at the new scheduling center, where operations schedulers work to fill shifts that day, handle requests, and plan out the upcoming weeks and months in a large room loaded with workstations.

Now, I turn right and go to Harbor House, where I stop to pick up any information (Cast Member Reference Guides, Disneyland Line, special bulletins, memos, etc.) I don't yet have. Exiting the other side of Harbor House, I'm now standing on the walkway that rises next to Harbor Undercrossing, where vehicles cross under the Disneyland Railroad as it moves from the Grand Canyon Diorama to the Primeval World.

Due to the steepness of the undercrossing, vehicles are given the right-of-way so that they don't risk rolling backward due to stopping for pedestrians. Vehicles trip a signal as they go under, warning pedestrians of their approach. I head under the train track and emerge up on the inside side the Berm, where I have to turn right and pass in front of the undercrossing.

Inside the Berm; Getting Ready

The Space Mountain complex is on my left, Pizza Port is up ahead on my left, the green, round, and large Innoventions building is in the distance as I walk next to the backstage buildings on my right. I pass by such places as Cast Cutters, where cast members can make arrangements for haircuts and the like.

I finally reach the stairs that take me up to the Men's Upstairs locker room, which I was forced to return to after about ten years away from it. It is no secret that another reason the downstairs locker room was eliminated is that management is pushing for hourlies to go on Fast Track, and then to find it easier to wash their own costumes. Everyone at DCA is on Fast Track. Fast Track is another reason why we see more costumes for entire lands as opposed to individual attractions. Also, downstairs lockers (or any "permanent" lockers) were not being issued to new cast members.

Swinging open the door to the locker room, I'm greeting by a pile of costumes on the ground, and stuffy warmth. Clothes hangers and debris are strewn about, and someone from Empire Maintenance is doing what Disneyland Custodial used to do - cleaning up the room.

There are two types of lockers in this room. There are tall, skinny ones with footlockers above, or short, wider lockers, one on top of another. The old locker room had the former; I have the latter in this room. I get the bottom locker, which barely has enough room for everything. A sweeper is likely to at least have two sets of costumes, a belt, a pouch (holds paper towels, maps, etc.), a jacket, work shoes, rain gear, and whatever he is lugging around for the day tucked into the locker. Without a footlocker, my shoes get shoved in with my costumes and rain gear.

Waaay back in training, we were encouraged to exchange our dirty costumes for clean costumes after our shifts. But these days, when I'm opening and therefore off anytime between 2:30 and 5:30 p.m., I know it is best to do it before my shift, before the crack of dawn, lest I be waiting in horrendous lines at Costume Issue long after I'm off the clock. Expansion of the Resort forced Costume Issue to stay open around the clock.

Now that I'm in the upstairs locker room, and now that Costume Issue is just east of the guest pet kennels at the Disneyland Main Entrance, I have quite a trek ahead of me. So, I open my locker, get out what I need to, and go back where I just came, all the way back through Harbor House, passing Harbor Pointe, walking the length of the old Administration Building until I pass by TEAM Center Parkside (a cast member store and paperwork center), which recently moved into the eastern end of the Costume Issue building. If this was later in the day, I could wave at guests going by in Monorails, all while holding my dirty costumes in my hands.

Cleaning the Kingdom

There is a line to approach the windows, even at this hour. To keep us occupied and informed, the 24-hour Cast Member Channel plays on the overhead television. The televisions in the backstage break rooms are all equipped to have this channel now, which shows what is happening at the Resort. Clever.

This building not only houses Costume Issue and TEAM Center Parkside, but it is where the new "day" lockers are located. Yes, if you don't put your costume on at home, and you need a place to put your clothes and other items, these day lockers are available to you for the length of your shift, as long as you use a company-issued lock. I think you buy it.

That particular locker room is co-ed, and there are "cozy" gender-specific changing rooms. Of course, if you are in Custodial and you aren't wearing your costume in to work, a day locker is very inconvenient because of all of the equipment and extras you lug around - it is good to have a "permanent" place to store them.

Well, I finally get to a window, offer my identification card to be scanned, and exchange my costumes, making sure I'm getting the right sizes and they are functional. Then it is time for the long trek back to my locker.

After changing, I need to hurry to make it to Custodial Central ("the office") on time. After passing Harbor Undercrossing, I don't turn towards Harbor House - I continue along the north side of the old Administration Building, past where Costume Issue used to be conveniently located. It was moved so that it would be conveniently located between both theme parks. Delivery trucks pass by parked cars, helping to prepare for the day ahead.

A bunch of Security Hosts stand around smoking. I finally reach the doors that I go through to get to the stairs down to the Custodial office, which was moved underground in January of 2000, under Security.

Over the years, more and more signs have appeared backstage. No doubt this has been done partially because of higher turnover. Most signs have some sort of Disney character or icon on them. The stairwell is no exception as direction signs inform you how to get to what in the building. Along the stairs, there are signs touting how many injury-free days the different divisions of Custodial (DL Days, DCA Days, DL Nights, DCA Nights) have behind them.

At the base of the stairs, I face a display case with pictures of new hires, retirement parties, award ceremonies, and occasionally, the recently departed. The cast member schedules for this week and next are on the wall as well. A long hallway stretches to the right, next to the stairs is a machine that dispenses such equipment as flashlights and squeegees. The office is on the left, and I hurry in to check in, as I'm supposed to before 6 a.m.

Custodial Central - A Busy Hive

Custodial Central is usually buzzing with activity. Round-the-clock Custodial operations for the Mickey and Friends Parking Structure, Disneyland Park, Downtown Disney, and Disney's California Adventure are based here, as are the outside contractors. Custodial now has a radio channel for Disneyland Park, one for DCA, and another for "chat" and contractor traffic. The command center is manned by a clerk or two, answering phone and radio (walkie-talkie) calls, checking people in, checking out radios and keys, keeping track of the hours cast members are working, etc. They are also the main communication link between Custodial and other departments.

There's not a wasted inch in the place. There are information boards; a large marker board with the daily assignments of managers and foremen; workstations for writing up needed materials, including parade and Fantasmic! clean-up assignments; large poster board cards to sign for people transferring, quitting, or retiring; the ever-important coffee machines, microwave, and water coolers; the copier; the conference room complete with marker board and television with VCR for training; the bull-pen of assistant manager desks in one room, the manager desks in others, and the office of the Director of Custodial.

Up until relatively recently, Custodial did not have a Director all to itself. Our overall manager, Ray Sidejas, was only the second person to permanently head up the department. Custodial has always taken pride in being committed to Walt's ideas and having a high number of people who have been in the operation for a long time, giving it a strong sense of continuity and legacy. When the management structure was set up for DCA and DTD, those areas were given to Mike Sweeney, a manager who was promoted from under Ray to a position parallel to him. Ray stayed put, and park veteran Matt Gray was placed over both of them in the new position of Director of Custodial.

I was assigned to be the foreman for Adventure / Frontier (one of my favorite areas) almost two weeks ago, when the schedule came out. Each area has its own personality, and as such, everyone has different preferences. I like Adventure / Frontier.

The Clock Starts

"Any radios?" I ask the clerk, who tells me they are all out. The two-way radio is our comfort blanket, our link to everything, *and* the bane of our day. It is our symbol of power and status. Indeed, when someone is disciplined and is relieved of Foreman duty (usually due to attendance problems), it is said that they've "lost their radio". We use it to get a hold of Security, the office, or our peers. It is also what is used by our managers and clerks to call us to relay messages.

The clerk checks me in and hands me the keys for my area. A competent, pleasant clerk with a sense of humor is priceless.

I pull my schedule for the day out of the folder and give it a quick look. "Who ARE these people? Anyone know who X is? Can she do trash? Oh no, I have Y in my area. Hey, at least Z is on

Cleaning the Kingdom

my crew today." These are just some of the things uttered at this point. Hopefully, I remember to grab a bunch of park maps to supply to my crew.

I make a few copies of the schedule in the copier. If I'd been earlier, I would have sat in the conference room with the rest of the leads and worked on the schedule, technically before being on-duty. As it is now, I take a quick glance at it to start toying with plans for the day. It is a little past 6 a.m. and most of the leads are still sitting around the conference room table.

We head off to our respective duties, dodging delivery trucks and other vehicles. The packer (trash compactor) behind Main Street is being put back into place after having been taken away and emptied. I go onstage by Lost & Found/Lockers, noticing the flyers on the backstage side of the door, and cut across the street, into the men's restroom, and out the back door to the backstage area on the Westside of Main Street. Large green dumpsters for recycling cardboard fill up the space between the building and the Jungle Cruise boat storage area.

I go this way to retrieve my hidden metal pan and broom. I have a locker for them between Fantasyland and Frontierland, but when work started on changing Casa Mexicana to Rancho Del Zocalo, it was too inconvenient to get to. For many years, Custodial Central was back there behind the Casa Mexicana / Mineral Hall facade, near Big Thunder train storage.

Metal pans are not being bought anymore. They are being replaced by plastic pans that are lighter, adjustable, and generally easier on the sweeper's arms. I want to end my days as a sweeper with a metal pan, so I can participate in the tradition of hurling my pan into the Rivers of America and having it quickly sink to the bottom.

After passing between Aladdin's Oasis and the Jungle Cruise, I walk through Adventureland, where Night Custodial is still doing their thing, as are Landscaping cast members. I go backstage via the door by Bengal Barbecue, navigating my way past everyone who is working back there while a radio (of the AM-FM type) blasts away.

Backstage

This particular backstage area is an "island". The only way to get to it or away from it is by going through onstage areas. There's a packer; drums for grease; an area with a hose and grated drain; access to the Golden Horseshoe, Bengal Barbecue, River Belle Terrace, Stage Door Cafe, and shop stock closets; cast member restrooms; stairs up to a semi-enclosed break room and offices, and stairs to an underground storage area (not a tunnel system!).

The break room has booths, a television, vending machines, a drinking fountain, pay phones, and an arcade game.

You can always find cast members smoking in an outside backstage area, and you can usually find official message boards and unofficial fliers of all sorts.

There's also the Custodial area locker.

Opening Up

I walk to the Custodial area locker (a supply closet) and unlock it, surveying the inside. Depending on how busy it was the night before, and who was working in that area, things could be anywhere from perfect to horrifying. The closet could be in disarray and depleted of stock, there could be no pan and brooms for the crew, stuff like that.

Ideally, the locker area is going to have a bunch of pan and brooms in good condition, mop handles, mop heads, and a mop bucket, pushbrooms, buckets, and long and a short handle picker, various chemicals, paper towels, cloth towels, a Lost & Found bag (hopefully empty), clip boards, and more. There are always signs and memos offering reminders about policies and procedures. Checking the packer to make sure it is empty enough and that it functions is a good idea. There's nothing like having your packer fill up on a busy day when the park is still open for several hours. That means hauling trash to a packer that's further away.

The backstage area can get quite cluttered with stock for the shops and restaurants that is being delivered and all sorts of equipment, including the large carts used by sweepers to haul the trash from the onstage cans to the backstage packer.

I plunk down the maps and the schedules and pick up a plastic bucket and the short-handle picker, ready to check out the damage from the previous day.

The closing shift Day Custodial is supposed to make sure the flowerbeds (generic term for landscaped areas, whether they have flowers or not) are picked clean of trash, that the waiting areas were swept clean, and that the trashcans were fairly empty. It doesn't always turn out that way. Night Custodial does the heavy cleaning, including hosing down the walkways. In the morning, we'll do things like check the building fronts, remove gum, check the flower beds, and take care of any standing water night crew couldn't get to.

It is good to check in the with the Night Custodial cast members and find out what is going on and what I need to be aware of. We see almost every inch of the backstage and onstage area every day, so we're up on what needs to be fixed and how to handle certain realities.

Magic Morning doesn't currently extend to this side of the park. All vehicles have to be moved out of the onstage Magic Morning areas, but they are still out in my area. Things are still in overnight mode, with doors to the backstage wide open and vehicles of various sorts zipping by. Food and drink products crowd the back area, waiting to be taken to where they'll be sold.

Preparing the Area

My first cast member is scheduled to come on at 7:30 a.m. Until then, I scour the area, methodically going through the landscaping to pick out the trash, stanchion plugs, looking for lost items, and restaurant trays, dishes, and silverware. If there was a late showing of Fantasmic! the night before, certain flowerbeds may be trashed. There are mornings when things are very clean, and mornings where it is so bad there won't be enough time to get most of it up before the park opens.

I'm understanding. I know it can be tough to close out during a busy season. The Foreman might be new to being a lead, may have been at the park for less than a year, and may have a crew full of people who are fresh out of training, some of whom won't care or won't be tough enough to stay a week. He or she might be inexperienced with this particular area and the specific characteristics it has. He or she might be too busy to remember to make sure they all use flashlights when checking their beds, and they might not think to get and use one, or they might not even bother checking the beds. The poor Lead isn't omnipresent, and it is hard to personally check the entire area each night. You have to choose your battles. Besides, even with a good flashlight, more can be seen during daylight.

Making my way around the area, I make sure there are no full trashcans, and generally survey the area. Usually, trash cans and benches will need to be placed back where they belong. Trash cans are often used as very expensive barricades on the part of Attractions cast members. We'll find two or more cans placed next to each other or in very close proximity, which is very inefficient, or "area" cans in the line or line cans in the area - yes, there is a difference.

You never know what you're going to find when you are opening up. I won't gross you out with tales of things we find that festered overnight. That's for chapter 5.

Places that definitely will need to be cleaned include the area by the McDonald's fry wagon (long-handle picker will be needed to get all the debris that will be down by the river), in the line for Big Thunder Mountain Railroad (time for some climbing), under the Tiki Room exit stairs, and the outside queue of Indy.

I try to make it back to the locker before 7:30 to leave a note for the 7:30 person to tell him or her where I'll need help with the rest of the opening procedures. While a 7:30 a.m. start time means they're supposed to be there at 7:30, they might not make it there until five or ten minutes later. That doesn't sound like a big deal, but when the park is opening at 8, it is.

But, you have to choose your battles. I'm usually not there to actually see them show up, because the moments are precious and they're dwindling. As 8 a.m. approaches, I might get a radio with a dying battery from a night cast member. Otherwise, I'll have to call the office and see if anyone has called in sick, been pulled to another area, or been added to my crew, as there should be another person coming on and I need to fill out the schedule.

Planning the Day

As with most things in life, planning can make all of the difference, even if things change. (and boy, do they ever change sometimes.) Scheduling well or badly can mean the difference between a safe, clean area or a shameful disaster of a mess. The trick is to make sure that every area is adequately covered at all times, at least as on paper, until the area can be handed over to the closing foreman.

I consider how many people I have, what their hours are, and who they are, and what the projected attendance for the day is. Fewer people on the schedule means more work for those who will be there, such as larger areas to cover. Certain people are more efficient at different tasks. It is hard if you don't recognize names on the schedule, because you have no idea what that person's experience, attitude, personality, age and physical condition, preferences, strengths, or weaknesses are. Ideally, on a very busy day, as Adventure/Frontier foreman, I'm going to have a crew of eight able-bodied, fairly competent cast members with good attitudes working with me on the day end

Cleaning the Kingdom

(meaning starting no later than 1:30 p.m.) It very rarely works out that way.

With eight people, one is going to cover Indy, which includes sweeping the line, taking care of Indy trash cans, responding if there is a hydraulic fluid spill from one of the troop transports, and making sure the cast member/Guest Who Needs to Go *NOW!* Restrooms are good, which means they get a "premium" (very slightly higher) pay rate.

Two people are going to end up dumping trash. They will be taking large metal carts with 3, 6, or 8 hard resin trash can liners through the area and emptying out the trash in the area cans. A "stomp board" helps them compact the trash somewhat, and the liners can be moved through the area on small wheeled platforms. They also are responsible for emptying the bagged trash cans in the lines and waiting areas, and the bagged recycling cans.

One person will end up sweeping lines. He or she keeps a record of which lines were done at what time.

Three people will each have a section of the area - Adventure, Frontier, and Alley/Trail. Frontier stops at the petrified tree and the wooden bridge on Big Thunder Trail, but is otherwise self-explanatory, as is Adventure. Alley/Trail goes from the entrance of Pirates to the wooden bridge on the Big Thunder Trail, and thus has some overlap with Frontier.

Finally, a breaker will cover those three areas during breaks and lunches and handle odd jobs.

Not too long ago, the schedules were modified to show how the shift hours had been designated, i.e. people are designated for trash removal, sweeping lines, and covering breaks. The Lead has the authority to assign people to wherever he sees fit, though. When it comes to something like Indy, however, there is a premium paid to the cast member, and if you move someone out of Indy, they may ask for their premium anyway, so I tend to leave that person in there.

After calling the office on a park landline phone to ask if anyone has been pulled, has called in sick, or whatever, I ask

86

any of my early crew members what their preference in assignments and break times are. It doesn't mean they'll get what they ask for, but the input can help. Looking down the list and seeing how many people I have, what their hours are, and who these people are, I formulate a plan for the schedule. Then, I run down the line, first filling in the assignments, then the break times for the assignments that will need a breaker in place when those people are on break.

While some managers consider breakers the last position to be assigned, I always try to have a breaker, unless my crew is so small as to render it impossible or unnecessary. It isn't that I don't want to cover the breaks myself, but a Foreman needs the freedom to answer radio calls and the like, and I know from experience that it stinks to return from a break or a lunch to find that your area hasn't been covered. My breaker is usually someone I trust, someone I think to be a good, experienced, competent worker, and someone I like to give a break to, because covering breaks is less monotonous than covering the same area for eight hours.

If it comes down to having the area split into three coverage areas or splitting it into two and having someone dedicated solely to sweeping lines, I'll choose the second option. Lines have gotten worse over the years, thanks to Vending, among other things, and FastPass can be a blessing or a curse. Some look at being assigned to lines as punishment. Some covet trash duty, which is less tedious and tends to be less supervised. I try to assign people to where I think they'll be the most effective.

When filling in the breaks, I try to make it so that the breaks will be comfortably paced for the cast member, will not overlap with another cast member's breaks, and if reasonable, back-to-back so that the breaker can be freed for longer blocks of time to do other tasks when not covering a break. An eight hour shift means a cast member will get a half-hour unpaid lunch (hence, full shifts are scheduled for eight-and-a-half hours) and two fifteen-minute breaks. Seven hours or less means two breaks but no lunch (mutually waived). Anything over seven hours means lunch is mandatory, so someone working seven hours and fifteen minutes makes less money for the day than someone working seven hours. Anything over four hours requires two breaks. Shifts are typically six hours and up. Some people work a four- day, ten-hour-a-day week.

Although breaks are officially 15 minutes, many Leads, myself included, assign the breaker to cover an area for a full 30 minutes commencing with the start time of the assigned cast member's break, and we tell that cast member, with a wink, "The breaker will be covering the area for 30 minutes." We won't actually *tell* them to take a long break. On the breaker's instruction sheet, which is not an official document but rather a scrap of paper, we assign them 15 minutes of "roam" time after their first break.

I don't write in when *my* breaks will be, as I tend to disappear on them, and I don't want everyone else to take the opportunity to slack off. Leads will often take a break along with their lunch out of convenience. I schedule my lunch first and my breaks later, as I might not get my lunch otherwise. By law and by union rules, we must take our breaks, or be compensated with overtime pay. I tell the people working with me to take their breaks no matter what (even late). If things go downhill, it isn't because they aren't doing their job - it is because there are either too many guests, or there has been a breakdown in the system, such as not enough cast members. My lunch may not actually happen until halfway through my shift or longer, and I may never get my breaks. We are often called off of our lunches and breaks for responsive calls or to meet a cast member.

After the break times are filled in, the breaker's direction sheet can be made. The breaker may cover an area until the other cast member arrives, will cover breaks, and may be assigned to such tasks as sweeping lines or shops, cleaning up the backstage areas, taking stuff to Lost & Found, getting stock for the locker, various odd jobs, going to parade clean-ups, pushbrooming, spot-mopping, etc.

Once I'm finished with the schedule and break sheet, I'll take it upstairs and make copies - one for our managers (I have to fill in my breaks on this one), and one for my pocket so I can keep track of everything wherever I am.

The King and Queen Arrive

As the park is now open, I pick up my pan and broom and head out to greet the early guests. Unless there is still opening clean-ups to do, there usually isn't a whole lot to do at this point. The park is a long way from being busy. Most of the activity at this time will be directing guests to where they want to go. Some want breakfast. Some are rushing to one attraction or another. Some are already looking for characters.

The Custodial Foremen are very visible, and must deal with guests, all levels of most other departments, their managers, their crew - in short, just about everyone. It is good to be flexible, knowledgeable about the Resort, and good with people.

I'm there first and foremost to assist guests, provide them with a clean and safe environment to enjoy their day, and to equip my crew to do the same. Throughout the day, I'm supposed to observe the individuals on my crew, especially the newer ones, for coaching and feedback purposes.

Even though I'm a Foreman, that doesn't place me above doing any task for which Day Custodial is responsible. We work as a team, even though I delegate various responsibilities and calls.

Back to the Hive to Check in with Management

Operating management meets for "Mickey's Roll Call" a half-hour after the park opens, and in Custodial, the Foremen meet with our management an hour after the parks opens for "Minnie's Roll Call". At Minnie's Roll Call, we go over what was discussed at their roll call and whatever is going on at the

Cleaning the Kingdom

Resort, in the Park, and in our department - gripes, concerns, questions, suggestions, praises, policies, whatever. We discuss our dealings with other departments, what do and say in certain situations with guests or cast members, specific cast members who are not up to standards, and so forth. Anything and everything happens during these sessions, from announcements of awards, to a shocking, terse statement that John Doe Assistant Manager "no longer works here".

Roll call may last ten minutes or over half an hour. Typically, we'll go over the roll call sheet that has official information on it, and then we'll go around the room and give everyone a chance to bring up their comments and questions. Sometimes there will be a demonstration or small lecture educating us about techniques, policies, or programs.

The length and tone often varies widely depending on who is there. Weekends are often different than weekdays, where you will find the most seasoned veterans. Vice-President Susan Cowan has been known to stop by on occasion. Department Manager Ray Sidejas stops in for pep talks and explanations, etc.

Ray is there, as he has been for recent Saturdays, bringing in donuts as a thank-you gesture to the Foremen. His attendance guarantees a much longer session, as he loves to explain his expectations thoroughly and discuss "how it is" with his front-line warriors. Ray is old school; he's a guy who cares about the Disneyland ideals, and well aware of the legacy that is in his hands while trying to please his bosses, who are relative newcomers. He frequently walks the park, inspects our onstage and backstage locations, and occasionally still gets into "whites" (Day Custodial Sweeping costume) to get a hands-on perspective. He has the respect and admiration of his veteran Foremen. When the other departments dropped their Foremen, he fought to keep his Foremen in place. As a result, Custodial was ahead of the game when the rest of Operations decided to bring back Leads.

Cleaning the Kingdom

When coming in for Roll Call, we turn in copies of our schedules if we haven't done so already, try to remember anything we needed to get or do at the office, pick up radios (batteries may be low), and the like. We try to give messages to the clerks, such as "give John Doe the trash equipment keys".

After Roll Call, I grab anything I need to take back to the area, sign any large or small (greeting) cards, talk one-on-one with managers if I need to, and escort any new cast member assigned to my area.

Operational Mode

Now it is a matter of sticking to the plan - patrolling the area, meeting cast members as they arrive, answering calls, meeting managers as they pass through, covering areas, etc. Some days you are runnin' around and need to be in several places at once, other days things are very slow and you need something to do.

This is the time you make sure your crew is performing well, that the area stays safe, beautiful, and clean. We monitor walkways, shops, landscaped areas, lines, ride vehicles, even backstage areas.

If you have a good crew, you've planned well, and nothing out of the ordinary is going on, this is where the day can get monotonous and long, as a lot of your work is done. Of course, there is always something to do; you just have to look for it. Different Leads have different pet projects, and this is often where the outstanding leads are separated from the rest. A lousy lead will try to get away with doing as little as possible, spending as little time on-stage, hiding, supervising as little as possible, and talking to their friends on their crew and in other departments all day.

Instead, they could be checking backstage areas, doing "utility" work, coaching a cast member, checking in with other departments working in the area, and initiating guest contact.

I've made friends with annual passholders who I knew were annual passholders only because I'd see them quietly passing through every week. They don't look or behave in an unusual manner, or call attention to themselves. Having them give a quick hello as they pass through is nice.

There are also some neat things to do while battling tedium that tend to vary by area, such as sweeping through the Indy line and using "performance theming". "Pirate TV" can be quite interesting. Yeah, in case you didn't know: just because you are "alone" with your honey on a ride, it doesn't mean that you aren't being watched ;-)

Laughing Stock & Other Entertainment

The guys from Laughing Stock crack me up. I make a point of "giving extra attention" to the area in which they happen to be performing. I love it when they come up with good ad-libs.

Woody and Jessie are very popular and can draw quite a crowd for autograph signings. I like it when it is earlier in the morning and they have more one-on-one time with the kids who happen upon them.

The Disneyland Marching Band likes to ride the front of the Mark Twain and interact with the steam whistles. We can hear the bands in New Orleans Square, and of, course, there's always the steel drum band in Adventureland above Tropical Imports.

The Fry Cart

Bussers handle the eating areas (any area with tables), sweepers don't. Years ago, Bussing was part of Custodial, now it is part of Foods. It is cheaper for Foods not to put tables by the McDonald's fry wagon, thereby giving all of the extra work generated by its presence to Custodial. Clever, huh?

The fry cart is one of the most challenging elements of that area. Clean that and the popcorn wagon, and things look pretty nice with a lot less effort.

Aladdin's Oasis

Once a restaurant with entertainment, the Oasis is now used for special functions and for storytelling with the characters from *Aladdin*. I loved using this place as a break area when I worked closing shifts. Strictly speaking, we supposed to use designated break areas only, but sometimes, some people just need to be in a quiet place where they can be left alone to read or write.

The Oasis has tile for flooring, and the covering of the patio is such that, if it has been raining, it can be near impossible to dry out. But the show is popular, so it is a given that we'll be called to dry it up, unless rain keeps coming down. We want to make it safe for the performers and comfortable for our guests.

Indy Oil Spill

It is actually hydraulic fluid from the mechanisms that give the vehicles their added movement, but "oil" is much easier to say, and fits in with the theme anyway. Occasionally, (used to be a lot more common), a vehicle will spring a leak, causing slipping and therefore a shutdown. If we're lucky, it will just be a small spot on a level surface. Sometimes, though, the vehicle traverses more of the track and leaves a long trail.

For the clean-up, the name of the game after safety is speed. The idea is to get the clean-up taken care of as fast as safely possible so that the attraction can be returned to operation for the enjoyment of our guests.

Especially if it is a busy day, the best thing for me to do is to head in to the attraction when the all-call goes out that the attraction is down. From our standpoint, it is good to have it go down for a long time for something else, and for the guests to be cleared out. That way, our people have an easier time of spiffying up the place. Attraction downtimes are the best time to go in and clean up any place. Although they are frustrating to the guests, nothing is better from a Custodial standpoint than to have an attraction break down a few times throughout the day.

My Indy person is supposed to meet me at the unload area so that, if we're needed, we can get tags (tag into the attraction) and get the necessarily equipment. It is essential to get a tag. The attraction will not be started back up unless all of the tags are returned. This is a safety precaution. The tags are rectangular, numbered, metal plates that hang on a board to the left, just out of the station. You pick a tag off of the board, and write your name and department in chalk where the tag was.

I meet my person and we either wait for word, or tag out and go to the spot in question. Walking instead of riding in a huge vehicle, the attraction's immense size is apparent. Some accessways cut down on the time it takes to get around, but some equipment won't fit, so if it is needed, we have to take it there by following the track.

There's a dust we put down on the fluid, requiring face masks. We pushbroom it into piles and vacuum it up with back-mounted vacuums. If it is a particularly large spill, we'll need to call for help and we may have two groups start at other ends and work in assembly-line fashion towards each other. Pools of the fluid are partially abated with pads and pillows. Several people will be there; people from Facilities, Attractions, and a Custodial assistant manager. The cleaned-up fluid and the dust can't be just thrown into the trash, but rather is taken to a special location backstage for processing and disposal.

After the clean-up, we put the tags back (this is very important!), and I wait with my Indy person to make sure that we aren't needed again for the attraction to be reopened. If it will be down for a while longer, we make sure everything is fine as far as Custodial's responsibilities and I can pull the Indy person to help out somewhere else.

Cleaning the Kingdom

Either one of us might have been called off of lunch or break to respond, or may have delayed our lunch or break until everything was taken care of. It sure is nice to have a breaker covering breaks out in the area when I'm stuck down in Indy. If I'm down in Indy and I get a call for an ice cream spill by the Big Thunder exit, I'll be asking the Fantasyland Lead to take care of that.

Speaking of Lunch

We get thirty minutes of unpaid lunch time. I try to get my lunch out of the way earlier in my shift, and will usually take it before I take any of my breaks. It isn't unusual for a foreman to have to answer a call and return to lunch later, or wind up taking lunch hours late.

A lot of cast members bring their lunches from home or some place they stopped at along the way, usually keeping them in small coolers. We have access to microwaves and refrigerators. Different departments have bake sales from time to time. There are, of course, sandwiches, meals, and snacks in the vending machines. Finally, there are the backstage eateries, where cast members can congregate to a somewhat fresh meal and watch television - the big game, even.

The key thing is that we have thirty minutes. We call our lunch in to the office over the radio, so everyone knows when we start. It isn't like we can sit around backstage and simply tell anyone who comes across us that we're on lunch. I try to get my lunch in when there won't be someone starting his or her shift in my area that I wanted to talk with right from the start, like someone who may be new. There isn't a lot of time to get to the restaurant, get the food, and eat it before it is time to head back.

Cleaning the Kingdom

Tasks in Other Areas

Indy oil clean-ups are one of my least-favorite things about the Adventure/Frontier area. Each area has its own specialized tasks.

Any area with a train station might get called to take care of something on a train, and if they aren't able to make it, the call is passed down the line.

In New Orleans/Critter, a sweeper might ride a Pirate boat for a trip to take care of a call, and the closing Foreman needs to make sure the Bear Band theaters are swept out when they close, usually at separate times. Sometimes, the ride operators will switch the theater in use so that we can clean.

On Main Street, there are the horses, of course, and parades.

In Tomorrowland, the Imagination Institute is swept out a couple times a day. The Foreman responds to calls in Innoventions, usually "biological products" in the Honeywell wall-crawl or on a seat at the GM exhibit. Something about the vibrating seats causes people to lose control.

Some of the other things that may be regularly encountered:

- Lost children, parents, items, or cast members
- Unsatisfactory cast member performance
- Schedule changes - call-ins, lates, no-shows, injuries or illness, pulls (to other areas), additions, shift extensions - getting another cast member can be a blessing or a curse, depending on the individual being sent to me
- Special management requests
- Cast member questions, requests, concerns, complaints
- Requests for First Aid
- People injuring themselves but declining First Aid
- Failure of the trash compactor

- Inquisitive, confused, upset, unstable, hostile, disruptive, or destructive guests, of many different languages, customs, and dispositions
- Various substances from various life forms (anything and everything, anywhere)
- Food, drink, and candy spills
- Vending carts leaking water, oil (very slippery!), frozen lemonade (very sticky!), etc.
- The rechargeable radio battery dying out - I hope Custodial Central has some others charged
- Low supplies at the locker - we trek across the park to get more

I'm probably forgetting a few dozen things. A foreman has to keep in mind such things as Federal, State, and local laws and regulations, Company, Resort, and Department policies, union contracts and rules, etc. Nothing is ever as simple as it first seems! When we don't know something, though, there are plenty of other people to turn to, like the on-duty assistant managers.

Finishing Up, Passing the Radio

The end of my shift draws close. Sometimes, I look back and wonder where the time has gone. Other times, it seems like the day dragged on forever.

Depending on the way the schedule is set up, there will usually be people coming on shortly before the closing Lead. I don't write down an assignment on the schedule for these people. I meet them or, if I know them and know they know what to do, leave them a note explaining what they should do, letting them know that the closing Foreman will determine their ultimate assignment and the timing of their breaks. If someone has a mid shift with a significant portion into the closing lead's shift, I tell them to check back with the closing Lead, because they may get moved, and because the closing Lead will have authority over when they will take their remaining breaks.

Officially, we have fifteen minutes of paid walking time. However, with all of the hassle and paperwork, opening Foremen are notorious for leaving the area a full 30 minutes before their off-time. Time is money to an hourly employee, and most will not do paperwork or anything work related after their walk time begins.

If I'm off at 5:00 p.m., and the closing foreman is on at 4:30 p.m., I will try to meet the closing lead face to face and discuss things with them. I make sure they know that I have provided extra copies of the schedule in case the one in use gets too messy. I hand him or her a note with pertinent information, such as ongoing problems, general conditions for the day, etc. The closing lead needs to know if or when the breaker will need more assignments, what breaks are scheduled but not yet assigned coverage, and what potential gaps there are in the schedule.

Ideally, a closing Foreman meets me there at this time, taking the radio and keys from me, which I will call the office to transfer to his or her name. Otherwise, I must stop at the office to check them in, or meet the Foreman down there. If it is parade time, we have to deal with crossing the parade route. This often delays the arrival of the closing Lead.

If it was a 7 a.m. to 5:30 p.m. shift, and the closing Foreman was on at 5, both he and I would have to deal with crossing the parade route during the parade. Fortunately, we don't have to do that today, and he arrives on time. He has his own radio, so I give him the keys and have to take my own radio back to the office.

Clocking Out

After making sure I haven't left anything at the locker, I leave the locker area to stash my pan. Hourly cast members never move so fast as when they are going to clock out and have somewhere they want to go. I wave to familiar faces that I bump into along the way, whether guests onstage, or cast members onstage or backstage.

I slip behind the western side of Main Street for a quicker way to go. I pass by the Jungle Cruise boat storage, past cast members lounging on a break. A small vehicle is being carefully backed up out of the dead-end alley.

I reach the unmarked door I'm looking for, one that gives me access to the back door of the Center Street restrooms and the restricted door of a merchandise stock closet. I remember walking through stock closets on my way to answer a call or fulfill a request made in person, but nowadays the doors are kept locked, restricted, and many have keypads on them.

Opening the restroom door, I walk back onstage, out of the restroom, and make my way across the parade route at the Center Street crossing. It is rather crowded on the other side with people crossing the route, walking up or down the sidewalk, at the fruit cart, or going to the Lockers/Lost & Found location.

Pushing open the large door with the "Cast Members Only" sign on it, I'm backstage for the final time today. From there, I can go through the area the parade floats and equipment will be heading to, past the large break room, past the Opera House building, back to the old Administration Building, down the stairs to Custodial Central.

It's a busy time again there with the changeover. I hand in my radio and tell the clerk the name of the Foreman who now has the keys I'd checked out in the morning. This is when I'll often see the closers, especially the ones who now work at DCA, for the few moments I'll see them this week.

After marching back up the stairs, I head quickly back towards my locker room. Along the way, I'll wave and nod to other cast members who are also leaving or some of whom are just coming on. Maybe we'll exchange a word or two.

Cleaning the Kingdom

Back at my locker, while changing out of my costume and emptying my personal items out of my pouch, I try to remember my car keys. In the old days, it wasn't as big of a deal to forget them, but now it means a lot of extra time if you don't remember them until you are heading for your car in the Katella Cast Member Lot (KCML).

I walk back towards the undercrossing, through Harbor House, to Harbor Pointe, where I can clock out so long as it is twelve minutes before my off-time or later. The allowance of early clock-outs started before the costuming and parking changes were made, back when some people were able to change quickly and be at Harbor House a few minutes before their clock-out time. The amount of time allowed has been reviewed and modified since. Many were suspicious when it first started that it was going to be used to take away walk time. Now, with the parking the way it is, early clock-outs are needed.

At Harbor Pointe, I check to see if I can clock out yet, press the button, and slide my card. I show my open backpack to the Security Host if he isn't too busy, and join the line for the cast member shuttle, under the monorail track.

Getting Back to the Car

Lines for the cast member shuttles can quickly grow. Tour busses were added to the rotation, but it takes them longer to get to the parking lot and they can only stop in one place, which may not be the stop you want.

If I had parked at the TDA structure, I could double back from my locker towards Custodial Central to take a minivan shuttle to Ball Gate, but I usually choose to walk straight from my locker and have to cross the parade route.

I pass up the chance to get on a larger bus, choosing to wait for the shuttle instead.

We all pile in, and away we go into Harbor Boulevard traffic. After enduring the traffic lights, the shuttle turns left onto what used to be Freedman Way, and we get to pass right by Melodyland. A right on Clementine takes us right past the fire station and aims us directly at KCML, though we have to make it through a traffic light.

The shuttle pulls into the lot, and turns right. At this time of day, there are a lot of cars pulling into and out of the lot, there are a lot of people looking for parking spaces. I get off the shuttle at the first stop and head for my car. It may be a little busy getting out of the lot, and I have to be extra careful at times like this with cars and pedestrians going every which way.

A few more traffic lights, and then I'm back on the freeway. In less than twelve hours, I'll be back on the freeway, heading to the park again.

And that was a typical day.

Chapter 4

It's Not Such a Dirty Job

Isn't it demeaning to be a janitor?

Introduction

Every Disneyland Custodial Cast Member has experienced it.

They're at a party, or in a class, or *anywhere* where they

Cleaning the Kingdom

meet someone they haven't met before, and the introduction goes something like this:

> Other person: "And what do you do?"
> Custodian: "I work at Disneyland."
> Other person: (excited) "Really??? What do you do there?"
> Custodian: "I'm in Custodial."
> Other person: (smile freezes, eyes glaze over): "...Oh."

You could show a picture to someone, a close up of a face, and ask someone to describe the person in the picture. Maybe the comments would be "friendly" or "thoughtful" or "handsome".

And if you pulled back to reveal them wearing Custodial Whites (or Night Crew Blue) and holding a pan & broom, the comments would likely change to negative ones.

R-E-S-P-E-C-T

I (Ken) used to be a frequent participant in online Disneyland enthusiast forums. If I had a difference of opinion with one guy in particular who was also a regular participant, he'd dismiss with me by knocking my job. Somehow, cleaning up after Disneyland guests made my opinion about Disneyland matters less credible than a guy who wasn't employed by Disneyland at all.

Then there would be people who'd do that to our faces. They were guests who'd ask us questions about something at the park, get an honest and truthful answer, and would then turn to a Ride Operator and ask them the very same question, as though we couldn't possibly know what we were talking about because we were holding a broom.

In case you don't know, a janitor, especially one who is a direct employee rather than with a contract company that

103

rotates people through, is probably *the best* person you can ask about what's what at any particular place.

Some of the ride operators they'd ask were relatively new and, perhaps, not all that personally interested in Disneyland. Sweepers like Lynn and I took a keen interest in everything at the park, both for our personal enjoyment but also so that we could answer any questions guests had.

No, being a jani is not the most glamorous job in the world. It isn't something to which people aspire. There were parents who would actually raise a stink with Disneyland management when their college kid would be cast in Custodial.

But the world needs janitors. Disney parks need Custodial cast members. Disneyland could operate without stores. It could operate without restaurants. It could even operate without attractions. But it could not operate if it got so dirty so as to run afoul of health codes. During a special VIP event in Adventureland I (Ken) had to dump some trash cans so they wouldn't fill up. I used a two-wheel cart because it was the smallest and quickest thing I could use. Someone working at the event descended on me and condescendingly told me to "get that ugly thing out of here."

When my manager caught up with me backstage, I was clearly irritated. My manager apologized up and down, but it wasn't her fault!

Just how "ugly" would it have been if the trash was overflowing in the middle of that party? What would that other woman have thought then?

Fortunately, most Disneyland cast members, whether our peers in Operations or retired executives, appreciated Custodial.

There is nothing immoral or unethical about the work of Custodial. It is an honest job.

Much of the job is doing other things than cleaning, especially assisting guests.

Yes, sometimes it was dirty, and you can read about the worst of the worst in Chapter 5, if you dare.

Cleaning the Kingdom

We would often get questions like "So, do you start by doing this and work your way up to working in the rides?" Well, the truth is, some people *did* transfer from Custodial to Attractions (or other Operations Departments), but it wasn't a promotion. In fact, it would usually mean losing seniority.

I (Ken) would get a chuckle when people who I knew were changing diapers, because they were pushing strollers, would tease us about cleaning up after the horses. I could clean up after the horses and never get peed on, and never touch feces, which from horses doesn't look all that different from what they'd eaten. How many people changing diapers could say the same thing?

I never wanted to transfer to any other Operations position. I liked the freedom of movement of Custodial, the variety, and the access. And the more seniority I got, the better. I didn't think it would be as fun to be stuck at a cash register or pushing buttons.

Usually, our equipment was doing the actual dirty work. And if we did get dirty, we could get a clean costume in the middle of our shift thanks to the massive Costuming Department wardrobe.

Equipped

The tools we used were, for the most part, basic, but some were unique to Disneyland, or Disney Parks. Using the right tools, there were many shifts during which we wouldn't get dirty and wouldn't directly touch the litter or dirt or whatever was being cleaned up. Most of cleaning up involved a pan & broom, meaning our hands and face were several feet away from the mess itself. Of course, there were also pushbrooms, trash pickers, and mops as well as many smaller tools, cleansers, heavy duty paper towels ("pro towels") and gloves of various kinds. Sure, there were many things a lot of us used to do barehanded. We lived *on the edge*, I tell ya. Visiting the parks now, you'll see the sweepers always wear gloves.

Cleaning the Kingdom

The pan we used when I (Lynn) first started was a metal pan with a long rod that bent at the top for your hand to hold up. I was on my second day of training and was in Fantasyland. The trainers gave us pans and brooms to use. I remember roaming around feeling very awkward, with this heavy metal pan. I remember how tired I got too. I thought *this is not going to be easy*. But I got the hang of it, quickly, and away I went - sweeping popcorn, and everything else in sight.

Now the sweepers get plastic pans, with adjustable handles. At first, many of us rebelled against using them, for some reason, including me. Then, after a while, I thought "Wow these are nice." But they weren't always. With the metal pans, if you knew what you were doing, you could scrape gum and candy off the ground with them, without even bending. With the plastic ones, it just wasn't effective. Also, the plastic pans warped easily. If left in a locker with it bent by another object, it would stay that way. If the lip of the pan got warped it was pretty much useless, because many items would slip right under the pan lip. With the metal pans, we could kind of bend it and form a better lip if needed. Also, some cast members would bend the rod outward an inch or so. This would help prevent them from hitting their ankle or shin with the pan, which did hurt, and was something I did often. Unlike plastic pans, the metal pans did not have adjustable handles and the handles came in two sizes. If an especially tall sweeper was hired, that sweeper could get an extra section welded into the handle to make it longer.

Another "improvement" of which I was not fond of was a foam grip pad for the broom handle. For me, it hurt my hand and wrist more, but many people used them, so they must helped them in some way.

There was a time when we got our own pan & broom that would be ours for as long as we were there or as long as they worked properly. We could write our names on the pan, and personalize it slightly. Many of us also had pan & broom lockers assigned to us for storing these items, and these lockers

Cleaning the Kingdom

were shared with another sweeper or two. I (Lynn) had a black metal pan, and a plastic pan, which I was able to take with me when I left Disneyland. I still use it today when I do yard work. It's very convenient.

Communal pan & broom lockers were brought into the Area Lockers vicinity, so a lot of people would not have their own personal set. They might, however, spend the start of their shift trying to find stray pans because there wouldn't be one in the communal locker. Other sweepers clung to their personal pan & broom set, and not long ago I saw a longtime sweeper who still had a metal pan. I (Ken) would try to find convenient places to hide the set I was using. Sometimes the pan & broom would be there when I came in for my next shift, sometimes they wouldn't. If I recall correctly, I had to do this because we lost our personal pan & broom lockers, or at least access to them. Although I sometimes used a plastic pan, I did prefer metal and I deliberately held on to having a metal pan until my last day (see Chapter 18 for why).

When we were dumping area cans, we usually needed to pack the trash down in the liners as we went along, so that we didn't need to take the liners backstage so often to empty. We used a plastic board about two inches thick, and maybe fourteen by fourteen inches. It was called a stomp board. When I (Ken) started, we used wooden stomp boards. Sometimes, the stomp boards would be accidently deposited in the packers and lost.

We set up lockers just for trash equipment, In addition to the stomp boards, we'd keep dollies in those lockers. This was not your normal looking dolly. It was more like a furniture dolly, with four small wheels. The trash can liner would rest right on top of this dolly as you moved around from trash can to trash can. So when they started, their shift the trash cast members were assigned keys and would go to these lockers and retrieve their stomp board and dolly. These were checked out on a clipboard in the locker for the area you were working. We would also use leather work gloves that we could get from a vending machine that was outside our office. This vending

107

machine had many of the items we used on a daily basis, from gum scrapers, gloves, tiny spray bottles, to flashlights and batteries. We would use a code to get these items, or ask for help from a Manager or Lead.

Once we got what we needed to dump trash we would head to the locker for that area or where the trash liner carts were parked. We would call them by how many plastic liners they held. For Instance an 8-liner cart, 6-liner, and 3-liner. We didn't have any special electric motor to help us. We would use manpower, or womanpower to be politically correct, because some of the women that dumped trash kicked some butt. These liner trash carts were made of metal, and could be heavy depending on the area and how much trash was in them.

Along with the tools that we had, we also have to throw the trash somewhere after we dump the trash cans. What we would do is take them to the trash packer. Every area had at least one nearby; they were spread out all throughout the park. We weren't the only cast members to use them. Any cast members, such as those from stores and restaurants could throw trash into them. In later years, however, a key was needed to activate the compacting process, rather than simply pressing a button, and only certain people (Leads, Trash Dumpers) had those keys.

Longtime, and now retired, Sweeping Lead Vern Hoiland came up with an idea that not only helped keep the packers from filling up as often as they did, but was something that went far beyond our operations at Custodial. He started the cardboard recycling program before we hired in. He realized that our packers were being filled by cardboard boxes. This did help with keeping the packers from filling up as quickly, and so green metal bins could be found in many backstage areas, filling up with cardboard.

Cleaning the Kingdom

Conclusion

I (Lynn) think custodial had it all. If you liked to socialize, then you could easily talk to guests. I found that most guests enjoyed talking to me; at least they did if they were on a bench relaxing or as I cleaned in the queues. In Attractions, you only had a brief moment to talk to the guests because you were either helping them board an attraction or directing them somewhere, or even pushing buttons, with hardly any interaction.

Yes, in Custodial we worked hard. We walked all day and were on our feet most of the day. I know most people think they could never clean up some of the things we did, but most people did get used to it.

Parents: don't be ashamed if your child wants to be a Disneyland Custodian. They know more than most cast members at the park, and get plenty of exercise. It is a good way to learn to talk with people, too, from all over the world. I think one can get many things out of Custodial as one applies oneself and works hard.

Cleaning the Kingdom

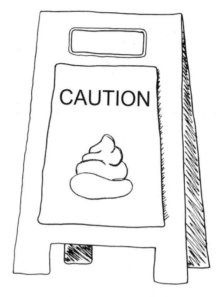

Chapter 5

Disgusting Things

It's not such a dirty job... except when it is.

*"There will be poop." -Jeremy Macera, Day Custodial
Sweeping*

Fair Warning: This is the chapter that contains all of
the really disgusting stuff - all of the stuff that is going to
gross out a lot of people. If you want to skip this chapter
entirely, we understand.

Cleaning the Kingdom

We mean it. This chapter talks about vomit. It talks about excrement from humans and other animals. It talks about body fluids little children aren't supposed to know about.

Are you still reading this chapter?

Of course you are. It's like a traffic accident. You just can't look away. Or maybe this is the chapter you REALLY wanted to see, right?

Introduction

Yes, sometimes, it could be a dirty job, if even for just the restroom duty alone. It's not a good idea to read this chapter while, or before, eating, but it might help you lose weight if you place copies of it on your refrigerator door.

Working as a Custodian at Disneyland could be like no other Custodial job. Sometimes, we had to clean up some of the most disgusting things I (Lynn) had ever seen. There were not only people to cleanup after, but animals too. People come from all over the country and the world and with them, along with all of the good things, they bring germs, bad habits, different customs, and some were just plain messy and disgusting.

Many of us in Custodial learned to cope and grew accustomed to dealing with these things, but some people never quite did that, and there were the rare instances that would gross out even the most hardened veterans of the broom.

The Circus Fantasy Affair

This incident took place in 1986, before we came aboard, and were going to let **Rob Goodale** tell the story.

* * * * *

112

Cleaning the Kingdom

In early 1986, Disneyland was deep into a campaign to rebuild its image. A painful labor strike had recently ended, and many thought that the "Disney Magic" had grown somewhat stale. While executives were feverishly working on restructuring the company, some immediate ideas were needed to jumpstart the process.

One of these ideas was "Circus Fantasy", a limited-time engagement that was to include circus themes throughout the park. Many experienced performers were borrowed from outside sources, a huge ad campaign was launched, and guests were invited to "be a clown for a day". Various acrobatic stunts were performed throughout the park, the most impressive of which, (and perhaps the least expected), was a human cannon ball that was shot over the Rivers of America.

In typical Disney style there was also a themed parade. Unlike previous engagements, this one involved a host of real circus animals: real tigers, monkeys, camels, extra horses, and of course, *elephants*! As far as anyone could recall, this was the first time elephants were used in a Main Street parade, or at least that was the rumor. Unfortunately, they were not entirely prepared to deal with these huge animals. Horses were commonly featured in parades and were always followed by a Custodial cast member who pushed a "honey bucket", a large green and yellow steel barrel with spoke wheels as if it were a Civil War caisson. The honey bucket was ceremoniously pushed down the parade route while the lucky Cast Member wore themed attire, typically a vest covered in sequins, feathers, gold fringe, whatever the particular parade called for so the Cast Member would "blend", of course. If you were really lucky, you might even get to wear a funky hat.

Someone must have assumed that following elephants in the parade would not be much different than horses. Apparently, this was not thoroughly researched.

When an elephant takes a dump it is no small matter. It is a HUGE pile consisting of numerous soccer ball sized lumps.

Cleaning the Kingdom

One good release could fill the honey bucket by nearly half. After two times, you got nervous because there were four elephants! However, this was not the real problem, it was the pee! When an elephant lets loose, they put out GALLONS! But fear not, someone thought of the perfect solution.

Alongside the honey bucket, another cast member, (in glorious parade attire), would push a mop and bucket installed in a specially built cart. The idea was that if a pee should occur both custodians would work together to quickly remove the bucket from the cart and quickly mop it up, replace the bucket, and resume down the parade route. To start off, the bucket was already filled about a third of the way with water and sanitizer, (something called A33), so that the mop could be rinsed and wrung out as we went along.

The parade had only been going for a few days, and in spite of a couple overstuffed honey buckets, there hadn't been any real pee emergencies.

But alas, it had to happen eventually.

I was told to report to the Circle D Corral, which was located in the maintenance shop area behind Fantasyland. This was where the horses were normally kept, but temporary accommodations had been set up for the elephants. Armed and ready, I manned the mop bucket apparatus while my co-worker took his place behind the honey bucket.

The parade stepped off without a hitch as we proudly strolled along in our glorious apparel before thousands of guests. In truth, I actually enjoyed doing this. If you took it in stride you could really have fun with it. It was a great break from my typical duties and we often got applause and hilarity from guests. Although we really were not supposed to, I typically bowed with the cheers after a clean-up which guests always seemed to appreciate. After all this was Disneyland; how many jobs in the world would allow you to dress up in ceremonious attire for the sole purpose of poo?

114

Cleaning the Kingdom

The parade proceeded as usual until we arrived at the Hub, near the Tomorrowland entrance. As fate would have it, one of the elephants took a **_massive_** pee directly in front of us.

An immediate "Oooohhhh" arose from the crowd as we sprung into action. With lightning efficiency, I pulled out the bucket and manned the wringer while my colleague frantically mopped. We wrung it out, mopped, wrung it out again, and mopped some more until we had completely filled the bucket.

There was still plenty to do but we were obviously not going to finish.

Furthermore, several minutes had passed and we were holding up the parade. We had to get out of their way fast. If an elephant took a dump and we were this far behind, it wouldn't be pretty.

Then came "the disaster".

At this point, with the bucket full, it was very heavy. It held five gallons, it was awkward, and there was still pee everywhere. In my haste, I suddenly slipped in pee, lost control of the bucket, and down it went.

It dumped over on its side and a massive wave of elephant pee rushed toward the Tomorrowland side of the crowd!

What happened next was beyond words; you really had to be there.

The air filled with a chorus of screams as people frantically stood up from the curb where they had been sitting, popcorn flying, mothers yanking their kids back, and myself with what must have been an expression of horror whilst wearing the ridiculous circus attire.

Simultaneously, a roar of uncontrollable cheers and laughter came from the opposite side of the street as guests watched a scene that could only be comparable to a Laurel & Hardy routine! I stood there for a brief moment as if time had completely stood still.

Obviously, the situation was hopeless and the elephants were now far down the parade route. We just threw all the gear together as quickly as possible and hightailed it out of there. As I recall, the remainder of the parade was uneventful, but I had plenty on my mind by that point.

When it was over, we stood backstage at Town Square completely relieved.

Shortly thereafter, the Custodial Department Supervisor, (Mr. L.H. smartly dressed in a tie with his trusty radio), rushed over to evaluate the situation. It was obvious this was not our fault and we could hardly be held responsible.

By then wearing pants smelling of elephant urine, we began to realize we had just contributed a short footnote for Disneyland custodial history!

Apparently a rush-order solution was assembled overnight. From that point on through the remaining duration of Circus Fantasy, the elephant crew included a third person pushing a machine that had been used for years for drying up excess water on rainy days, a battery powered wet-vac type machine fit with a large squeegee on the bottom. Modifications were made to the bucket cart to include two buckets that didn't need to be removed.

Tales circulated throughout the summer about other Cast Members' elephant pee experiences, but they were pale in comparison with ours.

In all seriousness, we should probably have earned some sort of arm patch for that one. Years later when asked "What was it like to work at Disneyland?" this is always the highlighted tale!

* * * * *

Code V

Ah, yes... vomit. With so many people, some are bound to be ill before they even arrive. Then there's the snacking and the excitement and the rides and flagrant price gouging, and so people puke. Some people just aren't used to standing for hours on end and navigating through dense crowds while stuffing their face with cotton candy after a spin on a flying elephant (even if the elephant pee never gets on them.)

We got used to cleaning up a Code V and we didn't let it bother us. We could eat lunch then go clean up a Code V or vice-versa.

A great option for cleaning up was Barf Dust, Pixie Dust, or "Dust" for short, was really Sani Sorb Bits. We'd pour it on, let it soak, maybe with the aid of gentle brooming, and then sweep it up. We might use a spray-on cleaner after that and make sure everything was dried up with moving a pro towel over the spot with our foot. But as far as that Dust, picture kitty litter, only finer. It could look like bird seed. It was in a thick plastic, two-layer bag, but its scent still filled the Area Closet. When we had slurry-covered walkways or smooth concrete all over the park, it was effective. It wasn't as good to use on carpeting, nor on paving stones, and so when various areas of the park switched over to paving stones, Dust was used less and less.

Sweepers knew how much to use of this stuff, and how to apply it just right. When people from outside of Custodial tried, they'd usually apply it wrong, or use way too much, or try to apply it from too far away, creating a new mess. We used it as efficiently as we could. We would trade stories about really bad Code Vs by saying "Oh, I had a four-bagger this morning. It was huge."

Sometimes the call to clean up a Code V would come with the advisory, "No dust required", meaning we didn't need to stop by the Area Locker to pick up any bags. There was even a Department newsletter for a while that had the title "No Dust Required".

One time I (Lynn) came across a huge Code V. It was in the walkway between Frontierland Shooting Exposition and Bonanzas Outfitters. I would say it was about six feet long and three feet wide. I needed help, and someone needed to stand watch so that guests wouldn't walk through it, because it was nighttime. So, another sweeper went to get some supplies to clean up the mess, while I waited by the hazard.

Some kids were running at me. I told them to "Stop running!"

One responded back saying "Try to stop me".

Well, I didn't stop them. But the chunky slick stopped one of them.

He slipped right in it and got it all over his clothes. These kids were about twelve or thirteen years-old.

I rubbed it in (figuratively): "I asked you to stop."

I helped him up and helped him get cleaned up as much as I could.

One sweeper, Vince Mitchell, got a memorable Code V not far from the one I had. This one took place during Fantasmic!, during its opening summer in 1992, so the crowds were huge at the time. Guest Control was still learning the ropes for the show, so to speak, and there were three shows that night.

Just before the second show was about to end, a group of sweepers, including Vince, were getting ready for the lights to come back on and do the cleanup. They were stationed between the Mark Twain dock and the petrified tree. But they noticed a terrible smell. Minutes later, the lights came on and people were slipping all over a huge splatter of vomit.

They started to use dust. Normally, half a bag, which was about six or ten ounces, did the job.

Vince & company needed **eleven bags** for this one.

They were in a hurry because Guest Control was holding back the crowds who wanted to get in place to get ready for the next show. The sweepers swept up as much of the used dust as they could, mopped the area as fast as they could, and then a huge crowd flooded the area. The sweepers pulled out of there.

After that final show of the night ended, the place was ripped, because the crew had been unable to complete the general post-show cleanup after the second show.

Cleaning the Kingdom

All areas can have some disgusting things to clean up, but some experiences I (Lynn) had in Tomorrowland were some I will never forget. Tomorrowland had Space Mountain, Astro-Orbiter, and Star Tours, all of which would bring about dizziness in some people. A man's got to know his limitations, but some people simply didn't. It was a very common thing to get a call to go to Star Tours for a Code V, normally at the exit of the attraction, but it was also somewhat common to have a mess *inside* one of the cabins of the attraction. If a guest does that during the ride, and it gets all over the floor, well, it ends up all over the cabin. The attraction is a (SPOILER!) simulator and moves quite a bit, dipping this way and that. Tossed cookies that were on the floor directly in front of the guest would soon be running all over, and possibly get on other guests' shoes.

Once that happened, that cabin would be closed and Custodial Central would be called. In turn, Custodial Central would radio the Tomorrowland Lead. A Code V in a Star Tours cabin could take a long time to clean up, which was unfortunate because one cabin is 25% of the attraction capacity.

Since it was a cabin inside a building, and not outside in the fresh air, the smell could be quite a problem.

One day I (Lynn) was Opening Lead in Tomorrowland and had a ten-hour shift on a busy Saturday. There was *something* about that day. I noticed after getting a couple of Code V calls. After about five or so I started counting them. It seemed like about every fifteen minutes or so I was getting a call for someone up chucking. We were short on sweepers that day, and I didn't have a Breaker to help me cover some of these messes. I responded to them in order as they came, and by the end of the day, I had a total of *36 Code Vs* that I had cleaned up.

I couldn't believe it. I'm not sure if it was a record or not, but it must have been close if it wasn't. A Lead affectionately nicknamed Foof once got so frustrated with the number of Code V calls she was getting one day that she remarked over the radio that they should change her call sign to Custodial Vomitland.

Usually, there was a nice barrier of towels or dust between us and the puke. But sometimes, not so much. There was a sweeper going through flower beds who found and picked out a popcorn box, which isn't unusual at all, but as she held it in her hand, she soon found that it has been used like an airsickness bag as the contents starting running down her arm!

If we found a Code V on the dirt in a flower bed, we might cover it with dirt or cover it with dust before covering it with dirt.

Toilet Tales

Everybody poops.

I (Lynn) have come across some of the worst things I have ever seen while working Restrooms. Guests sometimes love to be their own Picasso with their own feces all over the stall walls. I am not sure what kind of human being would do this for fun, but, these sorts of cleanups were part of the job.

One time I came across some pooh art in a stall, it must have been there close to an hour because when I opened the stall door there were at least a hundred flies swarming in the stall.

Yes, when assigned to Restrooms you can come across messes that some people would be incapacitated by encountering, but someone had to clean it up, and that someone was us.

I (Ken) was baffled by people who refused to flush, when it was so easy to flush without risking touching anything with your hands, even in restrooms that didn't yet have optical sensors for automatic flushing.

However, there were occasions when no amount of flushing would help, because these things were... *unflushable.* We were amazed that anyone could pass such fecal specimens without leaving a trail of blood out the door, but we've seen the results with our own eyes. When a sweeper assigned to

Restrooms would invite a passing area sweeper to come in and take a look, that area sweeper knew that they were about to see something impressive. In some of these cases, we literally had to use tongs to remove the object and place it in a trash bag because it wasn't going to exit the bowl any other way.

Some sweepers have encountered stalls where there was fecal matter splattered everywhere - the ceiling, the toilet paper holder, the door - everywhere except inside the bowl itself.

Poop Not in the Restroom

I (Ken) once had to climb into a crawlspace in the ceiling of the downstairs under Village Haus for I assume was leaking sewage. Whatever it was, I was there to vacuum it up. What made this task disagreeable were the general conditions of the space, and being hunched over, rather than the material being cleaned.

Some of the worst of the worst was when someone, especially an adult, evacuated somewhere other than a restroom. A couple of these incidents involved the Indiana Jones attraction. By the time the guests approached the loading area, they had been waiting for 90 minutes or so, and as far as they knew, they were a mile from a restroom. In actuality, there's a pair of individual-use restrooms just backstage from the north unload. It was mainly for cast members, but guests could and did use it.

A woman who did not know this burst into the control room for the attraction and deposited her gift right there. I (Ken) did not have the clean up on that one, though I was working in there that day. It must have been challenging for the ride operator to stay at their post in there before it was all cleaned up!

One I did have to clean up was left by the four emergency exit doors on the east side of the Rotunda, where guests who've just ridden the attraction pass by people still waiting. Fortunately, it was off to the side and not in the middle of the path, but it was bad enough as it was. It was a very large amount of diarrhea. Again, fortunately, it was in one place.

I wasn't so lucky with another situation in which a guest had diarrhea.

In what was my worst Human Code H cleanup ever, a woman wearing shorts had been on the highest of the three guest decks of the Mark Twain riverboat when diarrhea caught up with her and poured down her leg. She started walking, which meant she kept spreading it. As she descended the stairs to the lower levels, leaving a trail, she touched some white wire mesh protecting the propulsion system for the boat, leaving some of the fecal matter in the white wire mesh.

I felt for the lady. She was still on the boat when we got there, and the CFA nurses showed up with a towel for her.

I had one of my better crew members with me, and both of us had a hard time keeping the contents of our stomachs in place. It was a difficult cleanup because there was so much in so many places, but we eventually got it done.

There Will Be Blood

Leads would handle blood spills, having been trained to deal with bloodborne pathogens and having been given a series of Hepatitis shots. We'd use a special kit that had an unbroken seal, and when we were done we'd take the biowaste to a designated container at Central First Aid and replace the unsealed kit with a sealed one.

For me (Ken), the biggest problem wasn't dealing with the blood itself. That didn't bother me. It was that the process would take me out of the area for a long enough time that things could slip. We had to rely on a neighboring Lead to cover calls for our area.

One fateful day, there was a girl in a turret of Fort Wilderness on Tom Sawyer Island shooting the replica guns, which would give off a noise when the trigger was pulled. She jumped off her perch with her finger still on the trigger, which had a ring around it, and off popped her finger.

As is often the case, a sweeper was one of the first people on-scene. His name was An, and he preserved her finger in a pro towel.

When I (Ken) saw him later, I quipped, "I heard some little girl gave you the finger."

Poor An. His jaw went slack and he shook his head. "That's wrong, dude."

Code U

Unlike poop, which is very different from a horse than it is from a human, hence the different codes of "Code H" for horsecrap and "Human Code H" for... you guessed it, urine required the same tactics to clean up whether it was from a horse, a service dog, or a human, so it was simply "Code U". Of course, we'd never expect it to be large amounts unless it was at the top of the Hub or the bottom of Town Square, where our horses would stop.

Usually, but not always, it was a kid who needed to go *right now*. And usually, it was easy enough to clean up, thankfully.

Another Bodily Fluid - Yes, THAT One

With or without the help of another person, in rare instances, some guys would leave their ejaculate in places such as Pirates of the Caribbean boats. Sure, restroom stalls would seem like a more likely place, but some people do not realize when they are on-camera and others simply don't care, or even *count* on being on-camera.

One female Lead was called to clean up such a mess in Pirates and delegated the call to a male on her crew and quipped, "Your gender made it; your gender can clean it up!"

Dead Crows Aren't Much Fun

West Nile Virus hit southern California hard, and in the morning as we'd do our openings, there would be dead crows dotting the walkways, and we needed to sweep them up.

Snails and Slugs

There were parts of Disneyland where these creatures were abundant.

One night, I (Ken) was closing out Adventure/Frontier and I had made my way from the Big Thunder line, which involved a lot of leaning against rockwork. I did this so I could lean over, stretch, and grab litter in the flower beds. By this time I was checking flower beds in Adventureland. My hand casually brushed against my sidepack and I felt *slime*. Baffled, I checked my pack and there was a large slug, no doubt from the Big Thunder queue, and judging from the trail it had left, it had been moving all over the pouch.

In Fantasyland, a tomboyish sweeper had found a snail and put in on her finger. She motioned toward a male sweeper's face with that finger, just messing around. And he responded by moving his mouth toward her finger like he was going to eat the snail.

And then, before he knew it, her finger bumped his lower lip and the snail popped into his mouth!

He quickly rushed to wash out his mouth.

In the Event of Disaster

Rumor had it, and maybe it was actually written down somewhere, that in the event of a major disaster, it was going to be our job to set up makeshift potties by pulling the cushions off of dining area chairs - thereby leaving a wire frame - and putting buckets under them. We were also going to help haul off dead bodies and burn them, if necessary.

124

Sad But True

There have been people who have taken their own lives on Resort property. For example, there have been at least two people who've jumped to their death from the Mickey & Friends parking structure.

There was also a frequent Disneyland guest who killed himself by gunshot in that parking structure. The Custodial crew working the parking structure did encounter this scene.

Please don't kill yourself at Disneyland. Please don't kill yourself at all. Please.

Conclusion

Any Sweeper who has been on the job for a good chunk of time has these stories. It is a necessary part of the job. We learned to hold our breaths and breath through our mouths (years of competitive swimming came in handy for me, Ken) and simply look at the issue as something to clean up, rather than something disgusting. It reminds me of how during my Life Drawing sessions in college, I was looking at shapes, spaces, shadows, etc. rather than a nude body. It's the mindset.

Cleaning the Kingdom

Chapter 6

Bowl Games

(Don't worry, we leave the really disgusting stuff in Chapter 5.)

Just how are Disneyland restrooms kept so clean?

Introduction

Graffiti. Toddlers struggling with their potty training. Thousands of dollars in cash. Dead people.

Those are just some of the things a Sweeper may find in a Disneyland restroom. During park operating hours, cleaning restrooms was the responsibility of Day Custodial Sweeping.

Everybody poops. So restrooms are a necessary part of any venue, and Disneyland is no exception. Financially, they're a loss, of course, and a liability from slip-and-falls and whatever else. They don't generate revenue, but they're needed.

Like the rest of the park, it is a jani's job to keep them as clean and safe as possible, but keeping the floor clean and dry can be more crucial in a restroom than anywhere else, because it is easier to slip on tile.

Back when janitorial work at Disneyland was seen as a man's job, the only women on the crew were the restroom matrons who handled the women's restrooms. While in the past, Disneyland segregated the operation of certain attractions by sex (men on the Jungle Cruise and Davy Crockett Explorer/Indian Canoes, women on Storybook Land Canal Boats and Enchanted Tiki Room, etc.) the entire custodial operation was segregated.

Everyone who is in Day Custodial Sweeping for more than just a short stint is trained to clean restrooms. Our training on restrooms came later, separately, from general training, which was immediately after general cast member orientation. I (Ken) went an unusual amount of time before finally being trained on restrooms, which was just fine by me because, like some others, I didn't prefer to work in them. Eventually, though, when schedulers ran into that roadblock of trying to schedule me for Restrooms and not being able to because I didn't have the training, they scheduled me for a restroom training session.

Most cast members who like doing Restrooms put in a preference to work them. Some of their preference might have to do with the slight additional pay - which we understood was to compensate us for the risk of being stuck with a needle that could give us a fatal disease - or the freedom to roam from restroom to restroom, which was mostly a male privilege.

Getting Them Covered

A woman could sometimes be assigned to just one restroom for her entire shift, depending on how high the predicted park attendance was. Most of the time, men will have anywhere from two to five major restrooms per shift. That does not include the backstage (cast member) restrooms. Another advantage of restrooms could be time passing faster. Hourlong rounds are less monotonous than circling through the same area every fifteen minutes.

There can be twice as many women working restrooms as men. One reason is that women's restrooms are significantly larger than men's. Another reason is how many men and women use restrooms differently. It's not just that men's restrooms have some urinals while women's restrooms have places for women to get and to dispose of "feminine hygiene" products; it's that a lot of men may come into the restroom, walk to the urinal, relieve themselves, and then leave. *Yeah, without washing their hands.* Sorry ladies, but it is true. Guys also spend less time in front of the mirror.

Restrooms were assigned by "split sheets", as in, this was your split of the restrooms. The sheets would list your guest restrooms, with the biggest or busiest restroom first, and your cast member restrooms with the preferred number of times you were to clean those cast member restrooms during your shift. The busiest days would see an 8-way split for men, and a 16-way split for women. In addition to which restrooms they were going to cover, a split sheet would have their shift starting and ending time, assigned break and lunch times (usually coordinated with the other cast members' breaks so that the Foreman could at least cover the lunch), and whatever other restrooms they might need to cover at the start of their shift (if they were opening) or the close of their shift (if they were closing) if some of the crew was coming on later or leaving earlier.

The Routine

A typical day for a restroom cast member would start by going to Custodial Central to check in, pick up our split sheet, and appropriate key ring for the day. We might pick up clean, dry mopheads by placing enough into bags for our restrooms, but often a bunch of them would already be there. Then we'd proceed to our first restroom on our sheet.

Each on-stage restroom was to be cleaned at least once per hour. That means a cast member would have to plan things out and work quickly enough to accommodate for covering all on-stage restrooms once per hour while also taking the assigned breaks, and doing the cast member restrooms. There was some wiggle room as to when to take breaks (two fifteen-minute breaks for an eight out shift), but it was more important to take lunch (thirty minutes, unpaid) at the assigned time, as that was leaving the restrooms for longer. Lunches were more likely to be covered by a Foreman.

Large guest restrooms had fully stocked closets, complete with a mop bucket, mop handles. a water spigot and drain, boxes of paper products (paper towels, toilet paper rolls, seat covers, feminine hygiene), rolls of trash bags appropriate to the size of the trash cans, gallons of liquid soap, various spray bottles and dispensing containers full of concentrated cleanser to mix with water to make more for the spray bottles, and aerosol cans. There might also be plungers, squeegees, and "wet floor" or "stall closed" signs.

For some restrooms, men and women shared a stock closet, which had one door into the men's room and one into the women's room. This could lead to interesting situations, especially since a male and female could be together, alone, in private, could hear if someone else was unlocking the door, and was surrounded by the romantic ambiance of concrete and stacked toilet paper rolls.

On one occasion, the male cast member and the female cast member were conversing (yes, just talking) inside the closet, but the door to the women's room was slightly ajar, almost closed. A female guest pushed the door open and accused the male cast member of peeping at the women using the restroom. The door hadn't been ajar enough to even try, but even if it had been ajar, the only things he would have seen from that angle were ankles and feet. What was particularly amusing for fellow cast members about the accusation was that this was one of the many male cast members who'd made no secret of not being the slightest bit interested in the female body. For the record, no male guests reported any peeping on his part.

Opening procedures for a restroom would include making sure the correct paperwork was present and filling in the appropriate information, and setting up mops by placing clean, dry mopheads on the mop handles and filling up mop buckets. On the rare rainy days, we rolled out the "red carpet" for the guests, well maybe not red. These rain mats at the entrance of the restrooms helped keep the floors a little bit drier and made it less likely a guest would slip while entering a restroom. We might also place "wet floor" signs by the entrance.

A normal cleaning in the restroom would start by signing into that restroom, using a restroom coverage sheet paper on a clipboard in the stock (supply) closet in that restroom or close by. Sometimes, the route to that stock closet would take a cast member through the restroom itself first; other times, the cast member isn't going to get a look at the restroom until after signing in. Either way, it was important to get a look at the restroom as soon as possible to assess if there was anything in immediate need of attention, such as an overflowing toilet.

Then the cast member would sweep the floor to remove debris, perhaps testing the need to empty the trash receptacles by pushing the contents down with the broom. Sometimes they might look full but have just a few paper towels in them. In our day, the paper towels were of the c-fold sort that were in gravity dispensers, and we could check to see which ones needed to be restocked. As of this writing, many are motion-activated dispensers with rolls of towel that are torn off.

A wet restroom floor is always a potential safety issue. Many guests rush in use the restroom, wash their hands, *and*

Cleaning the Kingdom

dry off their hands by flinging their hands around to get the water off. After hundreds of people an hour doing that, that can be a slippery hazard. Of course, anyone who has lived as or with a male also knows some males sometimes have bad aim, which can also contribute.

We'd mop the floor with a dry mop to remove water and other liquids and perhaps mop to remove scuff marks or candy or whatever else might be sticking to the floor. Then it was on to stocking the paper towels, soap, baby changing towels, and wiping off the baby change table and sink-table surfaces to remove liquid and debris.

It was useful to take a dry mop and a cleanser spray bottle, along with a couple rolls of toilet paper, to go through the toilet stalls. If the toilet stall needed more toilet paper or seat covers, the mop could be used to mark the stall as closed while quickly slipping to the stock closet and back.

We'd spray the toilet seat down with the cleanser and wipe it off. After the toilets, it was on to the urinals to wipe them down. Ideally, every toilet and *every* urinal would be cleaned with each visit by the cast member covering that restroom, but were times when a "camper" was taking so long in a stall that waiting any longer to get to it would throw off the coverage rotation, so it would be skipped for that round.

Each stall would have two rolls of toilet paper, so that ideally, a stall would never be without enough for a guest. If a roll was very low, rather than waiting for it to become a cob, it would be removed, replaced, and used for cleaning paper. The rolls were always placed with the "waterfall" toward the seat rather than the partition.

One of the last things would be dumping the trash cans that needed to be dumped. Any trash receptacle with baby diapers needed to be dumped regardless of how empty otherwise, or it there was just one or two diapers we could use "salad tongs" to remove them, which was quicker than pulling off the bag and replacing it with a new bag.

Cleaning the Kingdom

We were supposed to hold the trash bags away from our body in case needles were inside. Yes, there were times cast members would get poked by a needle. When I (Ken) started, it was 1990, a time in which HIV/AIDS was still very much in the news and contracting HIV was considered a certain and soon death. In fact, one of our fellow longtime Sweepers died of complications from AIDS, although he'd probably not contracted HIV from a restroom needlestick as he was someone who led a very colorful life and is dearly missed.

The trash bags emptied from inside the restroom might be placed into the trash can in the stock closet so that it could be dumped, too, and just one large bag had to be carried. It might be good to go through the restroom with a deodorizer, too, although we did get automatic wall-mounted deodorizers while we were working there.

Once we'd completed the tasks for that restroom, we'd sign out of that restroom on the same log sheet on which they signed in. Guest restroom stock closets had a pad of them on the clipboard, and a new sheet was used every day. On each line of the sheet was not only our sign-in and sign-out time, but we'd write one or two words to describe the condition of the restroom when we got there ("busy, messy" or "dry, moderate" or "hellish inferno" - well, maybe not that last one), and we'd check off everything that we did for that round in the restroom. Some items on the list must be done every time, and some as needed. There would also be a space to write where we were going next, such as to put the trash in a packer or take a break or go to the office, and usually the next restroom after that, and finally, our initials. There were spaces at the bottom for notes and each cast member and Foreman working that restroom for the day would also have their full signature and shift hours on the sheet, and their assigned break/lunch time filled in as well.

These sheets are useful for many reasons in addition to being reminders of what needs to be done. Foremen and Supervisors (who would also sign in and check off what they did) might check on how effective a cast member is being, might leave notes, or might be trying to find the cast member and could figure out where they were based on the sheets (our time was before everyone was calling or texting each other on mobile phones).. The sheets also served as documentation in case of an accident or complaint.

Keep Moving

Once we were finished with a restroom, it was on to the next one, perhaps stopping by to throw trash in a packer or put some cardboard from dissembled stock boxes into recycling bins. On our way, we'd pick up trash we'd see on the ground. Usually, the walk would be short.

If there was a problem or we needed help, Custodial Central, Security, First Aid, and Facilities were just a phone call away. Knowing where the "park phones" were located was very helpful. The Dispatcher at Custodial Central could radio to our Foreman to let them know what was going on or to pass along that we needed help.

Second Shift

On most days, there would be two shifts working the same restrooms (opening and closing), with the closing shift person having a slight overlap with the opening shift person It was always good to catch up to each other, gossip, and pass along any relevant information ("Stall #3 has been closed all day in Space Mountain restroom" or "I've left an extra bottle of Jack Daniels in the Plaza Inn stock closet") OK, so of course we made up that second one. We were too stingy with our Jack to share.

Closing procedures included collecting each guest restrooms log-in sheet for that day, making sure everything in the restroom was fully stocked as far as soap, towels, toilet paper, and seat covers, emptying all trash including the trash in the stock closet, removing any used mopheads to take them to a collection point for cleaning, dumping out the mop water, and, if they had been used, rolling up any rain mats (bottom side on

Cleaning the Kingdom

the inside of the roll) and putting them away along with any sign.

Some restrooms, such as the Tiki Room waiting area restroom or the Tour Gardens waiting area restroom, were so small they wouldn't have their own stock closet. Rather, their log sheet and a spray bottle would be kept behind the mirror, which usually fronted a folded towel dispenser. Any needed supplies would be brought from the nearest large restroom, often carried in a small trash bag.

On slow days, restroom cast members could do extra in the restrooms and those tasks were on the sign in sheet in each restroom, referred to as "utility' work. One could wipe down the walls, clean out soap dispensers, or even organize the stock closet for that restroom. We were trained that the restroom supplies couldn't reach all the way to the ceiling of the stock closet, because the flammable material would be out of reach of a fire sprinkler.

Like just about everything else inside the parks, the deep cleaning is usually done by the Night Custodial cast members.

Backstage Restrooms

Cleaning backstage restrooms could be *more* difficult than some guest restrooms. For one thing, they could be hard to find. Keep in mind that there were as many as 16 splits for women, and 8 for men, meaning it could take many shifts before any given cast member had covered each area and become familiar with it. Restroom training at the time focused on guest restrooms, not showing us every cast member restroom. Sometimes the restrooms were squeezed into obscure corners; also, some buildings in the park had gone through multiple renovations, often making backstage portions more, not less, confusing to navigate. Often the location was discerned by its name. Coke Talent was *not* under Refreshment "Coke" Corner on Main Street but underneath the Tomorrowland Terrace restaurant, where the performance stage retreats after shows, as part of the Green Room. However, some restrooms, like this one, were nearby other restrooms, and so it was possible for Restroom cast members to go to the other restroom and think they'd done Coke Talent. Sometimes the names of the restrooms were old or new, causing confusion. When Innoventions opened in 1998, some Sweepers weren't sure if the Innoventions cast member restroom was inside the main building or another restroom somewhere nearby backstage.

There was a cast member restroom at the New Orleans Square train station, across the tracks, in the building that used to be the Frontierland train station. Like so many cast member restrooms, this restroom was small, consisting of a sink and a toilet. Some of them are small because they're not made to be used by all cast members, only those working a specific attraction or location.

While walking in the Westside backstage area, I (Lynn) discovered an older-looking building. This building appeared to be a restroom. While approaching it, it was clear this restroom had some years on it. As I walked inside, there was a heater attached to the wall, and all the fixtures appeared older and out of date. In fact, the whole restroom was like a time capsule. It wasn't dirty, but just... *older.* I used the restroom and moved on. Later, I found out from an older cast member that the restroom I had visited was the original restroom from Holidayland that had opened in June of 1957 and closed September 1961. If you are not familiar with Holidayland, it was not a Christmas-themed land. It was a picnic and recreation area that was sometimes used to be rented out by companies. This area also had a private entrance to Disneyland Park. To hear more about the history of this area check out episode #85 of The Sweep Spot podcast (<== Shameless Plug!)

Cast member restrooms had log-in sheets, too, but they lasted all week instead of just one day. They'd be deployed by the cast member working the split Sunday morning and collected by the cast member working the closing shift Saturday night - if they could be found!

Some backstage restrooms were like the small guest restrooms that didn't have their own stock closet, with their sheet and a spray bottle kept behind a mirror. Some of them didn't even have an opening mirror to stash things behind, and the log sheet might be kept folded and stuck in the tiny gap between the mirror and the wall! At least since these restrooms were backstage, extra paper supplies could be kept in a box or small bin in plain view.

Outsourcing

Or is that Outhousing?

Disneyland Day Custodial Sweeping used to clean all backstage restrooms, whether they were close to onstage areas or in more remote parts of the back area or offices. There would even be one male and one female sweeper who'd be assigned to do nothing other than backstage restrooms for their entire shift, and they'd usually ride around together on a small vehicle, taking supplies with them. This was considered a desirable shift on the busiest days, because the cast members would be getting restroom pay but have minimal interaction with the crowds.

During my (Ken's) time, the decision was made to outsource some of what Custodial covered (but please don't blame me). A company called Empire was the first outside company brought in. One of the things the outside companies were given backstage restrooms that did not take any on-stage presence to access. With that change, there was no longer a male-female pair of Sweepers assigned to backstage restrooms, and the guest restroom crew was only responsible for the backstage restrooms that the outside companies did not clean.

Read more about this in Chapter 17.

Restroom Leads

Restroom Lead shifts were sometimes hard to come by for people who were lower on the Seniority list, because they were slightly higher in their hourly rate. Not only would we receive the Restroom rate, but also Lead rate. The shifts were often long, too, which meant overtime pay.

There were typically two male Leads and two female Leads per shift, with the Leads splitting the park between Westside and Eastside. On less crowded days, there might be three male Leads total for the day instead of four, with one Lead having a mid-shift, and on shorter and even slower days, there might be two male Leads for the entire operational day, with one opening, the other closing, and much overlap in hours.

The job of the opening Restroom Lead would start by checking in to the office, getting keys and a radio, looking over the crew list for the day, picking the appropriate split sheet (for example, the day would have a six-way split), assigning the crew to their respective splits, schedule their breaks/lunches, and prepare their portion of the split sheets for them.

Once everything was set in the office, the Lead would head out to check the restrooms, place needed documents, and do some of the set-up procedures, and perhaps cover one of the splits until the crew member arrived. After the park was open and everything was in full swing, the Lead would go from restroom to restroom, checking in to see how the cast member was doing and to be sure he or she was making their rounds within the hour limit. We'd also help with the cleaning of the restroom. Leads would also cover lunches, absent some urgent matter keeping us from doing so. As a Lead, we'd help to be sure the right supplies were in each restroom, too. Normally a lead would make it to each restroom at least three or four times in a shift or as many as needed.

Sometimes there'd be confusion with a cast member on which restroom to cover and when, or whatever the case may be. I (Lynn) had a cast member once who didn't cover his restroom for *four hours*! I was unable to notice this because I was covering lunches and a big flood in the Critter Country restroom. Upon noticing the uncovered restroom, I found it trashed, or "ripped" as we referred to it. When I'd find this sort of thing, my first response was to get it cleaned and fast, rather than think about blame. After that was handled, I'd find out what happened with this cast member. In this case, his answer was that he simply forgot! It made me want to pull my hair out! What!?! *Forgot*??? That cast member was written up and a manager spoke to him.

Doing the Splits

Each restroom split had its own pro and cons, depending on one's personal preferences. One split might be close to Custodial Central, which could be a pro or a con, depending! Some restrooms had been more recently renovated than others, some seemed to have more plumbing issues than others. Some cast members preferred split near a specific break room or backstage eatery.

Most restrooms were themed with music piped in that goes according to that theme of the restroom; often it was the themed area background music. I (Lynn) personally liked the Village Haus restrooms music the best; who doesn't like polka? The Space Mountain restrooms were out of this world! The Big Thunder Ranch restrooms were in an old barn. They definitely have a great theming to them, fit for cowboys and cowgirls, with mining lanterns over stalls and sinks. The King and Queen restrooms on the backside of the Matterhorn, built into the side of the Castle, was themed to Alice in Wonderland, with giant playing cards for the stall doors, and heart tiles in the women's and diamond-shaped tiles in the men's. It was one of the better-themed restrooms. Not every restroom is themed in such detail, but they were color coordinated to match the areas.

New Orleans Square

One special feature of a New Orleans restroom split was access to **Club 33**. We figure if you're reading this, you probably have heard of Club 33, but in case you haven't, it's a private club upstairs in New Orleans Square with membership fees into the five figures, where members and their guests can eat and drink (including alcohol).

We knew full well that the last thing people dining in Club 33 want to see was a sweaty sweeper, so we'd always try to be as quick and discreet as possible when servicing the small restroom in there, making as little noise and spending as little time as possible.

The men's room was very small, had a nice marble or granite sink and counter. There was a urinal and a toilet with an elevated tank, complete with pull chain. In addition to the usual restroom hand towels, there would be Club 33 napkins. The women's restroom (which we men could see during hours the Club was closed) was more elegant. The toilets were wicker thrones; that's right women can sit on their own throne as they use the throne. There was also a vanity area for them to powder their noses.

The stock area for these restrooms used to be just up the stairs where The Court of Angels was, above the French Market. We shared an area with the stock for some of the shops and storage for Club 33, where the wine was stored. A recent renovation turned this area into part of an expanded Club 33.

Downstairs from the Club, the Blue Bayou restrooms were on the small side as well, as most restrooms have been at Disneyland when they're located inside a restaurant. It was usually pleasant to slip past the guests enjoying one of Disneyland's best restaurants under the Disney-created nighttime sky, the sounds from the peaceful beginning of the Pirates of the Caribbean attraction in the background.

The space above the Pirates of the Caribbean entrance, now a "Dream Suite" for lucky people to stay overnight inside

Cleaning the Kingdom

Disneyland (there's nothing quite like seeing a bunch of delivery trucks and people hosing down walkways), had originally been built as an apartment for the Disney family, used as office space, and then opened as The Disney Gallery in 1987. There were cast member restrooms in there, too, which had probably started out in the plans as the bathrooms for the apartment. Usually, the only people who'd use those restrooms would be people working in the Gallery, so servicing them was easy, although servicing them gave me (Ken) an excuse to say "hi" to my friends working there and see if any guests I knew were hanging around.

Baby Center and First Aid

We males were tasked with taking care of the Baby Center if we had a restroom split that included that portion of Main Street. So while parents were changing their diapered young'uns or trying to get a slightly older one to use the miniature potty, some big male sweeper would come through to stock the towels, check the toilet, and empty the trash (diapers!). It was cramped in there on a busy day. I (Ken) didn't look forward to it, but I did kind of like disappearing out the back sliding door like a secret agent.

Next door was First Aid, which at the time had a guest side in front and a cast member area in the back, each with restrooms to service. The guest restrooms were more like some backstage restrooms since they were private rather than communal.

Disruption

Sometimes working restrooms had its unfortunate side, from minor annoyances like ink graffiti to people having major medical issues, even dying right there in the restroom. We could run across some graffiti, plugged toilets or sinks, and of course

141

Cleaning the Kingdom

the dreaded special messes in the toilet stalls (see Chapter 5 for more on that).

Grad Nites bring many messes to the restrooms, including graffiti, broken mirrors, or scratched mirrors.

Speaking of mirrors, when we noticed a mirror was scratched, we'd notify a Lead to come and take care of it. They might find and bring a replacement, then swap them. If the etching was bad and there was no replacement, the mirror would simply be removed and there would be no mirror there until a replacement was ready. A special coating was used so that the coating could be removed and replaced instead of the entire mirror.

Ink or paint graffiti was easily removable, sometimes so much so that the vandal probably spent longer putting it there than it took us to remove it. When I (Ken) started, if the graffiti was more than a small scribble we'd block off the stall and call Security to come take a picture of it, with the goal of holding the culprit responsible for any & all graffiti they'd done on Disney property if they were ever caught.

Sometimes guests would like to partake in their favorite hobby or habit: smoking pot. Under California law, let alone Disneyland policy, smoking anything is prohibited in restrooms in businesses. We'd walk into a restroom and know right away what was going on. Anyone could even see the smoke rising from the stall, as if the aroma wasn't enough. We'd call Security, and sometimes the guest would get caught. It was not our job to get too involved in these sorts of things. It wasn't all that rare to find empty booze bottles crammed into seat cover dispensers.

A major issue that can happen in these restrooms is what we called a main line backup. This was something that would close down a restroom, sometimes *for hours*. When this happened, it was a major plumbing issue and we'd call Facilities immediately. Disneyland's plumbers would arrive to snake out the problem. In the meantime, it was our job to refer guests to other restrooms nearby. As you can imagine, sometimes these guests were not happy about it, but how happy would they've been in a restroom flooded with sewage water?

After the problem was fixed, we would clean up the mess by disinfecting pretty much everything. If we were lucky, other Sweepers from the surrounding area would join us and we'd end up leaving that restroom fully stocked, sparkling clean, and smelling nice, as if it hasn't been used at all yet.

In very rare instances, a wall-bolted toilet would actually come off the wall and crash to the tiled floor, causing a major headache for Custodial and Facilities alike. It was probably a surprise to the person sitting on it, too!

Sometimes we'd need to close off a toilet stall or urinal while keeping the restroom open. If there was a "Stall Closed" sign handy, it was convenient because it attached to the door and the partition and prevented the door from being opened. However, for urinals, we'd use a trash bag to block it off. Sometimes we'd have to use a bag like a rope to close off a stall. And sometimes, people would find a way to use the urinal or the stall even if it was closed.

Flush This Chapter

Cleaning restrooms, even at Disneyland, was not the most glamorous or desirable assignment, but it was a necessary and important one. However, one perk was being able to go places most cast members never see, whether we were supposed to be there or not. This was especially true before some of the backstage restrooms were taken over by outside companies. We had the keys, and the excuse, to go just about anywhere. If anybody asked what we were doing there, "checking the restroom" was the magic phrase.

Cleaning the Kingdom

Chapter 7

Land by Land - Westside

How did we cover the various "lands" in Disneyland?

Introduction

For some purposes, including Sweeping, Restrooms, and gang fights (well, maybe not that last one) Disneyland was split into Eastside and Westside. For reference, remember that Main Street, USA runs North-South with Sleeping Beauty Castle at the northern end, facing south.

Cleaning the Kingdom

The Custodial Sweeping areas of Main Street, Adventure-Frontier, and New Orleans/Critter were Westside. Tomorrowland, Fantasyland, and Small World/Matterhorn (yes, that's separate from Fantasyland), and were Eastside. Each area would have its own Opening Lead, who was there before or along with the earliest crew member, and each area would have its own Closing Lead, who was there until the end of the "Day" shifts. The Lead would divide the areas further into individual coverage sections. Depending on operating hours, the Closing Lead might spend the first hours of his or her shift as a non-Lead member of the crew, getting paid their regularly hourly rate, until the Opening Lead went home. Conversely, when the park would be open sixteen hours, such as 8:00 a.m. to Midnight, Opening Leads might start their shift at 6:00 a.m. and Closing Leads might end their shifts at 1:30 a.m., a span of 19.5 hours. Two have just two Leads cover that span, both Leads would work long shifts, such as 6:00 a.m. to 4:30 p.m. for the Opening Lead, and 4:00 p.m. to 1:30 a.m. for the Closing Lead.

The Westside of the park was our favorite side of the park to work. It contained so much as far as the architecture, attractions, restaurants, walkways, trees, and water. With the Rivers of America prominently placed, the Westside is a beautiful place to be in Disneyland.

Main Street

Main Street is one of the two areas through which parades and similar shows traveled, which significantly changed the entire tone of the workday in comparison to days without such shows or parades. Without parades or similar shows, on slower days, Main Street was busy for the opening and closing rushes but could get very slow and monotonous the rest of the time. Parades or shows on the parade route would not only break the monotony, but most sweepers on the Main Street crew would have pre-parade and post-parade

146

assignments. Much of the area would be viewing area anyway. For more information on Parade coverage, see Chapter 9.

Something Main Street had that no other area had: horses, which pull the trolleys. Big Thunder Ranch would have horses, but we didn't have to get anywhere near those.

Back in the day, there was a whitewing named Trinidad, who may have been the most photographed cast member. He was dedicated to cleaning up after the equine beasts. However, he was long gone by the time we showed up.

So, if the horses urinated... wait... *when* the horses urinated (Code U), that would be a priority clean-up. We had a dedicated mop backstage for horse urine, and a dedicated spray bottle of cleanser or deodorant. The horses would only urinate while stopped, which was usually only at the "bottom" of Town Square and the "top" of the Hub (Central Plaza).

But horses will poop anywhere they walk.

When a horse would poop (Code H), we'd sweep the road apples into our pan and go backstage to empty our pan into a the dedicated "honey bucket" and then hose out our pan. On some occasions, a horse would be especially prolific and it wouldn't all fit into one pan. A Code H, like a Code U, was a priority clean-up, not just because of smell but because it wasn't good to have guests walk through it, as many did, or trip over it or into it. Although that would be something to see, wouldn't it?

Sometimes, it was as though the Ranch hands had brought the horses onstage specifically to relieve themselves and then once they had no more to give, they brought in relievers with full bladders and full bowels.

Rain and parade or show preparations would mean the horse-drawn trolleys would not operate.

Since Main Street had a Disneyland Railroad stop, the Lead would occasionally get calls to clean up a mess on a train, and sometimes that would mean taking a trip. All aboard!

Main Street was also the last area of the park to close at the end of the operating day, usually with the stores remaining open an hour after the listed park closing time. As such, the

Cleaning the Kingdom

Custodial crews in the rest of the park would often send some sweepers to help out for the final 30-90 minutes of their shift. The Lead for those areas would radio the Main Street Lead and say "You're getting John Doe, who is off at 1:30. Where do want him to go?" This was done depending on how much need there was for Main Street to have help balanced with how much need there was for the other areas to keep their staff for their own closeouts. And sometimes, John Doe was someone another Lead wanted to unload onto the Main Street Lead just to be rid of him.

The Sweeping area for Main Street mostly lined up with the themed Main Street, USA area, with the addition of Main Gate and Parking Lot falling under the designation as well.

The Area Locker was on the east side, abutting the guest locker facility. This area would attract many sweepers taking their breaks, including Main Street and Tomorrowland area sweepers, Events crew, Restroom crew, and often sweepers who'd grabbed a meal from the Inn Between. Sometimes, this would give the impression to people outside of Custodial that there were a lot of sweepers sitting around doing nothing, and so there was at least once our benched table was removed. Meanwhile, if you were to walk into cast member restaurants you'd always see plenty of people from other departments in groups.

Main Gate

Before Resort expansion, when there was a flat parking lot stretching from the Disneyland Main Entrance south to Katella, "Main Gate" was one of the portions of Main Street, and covered the "red carpet" (red concrete) areas in front of the Main Entrance. Sweeping around the tram loading area, through the guest locker area and appropriate restroom, and around the ticket booths were a standard part of the coverage area.

The Picnic Area, having tables, was an area for the

Cleaning the Kingdom

Bussers. That was the general rule of thumb: Tables = Bussers (or Foods cast members). Sweepers and Bussers, even when Bussing was part of Custodial (into the early 1990s), had the same Supervisors but did not cover each other's areas, citing union concerns. If circumstances warranted, a Busser could be pulled to work as a Sweeper for the day, and vice-versa, but that was extremely rare.

It could get quiet out at the Main Gate, especially during private parties or slower evenings. One night, I (Ken) was sweeping by a flower bed which had a Monorail pylon in it. As the Monorail passed overhead, the bushes in the flower bed started to shake. It was a strange sight since I couldn't figure out what was happening - until I realized rats were running around in there.

On another night as I was doing a closeout, I was sweeping by the pay phones and one of them rang. Curious, I picked it up and said hello. The voice at the other end told me that Disneyland was closed and I should go home. A few yards away, a man promptly sat down in his vehicle and closed the door. I don't recall confirming if he was the prankster.

The trash cans outside the Main Entrance and in the Parking Lot were bagged, as opposed to the trash cans we had in most of our sweeping areas, which were unbagged, meaning inside the metal shell there was a hard resin "liner" but no bag. Disneyland used to have an abundance of bullet-shaped cans, mostly for waiting areas, and so bagged cans in Sweeping areas came to be called "bullets".

On some nights, especially during private parties, things could get very quiet out at the Main Gate. The quiet might be broken by what we used to call a pager ["pay-jurr"]. In case you're not an archeologist, a pager was a portable information receiver. If you could take your smartphone and fold it, you'd have something about the size and shape of a pager. This would be clipped on a belt or go in a pocket, and if someone called in a short audio message to it, it would vibrate, then deliver that short message. It was usually something like, "Drink spill at

149

exit" or "10-21 10-19". If we wanted to hear the message again, we could press a button and the device would repeat the message. The device would not send messages. It would not play music. It wouldn't play movies. It didn't even allow you to play Pong (look it up).

Parking Lot

Often, there was a cast member and a Lead assigned to "Parking Lot" and they'd take care of dumping the trash cans in the parking lot and sweeping up as needed, such as broken glass from busted car windows. These sweepers might also vacuum out broken glass from such a vehicle.

To do this, we used a plain white pickup truck with blue letters printed on the doors: CUSTODIAL. We needed a permission slip to take the truck, the costumes we were wearing, the rolls of trash bags (since all of the trash cans outside the Main Entrance were bagged), and a two-wheel cart out past Harbor House.

We'd park where needed, moving to several different locations throughout the round, and use the two-wheel cart to dump all of the trash cans in the lot and outside the Main Entrance, except the ones in the restrooms and Picnic Area. On busier days, we'd have to strategically create a hill of full trash bags in the bed of the pickup. Once we were finished, we'd haul it via Schumacher Road - a backstage road running along the east side of the park, along the west side of Harbor Boulevard and the offramp from southbound Interstate 5 - to the northern backstage area, where the DOB resided. As far as we knew, the DOB stood for the "Dump Out Back".

The DOB was a raised platform we'd reach via ramp, so we could toss our haul of trash off of the platform into large trucks, which would later take the treasure to wherever Disney and the City of Anaheim had arranged, whether a recycling, sorting, or landfill facility.

Cleaning the Kingdom

If it was the last Parking Lot dump of the night, we'd stop by the Main Street locker and empty the honey bucket, putting the pungent bag into the bed of the pickup so we could take it to the DOB instead of having leaving it to fester in the Main Street packer.

Working a Parking Lot assignment meant less repetition, often having a partner, which is more appealing to some than others, and less interaction with guests, which is also more appealing to some than others.

One November night, after finished at the DOB, I (Ken) just needed to get the pickup back to the Main Street locker and then I'd be done for the night. Unfortunately for me, it was the night the giant Christmas tree for Town Square was being moved into place after being decorated in the northern backstage area. Back then, a real tree was decorated from scratch every year. A crane carried the tree from one place to another. A slow... moving... crane. And I got stuck behind it without any other way around. It wasn't what I wanted to encounter after a long day, but at least I got to see it happen once.

That Time I Left a Huge Pile of Trash in Front of Disneyland

I (Ken) was once working a closing Parking Lot shift, which actually meant the end of my shift was on the early side compared to other closing Sweeping shifts, and had filled the bed of the pickup with a heaping hill of full black trash bags. I needed to get this haul back to the DOB and get the truck back to the Main Street backstage area before the end of my shift.

Then I went to turn the ignition. It physically wouldn't turn. I won't name the manufacturer of the vehicle, but it was an American automobile manufacturer that was later taken over by the federal government. I had experienced this problem with other vehicles from this manufacturer, but had always managed to get the ignition to work after a few more tries. Not this time.

I called Custodial Central and they summoned the

mechanical wizards from Facilities. I figured they would flick their wrists and the pickup would start, and I'd look silly.

Nope. They couldn't get it going either.

The end of my shift was upon us and I was not offered overtime, and given the OK to depart.

So, I waved goodbye to the guys from Facilities and a pickup truck piled high with full trash bags, right there in front of the Main Entrance. Come to think it, I guess that means the honeybucket at the Main Street locker remained full, too.

Changes

With the Resort expansion, the Main Gate area morphed and grew into the Esplanade, which became an area distinct from Main Street. The parking lot, of course, was replaced by Disney's (later, Disney) California Adventure, which needed its own Sweeping staff, and they got one. The new Mickey & Friends Parking Structure got its own Sweeping crew from Disneyland. For more about Esplanade and Parking Structure, see Chapter 9.

Town Square

Town Square consisted of the themed Town Square area as well as the inside portion of the Main Entrance, which was mostly taken up with people posing for pictures in front of Mickey Floral. The sweeper covering this area was responsible for sweeping all onstage areas, the Main Street Train Station, and any building interiors guests accessed. There were many benches and flower beds, and there was a popcorn wagon that was sometimes open. Whether or not a popcorn wagon is open makes a difference in how much effort it takes to keep an area looking clean.

Unique to this area was the Flag Retreat Ceremony and City Hall. Nowadays, there are Plaids placed strategically all over the park, but they used to be found only at City Hall, and

Cleaning the Kingdom

later at the information kiosk at the Hub. It was convenient to be able to escort a guest to City Hall if we couldn't take care of their issue ourselves. As far as the Flag Retreat Ceremony, it is one of the few times we were supposed to stand still, quietly, while we were working.

The Hub

The Hub was, perhaps, the most difficult sweeping area in the entire park. It's a large area with many walkways, flower beds, benches and it is very busy; most guests would pass through this area many times in a given day. There were food, snack, and drink carts all over the place. It's where Popcorn One was, and if any popcorn cart in the park would be open, it would be Popcorn One.

And then there were the horses.

There were shifts I (Ken) couldn't complete a round through the area without having to stop to deal with gifts from those horses. This is why if Main Street had enough sweepers, I'd assign a second person to the Hub.

The southern boundary of the Hub area was roughly the northern end of the Main Street shops. Moving clockwise, the Adventureland entrance bridge formed a boundary, as did the Frontierland entrance bridge, as did the bridges heading to Carnation Plaza Gardens, which is now Fantasy Faire, the Castle drawbridge, the edge of the walkway heading towards Snow White Grotto, the edge of the wide walkway heading toward the Matterhorn, and the edges of the walkways heading into Tomorrowland. Carnation Plaza Gardens was Bussing territory.

Center Street

Center Street was the "narrow" portion of Main Street between the Hub and Town Square. Other than keeping the trolley tracks swept out and horse droppings swept up, the unique aspect of this area was the high number of shops.

Eateries were not part of our coverage as sweepers, but we had the Penny Arcade and Candy Shop which were between two eateries and often had spills from them.

There's a guest locker facility in the middle of the area, which used to house Lost & Found in addition to the lockers. It was more convenient for guests, and therefore easier on us, when Lost & Found was still there because if there were problems with the lockers, we could walk the guest to the counter.

Directing guests to restrooms was never difficult because there are some in the middle of the area as well as the other areas of Main Street. With no lines, no vending food carts, the climate control of the shops, and the Area Locker close by, and no horse urine to mop up, it was, perhaps, the best part of Main Street to sweep. When we worked there, Disneyana was one of the shops and some of the other shops were fun for browsing as well.

On slower days, this area would be split between the Hub sweeper at the Town Square sweeper.

Dumping Trash

I (Lynn) think the two hardest areas to dump trash were Main Street, especially at night, and New Orleans/Critter Country. The descriptions below were written with Main Street in mind, but most of this applies to dumping trash anywhere in the park.

For most Lands, there were two modes of dumping trash. The main one was dumping the area cans (an area dump), which were the ones with the themed, boxy metal exteriors and hard resin interiors, which did not have trash bags inside of them. The secondary one was dumping "bullets" or "bullet cans", which essentially meant "can with trash bags lining the hard resin interior", so named because many of them used to be shaped like bullets: vertical metal cylinders with domed tops. These cans would be placed inside attraction waiting areas,

Cleaning the Kingdom

shops, and other interior spaces, but the ones that were actually shaped like bullets became few and far between, replaced by regular cans or cans that looked like half of the regular cans.

To do the main, or "area dump", the two sweepers assigned to trash duty would usually start by pushing out to the area an 8-liner or 6-liner cart: a big, themed metal box on wheels containing eight or six empty hard resin liners. We'd have them placed in the cart, which was open on one side, upside-down so people wouldn't put trash in them. Some people would try anyway. We'd find an appropriate place to park the cart for the next few minutes, and grab one of the empty liners, turn it right-side-up, and walk over to switch it out with the liner from inside one of the metal cans. Depending on how much trash was in the liner, we might push it down with a "stomp board" before moving on to the next can and pouring its contents into that liner. We did this until the liner was full, then took it back to the cart to place it back inside and take another empty liner out to repeat the process.

Depending on how busy the park was, we might be able to complete the area dump with one cartload. Otherwise, we'd have to take the cart back to the trash compactor ("packer"), which on Main Street was at the Area Locker, and take the liners up the ramp to empty them into the packer. We'd hose off the newly emptied liners before putting them back into the carts. We might either take the 8- or 6-liner back out to continue the area dump if we hadn't finished, or, if there were just a few cans left to empty, use a 3-liner cart or even a two-wheel (and later four-wheel) cart. Two-wheel/four-wheel carts were essentially large mobile rubber trash cans with no theming to them, just solid grey or blue color.

When I (Ken) hired in, there were just the heavy, hard-to-maneuver 8-liner carts and the two-wheel carts, and stomp boards. That was the extent of the trash-dumping equipment. There were no dollies, which in this case means a small platform with four small wheels on which to place liners to move them between the cart to the can and between cans and

up the packer ramp. We had the backbreaking method of
carrying the liners. We were never supposed to push them
along on the ground, although sometimes some sweepers did.
Women never, or at least hardly ever were assigned to trash
dumping back then.

In addition to more equipment choices, a couple of other
changes over the years included adding designated recycling
receptacles to the areas next to the regular trash cans, and
sorting the trash to get bottles and cans that had been put into
the regular trash cans instead of the designated recycling ones -
before putting the rest of the trash in the packer. The "sorting"
assignment was very controversial when it started, because it
was extra work and it meant picking through trash. The process
involved emptying the trash from a liner or a bag into the
"sorting table", picking out the bottles and cans, and then
pushing the remaining trash to one side of the table where it
would drop through a hole into another liner, which could then
be emptied into the packer. Protective gear was to be worn.

To dump bullets, the sweeper would line the four-wheel
(previously, two-wheel) cart with at least two or our largest
trash bags, and then attach a roll of smaller bags to the cart by
threading a bag through the cardboard core of the roll and tying
it to the handles of the cart. Then the sweeper would make a
circuit around the area to each bullet can, which was usually
double-bagged. If this person was thinking ahead to later in
their shift, they might, after emptying the bullet can, line it with
three or more bags so they could move quickly the next time
around by only having to pull a bag, not put in a replacement.

Liquid that would leak out the bags or otherwise find its
way into the hard resin interior of the bullet cans could get
mighty ripe. To remedy this, the entire bullet can would be
temporarily removed to the backstage and thoroughly hosed
out, cleaned, and disinfected, resin interior and metal exterior
alike. Then, it would be dried and double-bagged and returned
to its place. For bullet cans that were full-size and had clean
exteriors, it was easy enough to load up an 8-liner or 6-liner cart

with clean, double-bagged liners and take it onstage to switch them out with the liners inside the bullets.

Twice a week, the trash dumping sweeper would take out the 8-liner or 6-liner cart specifically to replace all of the area can liners, eight or six at a time, to bring them backstage to be scrubbed clean with cleanser and water. This might include breaking out a tool to remove gum or anything else sticking to the liner. This would be done until every liner in the area had been cleaned, and was called "eight-for-eights".

Depending on the condition of the area trash cans and staffing, the entire can might be pulled from the area to the backstage to be repainted (which our department ordered, but didn't do) or, more often, to be thoroughly cleaned.

Occasionally, a few cans in the area would need to be dumped while the rest of the area would be fine, so the trash dumper would do a "spot dump" using a three-liner cart or a four-wheel cart. Sometimes, a spot dump was done in response to a call from Custodial Central that a full can had been reported.

The responsibility of dumping trash would be a very different matter on days when there weren't any parade or shows compared to days on which there were.

One of the good things about dumping trash on Main Street was that the only stairs to climb were at the Main Street Station for the Disneyland Railroad, and the area is flat with a relatively smooth surface.

The actual placement of trash cans depended on several factors. Bullet cans were sometimes placed at the request of a manager of a location (such as a shop or attraction) but more often based on Custodial perceiving a need. Area cans were placed based on Custodial's determination of the need. They're not placed too close to other cans and not where they are likely to impede crowd flow or interfere with anything else. They might be moved a bit based on the preferences of the area sweeper or the trash dumper, or the Lead, but generally, the opening Lead regularly assigned to that area would determine the "permanent" placement. Guest Control might regularly move the cans back and forth as needed for handling parade crowds, and Security or a sweeper might move them temporarily in the event of an emergency to act as a barricade or to cover up a slip or trip hazard until the problem could be remedied.

Give Me a Break

It was common for people to take their breaks at the area locker for Main Street. Official break areas, though, included the Inn Between (the cast member restaurant on the backstage side of Plaza Inn), a break room behind the south eastern block of Center Street, and a break room behind the northern side of City Hall, up against the Jungle Cruise.

However, a mighty nice to place to take a break, when it wasn't open to guests, of course, was the Main Street Opera House, there the Abraham Lincoln show was. It was very comfortable in there, and nice to be around the artifacts of company history.

Adventure/Frontier

This Sweeping area deviated from the namesake themed areas in the following ways: 1) The northern boundary was the wooden bridge on the Big Thunder Trail, whereas the themed area of Frontierland continued on the trail to where it reaches Village Haus Restaurant in Fantasyland; 2) Tom Sawyer Island was separate (see Chapter 9); 3)The dock for the Tom Sawyer Island rafts, along with the nearby walkways, was in New Orleans/Critter (NO/CC); 4) Responsibilities for Pirates of the Caribbean were split with NO/CC.

Custodial operations for Adventure/Frontier were based out of the island ring of buildings that includes the Golden Horseshoe Saloon and the Adventureland Bazaar. There's an open-air backstage area in the midst of that ring of shops and eateries, and it was crammed with restaurant and shop supplies, two staircases heading to the upper level (to offices and a break room), a packer and related elements, and our Area Locker.

The main ways for cast members to access this back area was a swinging door between Bengal Barbecue and River Belle Terrace, and the large gate between Stage Door Cafe and River Belle Terrace. Other than that, entry could be gained if you had the right clearance and keys through the shops and restaurants, and if you were in Custodial, through the Adventureland guest restroom stock closet, which had a door that opened into a cast member restroom. When I (Ken) started, there was another way, which was the preferred way for Custodial, and that was a swinging door by the Adventureland men's guest restroom. But that disappeared when the restrooms were rebuilt in the early 1990s, which meant that carts full of trash had to be pushed close to diners at the other access points.

Being a Lead in this area often meant getting called to clean something out of a Jungle Cruise Boat, which might mean a trip around the jungle with just a ride operator. It also meant getting calls to clean up messes in Big Thunder trains that were pulled to storage, even though the Fantasyland Lead might be in a much better position to handle that call.

Leads in this area usually responded to hydraulic fluid clean-ups in Indiana Jones (see later in this chapter).

At night, if Fantasmic! was scheduled, the Adventure/Frontier Lead could defer calls to the Fantasmic! Lead during lunch or when there was some other need to do so, so that was convenient.

One of the nicest features of the area was the beautiful Golden Horseshoe Saloon, which is a living piece of Disneyland history. I (Lynn) enjoyed sitting in the Horseshoe after it was closed to guests. I would go upstairs and read or study for a test I had to take in college the next day. It was neat to sit in there all by myself at night, but sometimes it felt like I was not alone, if you know what I mean.

Although not as old as the Horseshoe, Walt Disney's Enchanted Tiki Room was something that gave off the same vibe for me (Ken). It would often close before the park did, and it was a great, quiet, comfortable, climate-controlled place to take a break to read without being disturbed, and we had the excuse of needing to make sure the room was clean.

A long-running entertainment offering in this area was the Laughing Stock Company. Although the nature of the live shows didn't lend itself to any occasional inclusion of sweepers, the shows done out in front of the Golden Horseshoe were often entertaining even if we'd seen them hundreds of times before, because sometimes the performers would ad-lib and sometimes they had guest participation, and you could never be sure how the guests would handle it. I (Ken) had my favorite performers and we'd sometimes shoot the breeze backstage. I'd do what I could to encourage passers-by to stop and watch the performances, even though it created a crowd flow bottleneck in the area.

Adventureland

The area from the Adventureland entrance to Tarzan's Treehouse, about halfway over the bridge in front of Pirates of the Caribbean, was the Adventureland sweeping area. This area was packed with four attractions: The Enchanted Tiki Room, Jungle Cruise, Indiana Jones Adventure, and Tarzan's Treehouse, and also shared Pirates of the Caribbean with NO/CC. Then there were the shops, places for people to buy food, and Aladdin's Oasis. There wasn't a lot of room for vending carts. There's a busy restroom close to the entrance of the land.

The crowds could get very thick in Adventureland, especially with rows of parked strollers, because it is a narrow area.

Although a sweeper assigned to an area would generally be responsible for "edging out" lines and waiting areas as part of their fifteen-minute round, the Adventure sweeper would not go inside the Indiana Jones interior, as it would take them too far away from the rest of the area and another sweeper was dedicated to keeping that attraction clean. One of the hidden treasures of Adventureland was near the Indy FastPass: the **Dominguez Tree**. This palm was on the land before it became Disneyland, as it was near the Dominguez family's house. The trees of Adventureland, like the shops, were a positive for sweepers working this area as we could stay cool on hotter days.

Just Following Instructions

Sometimes a sweeper would get into autopilot mode.

A sweeper covering the area was usually not going to see something that needed to be cleaned upstairs in the Treehouse (originally the Swiss Family Robinson Treehouse, later Tarzan's Treehouse). The Lead would usually get that call. Back when it was Swiss Family, Ride Operators would have it on their rotation to be there to answer questions and make sure everything was alright. One day, someone came down the stairs and told the Ride Operator that there was a deposit of human fecal matter upstairs.

The ride operator called the Custodial office to report a "Code H", which is code for horse droppings.

The Custodial office called the Adventure/Frontier Lead to report a "Code H" in the Treehouse.

The Custodial Lead took a pan & broom and climbed the stairs of the Treehouse, as a pan & broom is usually all it takes to completely clean up a Code H.

The Lead came down the stairs and said to the Ride Operator, "That's not horsecrap. That's human!"

The ride operator looked up through the Treehouse and asked, perplexed, "How would a horse get up there anyway?"

We would call that "Human Code H".

Cleaning the Kingdom

Live Entertainment

For many years, a steel drum band played in front of the Bazaar. When Adventureland was renovated ahead of the debut of the Indiana Jones Adventure, a space was built into the second level of the new Jungle Cruise for the steel drum band and other performers. One of those other bands was accompanied by an actor or two to add some humor. One of their gimmicks was to take requests from guests to see if anyone could stump the band. No matter what song anyone requested, the band would actually play the tune "Zip a Dee Do Dah" and one of the actors would improvise rhyming lyrics using the title that the guest had suggested.

Either a guest would catch on and request "Zip a Dee Do Dah" or the actor would pretend a guest in the line behind them had made the request, and after it was announced, the band would act stumped. Since the performers recognized and trusted me (Ken), they would ask me to "stump the band" when they wanted to end the bit, and I would make the request.

An Oasis Indeed

When I (Ken) hired in, the Tahitian Terrace, connected to the Tiki Room, was still considered a popular dinner and entertainment option, and it wasn't something for sweepers to worry about as it was covered by Foods cast members.

With the arrival of the hit animated feature "Aladdin", the venue was rebuilt into Aladdin's Oasis, with the same general idea of a table-service dinner and themed show.

It appeared to be popular at first. Eventually, though, the dinner and show went away and the venue was used for things like private events, including a lunch I attended thrown for cast members who'd been around for five years, and for a lower-production storytelling show aimed at kids.

Since it was no longer being treated as a restaurant, it became our responsibility to clean up any messes there. Usually, this was not a problem, but it became so on rainy days. With smooth tile for flooring and a cloth canopy, a little rain could mean a lot of work for us as the dripping continued long after the liquid sunshine was finished falling from the sky.

Rainy days generally meant less of a crowd, but especially when the showers are intermittent, sweepers had a lot of drying to do, and this location was a prime example.

The place did make for an excellent unofficial break area, especially in evenings. There were the separate men's and women's restrooms in the back, as well as the one near the entrance that was designed to accommodate guests with disabilities and an assistant, and thus could lock from the inside. There were plenty of tables and chairs, and a park landline phone was there, which was handy in responding to any request from Custodial Central to 10-21.

Not as obvious was a space above the disability restroom, as the structure was a small tower. This space was accessible via ladder, one facing the Jungle Cruise. It was a very private space, but of course the trick was getting there without being seen in the first place.

When I spent a week on Limited Work due to a sprained shoulder, there was a day I dressed up in a themed costume for Aladdin's Oasis and then was placed at the entrance to the venue to keep people out and answer their questions. The timing was right for me to end up in a picture that, last I checked, was still used on the Yesterland website.

Indy

When the Indiana Jones Adventure was added in March 1995, Day Custodial responded by assigning several sweepers to the attraction. They were split between Adventure/Frontier and NO/CC areas and would work on tasks in those areas until they needed to respond to clean up hydraulic fluid from the attraction's track.

Cleaning the Kingdom

After things settled down, there were two sweepers per shift assigned to Indy for several years, and eventually it was down to one.

If you're not familiar with attraction, the show building for it, where the ride actually takes place, was built outside the berm, taking up what used to be the Eeyore section of the original Disneyland parking lot. The Disneyland Monorail track had to be moved to accommodate it, and for guests to get to the ride, they have to walk an eighth of a mile from the Adventureland area to the show building, and after the ride, they have to walk an eighth of a mile back. This was all themed as an ancient temple and the waiting area was carved out of what used to be part of the Jungle Cruise, an extended portion of the Pirates of the Caribbean waiting area, and backstage area.

It was a huge building and the queue was one of the longer lines to sweep. The Custodial sweepers working in there would sweep the line, dump the trash cans, which were bagged (bullets), and clean the restrooms and break room inside the attraction. The restrooms, each "private" in that someone could enter either and lock the door, were officially cast member restrooms but ride operators and sweepers would readily let guests use them rather than sending guests all the way back to the Adventureland restrooms. They're right behind the elevator that is on the north unload side of the loading area. The attraction break room was past the restrooms.

We had a small room (a closet, really) to ourselves right behind the stairs the guests took to go up over the loading area, where we'd keep our supplies and where we could read if we didn't want to be in the noisy, crowded break room.

One of the doors in the line literally opened into a cramped back area at the Pirates of the Caribbean loading area, and across from the door is another one along the exit that grants access to stairs that connect to an upstairs back entry into the Pirates building, to the control tower area. This was convenient if there was a call for the NO/CC Lead to get something at the load or unload of Pirates and they couldn't, as the Indy person, who was also equipped with a radio, could do so.

Another convenience was that there was a packer in the back area between the line for Indy and the New Orleans building, so the bagged trash could be taken there rather than all the way back to the Adventureland packer.

When the attraction was opened under the sponsorship of AT&T, decoder cards were passed out for advertising under the guise of helping guests translate the "Maraglyphics" while they waited. Of course these cards would find their way to the ground and everywhere else, and we were there to clean them up. Later, FastPass meant (as it did in many other places in the park) many little paper rectangles ended up everywhere, and a change in the flow of the waiting area, since stand-by lines moved more slowly and certain gaps in the waiting areas were created to benefit guests using FastPasses.

For at least the first couple of years of operation, the attraction would draw a line at the start of the day that would extend through Adventureland and into a snaking layout in Frontierland.

The vehicles guests ride had on-board hydraulics, and early on, they'd leak often, and the leaks would get big enough to cause the attraction to go down. We'd have to get onto that track and get those spills cleaned up using protective equipment, dust, vacuums, and absorbent pads. If you've never been evacuated from the ride or otherwise had an opportunity to be on that track, walking it really underscores just how massive that attraction is. Zipping through it on a large vehicle somewhat obscures that from your perception.

Speaking of the vehicles, if there was some mess on them that was going to need more than a few seconds of cleaning, they would be pulled off to their maintenance area and that is where we could clean them. So, there were no ride-arounds under the excuse of cleaning a troop transport.

Indy was one of the first, if not the first, attractions we can recall with lockout-tagout procedures. Just after dispatch, there was a board on the left side for this, and it was designed to keep the attraction from being started when anyone was still on the track. There was at least one longtime Foreman who forgot to return his tag and had scribbled his name in a way that when the radio call went out searching for the person to get them to tag back in, he didn't realize for a while that he had a tag in his pocket that needed to get back to its home ASAP!

Frontier

The second main sweeping area for Adventure/Frontier was, appropriately enough, Frontier. For our opening shifts, the first sweeper on duty after us Leads would usually be assigned to sweep (after finishing the opening procedures) the busiest area. During my (Ken) time, that switched from Frontier to Adventure due to the addition of the Indiana Jones Adventure. But Frontier was nothing at which to sneeze.

This area was from the entrance of Frontierland past Big Thunder Mountain to the wooden bridge. That bridge separated two custodial areas Fantasyland, and Frontierland. The other boundary usually was around the petrified tree.

The Frontier area had several attractions. Big Thunder Mountain Railroad is the largest, but there is also the Shootin' Exposition, the Mark Twain riverboat, and the Sailing Ship Columbia. Much guest traffic flows through this area, and Big Thunder Mountain, on a busy day, could have its line extend out into the area. Frontier also had many flower beds (though few actual flowers) and benches, There were just a few shops and a few restaurants.

Some of the flower beds were hard to reach, especially one that is along the Rivers of America off the side of the Big Thunder Trail, and we'd have to climb down before the park opened to make sure they were cleaned up. One morning, after the area had been re-landscaped, I (Ken) found that the mud was lightly placed rather than packed down, and my feet were sinking into the mud! I got about a foot down into it. I was wondering if I was going to stop sinking or if I was about to disappear there. I was wearing shorts, so at least I wasn't soiling white pant legs, but it sure wasn't good for my shoes or socks.

In 1998, as part of a long and extensive corporate agreement, McDonald's moved into Disneyland, but only selling their French fries. One location for this was a covered wagon placed across from the exit of Big Thunder Mountain. Along with the fries, it served soft drinks and water.

It was a mess.

Since there were no tables, it was left for us sweepers to handle it, rather than Bussing. Fries frequently littered the ground, along with napkins and straw wrappers. In 2001 an identical menu went in at the Harbor Galley at Fowler's Harbor in New Orleans Square. In January of 2007 both locations closed. The Conestoga wagon went away. The Harbor Galley changed its menu to seafood.

Another blight on the same area of the Big Thunder Trail had been a "lemon quench" cart run by the Outdoor Vending Department. We used to call those "lemon stench" for good reason. Frequently, the sticky concentrate would leak and make its destructive way down the slope of the trail.

Frontier had a popcorn wagon across from the entrance of Golden Horseshoe, and it was one of the popcorn carts that was pretty much always open, and an open popcorn wagon always meant there would be bits of popcorn everywhere, and spills of various sizes. I (Ken) was working Adventure/Frontier one day when a large tree fell over. Now, that could happen from time to time, as there are so many trees throughout the park, but this particular tree clobbered the popcorn wagon. It had happened as I was leaving for the day, and when I heard about it, I just had to make my way back to the area to see for myself and maybe give the tree a thankful pat. Unfortunately, the tree had trapped and/or injured a few people as well, and so guests were being redirected away from the scene of the incident, but I did get a good look. We heard that after the damaged popcorn wagon was moved backstage, it was hit with a lit firework! Of course the wagon was quickly replaced. Those things generated far too much revenue to leave a gap in where one would normally be.

I was also the Lead in the area on the evening of May 17, 1997, when the Keel Boat attraction met its demise. Around 5:30 p.m., one of the two boats, the Gullywhumper, capsized. Guests were dunked into the Rivers of America and the boat was on its side. As we stared at what we knew would be Disneyland history, with Tom Sawyer Island rafts being used in the response, I certainly did *not* see a certain person on my crew taking out a camera and snap some pictures. And his initials were not V. M. Fortunately, nobody was seriously injured, but it was a sad end to an attraction I personally enjoyed.

Although we were witness to the aftermath of that accident, I once went to court as a defense witness for Disney in a civil lawsuit even though I had not been a witness to the incident itself, which was a woman twisting her ankle at the Shootin' Exposition. Harry Hemhauser, being the longest-employed sweeper at the time, and being the opening Foreman for that area, was usually tapped for testimony in these situations, but he wasn't available so I got the task. This mother was taking video of her family using the attraction at night, and she backed off the boardwalk and twisted her ankle. From what I understand, which could be completely wrong, Disney offered her a couple of thousand dollars for her troubles, even though Disney was not admitting fault. She rejected that, wanting five figures. Her lawyer left the case, so she was representing herself.

Now, I'm the son of a civil law attorney. I thought this woman was being very foolish pursuing the case in the first place, but even more so that she was representing herself. Disney's lawyer was good at what he did. He asked me about our fifteen-minute rounds. He asked me what was at the left end of the attraction, which was a door Custodians used all of the time to get back to Custodial Central, which was in that back area at that time. The point was, if something had been wrong with the boardwalk we would have noticed it quickly and placed a nearby trash can in the way to prevent a problem until Facilities could get to it. I had a hard time keeping a straight face as the plaintiff cross-examined me, but I think I pulled it off.

The jury sided with Disney and the woman got *nothing*. Good day, sir!

Big Thunder, Big Line

While we usually had someone designated to sweep through the lines on busier days, the waiting area for Big Thunder Mountain was, perhaps, the toughest thing about covering the Frontier area, especially for closeout and opening procedures. The landscaping for the attraction, the props, and the rockwork with countless crevices were popular places for people to shove things when they couldn't be bothered to hold on to them for a few minutes until they reached the next bullet can. The staircase to the loading platform was split into two sides by a rail, and each side was too narrow to do anything but follow the guest flow, rather than sweep against the flow, which is what we did for most of the line.

The Alley

The third of the three areas for Adventure/Frontier was the Alley, also known as Bridge to Bridge, Pirates-Alley, Thunder-Pirates, or even Harry's Jail. That last name was because that's where Harry Hemhauser put people he wanted to watch like a hawk. With the other two areas, it was plausible Harry could be unable to see a sweeper on his crew because they were sweeping through a shop or they were around a corner, but with the Alley, if Harry couldn't find you quickly it was because you were stiffing (goofing off) somewhere. It was also the area with the least amount of shade and no air-conditioned shops to sweep through.

As the names imply, the area stretched from the Pirates of the Caribbean entrance (a bridge) to the wooden bridge on the Big Thunder Trail. This meant that a good portion of the area overlapped with the Frontier coverage area.

On slower days, the Adventure-Frontier was split into two sweeping areas and Alley was not an assignment. The Adventure person would sweep "Adventure Circle" meaning Adventureland, the portion of the Alley that extended to the Frontierland popcorn wagon, and along the Frontierland shops to the Adventureland entrance.

Lines

Since the Indiana Jones line was covered by the designated Indy person or pair of people, someone assigned to sweep out lines in the Adventure/Frontier area would sweep the Big Thunder Mountain line, the Pirates of the Caribbean line, Jungle Cruise line, Tarzan's Treehouse, the boat dock, and the Tiki Room waiting area. Of course, they would take care of anything they saw as they moved from location to location as well. For the most part, sweeping lines meant going against the flow of the line. People could see you coming, which meant many of them would get out of your way (other people preferred to pretend to be a wall), and you could move through the line faster than going with the flow of guests. Some portions of lines would be too narrow to go against the flow, however.

Sweeping lines in this area often mean crossing Big Thunder Railroad tracks in the loading area, or crossing through a train, sometimes where the prop engine met the passenger cars. It also meant crossing Pirate boats. We used to be allowed, even encouraged, to take calculated risks that are not allowed now.

Cleaning the Kingdom

Dumping Trash

The packer for Adventure/Frontier was in the backstage island behind the Golden Horseshoe, River Belle Terrace, Adventureland Bazaar, etc. Not only would the area trash and the trash from attractions (bullets) go there, but so would the trash for much of the Fantasmic viewing area, the Golden Horseshoe, the Stage Door Cafe, River Belle Terrace, and Bengal Barbecue.

Sometimes the packer would get full. And by full, we mean *full*. The compacting function for it would no longer work. That meant the trash would have to be hauled elsewhere to be dumped, such as the Critter Country packer (which we discuss below). For most packers, if they got full because either they weren't emptied overnight or there was just too much trash, they could be switched out or emptied per request, but since this was one in a backstage island, it had to wait for the park to be cleared of guests. That's because getting it emptied meant bringing in a large truck to haul it out.

Absent a full packer, dumping the area trash in Adventure/Frontier was straightforward and much as described for Main Street. Some of the area cans would become part of the Fantasmic! coverage area in the evening. The Indiana Jones cans were handled by the assigned Indy person. There were the Tiki bullets to get, as well as Oasis, Jungle Cruise, and the Big Thunder bullets, which could be a real challenge because there were many of them and we had to haul the bulging bags up some side stairs to our cart. We'd also cross to the middle of the load area to take care of the can(s) there, which usually meant stepping on a designated yellow pad on the coaster tracks after a train was dispatched, and doing so in communication with the ride operators. It wasn't all that unusual that a bag would spring a leak, and that meant having something to clean up, of course.

Coverage of Pirates has varied over the years, but the exterior waiting area was generally the responsibility of

Adventure/Frontier, and that included dumping the bullets there.

Last but not least, there was dumping the bullet cans in the waiting area of the Mark Twain riverboat and Sailing Ship Columbia and the cans on-board the ships themselves. Every once in a while, this resulted in a trip around the River. Oops!

Ever since the Adventureland restroom renovation that eliminated a door wide enough to take the trash carts through, carts had to be taken out by Stage Door Cafe, past the dining area, with smaller carts able to go through a door by Bengal Barbecue.

Big Boats

Speaking of the Mark Twain and the Columbia, if there was a spill or some mess on one of the ships or boats, then when docked, a sweeper would clean it up. Every now and then it required more than a quick cleanup, so we were able to ride the boat around the River. Leads would get these calls, and if they didn't have someone on their crew who was around and would be convenient to spare to take care of it, the Lead would do it.

Little Boats

A unique aspect of closing out Adventure/Frontier on any night the park closed before midnight was doing Pirate boats. This meant that the area closeout would largely have to be completed ahead of time except for a sweeper or two who could be left to complete or double check the closeout while the rest of the crew hit the boats.

NO/CC would generally respond to calls to clean up something in a Pirate boat during operating hours, but Adventure/Frontier handled this end-of-night cleaning on these days. When the park closed at midnight or later, Night Custodial would handle this task.

After park closing, we would head over to the Pirates of

Cleaning the Kingdom

the Caribbean attraction, to the unload side. Once the last guests had exited the boats, we started our cleanup.

We'd tie a towel around the first boat to indicate where we'd started.

Since two boats are in the dock at once, and dispatched together, we'd have four or five of us there so two people could get the first boat, and two people would get the second. A fifth person would be ready to vacuum out water, mop out water (we had to roll a mop bucket over there) or pan & broom. The two people on each boat would grab whatever debris we could and toss it on the unload dock and use cloth towels to wipe down the seats and rails.

Yes, some boats would get a lot of water, mainly due to going down the waterfalls in the attraction all day and splashing into the boats, but some of it appeared to be from leaking. If a boat was too flooded with water, we'd tie a towel on it to indicate it should be pulled for extra attention. This seemed to happen more and more. as the fleet aged. It has since been replaced.

We would find lots of maps, bottles, and whatever else the guests have left behind.

Once those two boats are cleaned, the lead would yell up to the tower "Clear". That meant the boats could be dispatched, usually by a ride operator who was working later than others, and the next boats could arrive to the dock to be cleaned. We'd do this until all of the boats in use had been cleaned. It could take twenty minutes or it could take a lot longer if things were really bad.

Fantasmic!

There was a time when Adventure/Frontier and NO/CC were very quiet at night, especially when NO/CC was NO/BC, meaning Bear Country instead of Critter Country. Back then, if things were slow enough, those two areas were put under one Lead. That was before either of us were hired in.

173

Someone could take a quiet, romantic nighttime trip aboard the Mark Twain as it plied the Rivers of America.

Fantasmic!, the nighttime water-light-pyro on the Rivers of America, changed a lot. One of the things it changed was making these areas very, very busy at night. The show premiered in 1992 and, until recently, the viewing areas were claimed on a first-come basis. So if the first show was at 9:00 p.m., people might start claiming spots at *4:00 p.m.* Frequent guests would do this. At least one group in particular would spread out a blanket or tarp and then as the minutes to showtime shrank to a few, they'd scope out some desperate tourists fruitlessly seeking a spot with *some* view and the squatters would invite them to some of the best viewing possible for the show.

Now, squatting is prevented through a FastPass distribution system.

But for over twenty-two years, thousands of people waited for a very long time for the first show, and then after the show was over, piles of trash were left behind which had to be cleaned up before people were allowed to claim their spot for the next show.

Most Custodial cast members in Adventure/Frontier and NO/CC would get pulled to post-show cleanups.

For more about cleaning Fantasmic!, see Chapter 9.

New Orleans/Critter Country

The other area that dealt with Fantasmic! was the remaining area on the Westside of the park, New Orleans/Critter Country (NO/CC). As with Adventure/Frontier, having Fantasmic! drastically changed how the area was covered. The Custodial area mostly conformed to the themed areas of New Orleans Square and Critter Country, although Pirates of the Caribbean was partially handled by Adventure/Frontier and the mainland-side Tom Sawyer Island raft dock and everything along the Rivers of America from the Pirates of the Caribbean entrance area was part of this area, even if Tom Sawyer Island and the departed Keel Boats were listed as Frontierland attractions.

Technically, Tom Sawyer Island was also under the jurisdiction of NO/CC but that hardly ever came into play as the Island was covered by a pair of sweepers, one of each gender. (See Chapter 9.) Every now and then, I (Lynn) liked to surprise the sweepers over there and check on them. If there was something they needed or couldn't do, the Lead would have to go over. The problem with that was having to wait for a raft to get over there, which could take fifteen minutes. Then there was the task itself, which might include finding a sweeper who wasn't being responsive to their radio (dead battery, it was turned down, or on the wrong channel), then getting back to the mainland; that could take an hour in total. In the meantime there were breaks to be covered or calls to which the Lead couldn't respond.

So the area stretched from the bridge in front of Pirates of the Caribbean all the way where Critter Country dead-ends. It's a large area, but Critter Country still got very quiet most nights.

The Area Locker was to the immediate left when exiting the Haunted Mansion. There was a dead-end back there, and without climbing into the elevated landscaped areas, the only way out was either by the Haunted Mansion exit or going into an access door, downstairs to the Haunted Mansion and navigating through the Haunted Mansion show building into the beyond-the-berm backstage area. The packer for the area was past the gate at the dead-end of Critter Country.

The Lead for this area was one of those who might get calls to clean up something on one of the Disneyland Railroad trains, which could mean a trip around the park. We also used to sweep through the Haunted Mansion ride *as it was running*. The ride operators would leave a break in seating guests in Doom Buggies and we'd sweep through, following the flow of the ride. This is one of those things that would probably get people fired now. We'd also ride through in a buggy to clean up something in it.

For some things, the attraction would have to be shut down entirely, like when people spread the ashes of their deceased loved ones. Yes, people have done this. When terrorism became a concern, some people might see a powdery substance and think it was Anthrax. Unfortunately for those spreading ashes, the remains were cleaned up and did not meet a pretty fate.

Then there were the people who took advantage of the seeming privacy of the Doom Buggies to, *ahem*, make a family in a family park. Early on in my (Ken's) time, video cameras were added and the monitors were in the control "room". They were pretty clear in revealing what some people were doing, who we could then meet at the unload with a quip or two. This is not simply a matter of giving people a hard time, uh, so to speak. People can leave things behind that need to be cleaned up and even though they think they have privacy, it is possible for kids to see what is going on.

There were a pair of basic, small restrooms for cast members in the Mansion, and that was a convenient location for a sweeper to access during a visit back to the area locker. I (Ken) really needed the privacy in order to feel comfortable. So I was horrified after I used the restroom, as I had many times before, only to notice afterwards that part of the wall had recently been torn out, presumably for repairs, and any cast member walking by could easily see everything I was doing, and could still be having nightmares to this day. Appropriate enough, given the location, no?

At the end of the night, we would likely sweep through the ride to remove any little trash we could find. The sets were something to behold even with the lights on.

Some other fun calls would be to clean up something in a Splash log, a Pirate boat, or, rarely, a canoe. The Splash logs would be pulled to the side flume and we could comfortably take as long as we needed to clean it right. A cleanup for a Pirate boat would usually mean a trip on the ride. Sometimes we'd finish the clean up before we'd even reached the first drop, and we could relax and enjoy the rest of the trip. We'd usually ride all the way back to the unload, but there was at least once that I was in a hurry and I bailed out after the jail scene, in the "burning embers" area. There's an emergency exit door that leads to a staircase up to the area that used to be the Westside Diner. That's another one of those things that would probably get someone fired these days.

New Orleans

This area would be from the Pirates bridge over to the imaginary line from the Disneyland Railroad Station down to the Tom Sawyer Island raft docks. That meant the sweeper had those pathways and terraces running along the River, and the streets of New Orleans Square with all of their shops.

There's a popcorn wagon at the imaginary line forming the border, so it was shared with the person covering the Mansion.

One of the great things about sweeping this area was getting to listen to the live music of the Royal Street Bachelors.

This specific sweeping area is one of the greatest examples of theme park design. As a student of theme park design (I, Ken was) I still marvel at the intricate layout that completely immerses the guest in something evoking a famous part of distinctive American city. The structures housing the Pirates of the Caribbean load and unload, Cafe Orleans, and the French Market appear to be three different buildings but are really all one large building with each least four levels. One could literally get lost in the backstage areas of the buildings, and I'm sure some cast members have. This design also allowed someone to disappear if they wanted to. I sometimes would take my break right by the first drop of Pirates of the Caribbean, concealed from guests by an emergency exit door, and concealed from fellow cast members by another door.

Mansion

This area picked up where New Orleans left off, with the Railroad station, the area with the decorative fountain, down to the Tom Sawyer Island raft dock, the pathways between the Haunted Mansion and the Rivers of America, and to the border with Critter Country.

Aside from the popcorn wagon, the big things about this area were the smoking area (on the former Keel Boats dock) and keeping an eye on the waiting areas for the Railroad and the Haunted Mansion and sweeping those out whenever the crowds receded. A lot of people would also sit along the lower brick wall between the Haunted Mansion entrance and exit. We'd sweep out the smoking areas and empty urns.

On slower days, this area was split between the New Orleans and Critter Country sweepers.

Critter Country

The sweeping area was the same as the themed area. Of course the Hungry Bear Restaurant was Bussing territory. There used to be more Bussing territory towards the end of Critter Country for people eating from the Brer Bar (formerly the Mile Long Bar), but those tables were removed and then that area got Pooh all over it, making the Bar disappear.

Splash Mountain and its line dominated the area, but there's also the Davy Crockett Explorer Canoes and the Winnie the Pooh attraction.

Before Pooh, there was the Country Bear Playhouse, which, during the years we were there, featured the Country Bear Vacation Hoedown and the holiday special during the right time of year. The Playhouse was removed in 2001 for Pooh not too long before Disney put out a movie based on the Country

Bears. The movie was a tad less successful than turning the Pirates of Caribbean into a movie, but it probably wasn't due to the Playhouse being gone. Things got slow enough for our beloved Bear Band that only one of the two identical theaters would be used, to the point that one theater was kept in the holiday dressing year-round so that there wasn't even a need to do a changeover to start and end the season.

After a theater was done being used for the day, we'd sweep it out, and of course we'd respond to any calls to clean up as necessary during the operational day. Having the attraction closed before the rest of the park or having one of the theaters closed to guests made the Playhouse a nice climate-controlled, quiet, well-lit breakroom... as long as you didn't feel creeped out by Max, Buff, and Melvin staring at you.

One night I (Lynn) was in there sweeping by myself, and it was maybe a bit after midnight, and all of a sudden the animatronic figures started moving, but without sound. I ran out of there!

There was also an official breakroom through the doors at the end of the Playhouse waiting area. Nothing was creepy there, except maybe some of the other cast members.

Something unique to this area was the combination of smooth concrete walkways and many trees shedding needles. This was a slippery combination, especially with the elevation changes of the walkways. One day, the first strong wind of the season was causing dried needles to rain down on the area in such volume that literally all we could do was work in high gear and create large "haystacks" by continuously pushbrooming the needles into piles. This seemed to go on for hours and hours. There could have been quite the bonfire at the end of the day.

Lines

A designated Lines sweeper was certainly busy in NO/CC. We had Splash Mountain and the Haunted Mansion lines to sweep, and sometimes the Davy Crockett Explorer Canoes line needed attention, too. Pirates was mostly covered by Adventure/Frontier. The waiting area for the Disneyland Railroad and for Country Bears, and later, Pooh, were part of the round of lines, too.

In my (Ken's) first Summer season, I often had the Lines assignment in NO/CC as my usual shift was 11:00 a.m. to 7:30 p.m. and the areas were usually covered by earlier shifts. This was 1990, so Splash Mountain had only been open a year and the Line was extensive. The Lines assignment was considered one of the less desirable ones, but I actually liked doing this assignment because I found sweeping out the lines less repetitive than 15-minute rounds and I enjoyed interacting with guests and easing their wait a bit. Considering I'd been obsessed with the construction of Splash Mountain before I was hired and had ridden the attraction hundreds of times, it seemed only fitting that my second day out of training, I was assigned to NO/CC under the watch of Harry Hemhauser and got paid to sweep the line I used to pay (well, my parents used to pay) for me to stand in. Harry was Opening Lead for NO/CC for my first couple of years before being rotated to Adventure/Frontier, and ended up being my Summer Foreman until I became a Foreman myself.

Sweeping the lines included sweeping the load/unload areas of Splash Mountain and the Haunted Mansion, and doing so efficiently often meant doing things that are probably no longer allowed, due to safety restrictions. For example, with the Haunted Mansion, we'd go in a side staircase by the exit, to the unload area, sweep that, and then walk alongside the Doom Buggies as they passed the control "room" and down the slope to the loading area. From there, we'd sweep against the flow of people back to the Stretching Rooms, so we could enter the next one after guests were emptied from it into the final part of their wait before boarding their Doom Buggie. We'd sweep out what was suddenly the Quickly Shrinking Room as it reset for the next batch of guests. Then, after the guests came into the room, we were able to slip out and sweep the empty-for-a-moment

Cleaning the Kingdom

entry room. Finally, we'd move from there through the outdoor portion of the line, against the flow of guests.

Dumping Trash

Dumping trash in this area could be a challenge and normally required two cast members, even more often than other areas (Fantasyland was the only "full" area that could usually get away with just having one trash dumper.) Since the trash packer for this area was behind Splash Mountain, all, or at least most, of the trash for this area would have to be hauled over the hill in front of the face of Splash Mountain.

To risk sounding like old men: In our day, none of our trash carts were motorized. We had to use brute strength to push the fully-packed eight-liner carts up the hill through the crowds, and then keep it from rolling over people and crashing on the downhill portion.

Getting to some of the bullet cans could be difficult, so in some cases we had some shortcuts, such as using emergency exit doors that wouldn't set off alarms. In the Haunted Mansion, we'd reach a can at the loading area by using a door by the tombs alongside the outside line switchback area. We would also climb the wall right there to get to some of the outdoor bullet cans. There was a can at the unload we'd get by going down some backstage stairs next to our area locker. In Splash Mountain there were several bullet cans, and most could be accessed easily, but there were a few which weren't. One of them we had no option to reach other than by going through the guests.

Again, I (Lynn) think the two hardest areas to dump trash were Main Street, especially at night, and NO/CC.

Logging Operations

Just as the Adventure/Frontier Day crew cleaned Pirate boats if the park closed before midnight, and Night Custodial

181

handled them if park closed at midnight or later, the NO/CC crew had the considerably easier Splash Mountain logs to clean out. There was the same basic idea: tie a towel around the first log to mark it, and clean out and wipe down the logs two at a time until the entire on-circuit set had been cleaned.

Eating on the Westside

We were supposed to take our breaks and our unpaid lunch in official break rooms. We could eat food we'd brought from home, something resembling food that came from a vending machine, or eat food purchase at cast member restaurant. Official break rooms on the Westside that were not restaurants existed behind the Main Street Fire Station, upstairs over the River Belle Terrace, and behind the Country Bear Playhouse. Sometimes, we'd hang out with the ride operators in a small room with a sofa and television crammed into the actual mansion portion of the Haunted Mansion.

Leads would often go to the Inn Between (the backstage part of the Plaza Inn) to meet up with other Leads. However, if the hours were right, those of us working in Adventure/Frontier, NO/CC, or Westside restrooms might hit the Westside Diner, which was called the D.E.C. before that ("Deck"), which I think stood for Disney Employee Cafeteria. Before we were there, it was The Pit, hence the racecar theming that lasted through the DEC days. The Westside Diner took on a 1950s theme.

This place was in one of the underground levels of New Orleans Square, connected to the kitchen of the area that was supplying food for the various restaurants above. For my (Lynn's) first few years working there, the food was very good, because it came from the same kitchen as the Blue Bayou. Sometimes they would have fish, chicken, dinner entrees, chicken tenders, and made-to-order burgers. Over the years, someone had an idea to make all the cast member cafeterias the same menu, so out went some of those yummy choices.

Cleaning the Kingdom

Every once in a while a flood would close the restaurant. It was later replaced by a new building on the outside the berm, not far from the Monorail track, to make more room for backstage operations to meet the needs of guests.

Cleaning the Kingdom

Chapter 8

Land By Land - Eastside

You've read how we covered the Westside. Or maybe you haven't, Well, here's how we covered the Eastside.

Introduction

The areas of the Eastside, as broken down to be assigned to a Sweeping Lead, included Tomorrowland, Fantasyland, and Small World/Matterhorn, with Toontown being introduced as a quasi-autonomous territory.

185

Cleaning the Kingdom

Tomorrowland

The Custodial Day Sweeping area of Tomorrowland was synonymous with the themed land by the same name. As such, the area included all of the guest areas east of the Hub and east of the Matterhorn, except, of course, for the Bussing areas.

The Area Locker for Tomorrowland moved over the years. When I (Ken) hired in, it was up against the backside of Space Mountain, right next to where the 3-D glasses were cleaned for the Magic Eye Theater (then featuring "Captain Eo"), which was near the gate that's at the Space Mountain exit. By the time Lynn had hired in, it had been moved a bit behind The Center, a backstage building between Tomorrowland and Main Street. It was later moved to behind the Innoventions building.

The main packer for the area was also behind the Innoventions building, but the Main Street packer was also nearby, as was a packer behind Plaza Inn on the Star Tours side.

The last time most of Tomorrowland was significantly overhauled structurally was for the renovation that debuted in 1967, which was right after New Orleans Square opened. Much of the same kind of thinking was applied to the layout of Tomorrowland, in terms of there being multiple levels built, including development underground. Of course, the Space Mountain complex was added in 1977 and there was some additional work for the 1998 renovation of the area that added a small tunnel. Some of the buildings had undergone multiple renovations by the time we were around, such as the building where Star Tours is now and the building where the Buzz Lightyear attraction is now. All of this work, and the distinctive shapes of the buildings, created many odd spaces backstage, some of them appearing to have been forgotten.

Whether trying to get somewhere quickly to respond to a call, sweep a line, or dump some trash, or if one just wanted a place to take a break, it was helpful to be familiar with all of the doors, all of the ways from here to there, and all of the odd and hidden spaces.

Cleaning the Kingdom

In the middle of the area was a Bussing establishment, Tomorrowland Terrace, temporarily renamed Club Buzz for a Toy Story-based live show. Later, the Jedi Training Academy would be held there. These were daytime shows, as the nighttime entertainment consisted of live bands, including cover bands and tribute bands (a Beatles tribute band played there for a while). These shows didn't have an impact on Sweepers beyond attracting a crowd to the area or filling the air with music and sound.

A couple of Entertainment Department offerings in Tomorrowland did Custodial themes. One was PUSH, a moving, talking, interactive trash can, who got his name from the word on the flap of the can. This little guy looked like an area can but would literally roll around the area interacting with guests. This was not a recording; it was live. Although, PUSH could play music. Someone who could pull their eyes away from PUSH and look around the nearby area carefully might be able to figure out how this fun diversion was accomplished. The other tie-in was the Trash Can Trio, consisting of three drummers. They would be dressed as sweepers, pushing what looked like round metal trash cans through the area, then they'd stop to "take a break". Then they would launch into their set by whipping out drumsticks. I (Ken) got a kick out of this and I would interact with them whenever I could by loudly telling them to take a break when I knew they were about to start a set.

As a fully functioning area, Tomorrowland was large and busy. Throughout our time there, though, various parts would be closed for renovation or just to sit idly while corporate politics churned. It lightened our load as far as cleaning, but when vacant space was idle rather than being actively renovated, it was mind-boggling to think that such valuable real estate was not being used well.

Tomorrowland was usually divided into three basic areas for sweeping, and each had its own guest restroom the sweeper could help out in by sweeping through.

187

Entrance

As the name implies, this was the area that covered the Tomorrowland entrance, from the Hub to about the Star Traders shop.

Until Tomorrowland was renovated for the 1998 overhaul, the actual entrance of Tomorrowland was fairly quiet, especially at night. There were a pair of flower beds fronted by sculpted benches. Here, and along with seating that was adjacent to Tomorrowland Terrace, a group of teenagers who were regulars (annual passholders) and referred to as "wall kids", would congregate on weekends and summer nights. Their garb ended up being along the lines of "ravers". Some of their loose jeans had so much extra material they probably could have clothed entire third world countries if repurposed.

There was a time the Entrance position had a pager. If you don't know what that is, ask an old person or read about "Main Gate" in the previous chapter. If someone called in a short audio message to it, it would vibrate, then deliver that short message. If we wanted to hear the message again, we could press a button and the device would repeat the message.

There was a sweeper who was annoyed enough by the wall kids that he called his own pager with the message, "10-4 Security is responding." He did this so he could pretend it was a radio, talk into it requesting Security, then press the button to have the message play as though it was live.

The pager allowed the Entrance person to be a kind of backup to the Foreman by responding to calls the Foreman couldn't get due to responding to something else.

The Entrance could sometimes get very busy, especially when Rocket Rods was there, like when I (Lynn) started. Rocket Rods was a fast-moving attraction on top of the old Peoplemover track. The entrance to the attraction was where Buzz Lightyear is now. Between the addition of the Rocket Rods and the Astro-Orbitor being planted at the entrance to Tomorrowland, the area was much more to deal with than it had been before 1998.

Space Mountain

Space Mountain area, or just "Space", was the area from around Star Traders to the entrance of Innoventions, and included the entrance and exit of Space Mountain.

This area could be a challenge because it was right in the middle of Tomorrowland. On busy days this area would often be very congested. Guests would be entering Space Mountain and gathering FastPasses and dropping related notices (you know, those rejection notices from FastPass machines) near the entrance to that attraction. Then on the other side, guests would be constantly exiting Space Mountain, and then there would be the rush of people exiting the Magic Eye Theater every 20 minutes or so, after a screening of "Captain Eo" or "Honey, I Shrunk the Audience".

Innoventions, which was part of the 1998 renovation of Tomorrowland, never had a long wait, so that attraction didn't add a lot of work for sweeping and dumping trash in comparison to when the building had been closed to guests, as it had been since 1988. There was some controversy as responsibility for cleaning Innoventions during third shift (when the park was closed to guests) was given to an outside company rather than Disneyland Night Custodial (see Chapter 17). As a result, some Day Custodial sweepers resented covering it during the day. To further add to the negative feelings, rather than having a sweeper regularly sweeping through, Custodial was contacted on what the Innoventions cast members, who were a specially picked and trained group, perceived as an as-needed basis. For example, a vibrating effect on a seat in a General Motors exhibit often caused guests to, how shall we put it, *leak* a bit. So the Code U call would go out.

Usually, when a sweeper was covering an area and sweeping through shops and attraction waiting areas, they were going to encounter and take care of most messes before anyone could call Custodial Central. But with Innoventions being closed off, the staff there became famous for calling Custodial for the smallest cleanups, and that meant more radio calls to the Tomorrowland Lead. Then, when the Lead or the sweeper sent by the Lead would be in there responding to the request, it seemed as though there was this *look* we'd get, as if the Innoventions cast member was trying to get us to be finished faster so we could disappear faster. Even bussers, who were protective of their territory when they were actually working their territory, would be more welcoming of the presence of sweepers.

Another element of the 1998 Tomorrowland renovation that had an impact on the Space area was Cosmic Waves. This was a fountain-play feature that was added to the middle of the area. The original idea, as far as we could tell, was for young-at-heart guests to try to *avoid* getting caught in the field of mini geysers by running to the ball in the center, itself spinning on water, before they could get soaked. And if they wanted to catch some of the water, well, that was their option. This sort of thing seemed to work better at Walt Disney World.

Many sweepers called Cosmic Waves "Cosmic Bidet", because of some of the things kids would be doing there, often at the direction of a parent. Some children would take their clothes off. The worst was seeing grown men take their shirts off and play in the fountain. We would have to ask them to put their clothes back on, per the dress code. Yes, some kids would use it as a restroom. Another problem was that people would get soaked, and then would walk through a store or sit down someplace, and then we'd need to dehydrate the floor or the seat.

The very heavy ball spinning on water is still there, but the fountains were removed to put in benches and make it a place to rest.

Cleaning the Kingdom

Sub/Mono

Yes, it sounds like a disease, but it is named for the Submarine Voyage and the Monorail. I (Ken) used to call it "Train to Triton" back when the area near the south of the Matterhorn was Triton Gardens, where Ariel the Little Mermaid would sit for pictures with guests.

This area had some overlap with the Matterhorn coverage for the Small World/Matterhorn area, as the sweeper would sweep as far as what is now the Pixie meet-and-greet area, then eastward past the Submarine Voyage and Autopia, back to the Disneyland Railroad station. The area would extend southerly as far as the Cosmic Waves feature.

This area, during the time I (Lynn) was working there, was mostly calm. The Subs closed a month after I started in Custodial, in September 1998. They remained closed until June 2007, near the time I when I quit. Then for a period of time Autopia was closed for its rebuilding and re-opening in 2000.

When the Autopia did reopen, it shared an element with Indiana Jones: wallet-sized cards distributed to guests. Under Chevron sponsorship, "driver's license" cards were handed out. A lot of these ended up on the ground, or in the flower beds. Since the new waiting area for the Autopia was over some flower beds, it was very easy for the cards to fall into them or be thrown. This meant that the opening Lead or the sweeper starting their shift before the park opened would have to quickly pluck the cards out of flower beds every morning.

A World - and a Jani - On the Move

The 1967 Tomorrowland was dubbed "A World on the Move" and it remained as such for a long time. The place had a kinetic look to it.

It was one of the areas with the highest number of attractions to which a Lead might get called to do a clean up,

191

Cleaning the Kingdom

frequently in a vehicle. Leads would often do such clean ups themselves, At other times, they'd send someone on their crew if it made sense to do so, such as if they happened to have someone sweeping Lines and they saw them at the right time.

While operating, the Submarine Voyage ride operators might call Custodial to come clean up something in a submarine. This could mean taking a ride around the attraction to get the cleaning done right, so it would be just the sweeper and the ride operator in the vessel.

Sweepers would also sweep out monorail trains while they were in the Tomorrowland station, and when I (Ken) hired in, in 1990, sweepers would still, from time to time, ride the Monorail to sweep up the platform at the Disneyland Hotel station.

Autopia cars would be pulled off the circuit if there was a mess inside that needed to be cleaned up.

Of course, Tomorrowland was also one of the areas where the Lead might get a call to catch one of the trains on the Disneyland Railroad for a clean-up, and sometimes that meant taking a ride.

The Skyway was closed in 1994, but when it was operating, it was easy for a bucket to be pulled offline there at the Tomorrowland station so that a sweeper could clean it.

Peoplemover shuttles would usually not be pulled. Instead, we'd get to take a ride. It sure was nice when Disney paid us to ride instead of the other way around! This attraction closed in 1995.

A cleanup at the Rocket Jets attraction meant a trip in one of the two guest elevators. Responding to a request at the success attraction, Astro-Orbitor, just wasn't the same, since that was placed at ground level.

Space Mountain rockets could be pulled to the side, which was convenient but that, of course, meant no "paid rides" for us.

There were only the four cabins for Star Tours, so we were always mindful that if one of them was being kept idle for

192

a cleanup, that meant the attraction was operating at 75% capacity at best, so that cabin needed to be returned to service ASAP. However, it wasn't like we were dragging our feet about cleaning ride vehicles on any other attraction. Our goal was to let the ride operators have their vehicle back, spotless, as soon as we could, because we cared about the guest experience.

Rocket Rods

As had been done with the Indiana Jones Adventure when it opened in 1995, Rocket Rods got a dedicated Custodial presence when it opened in 1998. That cast member had a radio on them so they could respond to calls for cleanups within the attraction queue and in the vehicles, and if there was something in another part of Tomorrowland that the Lead delegated due to priorities. They would dump the bullet cans and sweep the extensive, slow-moving line, which would stretch from the load/unload area on the former Peoplemover platform, back through a new tunnel under the main level of Tomorrowland, back into and through the old CircleVision building, which is now the Buzz Lightyear attraction.

One morning before the park opened, the Rods were cycling and one of the vehicles, while going over a high, exterior section of the track, threw a part down near the opening sweeping Lead. The attraction was plagued with problems, and without a sponsor, Disneyland management must have figured the costs of operating and maintaining the attraction weren't justified. It was there from the premiere of the 1998 Tomorrowland until September 2000. It was a short stay for the attraction. I (Lynn) will never get the noise it made out of my head.

It officially went on "hiatus", but we'll go out on a limb and predict that it isn't coming back.

Space Mountain

Like the Indiana Jones Adventure and Rocket Rods before, when Space Mountain re-opened in 2005 after the entire attraction (other than the exterior shell) had been rebuilt, a sweeper was assigned to be solely responsible for the attraction. This person would sweep the line, dump the trash (bullet) cans within the line, and respond to calls - that is, if they had a radio, which many times they didn't.

Lines

A sweeper assigned to Lines for their shift had no small task in Tomorrowland. Before Rocket Rods, there was CircleVision, which was one of the nicer tasks because of the climate control. It was entirely carpeted, which could pose a challenge, but both the waiting area and the theater itself were usually relatively clean. After Rocket Rods, Buzz Lightyear was added to the rotation. When the Peoplemover was open, it was also a generally easy pass since it was a very high-capacity attraction, so even when there was a line, it was fast-moving and short.

Before the renovation of Star Tours in in 2011, the flooring in the first part of the interior queue had these long rubbery grooves that stretched from one side to the other. Perhaps this material was chosen to prevent slips? We don't know. We just knew that it was not the friendliest material when trying to keep a waiting area in a theme park clean. Stuff would get trapped in the grooves, so rather than being able to pass over this portion of the line in a couple of minutes, if a sweeper was going to clean it thoroughly, he or she would have to sweep out the grooves a few at a time. This became tiring after five minutes or so.

One night after the park closed, I (Lynn) was in there to close out, sweeping away at a huge popcorn spill that spread for at least 30 feet. My arm was getting tired, and I was getting frustrated. All of a sudden, as I was almost finished, a Night Custodial cast member came along and vacuumed it up within seconds! I should have just waited to have him do it, but had no idea the night crew did that. Sweepers are supposed to sweep up as much as possible in preparation for the night crew and not simply leave stuff for them. They were going to have enough to do without having to get stuff Day Custodial normally got.

The waiting area for the Magic Eye Theater, ideally, was swept by the Lines person as well as the Space person.

Before Space Mountain had its own sweeper, it was part of the lines rotation. We would use our knowledge of how to get around to start at the loading area, where we could cross over to the unload to check that before crossing back to the load side. As with other areas, this involved knowing when to cross and when not to cross, and having visual and auditory confirmation with the ride operators. The last thing we wanted to do, aside from injuring ourselves, was cause a downtime on the attraction. Crossing active attraction tracks was something we did all of the time in those days.

Mission to Mars - where Pizza Port currently resides - was open during busier times when I (Ken) hired in. It was another easy, climate-controlled place for the lines person to check. It stopped its run in November 1992.

Sweeping the exterior of Innoventions was something added to the lines list when that opened in 1998.

The Skyway line, which went away in 1994, was the only one in Tomorrowland to have stairs until Rocket Rods opening in 1998. Space Mountain used "speed ramps" (rubber escalators that are "flat" instead of like stairs) and, later, a static ramp. Monorail and Peoplemover used speed ramps. When the Autopia was overhauled in 2000 and became a multi-level waiting area, it did get some steps.

Next to the Skyway was the station for the Disneyland Railroad.

The nature of the Autopia wait changed drastically with the 2000 renovation. Before the renovation, it was a simple area of metal-railed narrow switchbacks. After the renovation, there were entrance and exit ramps, switchbacks, staircases and multiple load/unload strips, and a small elevator.

The Monorail station was simple enough. We were free to emerge from the guest waiting area onto the loading area of the platform even if there was no train in the station, meaning it was possible for us to jump onto the beam or fall between the beam and the platform, but *somehow* we managed to avoid falling, I wrote sarcastically.

The Submarine Voyage usually had a long wait, and it was packed with those metal-railed narrow switchbacks.

Dumping Trash

There were a lot of very busy bullet cans in Tomorrowland. When dumping bullets, it was easy for the Trash Dumper to empty their cart at the packer in the backstage area between Star Tours and Plaza Inn.

Tomorrowland used to have the only place in the park for a Trash Dumper to unload bullet bags into a packer from the second level. There was a chute located in a room upstairs over what is now the patio seating for Pizza Port. At one time, this was seating area for the Space Place restaurant. It was helpful to have this place to unload the bullet bags from Space Mountain, and, when it was there, Toy Story Funhouse.

Aside from these two places, there was the main Tomorrowland packer behind Innoventions and the Main Street packer came in handy for Tomorrowland at times.

Scheduling Priorities in a Changing Land

Tomorrowland had its very slow times. At one point, the Submarine Voyage was closed, Rocket Rods was closed, and Autopia was down for a lengthy refurbishment. There was only Star Tours, Astro-Orbitor, Space Mountain, Honey I Shrunk The

Kids, and Innoventions. The Monorail was down for a bit too, due to the construction of DCA and the Grand Californian.

On a weekday in the off season, which used to be from January to Spring Break, there would be maybe a couple hundred guests in the area at any given moment, which was nothing. Custodial management adjusted by cutting the hours assigned to the area.

One the responsibilities of a Lead, not just for Tomorrowland but any area, was making judgement calls as far as how the crew was assigned. This was based on how busy and messy the crowd was, and who was on the crew and what their hours were. Every sweeper had their own strengths and their own preferences. There were days we knew we were going to be stretched thin ahead of time and days on which our crew was thin due to people calling in sick. There were also days we had an abundance of people on the schedule, but sometimes that was a mixed blessing because of the rare bad apple who was trouble and seemed to generate more work for us than they handled.

Tomorrowland might end up with only having three people covering the area and a trash dumper. The Lead, ideally, would cover breaks and lunches, but a call could take us out of the area for ten to fifteen minutes.

Sometimes if I (Lynn) had extra cast members, I would put someone on Roam. That meant to just roam the whole area, sweeping. This was nice because it helped out, not only the sweepers within each area, but the Lead. Tomorrowland would usually need two trash dumpers on busy days. It was always good to have both a Breaker and a Lines person, but it wasn't always possible, and we would often have the Breaker sweep out lines when they weren't covering a break. If we scheduled breaks just so, we could create longer blocks of time for the Breakers to sweep out lines.

Cleaning the Kingdom

Speaking of Breaks

Tomorrowland had many, many places over the years suitable to be unofficial break areas. Leads and other assignments that had keys (such as Restrooms) had more access than other roles, but before high turnover, terrorism concerns, and increased safety regulations, it was easy to find a place to hide or to relax that didn't have a bunch of people wanting to start conversations, or at least no televisions or vending machines.

Sometimes when I (Ken) would be called to a maintenance area, such as where the Space Mountain rockets were stored and serviced, to clean up something, I might take my break after I was done right then and there. After the 2000 overhaul of the Autopia, there was a small room for resting that was added by where we'd clean a car.

The ideal places were those that didn't take us too far out of our area, if at all, and allowed us to read, study, or chat with a friend without being interrupted. Also, they were usually climate-controlled.

Before it was transformed into Innoventions for the 1998 Tomorrowland, the former home of the Carousel of Progress had last featured the show America Sings in 1988. That was a long time for it to sit "empty". It wasn't really empty, though. There were six audience areas, and they were sometimes treated like classrooms for training or presentations, There had been offices on the upper level already, in the space not taken up by the Peoplemover maintenance area or Speedtunnel, since the America Sings attraction didn't use the remainder of the upper level. When the audience seating areas were not being used, it was a good place to relax. After the building was gutted and turned into Innoventions, there was still a staircase that came up from the underground area (utilidor) up to ground level, and kept going up to the upper level, where the Rocket Rod maintenance bay was. This was a great place, especially after the Rocket Rods went on hiatus -

both the stairway and the maintenance bay.

After Mission to Mars ceased opening sporadically, the attraction rooms had so many empty seats just begging for a weary cast member.

The Space Mountain complex, meaning the attraction itself, the Starcade, and Space Place were excellent places to find a quiet corner, especially in the upper levels. There were emergency exit staircases that went completely unused, and there was at least one space that was difficult to reach, but when found, revealed a makeshift mattress that was probably used for napping.

There was a Night Custodial closet in Star Tours which was great for a break since it was easy to go from that location to respond to calls in the area or to head backstage.

After the Rocket Rods "went on hiatus" and before construction began on the Buzz Lightyear attraction, that building provided a cool, dark, quiet, comfortable place to kick back. The tunnel that was built especially for the Rocket Rods queue, leading from the former CircleVision room to the load/unload area, was still there. Before Rocket Rods, a closed CircleVision couldn't be beat as far as comfort.

Honey, I Swept the Theater

Something unique to Tomorrowland was doing a sweep of the Magic Eye Theater. At the time I (Lynn) worked there, it was Honey I Shrunk The Audience show. So, we would call it a Honey Sweep or HISTA Sweep. Before that, it was an Eo Sweep. This was a sweep of the theater which happened at least once in the middle of the day on a longer day of operation, then again in late afternoon or early evening, then at closing time. I would put a note on the assignment sheet specifying who would have to report for the sweep. This would usually involve at least the Breaker and the Lines person, maybe one of the people on Trash and the Space person. We would report to the attraction at a time set up earlier with the Honey cast members.

Cleaning the Kingdom

We'd enter the back of the theater as inconspicuously as we could. Once the show ended, we would go in and go up and down each aisle sweeping trash, and picking up bottles left behind by guests. Sometimes we would find sunglasses, cell phones, small children, etc. We would then turn those into the attractions cast members. Well, not the kids. We'd keep those and make them our apprentices. Once we were done, which would take anywhere from five to ten minutes depending on how much of the crew could be there and how messy the guests were being that day, we would exit the theater and go back to our assignments.

At one time, there was competition and bragging on who could do the Honey Sweep faster. One Lead, Vince, got together almost every sweeper on the Eastside of the park to do the Honey Sweep and it took them about two minutes. He bragged about that for years, and still does to this day.

Toy Story Funhouse

For the earlier part of 1996, as Disney was riding high on the success of Toy Story, the Toy Story Funhouse was cobbled together from what had been previously offered at El Capitan. It was completely out of place for Tomorrowland, save the character Buzz Lightyear, and it was not the quality of a permanent attraction ("Toy Story Outhouse"), but it could still be fun for the guests. There was a stage for a live show in front of the shuttered Mission to Mars entrance, and then the rest of the Funhouse was in what is now the patio seating for Pizza Port and the entrance area to Space Mountain, including up on the second level.

Custodial assigned a couple of sweepers to sweep up in the attraction and dump the trash cans, and I (Ken) worked some of those shifts. We were given radios, and it turned out to be an omen of what was to come that Summer season, when I became a Foreman.

Cleaning the Kingdom

Radio Disney

There used to be a small refreshment stand called the Lunching Pad. It was under the Peoplemover loading/unloading area, which was under the Rocket Jets, and it faced eastward towards what was then American Sings (or, after it closed, America Sang or the Carousel Theater). So when I (Ken) was hanging around as a teenaged Annual Passholder and perhaps for a bit after I hired in, Tomorrowland had the Tomorrowland Terrace, the Lunching Pad, and Space Place for guests to get food and refreshments, and all were covered by Custodial Bussing.

In the Tomorrowland 1998 renovation, what had been the Lunching Pad was closed off and became a broadcast facility for Radio Disney. I thought it was great to have people broadcasting from Disneyland on a permanent basis and then people listening across the country could drop by and see the place on their next visit.

Mark and Zippy were the two disc jockeys I remember working in there. I would see them at the Inn Between and they didn't seem to mind associating with Custodial. In fact, they had a recurring bit on their broadcast in which they pulled in someone to talk about what they'd found in the trash. If I recall correctly, it was a busser from Tomorrowland Terrace, and by then they were no longer part of the actual Custodial Department, but you get the idea. They didn't have this attitude of being big-time broadcasters who were too good for the people cleaning theme parks.

When the plug was pulled on the show and the facility, Mark and Zippy gave props from the show (yes, even though it was a radio show they kept props) to some sweepers, who stashed the props in the locker. After a little time passed, there was one sweeper who knew a guest was visiting from out of state and had been a huge fan of Mark and Zippy, and slipped that guest one of the props to take home.

Cleaning the Kingdom

With Radio Disney gone, it was just more space to take a break, until that place was turned into a shop.

In the Future, Nobody Can Hear You Eat

The only full cast member restaurant around Tomorrowland was the Inn Between, which was the backstage portion of the Plaza Inn. Sometimes we'd eat there, sometimes we'd take our food to the Main Street locker or the Tomorrowland locker, when it was on that side.

There was an official break area by the parade step-off on Main Street (behind the Magic Shop), another under Tomorrowland Terrace adjacent to the prototype utilidor, another in the back of the CircleVision/Rocket Rods building (facing the Matterhorn), and there had been one in Mission to Mars accessible after the attraction closed, but when a photo processing operation moved into the building, the smell could be awful. The loss of that breakroom was mitigated by the addition of one behind Innoventions in a mobile building.

When Space Place which is now the Space Mountain entrance and Pizza Port seating, had been open to guests there was a backstage window for cast members to get the food at lower prices than guests.

Fantasyland

Fantasyland, from what we understand, was one of Walt's favorite places.

Back before I (Ken) hired in, there were slower times in which this area was almost the same as the themed area of Fantasyland. However, it was permanently divided and so "Fantasyland", in Sweeperese, became the area stretching from the wooden bridge on the Big Thunder Trail through the area with King Arthur's Carousel and Sleeping Beauty Castle, over to the western edge the parade route, meaning that the Storybookland Canal Boats, Mad Tea Party, and Alice in

202

Wonderland attractions formed the eastern edge of the area. "Small World/Matterhorn" is the other general area we will talk about later in this chapter.

It's a beautiful place. There was one quiet night I (Ken) was standing behind (north of) the Castle, and it was a clear night. The full moon was directly overhead, and as I gazed straight up, my sight of the moon was framed by the tops of the Fantasyland buildings and a giant moon ring. Fantasyland was full of charm. It was also full of little kids and strollers.

One of the good things about the area was that it wasn't hard to direct guests to nearby restrooms. There were some at the Big Thunder Ranch (if it was open), by Village Haus, at Carnation Plaza Gardens, and adjacent to the Alice in Wonderland attraction.

One of the *bad* things about Fantasyland is that it was an awful place to be a Sweeper on days with intermittent showers. Dumbo and the Mad Tea Party were both open-air attractions and Alice in Wonderland had a portion of the track that was outside and uncovered. Rain would close the Tea Cups and Alice, but if the showers let up, then we were summoned to dry out each tea cup and dry off the Alice track. We'd get called back if it rained and stopped again. There were times we were on the Alice track over and over again, and times we'd just finish drying off the cups and track when it would start raining again. And you know what? We never once fell off the track at Alice, even though the safety measures that were added in recent years were not there.

There were some advantages to sweepers in this area. The Area Locker is on the west side of the Village Haus restaurant and adjacent restrooms, behind those large wooden gates. The area packer was right there, too. This placed the area locker close to a backstage window for Village Haus restaurant. As had been done with Space Place, this window was for cast members to order the same food served to guests for a lower cost. When we worked there, it was burgers, personal-sized pizzas, chicken nuggets, fries, and salads. There were tables and umbrellas in an area that appeared to be carved out of the side of Big Thunder Mountain. Custodial Central used to be located just a short southerly walk from there, but was later moved under Security in the old Administration Building when Casa Mexicana was renovated into Rancho Del Zocalo.

Under the Village Haus side of Fantasyland was a very large basement. Down there were offices, kitchen prep areas, control rooms for the attractions, a cast member restroom, and a break room. The break room was unique. In addition to the standard television, tables, chairs, and vending machines there were video games and a ping pong table (look it up, kids). Some sweepers and other cast members would bring their own paddles and have competitions - during breaks, of course. Going underground might mean loss of radio contact, so it could be problematic for a Lead. When a Lead didn't respond to calls, people might assume they were simply absent-minded or had turned down their radio so as to talk with someone without being distracted and had forgotten to turn it up. Sometimes, they were on the wrong channel.

We never really had good places in Fantasyland other than the official break areas to take a break. The one place that was good was the Big Thunder Ranch when it was closed and at night, such as the stock closet for the restroom. With it closed, it was unlikely even someone assigned to restrooms would be by.

A unique thing about working in Fantasyland at night was seeing Tinkerbell land at the tower, right by our area locker. It was always exciting to see this no matter how long we worked there. During my (Lynn's) training, our trainers took us to watch it. More recently, the fireworks shows have changed and Tinkerbell no longer makes a direct flight and landing there, and a good portion of Fantasyland gets closed down for the show.

Cleaning ride vehicles in Fantasyland usually meant taking a ride, and since most of the rides were not very long, it meant working quickly.

Cleaning the Kingdom

Fantasyland was divided into two basic sweeping areas, although on especially busy days with a large staff, a third, overlapping coverage area could be added.

North/Ranch

This area was from the wooden bridge on the Big Thunder Trail to around Dumbo. The Ranch portion could be pretty slow on most days because it was mostly a walkway people were using between Fantasyland and Frontierland, but we did have the dusty petting zoo area and the Big Thunder Ranch Barbecue. As always, the restaurant itself was not our domain. It was great to see horses and goat and other live animals in a setting that was mostly peaceful, except for the Disneyland Railroad trains coming through.

The Ranch itself was altered in 1996 with the installation of the Festival Arena, the performance venue for the Festival of Fools from "The Hunchback of Notre Dame". Shows ran in there until April of 1998 and cleanups were handled by the Events crew (See Chapter 9).

The North portion ran past the Skyway (when it was still open), Village Haus Restaurant, Casey Jr. Circus Train, and Dumbo's Flying Elephants. It was a great place to interact with guests because you were never far from refreshments or a restroom, which is what many guests wanted to find when approaching us, and nothing in the park was too far away.

It was a little sad, after the Skyway closed, to have the Fantasyland station just sitting there, unused, on a hill. With some work, it could be a nice place for a Dream Suite. On the plus side, sweepers no longer had to climb those stairs to sweep the line and station.

South/Middle

This area picked up, so to speak, at Dumbo attraction and went around the Mad Tea Party and by Storybookland

Cleaning the Kingdom

Canal Boats and Alice in Wonderland, and also around the King
Arthur Carousel and through Sleeping Beauty Castle to the
courtyard and Snow White Grotto.

This area was loaded with attractions, including
Dumbo, Storybookland, Mad Tea Party, Alice in Wonderland,
Mr. Toad's Wild Ride, the Carousel, Peter Pan, the Castle, Snow
White's Scary Adventures, and Pinocchio's Daring Journey.
There was no guest restroom in this area, but the guests could
be directed to the one adjacent to Village Haus, near Alice, or at
Carnation Plaza Gardens/Rancho Del Zocalo.

With the transformation of that Plaza Gardens area into
Fantasy Faire, we understand that Fantasyland will have a
sweeper dedicated to that area during the day, when it is full of
activity and guests, and that the South/Middle person will cover
it at night.

Lines

Doing lines in this area was a challenge due to the fact
that many of these queues were so narrow and slow-moving.
For most attractions, the sweeper had no choice but to stand
with the guests in line rather than "backsweeping" or going
against the flow. Because there were so many lines, if staffing
permitted, a second lines person could be assigned. When the
Castle walk-through was open, that would mean regularly
climbing stairs to sweep inside, and the Skyway, when that was
open, was another place where stair-climbing was another
regular part of the cycle.

Dumping Trash

Dumping trash in this area was done mostly by one
person, but at times two may help. Due to the crowds, it could
be difficult to use large carts in the area and find a place to park
them. There were also bullets at most attractions, and getting to

some of them would mean coordinating with the ride operators as it would mean maneuvering around ride vehicles.

Having the area packer behind Village Haus meant it wasn't far away. However, since it was also getting trash from the Village Haus restaurant and the restrooms, it was possible for it to fill up. If that happened, there was another packer down by Rancho Del Zocalo, but a truck could be brought into dump the Fantasyland packer. It involved opening the large gates to temporarily close the Trail twice: once to get the truck in, then once to get it out, and then repeating that to get the packer back.

Closing Out Fantasyland

Every area has some music somewhere, some of the time, but the music in Fantasyland was loud and constant, coming from several different attractions, and there was the music loop from the Carousel, Casey Jr., and calliope by Dumbo.

It didn't matter how empty Fantasyland was. If that music was playing, it seemed full enough.

Once the park was closed and the attractions were cleared, there were times we'd explore them. There wasn't much to the center of the Carousel, but it was fun to walk through the dark rides. We (the authors) always had respect for the show and so we never wanted to do anything that would damage any of the elements in the attractions. That is why when we found white trash bags just sitting on the floor of one of them, we left them there! (Think of a wonderful thought.)

Small World/Matterhorn and Toontown

The remaining area on the Eastside of Disneyland was an area we called, in Custodial, Small World/Matterhorn. We called it that because that's where the Fantasyland Theatre was. (Just wanted to see if you were paying attention.)

This area was the other area, in addition to Main Street, that was the stage for parades and similar shows, and so the operation of the area would be very different on days and nights with those shows than days without them. It stretched all the way from the Hub, completely around the Matterhorn, northward past Alice in Wonderland, Mad Tea Party, Storybookland Canal Boats, up to It's a Small World, and up to Fantasyland Theater. Mickey's Toontown was a somewhat autonomous extension of this area, meaning the Toontown crew was listed on the Small World/Matterhorn assignment sheets, but separately from the rest of the crew, and Toontown had its own Leads. Before we hired in, before Toontown was "opened to non-toons", this area would sometimes be part of the Fantasyland coverage area on slower days, especially before the amphitheatre was built in the mid-1980s, just like New Orleans/Bear Country would be bundled together with Adventure/Frontier.

The Area Locker was literally right behind the Casey Jr. attraction, right next to where the trains get parked for that attraction. The access from the area is the large gate to the left when facing the Small World attraction, and to the left when facing the Fantasyland Theater standing next to Small World shop. Immediately behind the gate, on the left, was a breakroom attached to boat storage ("Neverland") for the Storybookland Canal Boats. Past that on the left was the area packer, and then the area locker. On the right were cast member restrooms and then stock closets/back access to the guest restrooms that were up by the Fantasyland Theater.

This area saw a lot of change during my (Ken's) time. It was where I spent my first day out of training, on Vern Hoiland's crew. It was also Lynn's first assignment, as he mentions below. In addition to the opening of Toontown and the various live productions at the Theatre and related elements that spilled out in front of the Theatre, there was the temporary installation of Afternoon Avenue in 1991 and the overhaul of the parade route for 1997's Light Magic. Light Magic was probably intended to be a parade-like show that lasted for many years to come, but it went on hiatus... and we're going to go out on another limb and say it isn't coming back.

Afternoon Avenue was *not* intended to last, and that was very obvious. If the subsequently opened Mickey's Toontown could be likened to caviar (it's a stretch but stick with us), then Afternoon Avenue was a drive-thru fast food fish stick. It was installed to promote a syndicated Television Animation block of programming. It belonged in the same category as the Toy Story Funhouse, which was temporarily installed in Tomorrowland several years later. In addition to creating more work for sweepers by drawing more children to the area, Afternoon Avenue also had miniature building fronts, and those needed to be kept clean, and things like a giant hunk of plastic cheese with holes through which kids could actually climb. One sweeper who was sent to get in there and clean it out reported getting high off the fumes from the cleaner he was using in the confined spaces.

Small World/Matterhorn usually had a heavy presence for Outdoor Vending, with popcorn wagons, drink carts, ice cream carts, etc., and that always meant work for sweepers, since popcorn was topped off and bound to fall, carts leaked, drinks spilled, churro bits fell, and ice cream dripped.

Much of the area would become the performance corridor and viewing area for the parades, on days those ran. Some of area crew would be given pre-parade assignments and then take part in the post-parade clean-up (see Chapter 9.) The parade crew, and those pulled from the area, would work together to leave the area as clean as it was before people started crowding to wait for the parade, if not more clean.

A unique thing about this area included being called to clean up a Small World boat, and getting to ride through the attraction while doing that. It recently occurred to us while we recorded an edition of The Sweep Spot podcast that although Day Custodial Sweeping would clean Pirate boats and Splash logs at the end of the operating day, if the park closed before midnight, we didn't clean Small World boats. We're not sure

Cleaning the Kingdom

why. Maybe it was because, unlike the other two attractions, there wasn't likely to be much water in these boats?

We did not get to ride through the Matterhorn if a bobsled needed cleaning. Rather, the bobsled could easily be pulled to a side track and we would, with the cooperation of the ride operators, cross the track to get to them and have all of the time we needed to clean them.

On busier days, Small World/Matterhorn could be split into four sweeping areas.

Meadow or Video

The places that was quickly built in 1985 on the vacant land west of It's a Small World was originally called Small World Meadows Amphitheatre. There's some trivia for ya. Nobody called it that. Everyone called it Videopolis, which was really the nighttime music and guest-dancing thing that took place there. So, some people called the sweeping area Meadow and some Video, but it was the same thing.

It started at the Toontown entrance, went to the Toontown Depot for the Disneyland Railroad, covered the area in front of the Theatre over to the restrooms, and extended to the edge of the parade route. It was a fairly simple area, albeit an area where we'd constantly be sweeping uphill and downhill, and there were often many fallen leaves to sweep up. It happened to be my (Lynn's) first sweeping area.

There was often a popcorn wagon (boo!) operating near the gate that heads back to our Area Locker, and coverage of this would overlap with the Small World coverage area.

On slower days, Meadow was absorbed into the Small World coverage area.

Small World

This area extended from the parade step-off and the It's a Small World attraction down the parade route to where there's a popcorn wagon (boo!) across from Storybookland

Canal Boats.

Matterhorn

On busier days, this was the area covering the space north of the Matterhorn from the parade route to, about the Submarine Voyage Lagoon, where there are several walkways formed by flower beds and benches.

Extension or Backside

Combined with the Matterhorn coverage area on slower days, this basically covered the parade route from the Hub to where the Small World area coverage ended, around the "backside" of the Matterhorn, to where the Matterhorn coverage area ends by the Submarine Lagoon.

Portions of this area were quite a ways from the area locker, so usually there would be a mop and bucket stashed in a maintenance bay behind the Alice in Wonderland attraction, behind a door that is next to the guest restrooms.

Dumping Trash

There wasn't much unique to dumping trash in Small World/Matterhorn. There were bullet cans that would be across the track at the Matterhorn Bobsleds for ride operators to put trash they'd pulled out of bobsleds. Crossing the track had to be done in communication with the ride operators so as to not get injured or disrupt their operations.

As with Main Street, working around a parade schedule was crucial.

Lines

With the closure of the Fantasyland Autopia and the Motor Boat Cruise in the early 1990s, there were only three

Cleaning the Kingdom

ride-through attractions in Small World/Matterhorn: It's a Small World, the Matterhorn, and the Disneyland Railroad. The Matterhorn had two sides and usually had two lines, although sometimes, like during a parade, one line will feed both tracks. Sometimes a line would form for whichever show was at the Theatre. The lines person for Small World/Matterhorn would also sweep lines in Toontown, including for Roger Rabbit's Car Toon Spin and Gadget's Go-Coaster.

Most of the line for the Matterhorn was easy enough for the area sweeper to edge out, because it consisted of a single-file line against the base of the mountain with a single chain keeping the line in place. However, the last portion of the line, under the roof, could be difficult because it was narrow and had to be swept going with the flow of the guests rather than backsweeping, and because the ground was covered with a black sandpaper-like material that doesn't work well with a broom. So, whenever the attraction would stop operating and the line would be cleared out would be great for us.

Taking Breaks

In addition to the official break room attached to the Storybookland Canal Boat storage, there was the break room in Tomorrowland that was at the back of the CircleVision/Rocket Rods building. We might want to hurry over to Village Haus or Inn Between for lunch. There were times there would be a roach coach food truck behind the Theatre, and that was popular with sweepers.

One great place to take a break was the backside of the Alice/Toad/Pan building. A joint maintenance area for Toad and Pan could be accessed by doors on either side of the guest restrooms there. We had legitimate reason to be in there because there was a mop and bucket we kept there and a small (one person) cast member restroom. Inside there, when the park was open, we could constantly hear certain sounds from Peter Pan's Flight, Mr. Toad's Wild Ride, and Alice in

Cleaning the Kingdom

Wonderland. If we wanted fresh air, there was a secluded outdoor staircase that led up to the maintenance area for Alice.

Toontown

Finally, there was Toontown, which used be far enough from Custodial Central, but then was literally at the other side of the park from the office after the office was moved to the Old Administration building.

This Sweeping area was synonymous with the themed area of Mickey's Toontown, if you don't count the Train Depot as part of the themed area, since it is outside the Toontown gates. Opened in 1993, it was the first extension of the park's guest area in the park since the 1986 opening of the Big Thunder Ranch.

When it first opened to non-toons, it was packed!

The Area Locker was right behind Minnie's House, so we'd get there either by walking through the area and behind the large gates by Minnie's, or we'd use the back area tunnel between the Fantasyland Theatre and the Big Thunder Ranch. The area packer was near the area locker, and was also constantly used by Bussing, which kept the food locations clean. There was also an official break room back there, and a cast member restroom.

I (Lynn) worked as a Lead in Toontown for two summers in a row, and being up there that much, I discovered a few things by talking to ride operators. For example, Roger Rabbit's Car Toon Spin was, at one time, going to have a second level to it. You can still see the balcony where the cabs would have passed by outside. During the early days, there would be a band playing up there.

Except on the slowest days, there was a Toontown Lead and a couple of sweepers, so a crew of three for a shift. Also, the Small World/Matterhorn lines person would sweep lines in Toontown. Usually, one of the non-Lead crew members would dump the cans, which were all bagged the first few years. This was the only sweeping area in the entire park where all of the cans were bagged. The ideal was to have two people sweeping Toontown at any given time, especially when the popcorn wagon by Mickey's garage was open.

Sweeping Toontown could be challenging for a few reasons.

There were a lot of places for people to sit, and along with a popcorn wagon that would operate near the exit (garage) of Mickey's house, that means there was a lot to clean up.

It is a small area, and in the middle of the day, it could get very crowded. During summer months it is always warmer in Toontown than other areas, probably because of all of the concrete and the lack of trees. When Toontown opened in 1993, sweepers had to wear, over their Custodial Whites, a checkered cap, a checkered vest, and a bow tie, which made the heat so much worse for us. It was the only time, other than being in the Very Merry Christmas Parade, sweepers wore themed costumes, which bussers wore all of the time. Mercifully, the requirement we wear those extra costume pieces was eventually lifted. And yes, we do realize how fortunate sweepers are when it comes to costuming in general.

There were two decorative fountains in the area, one on each end, and those fountains could cause issues. I (Lynn) remember being up there when one overflowed. Water was spilling out into the area. Finally, someone from Facilities came to shut it off.

Another problem with Toontown was the noise. The music was annoying after a while, and noises came from several of the interactive attractions and elements. There was the exploding sound coming from the Fireworks Factory, the manholes and metal pavers around the fountains that make noise when you step on them, and Donald's Boat. There was a mute button that I (Lynn) found for Donald's Boat, which I may or may not have used several times.

The area also had characters and attractions for smaller

children, which meant more kids, which meant more of a mess and more difficulty maneuvering around the crowds. More kids also meant finding diapers on benches, in flower beds and on the ground. What parent would do that when there were trash cans everywhere?

There were many attractions in Toontown, but many were walk-through type. There was Roger Rabbit's Car Toon Spin, which had a very detailed queue, with some interactive features. This attraction had a FastPass, which always meant little paper cards to sweep up, and was popular on busy days. There was Goofy's Playhouse. This used to be called Goofy's Bounce House and was a popular place for kids to collide and get bloody noses. Then there was Donald's Boat which was a play area and used to have slides. Gadget's Go Coaster was in the back corner, and although it is a small, very short roller coaster, it could get huge lines.

Chip 'n Dale's Treehouse was another play area that used to have a slide, and next to it was the "acorn crawl". This was like those play areas you'd see in a fast food restaurant with plastic balls where kids would sink into and hide under. That area is still there to this day, but you can't enter it anymore. It was a mess if a child had an unfortunate accident then the attraction would have to be closed down while sweepers emptied all of the "acorns" cleaned the rubbery surface of the pit, and then brought in a batch of clean acorns.

Mickey's House and Minnie's House needed to be swept through, but that could be fun and, especially with Mickey's, it was a nice way to get out of the sun.

Another place to take refuge from the sun was the shop, which needed to be swept through anyway.

As we detail elsewhere, there's a Night Custodial closet inside the "island" of building in the downtown section, at the Post Office, and that could be a great place to duck away from the crowds for a break, but another place was some stairs at the back of Mickey's movie barn. These stairs lead up to the roof of the building. Toontown would close down for Fantasy in the Sky fireworks due to fallout, and subsequent fireworks shows have meant the same thing. Management warned sweepers to take shelter and stop watching the fireworks from Donald's Boat, but an even riskier place was on that roof over Mickey's!

Chapter 9

Landless

Is there more to Custodial than sweeping or dumping trash in a land?

Introduction

Part of being a Custodian at Disneyland could be working outside of a land. Sometimes it meant working in and around the Mickey & Friends parking structure, Esplanade (between the theme parks), parades or shows, or working on projects, scheduling, training, or a as a Dispatch clerk in Custodial Central.

For some, these were preferable assignments. Maybe they enjoyed being away from the constant crowding of guests, or liked working in larger open areas, or just a change of pace or scenery.

These assignments were not your authors' favorites. We preferred to each be Lead over an area inside Disneyland, especially areas neighboring each other because we could wreak more havoc that way. Or maybe it was because we liked the ambience and being in the thick of the show, with plenty of guest interaction.

Most of the assignments in this chapter involved working in pairs or groups, rather than being solitarily responsible for a portion of an area, as sweepers are when they're assigned to cover the Hub or to a Restroom split.

These assignments were also important to keeping the Resort clean, safe, and pleasant.

Parking Structure

If you've driven to the Resort, this might have been your first experience and impression.

The Mickey & Friends parking structure was built with the Disneyland Resort expansion that added California Adventure, the Grand Californian, and Downtown Disney. The structure was one of the first things built because Disneyland would lose most of its big parking area in front of the park to make way for California Adventure. The parking structure was opened in 2000. There were over 10,000 parking spaces total on seven levels. At the time of its opening, it was the biggest parking structure in the world.

While the old parking lot had trams, it was much easier to walk to the Disneyland entrance from the old parking lot than it became to walk from the parking structure to the entrances of the parks, since it was about 3/4ths of a mile away. So, the trams became much more important.

I (Lynn) remember before the structure opened, having

the chance to take a tour of it, because Custodial was going to be working there soon.

There were some similarities with working inside the park, but there were many different tasks.

There were guest restrooms at the bottom level near the tram pickup and drop off. These restrooms were busy in the morning and could be busy at night, but during the day, after the main rush, they stayed pretty quiet. There were also cast member restrooms inside of a small building near the parking toll booths, with a break room inside, too. Then, on the other side of the structure, there was a bigger breakroom with restrooms and offices. It was near there that we had our Area Locker, where we had the majority of supplies for the structure.

We did have a cart to drive around the structure, which was something that was definitely needed for covering such a large building. At first, we had a small electric vehicle, kind of like a golf cart, but we found it barely made it up the ramps, so we switched to a gas-powered vehicle.

Every morning, we would meet with the Night Custodial cast members to take the vehicle from them for our use that day. We would check the flower beds around the tram loading area, and throughout the day we would sweep that area for debris and spills. The guest restrooms in the tram area were checked and cleaned every hour like the restrooms in the parks. Every so often, the walkways on each level were to be checked for debris, not in the actual parking areas, but the walkways leading to the huge escalators and elevators.

Dumping the trash was a big task. We can't remember how many trash cans there were, but it was more than 40. All of them were bagged. These were to be dumped at least twice a day; sometimes they needed it more. We would drive to each trash can and throw the trash bags in the back of the vehicle. Usually, the vehicle would quickly fill up with trash bags and we'd have to dump it before continuing. To dump the trash from the vehicle, we would drive along the tram route to a backstage gate. Then once inside, we were behind Frontierland and would dump the trash in the DOB.

Another task was cleaning up the trash along the tram route. So, a few times each day, we would drive along the tram route and remove any debris along the route or in the flower beds nearby.

Sometimes, we would get a call to clean up oil spills or glass in the parking areas. Custodial Central or the person calling us would give us the parking level and aisle number so we could quickly find it.

In the middle of the day, the structure would stay pretty quiet, but then at closing time, guests would come back to their cars in droves, leaving trash and spills along the way. Trash cans would fill up fast again, and the final trash dump for the night would start. Many of the guests would be tired from the day, and for many it would have been 16 to 18 hours since they parked their car and wouldn't remember where they parked. They would become easily frustrated and not even remember what level they parked on. The parking cast members kept a log as to what levels were being parked at what time. That narrowed it down to what level they were parked on, if the guests could remember what time they'd arrived.

When I (Lynn) was first assigned at the structure as a Lead, we would normally have a Lead, a female cast member, a male cast member, and another cast member to help out. We needed both genders on the crew for the sake of cleaning the restrooms. Near the end of my career there, management had eliminated the extra cast member leaving it to just three at one time. Then in the late afternoon, another crew would arrive to take over and they would work until after closing.

Esplanade

When the old parking lot was eliminated and new tram and shuttle areas added, the new area in between both parks, where admission passports are sold, became the Esplanade. The Esplanade was bordered on the west by the Downtown Disney area, which was covered by California Adventure sweepers, but the Esplanade coverage area did include the loading/unloading area for Mickey & Friends trams. Esplanade extended past the park entrances all the way eastward to Harbor Boulevard. It covered the loading space that accommodated taxis, buses, shuttles and trams. It was a huge area and was busy in the mornings and at closing.

The Area Locker was under the Monorail track as it passed by the shuttle zone, headed in the direction of Harbor Boulevard on the way back to Tomorrowland. The locker was hidden behind tall, fully grown hedges. It was kind of a neat trick to disappear into the hedges or appear into the area from being out of view.

Everyone on the crew had a radio, because the coverage was over such a wide space and there were many visual barriers.

There was the Lead, East Esplanade sweeper, West Esplanade sweeper, and a Trash Dumper. Esplanade had many trash cans, all bagged, and they could fill up quickly depending on the conditions of the day. When the trash dumper needed to empty a cart, they could do so either at a packer in the Hollywood back area at California Adventure or at a packer in a special fenced-in pocket of the Disneyland backstage area, near the Indiana Jones show building, accessible from the northern part of the Mickey & Friends Tram loading area.

There were two sets of restrooms, one set to the left of the California Adventure entrance and one to the left of the Disneyland park entrance, and they were covered by Restroom cast members, but when we swept at the Esplanade, as with any other area, we'd sweep through the restroom.

A supply closet used by Night Custodial near the Disneyland-side restrooms was handy for grabbing a mop or anything else we needed to respond to something near there. It was also a good place to take a break if you wanted to sit alone and read.

Cleaning the Kingdom

There was the Dog Kennel to the right of the Disneyland entrance, and we would dump their trash at the end of each night.

Once the terrorist attacks on September 11, 2001 happened, bag-check tents were added to the Esplanade, one set on the western side and one set on the eastern side. The tents were there to have cast members search backpacks, purses, fanny packs, etc. I (Lynn) am glad they added them, because it is for the guests and cast member safety, but it was an obstacle when we were doing our work. Now it is something normal in our society, unfortunately.

When the Lion King parking lot was behind DCA where Carsland is now, I (Lynn) had a call for broken glass in a car in that parking lot. For calls out there, we had to get on a tram and ride out to the location. It was maybe a five-minute ride, but guests were trying to board the trams to get home. There were normally long lines at closing time. I had to jump in front of the guests and get on a tram. I had no idea how bad it was, so I brought just my pan and broom. Once I arrived, I realized someone had broken into their car and shattered the window in the process. There was glass all over the seats and floor. It was also a cold night, so with no side window it was going to be an ordeal for them.

I then had to go back to the Esplanade locker and get a vacuum. By this time it was getting late, maybe 1:00 a.m. Which was almost my walking (go home) time. Then a manager called me on the radio and said he would come out and help me. We had to vacuum the car out and get some cardboard and put over their window. The guests were very thankful and it is just part of our job, which sometimes requires us to stay overtime to make it right for the guests, and that is what makes Disneyland cast members extra special.

Some sweepers enjoyed the area because of the open space. There were no attractions and no food or vending locations, just the Picnic Area that Bussing covered.

One longtime sweeper in particular had very good

reason for working Esplanade. Billy's wife of 35 years (and counting), Karyn, is a "ticket taker", one of the cast members working the entrance turnstiles. Working the same days and either the same hours or almost the same hours, these lovebirds continue to be able to come to work together, work all day near each other, and go home together. They're so cute and sweet it just might send your pancreas into shock.

Parades

Officially, there was an assignment called "Events", but it usually meant someone would say, "I'm on Parades."

Parades are a big part of the Disneyland experience. These parades attract thousands of people, and with people, comes trash. Perform it, and they will come. With trash. Sometimes, it was not just the guests who leave behind their trash; the parade itself might leave confetti, "snow", and even poop.

Part of the Disneyland Custodial method of keeping the parks clean is a well organized, precisely coordinated preparation and response to parades and cavalcades. "Cavalcade" was Disneyese that roughly translated into "a very tiny parade".

The Parade crew would work hard to make sure the parade route would look as good-or better-than it did before guests started crowding for the parade.

On a daily basis, it started with the Parade Lead, who'd make schedules for parade assignments based on his or her own crew, and also pulling from the area sweeping crews for post-parade cleanup, especially Main Street and Small World/Matterhorn. Main Street and Small World/Matterhorn sweepers were also likely to have pre-parade and during-parade assignments. When Bussing was part of the Custodial team, roughly half of the Parade crew was bussers and bussers would also be pulled from their restaurants just as sweepers were pulled from their areas to assist with post-parade

Cleaning the Kingdom

cleanups. After Bussing was ripped away from Custodial and given to Foods that continued ...for about five minutes. Then it became entirely up to Sweeping.

Pre-parade assignments would cover inside the parade route as well as areas behind the crowds. Someone doing "preliner" would be inside the parade route, passing along the waiting crowds, using a two-wheel (in earlier years) or four-wheel cart, which is essentially a hard rubber trash can on wheels. The purpose was to collect as much big stuff from the guests before the parade started so there would not as much after the parade. Since some of these guests had been sitting down waiting for the parade for hours, they may have eaten entire meals in that spot and they might not have wanted to move for worry of losing their view. Sweepers using their pans and brooms would also patrol the inside of the route and behind the crowds. If needed, a sweeper would bring a mop to clean up spills. As a Parade Lead, we'd walk the parade route and help out sweeping, and also checking to be sure all our cast members were out doing their jobs. We'd assist them as needed and we'd respond to calls.

During-parade assignments would include things like sweeping through shops or mopping the guest Locker building.

Post-parade assignments, which would be spelled out on the assignment sheet as determined by the Lead, would include pushbrooming, pan-&-brooming, linering, and, depending on the parade, mopping, vacuuming, and using leafblowers. Who was doing what could be flexible, and it was fair for Area Leads to substitute a different sweeper for the one requested when they sent someone to help with the parade assignments.

After the parade had started and any during-parade assignments had been completed, the parade crew and anyone lent to parade duty would gather backstage, usually at two key locations: where the parade had stepped-off, and the Fantasyland Area Locker (backstage by Village Haus restaurant).

Cleaning the Kingdom

Usually, the first parade performance would proceed from the gate to the right of It's a Small World and the second running of the same parade would proceed from the Town Square Gate by the Main Street Mad Hatter shop. If at Small World, the sweepers from the Small World area would join the Parade crew there, behind the gate where the parade would step off, and would be done with their part at the Hub, returning back to their area, replaced by sweepers pulled from Main Street. Likewise, when the parade stepped off from Town Square, the Main Street sweepers would join the Parade crew for post-parade clean up by meeting at the Main Street Area Locker before following the parade out the Town Square Gate, and then be finished at the Hub, replaced by Small World sweepers.

The teams who'd met at the Fantasyland Area Locker would emerge onstage near what used to be Carnation Plaza Gardens (now Fantasy Faire), and head to the Hub portion of the parade route.

Some of this would vary for special parades or extra busy days, as sometimes there would be more teams coming from more backstage access points.

As you might imagine, we became very familiar with the parades.

The goal would be to make the parade route and immediately surrounding area look as good as it did before people started crowding for the parade, and sometimes better. The guests would almost always move out of our way and some watched the cleanup like it was a ballet, and few would even express their surprise at just how effective it was.

If there was no confetti or snow, the post-parade clean up would have teams on both sides of the route that consisted of a pushbroomer, a liner or two, a pan & broomer or two, and maybe someone with a mop. Liners, in this case, were hand-held hard rubber trash receptacles. They were double or triple-bagged, usually with pro towels hanging down from the lip, held in place by the bags. These were handy when towels were needed for spills or to clean off a bench. A liner would usually go first, collecting all the bigger items on the ground, on or under benches, or in flower beds, like cups, food boxes, popcorn boxes, etc. This would help clear the way for the next person, the pushbroomer. This person would put the rest into piles for a pan & broom. Sometimes there would be several pan & brooms to make sure everything is collected.

If things were really bad, the pushbroomer would make piles and an additional liner would scoop up as much of the pile as possible by hand, and the pan & broomers would get the rest.

When there was confetti or snow, we used to have large gas-powered (noisy!) industrial vacuums and gas-powered, hand-held leaf blowers, which could be reversed for the day into hand-held vacuums, in order to get stuff out of flower beds. The leaf blowers and pushbroomers would get the confetti from the sides of the route or off the sidewalks of Main Street and the vacuums, sometimes a wall of them, would methodically go over the route until it was clean. Things could get a little smokey when a gas-powered vacuum full of confetti would pick up a still-smoldering cigarette! We did get electric models of these pieces of equipment, and they weren't nearly as noisy.

Sweepers would have to blast lingering confetti off of the upper levels and awnings of the Main Street buildings. In order to prevent us from tumbling off and maiming a guest, we'd wear a harness with a small cable. We'd test the cables for fraying just before using them by having one person hold the device, allowing the cable to pass between their finger and thumb as another cast member backed up or pulled out the cable quickly, fully extending the cable and then letting it quickly recoil. If the metal cable was frayed, we'd know!

In addition to making the assignment schedules, the Parade Lead was responsible for getting assignment sheets, with the relevant names highlighted, dropped off at the Area Lockers. There was often more than one Lead, working in staggered shifts. They were also responsible for getting equipment clean, working, and prepared for the day. The equipment was stored in a locked, roofed Parade Cage, which was a few yards west of the Small World Area Locker, placing it close to the Fantasyland Theatre. The cage had everything needed: vacuums, blowers, liners, pushbrooms, fuel, mops, etc. The cage also accumulated some items Disneyana collectors might drool over, such as signs. Prepared liners and pushbrooms (and if needed, vacuums) would be taken by the crew to various places around the park, such as the parade step-off locations and the Fantasyland Area Locker, to await use later in the day.

There were times when the parade crew would be well-staffed and have gaps in being needed for parades and shows, and so we'd get temporarily distributed to areas to sweep lines, or would clean back areas, and we'd even go through cast member costume locker rooms to clean up. I think we stopped cleaning locker rooms when outside contractors started to come in.

Special Cavalcades, Parades, and Events

There were special parades over the years that could be shorter but much more of a cleanup, usually due to the abundant confetti. One of these I (Lynn) experienced was the Angels World Series victory celebration in 2002. The Company owned the MLB team then and made the most of it. The baseball players were on floats waving to the guests along the parade route, with confetti just pouring out all over Main Street. It covered the ground, and I thought it would never end. It seemed like weeks later we would still find confetti in flower beds, sometimes as far as Critter Country.

The Parade Crew was used not only for parades, but pretty much any special event that required cleanups. In 2004 was one of those times, they set up a swimming pool on Main Street. Yes, a swimming pool measuring 50 meters long, and 3.5 feet deep was set up on Main Street just for a special event. Olympic Gold Medalist Michael Phelps and other swimmers

Cleaning the Kingdom

from the U.S. Olympic team were there to show their skills. Many guests stood alongside the pool, which was literally in the middle of Main Street. After it was all over, the Parade crew came through to clean it all up.

It seemed like there was always a special parade or event going on, and our great Parade crew was there to clean it up, adapting as necessary to get the job done. The ability to effectively adapt to changing situations was always a good skill for a Disneyland Custodial Cast Member to have, but especially so for an Events assignment.

Fantasyland Theatre

Usually, the very same crew that covered parades on any given day would also cover cleanups after shows at the Fantasyland Theatre. Sometimes, there would be a time conflict and so the crew would be split.

Conveniently, the venue was mere yards from the Parade Cage. It's a 5,000 square-foot space and started out as the Small World Meadows Amphitheatre in 1985, but nobody called it that. Instead, it took on the name of the nighttime music, dance, and video experience called Videopolis. It was *so* 80s. So... *rad*.

In our time as cast members, it was mainly used for live stage productions that ran mostly during the daytime. "One Man's Dream" was the first of these that I could recall, other than the holiday shows. Then there was "Diamond Double Cross", a popular Dick Tracy show using actors cast from theater, as opposed to sticking with Entertainment cast members who were already familiar faces at the park. Then there was quite the pullback with "Plane Crazy" in 1991 for the Afternoon Avenue overlay. The bigtime was back with "Beauty and the Beast", and that lasted for years. "The Spirit of Pocahontas" started in June of 1995, and that lasted into September of 1997. Then, in early 1998, the venue was upgraded, complete with a covering and the next show there was called Animazement.

There were other shows after that, but through all of it, our cleanups pretty much stayed the same. We'd have half a dozen or more people, most from the Events crew but maybe someone from the Small World/Matterhorn area, too, and to clean the audience area of the theatre we would take liners and pick up the big stuff like cups, popcorn boxes, and thermal detonators. Once the liners were done picking up the larger items, they'd go get another piece of equipment, such as a pan & broom.

If it was a show that used confetti or some variation of confetti, we'd use vacuums and blowers in addition to the other equipment, blowing everything the liners didn't get from the upper level down to the lower level for the walk-behind vacuums to get. Blowers might be used even without confetti.

The crew would use pushbrooms, pan and brooms, and mops to complete the cleanup, and the trash cans would get dumped, too.

This venue would be used for many other things throughout the years. For a while they were doing cheerleading competitions there. Now, that was one of the worst messes I (Lynn) had seen working at Disneyland. The competition started at about 8:00 or 9:00 a.m. and went until about 9:00 p.m. There was never a good chance for us to get in there and really clean the place because it was constantly occupied. We were able to get to some of the trash cans, but as far as the floor and benches in there, well, it got ripped.

When all the people left at the end of the day, it was a total mess. We called in Custodians working in other areas to come and assist. It was bad! Cups, boxes, popcorn, drink spills, corpses, you name it, it was there. Well, maybe not corpses. There was even a Code V nobody had reported.

That theatre has also held concerts. I remember the band No Doubt did a concert there for the local radio station

KROQ. That was a lot of fun to hear them play at Disneyland, which they were known for doing at Grad Nites.

Festival Arena

In 1996, Ten years after Big Thunder Ranch opened, a large chunk of it was replaced with what was called Festival Arena, because it was where the Festival of Fools show was staged as a tie-in to "The Hunchback of Notre Dame". It was a show that literally put the guests in the middle and encouraged audience participation.

Cleanups for this were much like cleanups for the Fantasyland Theatre, but there was also some pre-show work to collect trash from the crowd. This was one of the rare situations in which sweepers would wear themed costumes.

One of the nice things was that this location was accessible from the same backstage area as Fantasyland Theatre, where our Parade Cage was.

Parade Building

Another part of Events crew was being assigned an early shift at the Parade building, where the parade floats were stored. The building is in the northern backstage area, near Mickey's Toontown and Circle D Corral (the pony farm). This was a highly desired assignment because it was "cake" as the saying went. There was virtually no supervision and definitely no guest interaction.

The main task was cleaning the parade floats. As such, we got to get onto the floats themselves and see things from the vantage of the performers, and get a very close look at whatever we wanted to see on the floats. How dirty do you think those floats got? Not very, especially in comparison to a bench by a popcorn wagon or the Big Thunder Mountain queue.

There were other tasks in addition to cleaning the floats. I (Lynn) remember we would go dump the trash cans where the

Cleaning the Kingdom

Fantasmic barges would be parked. This was on the backside of the Rivers of America.

One morning, on my way to the parade building, I decided to take a different route and explore a bit. Behind where the McDonald's French Fry cart in Frontierland was, across from the Big Thunder exit. There was a dirt trail over the remainder of what used to be the Nature's Wonderland attraction. You could tell it had been an established trail at some point, like it was something bigger from the past that was no longer used much. I finally realized it was the old trail for the mules and wagons they had years ago. This trail is still there, a nice piece of Disneyland history, but secluded. In case you're thinking about going there to check it out, it is also secured.

The parade building was a huge hanger-like structure to hold as many floats as possible. We had a locker in it, which was kind of a cage. It was locked up, but you could see into it. We had a desk, and places to sit and store some equipment. It was no bigger than a walk-in closet. Then there was an upstairs to the building that was set in one corner. In this area was a break room and some offices. We weren't sure whose offices those were and it didn't really concern us. We just figured they were for the Entertainment managers. The break room was our responsibility to clean. There were several tables and chairs, and a small kitchen area. Near the bottom of the stairs were the restrooms for the cast members who worked in the building. There were electricians, painters and techs who worked in the building full-time. They did all the maintenance to the floats.

Depending on the floats, we would have to use lifts, ladders, and more. Much of the cleaning was done by climbing up and around the float. We had blowers that we would hook up to air compressors. This was so we could blow any dirt or confetti off the floats. Much of each float would get wiped down. Occasionally, the floats might require a washing and that would be done outside, near the building. Some of us, not me (Lynn) were trained to drive the floats; that would have been fun.

There are many trash cans on the building that would be used by the crew, so those were something we would dump before we went home. The shift was a nice shift to have if you didn't want to work around the guests. I (Lynn) enjoyed it every now and then, but I think I enjoyed working around the guests as well. The shifts were normally given to higher seniority cast members, so there were some that never got to work out there, and some that never wanted to, but for those of us who enjoyed it, we got to see a bit more behind the scenes.

Fantasmic!

Fantasmic! physically changed the Westside and greatly changed the overall nighttime feel. Some of the physical changes came after the 1992 debut season because the popularity of the show cried out for more crowd accommodation.

I (Ken) was with the last guest to stand in the old mill on the southern tip of Tom Sawyer Island before it was torn out to make way for the new mill that would house the show equipment. When the Rivers of America were drained for initial installation, some of us in Custodial rode in a pickup truck in the riverbed to tend to something on the Island. I was asking myself, "How many people have been able to do this?" Not a lot. Back then, the River was mostly soft-bottom with a concrete strip along the (SPOILER!) track that guides the Mark Twain and Columbia. Concrete was added for the show area, and then, eventually, the whole River was concreted, and then even that wasn't good enough and the dirt-mud shore along parts of the waterway were replaced with a concrete lip, albeit themed. Then swimming lanes were installed on the tiled bottom of the River. Just kidding about that last part. I think.

Along with the huge crowds for Fantasmic, which included people waiting for several hours and eating their dinners, came the need for an Events crew dedicated to the standard three showings. (For extra-busy nights, such as New Year's Eve, you could get five shows.) There were two Leads for

Cleaning the Kingdom

this at first, along with assigned crew members for the shift and people pulled from the areas for the cleanups. The Fantasmic! crew would get things prepared, including boarding the Columbia as it was in Fowler's Harbor and would clean it up and dump the bullet cans. Then the crew would do pre-show work, sweeping the walkways and waiting spaces and dumping the trash cans.

Maps depicting where the various teams were to start their cleanups and the courses they would take were drawn up and laminated. The lightest cleanup would have four teams, but on the busiest nights there might be up to eleven teams to do the first show's clean-up. We'd meet at the Adventure/Frontier and New Orleans/Critter Country area lockers, officially at fifteen minutes after the show started (when the villains take over) but some would try to get there earlier for the sake of socializing or making a bit of a break out of it. At the moment the villains were defeated, we'd head out and take our strategic places in the crowd, which means we'd get to watch the celebratory finale.

Like the post-parade cleanups, we'd form teams at the scheduling and direction of the Fantasmic! Lead, with pushbrooms, liners, and pan & brooms. Sometimes the liners would fill up and the jani handling them would pull the bags and leave them somewhere they could be retrieved later, which is one reason the liners were often triple-bagged or more. This way, they could continue to be part of the active cleanup. There could be piles of trash, trays and silverware from restaurants, guest belongings, uranium rods - you name it.

The final cleanup of the night was much more relaxed, but when there was a subsequent show scheduled, it was a race against the clock, especially after the first show. That was a main difference from most post-parade cleanups, except for those leading into a fireworks show. The crowds from the first show would be shuffling out at the direction of a precision Guest Control team, who were literally keeping mass tramplings from breaking out. Another part of the Guest Control team would be

233

holding back the masses itching to grab spots for the next show. They could only hold back the next audience for so long. More often than not, it was long enough because we were working at the speed of cheetahs on steroids, but sometimes they just had to let the throngs descend on us before we were far enough along. Then, it was a matter of trying to get whatever trash was left over as guests were flinging themselves onto their desired chunk of the pavement. The Fantasmic! Lead might switch over the radio to the Guest Control channel to be tipped off as to when the hordes were going to descend, then would switch back to the Custodial channel to warn the area Leads.

There were also the rare occasions the performance of the show would stop instead of completing, and we had to scramble to clean up, at least where guests abandoned their space rather than wait for a subsequent showing.

I (Ken) spent at least a couple of Summer seasons (and other times of the year) in the late 1990s being a closing Lead in Adventure/Frontier and New Orleans/Critter County. A sweet woman by the name of Joanne was the main Fantasmic! Lead at those times, and we got along fine. She was seeing, and then married, a fellow who was involved in the show. Joanne was famous for baking cookies and brewing up sugary punch, so while most Area Lockers had ice water in their thermos kegs, the Adventure/Frontier one would look like Jim Jones has been by. Only, without all of the murder and suicides. Usually.

While we were writing this book, the Fantasmic! viewing areas were switched to a FastPass distribution system and guests were prohibited from staking out spots too early, needing a FastPass and then only being allowed to take their spot at the designated time.

Fireworks in the Sky and All Over the Place

With the more simple fireworks shows, such as the long-running Fantasy in the Sky, the Parade and Fantasmic crews could do the cleanup along with the area sweepers. A special response was needed for the fireworks on New Year's Eve (see Chapter 10). In our later years, we were mostly working opening shifts, so we weren't dealing with the more elaborate, more popular fireworks shows, which we expect take an effort more involved than Fantasy in the Sky did.

Utility

Since we hired in long after the park went to an every-day-of-the-year schedule, the Utility assignment was either taking care of things backstage, or doing tasks onstage after park closing on days the park closed at 6, 7, 8, or 9:00 p.m.

Each night we did this there was an assigned area or two, depending on how many people were scheduled. There was a Lead and he or she would put the sweepers into groups and inform them on where they were going and what they would be doing for the night. Sometimes it would be cleaning light lenses on Main Street, or in any area. Sometimes it may be inside.

One time I (Lynn) was on Utility and we had to vacuum inside Star Tours queue area, but on the areas the guests didn't walk. There were ways to climb around down there with vacuums on our backs. It was fun, because it was an area that you could see, but not go as a guest. Another time we cleaned lights in Fantasyland.

I (Lynn) didn't have this shift too often, but the few times I did, I didn't really like it. I was a Lead once and it started with me helping with parade cleanup, because on weekdays the parade would be at maybe 6:00 p.m. After that cleanup, I would organize the equipment for Utility cleaning. The cast members who had this shift only had maybe a four to six hour shifts, which meant no (unpaid) lunch, and or a break or two, depending.

Sometimes this assignment would mean picking up dented or chipped themed trash cans from the different areas with a truck. The trash cans were taken to the Paint Shop behind Critter Country. There, the painters would paint the trash cans like new and repair them too. Then the cans would be dropped off to go back into the areas.

Like Lynn, I (Ken) had a few Utility shifts and they weren't my favorite. They were fine as bonding time, as we usually worked in teams. In one shift, we detailed the old Autopia queue area by giving all of the railings a good scrub and removing any gum or stickers that had been pounded into the flooring. There was another time when we were going through all of the restrooms, male and female, and prying off signs that had been on the inside of the stall doors. The signs were in English and Spanish, and we were removing them because some Spanish readers had an understanding of the signs that was different than intended.

There was a lot of this type of work going on backstage; it was all part of maintaining the show, but not seen by guests. It was just as important as any other shift in Custodial.

By far, my (Ken's) favorite Utility assignment ever was spending a full week, on a four-day, ten-hours-per day shift, cleaning out Space Mountain. This would have been in 1999 or early 2000.

The attraction was down for refurbishment, and our job, as a team of maybe half a dozen, was to dust and degrease the attraction.

By dusting, I'm not talking about taking a rag or a feather-duster through there. Rather, we suited up in jumpsuits (and harnesses, if I recall correctly) and had rubber breathing masks that looked like old gas masks. They were supposed to keep us from inhaling dust. Then, we took air hoses hooked into the pressurized air system in the track, and started to dust the ride literally from top to bottom.

And there was a *lot* of dust. Clouds of it. There were dust bunnies the size of elephants. I figured a lot of it had to be from the welding.

After we completed the dusting, we went on to degreasing *the entire track*, carrying buckets with us and moving them as we moved.

This assignment did test my fear of (exterior) heights a bit, but I was happy to do it, because I was getting to scrutinize the attraction in a way few people have, even more than some ride ops who have worked the attraction have. I even left my signed mark on the ride.

But in 2005, the attraction reopened after everything inside there was torn out and rebuilt with the same layout.

Tom Sawyer Island

This assignment was unique. Technically, the New Orleans/Critter County area had jurisdiction over TSI, but the NO/CC Leads rarely went to the Island.

A restroom-trained sweeper of each gender would be assigned to TSI and a radio would be used for communication with Custodial Central and the rest of the mainland.

This assignment included sweeping up the dirt-covered walkways, caves, and the Fort; dumping the bagged trash cans and taking the cart to the mainland to be emptied; responding to calls; and cleaning the small restrooms. There were two restrooms: one was on the side of the Island facing the riverboat landing, and another was in the Fort.

Our closet was under the outside staircase in the Fort, where both of us could sit down and take a break. We could get free drinks in the adjoining snack shop, and I don't know anywhere else sweepers could do so. Bussers got that perk when their operation was moved from Custodial to Foods.

Fantasmic! and maintenance issues changed TSI, and eventually the Fort was closed to guests. The show did add the large mill at the southern tip, and that was an air-conditioned structure with a dragon inside! Of course we explored that!

Cleaning the Kingdom

Scheduling

Another job that was part of the Custodial Department that would not have the cast member in the area or interacting with guests or even cleaning up was Scheduling. When we hired in, our schedulers were sweepers who usually wore whites and were tucked in a corner of Custodial Central, which was behind Casa Mexicana. In fact, the schedulers sat at a desk that was just inside a themed door that had a reference to the old Mineral Hall. Standing in the middle of the old west, we'd open a door and there would be a modern office.

Greg King was the primary scheduler when I (Ken) hired in. I have nothing but good things to say about Greg. I always saw Greg in whites, but I can only recall seeing him actually cleaning once or twice, assisting with a post-parade cleanup. He knew everyone's name and Social Security Number off the top of his head, and knew where they were all scheduled to work. When we were there, the Scheduler would configure weekly schedules and post them, usually a couple of weeks in advance. "A"s would tend to work the same days and same places week in and week out, although they might get scheduled for extra days. Other custodians, especially in the Casual status, would get moved around both in time and location. However, for the Summer season, just about everyone got to pick their shift from the ones available, and that was done by seniority.

After a weekly schedule was posted, the scheduler was likely to be inundated with shift change requests by people wanting to trade shifts, and would have to make other changes because of illnesses, injuries, suspensions, terminations, or changing conditions (such as increased park attendance estimates).

Bussing had their own schedulers who worked side-by-side with the Sweeping schedulers when Bussing was part of Custodial.

Schedulers did not have a space in the new Custodial Central location under Security in the Old Administration

238

Building. Our schedulers ended up in a centralized scheduling office, which was upstairs in the building and on the south-facing side.

It was to our advantage to be friendly with the schedulers because they were in charge of our destiny in the park and our days off.

In my (Ken's) last five years as a cast member, the schedulers accommodated me (and a few others) as we avoided the official required minimum availability. I could work weekend and holidays, and do so regularly, and they scheduled me as such. In those last years, Mel was one of the schedulers who did this. I think it is possible I never met Mel face-to-face due to opposite work schedules, but I remember leaving a present for Mel at least once. I told the schedulers I preferred an Area shift, and for those last years I was almost always an Area Lead, and when I wasn't, I was Esplanade Lead.

Trainer

Another assignment in Custodial that would leave you landless was to be a Trainer. This was a very important role. Trainers were people who worked among us, not a separate group of cast members. However, there might be some months of some years they mostly did training and nothing else, because of all of the new hires. They could do their training in their Custodial whites costumes, getting the new batch of custodians after they'd been through Disney University orientation and they'd go through classroom material as well as hands-on training.

Some really enjoyed doing this and my (Lynn's) trainers who were Brian and Petra were no exception. They were good at what they did, and you could tell.

Cleaning the Kingdom

Clerk

Along with the Schedulers and Trainers, Dispatch Clerks were essential, foundational support staff. Some clerks were permanent secretaries, but others were people who wore whites as they were veterans of the trenches and still identified as such. They'd sit at a desk that was more like a command center, just inside the entrance of Custodial Central. A good clerk was priceless, juggling tasks like checking in each Custodial cast member as they arrived, checking key rings and radios in and out, fielding phone calls from inside and outside the berm, making phone calls, and initiating and responding to radio calls. It could get mighty busy in Custodial Central, especially when Disneyland and California Adventure were run out of the same spot.

There were many outstanding clerks over the years, but one I (Ken) wanted to mention is Donna. She was kind and friendly, and to this day, she helps organize a monthly, informal get-together for current and former Custodians and any family they want to bring along, usually just to chat and eat together at a restaurant. I remember when she was pregnant with her daughter and working Dispatch, and daughter has since grown up to be a cast member herself! I'd tell you what her daughter does, but I can't because I "value the magic." Let's just say she's a friend of a princess.

Conclusion

There was a lot more to being an hourly cast member in Disneyland Custodial than sweeping up popcorn or mopping up a spill. To keep Disneyland clean took a variety of activities both onstage and backstage, around the clock. If a Custodial cast member needed a change in pace or scenery, they could find one without leaving the Department.

Chapter 10

Business Is Always Picking Up

Have you ever had a day at work that was so exhausting you ached all over?

Introduction

Disneyland is a place where people come from all over the world, and sometimes it felt like it. If you've never been to Disneyland on one of those extremely busy days, well, lucky you! Those of us who were paid to be there, and paid to keep it as clean and friendly as possible, usually knew what we were getting ourselves into after having worked through a few high attendance days. Some of us actually looked forward to these days because we wanted the overtime. Also on the plus side was that, once it got busy enough, nobody could see trash on the ground anyway.

I (Lynn) remember working during these times and the park closing its gates to guests by Noon. This was due to the park hitting capacity. There were progressive reactions to the crowding, including stopping ticket sales first before actually barring people from coming inside the park. After some of the crowd inside the park left, the turnstiles would start clicking again.

During these times, we were offered extra hours and sometimes just given extra hours with "mandatory" extensions of our shifts. Any shift shorter than eight hours would be extended, and then overtime would be offered, and if that still wasn't enough, "mandatory" overtime would be imposed. As with so much, overtime was offered by seniority.

One distinct memory I (Ken) have was being on the closing crew of one turtleneck-wearing Lead I will call the Notorious JVW. He was the Small World/Matterhorn Lead that night. He asked me if I'd extend my shift because he was short on crew members on a busy night. I ended up extending to twelve hours, which was the longest shift I'd worked until then. JVW and I were the last of the crew that night, and we actually ended up working past that twelve-hour point by almost another half hour, so we had to get a manager to note the adjustment so we could get paid. The Notorious JVW was very thankful for my willingness to work late.

We usually expected the crowds and were somewhat prepared, but that doesn't mean it was easy. It was very hard at times to keep up our areas, but for the most part, we did well. Even when the area looked sloppy to us, some guests would compliment us on the park being so clean. It was a matter of perspective; we'd see every piece of trash because that was our

Cleaning the Kingdom

job, while the guests would expect that there would be much more litter, so the place looked clean to them..

It was often hard to maneuver around guests while sweeping the areas on those busy days, but as long as we were onstage and trying, the Lead or manager didn't say much other than giving encouragement. They understood how hard it was to deal with the crowds on these days

Trash cans would fill up much faster, so in most areas we would have two cast members dumping trash, sometimes even three. Ideally, we'd have a Breaker and a Lines person, but then again if we were short on cast members due to call-ins then we had to just deal with what we had. Restrooms took priority, meaning that if there was supposed to be an 8-way split for Men's Restrooms, then if one of those eight called in sick and there were no Undistributed sweepers available, then some male sweeper would be pulled from an area to fill that hole in the Restroom coverage. It was more important that guests have clean restrooms than litter-free lines and walkways.

Busier days meant more vending carts selling popcorn, drinks, ice cream, cotton candy, churros, and other snacks, and more vending carts definitely meant more mess!

The Contrast

Working busy days takes a great deal of patience. This job taught me (Lynn) things I could use in many of life's circumstances. Yes, working busy days could wear on us as we went through day after day dealing with so many guests and the constant pace of the work. There always seemed to be more people calling in sick late in the Summer season, because we were so worn out.

That is why we looked forward to the slow season.

On those days, our crews would be down to the bare minimum. Many times we could even go home early, or not come in at all for our shift, if that ER or instant ADO was OK with a manager.

Cleaning the Kingdom

One time, I (Lynn) didn't even get off the shuttle. I was riding on the shuttle from the Katella Cast Member parking lot to Harbor Pointe and sat next to a manager on the shuttle. I told this manager I had a test the next day at college and needed to study. The next thing I knew, I was on the shuttle back to the parking lot and went back home.

Many cast members on slow days would ask me or a manager if they could ER. I couldn't approve that, but I could call a manager for them to see what they say. Most the time, if all was well they would get to go home. ERs meant those hours cut off the shift went unpaid, which was management's incentive to grant them. Sometimes we could influence the manager by convincing them that we had things more than under control, but the risk was that instead of granting an ER, the manager might pull someone from our crew to Restrooms or another area.

Working on rainy days was normally a slow day.

We were told in training to call ahead to see if our shift was cancelled, if we weren't proactively contacted by a clerk or scheduler. Custodial had less of certain work to do on rainy days but also would have things to do we didn't have on dry days.

Shops needed to be mopped, water puddles would be pushed into drains, and when there was a popcorn spill on the wet surface it was harder to sweep up. The maps handed out free to guests would fall on the ground and start to deteriorate, but not enough to disappear. Plastic rain poncho wrappers would fill our trash cans.

The restrooms would also get slippery, so we would put out extra rain mats inside and in front of the restrooms.

Days with intermittent showers were the worst as far as dealing with the rain. It was better to have it rain constantly rather than stop for a while and then start again. We'd get called to dry out Aladdin's Oasis, which had tile for flooring and dripping cloth canopies. In Fantasyland, we'd have to go dry out the Tea Cups and the outside portion of the Alice in Wonderland track. We would take towels and mops to dry everything up,

Cleaning the Kingdom

and even sometimes a wet vacuum. Then, thirty minutes later, it would start to rain again and the attractions would shut down. This cycle could repeat and go on all day.

One of the benefits of the rain was that it would clean things off, of course. One radio call that sticks out in my (Ken's) mind from a rainy day, when it was pouring consistently, was to clean up a drink spill in the middle of my area.

My response on the radio? "Really?"

Any drink that had been spilled would have been washed away.

There used to be more parts of Disneyland that could not handle the rain well. We were constantly pushing puddles toward drains with pushbrooms. It only made a difference if the rain was light or had stopped, but we'd do it when it was pouring, too, because we were supposed to. As various parts of the park got resurfaced away from slurry covering to pavers or textured concrete, some of the flooding and puddle problems were eliminated or at least reduced, thankfully.

Changing Attendance Patterns

Up until the latter part of the first decade of this century, Disneyland had distinct, predictable off seasons. During the off season, general admission hours for the park were shorter, sometimes as short as 10:00 a.m. to 6:00 p.m. during the week (with some private parties in the evenings). Some attractions, shops, restaurants, and restrooms would be closed for refurbishment, parades and shows would be dark, and there would be less entertainment in the park in general. (Management used to avoid having attractions closed during the distinct "on" seasons.) The crowds would be light, with projections as low as 10,000 guests for a weekday, and it was easy to get time off for vacation. It used to be that immediately after Summer season ended with Labor Day, guest attendance would go from 50,000-70,000 per day to perhaps 30,000 on weekends and 10,000-15,000 most weekdays, and the refurbishment walls would go up. Of course Friday, Saturday, and Sunday would be busier, but the crowds would stay on the light side until Thanksgiving Day. Thanksgiving Day and the following three day weekend would be so busy that Casual Seasonals would be brought in. That would also be the start of the Disneyland holiday season. The crowds would shrink back down again, although not as much, until the two weeks containing Christmas and New Year's Day. Those two weeks would be packed, and some of it was fans of the teams playing in the Rose Bowl and the bands from those schools. After those two weeks, except for some three day weekends, things would be very quiet again until two weeks in March or April for Spring Break. After that, things would start picking up again for Grad Nites. June would bring the very busy Summer season back.

Not only was it easy for us to take vacations in the off season, but visiting Walt Disney World Resort was good because crowds have roughly the same patterns there and so we could get full use of our discounts and avoid the crowds. Cast members and guests both took advantage of the reliable patterns of the off season vs. the on season and the extra busy weeks.

Things changed, however. Some of it could be attributed to the expanding winter holiday season, as detailed in the next section of this chapter, but there were many other factors that contributed. The Disneyland Resort had been maturing. When it was pretty much just Disneyland Park, someone who would only be visiting once every few years could, if they did it right, get their fill in a single day. One of the primary reasons for expanding with a second theme park was to get more people to stay (preferably in a Disney hotel) for multiple days. School schedules became less uniform, expanding the winter holiday breaks, spreading Spring Break over more weeks, and expanding the Summer season. Some schools might start earlier in August, but they'd be out earlier in May or June, or have adopted a "year round" schedule. Another factor was the heavy marketing of the multiple tiers of annual passes, and allowing monthly payments for them rather than the entire cost being paid upfront. The number of annual passholders increased tremendously over the years, and even if they would just drop in for few hours, if they were doing so every couple of weeks or multiple times per week, it added to the crowding. Even for southern California residents who didn't buy annual passes, there were frequently heavily-marketed "off season" ticket discounts to counteract the ever-rising admission prices.

We Won't Be Home For Christmas, You Can Count on That

The two weeks around Christmas are always busy in Disneyland, but especially from Christmas Day through New Years Day. We would never suggest anyone go during this time, unless you absolutely have to or are fine doing only a few things there. Some people just wanted to be inside Disneyland on Christmas, or to countdown to the New Year, and didn't care about doing much else.

Because these days were ridiculously busy, it was very rare for anyone without many, many years of seniority to get Christmas Day, New Year's Eve, or New Year's Day off. The better plan, if you actually wanted to spend the holidays with family, was to try to get a shift that would end as early as possible or would start as late as possible, and maybe family could work a plan around that schedule. The exception used to be Christmas Eve, because while the rest of that two week block would usually have the park closing at Midnight (2:00 a.m. for New Year's Eve), the park used to close at 7:00 p.m. or 8:00 p.m. on Christmas Eve, which was nice.

We enjoyed the holiday pay rate, and could work seven days per week, ten to twelve hours each day. These were the weeks for which we'd typically get our biggest paychecks of the year.

There was a time when the holiday seasons at Disneyland Park ran from Thanksgiving through New Years. Main Street, U.S.A. was decorated, there was a giant tree placed where Town Square met the rest of Main Street, and a pair of white Christmas trees in the castle moat.

There was a very extensive parade, called the Very Merry Christmas Parade, featuring live horses and live bands, and the first half of the parade featured floats and characters from classic Disney animation, and the second half featured more traditional Christmas/holiday setting and characters. Three Disneyland Custodians were in this parade behind a unit that included horses. I (Ken) did this a few times. We'd wear extra costume pieces to help blend in with the parade. One of us would have a pan and broom, the other would push the honeybucket, which had a shovel, and the third person had a shopvac to get up any horse urine. The shopvac wasn't used much, but the honeybucket was almost always used. The person pushing it would open the lid, get as much of the road apples up with the large shovel as was practical, and then the pan & broom person would get the rest, dumping it into the honeybucket. We had to work quickly so as to not hold up the parade. We'd get applause, whether or not we were actually cleaning up anything, which was nice.

In 1984, the Country Bears got a holiday special program that returned every year for most of the rest of the life of the attraction.

Sometimes, there would be a holiday-themed live show at the Small World Meadows Amphitheater (now known as the outdoor Fantasyland Theatre) In 1991, a particularly Disney-themed holiday show, "Mickey's Nutcracker", performed there.

People could also lineup and get pictures with Santa, or listen to the Dickens Carolers, or listen to the heralders blast out traditional Christmas music from the castle or from the Main Street railroad station.

One holiday tradition in high demand and short supply through the years had been the decidedly Christian Candlelight Procession, which only happened one weekend out of the year in the original Disney park. Since it happened only one weekend and wasn't something a significant number of park guests would get to experience, it wasn't marketed to the general public as something to draw people to the Resort for the holidays.

In 1994, the Very Merry Christmas Parade was replaced by the Christmas Fantasy Parade, which was completely holiday themed, shorter, and had no live animals and no live bands other than the marching toy soldiers. Still, it was a Christmas parade.

The holiday season was contained to those shows and the one parade, and the decorations on Main Street for many years - though the white trees in the castle moat went away after being toppled in the wind one year.

However, in 1997, Disneyland management discovered something about Disneyland guests - they can't get enough of the holiday spirit while visiting the Happiest Place on Earth. This was discovered when the Small World attraction received a temporary holiday retheming, which proved to be wildly popular. It has since been brought back every year, complete with wreaths on the boats, an elaborate display of "Christmas" lights on the exterior, holiday traditions from around the world inside, and holiday music intertwined with that familiar Sherman Brothers tune.

The weeks containing Christmas Day and New Years Eve were already the busiest weeks of the year, and so the logical conclusion was to make the most of that by bringing the rest of the park into the season and making the season itself longer. Now, the season goes parkwide at the start of November. Actually, when you consider the Nightmare Before Christmas overlay the Haunted Mansion has been featuring every year since the 2001 premiere, part of the park gets into the season in October.

It should be noted that neither the Small World nor the Haunted Mansion overlays would have been possible and successful if the attractions didn't have their expensive infrastructure - large show buildings, good ride systems, extensive sets, animated characters, and all of the lighting, audio, and electricity that goes with those things.

The pyrotechnics-snow-light show, "Believe... In Holiday Magic", was added in 2000 as a special version of the popular pyro show from that year's 45th anniversary observance.

The decorations have spread throughout the park, and recently, even the Jungle Cruise has been turned in Jingle Cruise. We're still waiting for Presents of the Caribbean.

Guests have responded by showing up by the thousands every day. No longer is the busy Holiday Season confined to just two weeks at the end of the year and part of Thanksgiving week.

When 1999 Became 2000

I (Lynn) remember a day it was extremely busy, and that was New Year's Eve 1999. Yes New Year's Eve was normally busy, but this one seemed more so than normal and it stuck out to me because of the whole dawn of 2000 thing, and because of the "Y2K" thing.

If you remember or know what the whole Y2K scare was, you can skip this paragraph. Believe it or not kids, there were people very, very concerned that computers, which of course meant just about anything with a processor or microchip, would go haywire as the year switched to 2000, since old programs that included dates used two digits instead of four, such as "85" for 1985. The fear was that as "99" went to "00", computers would crash, airplanes would fall out of the sky, prison cells doors would unlock (we're not kidding), power utilities would fail, and there would be a Carrot Top-Pauly Shore cop-buddy movie - you know, worldwide catastrophe. There were people making a living working on fixing systems to handle the New Year, there were people stocking up on emergency supplies to last them years, and even moving to the boonies, and people making money on that as well, stoking fears.

Cleaning the Kingdom

A lot of people were worried or unsure. I remember I was on Restrooms that night. I had a long shift: 5:00 p.m. to 3:30 a.m. as Disneyland was open until 2:00 a.m. We were given flashlights, and at the Main Entrance, guests were given glow sticks that said "Happy New Year 2000". While it was presented to guests that these were to welcome that long-dreamed about year, 2000, with glowing light, one does not need to be a cynic to think the real reason each guest was given a source of light was "just in case". 80,000 guests with glow sticks would surely provide some light.

I remember our Leads were giving us instructions on what to do if the electricity did go out. We were to get everyone out of the restroom, then go see if help was needed out in the area at attractions, stores, etc.

Just like every other NYE, it was an extremely busy night. Disposable hats and noisy horns were distributed free to guests, most of whom were planning to stay until after Midnight.

My Restroom split was a small one, but hard to do. I had Adventureland restroom, and Tiki Room restroom. It was just two restrooms, one of them tiny, and they were mere yards apart, but each time I needed to get from the Adventureland restroom to Tiki, it took about twenty minutes. We're talking about 30 feet, but it was where Adventureland met Frontierland and the Hub. I was packed into the crowd trying to move, and the guests were not happy. I hid my name tag because I didn't want anyone yelling at me, certainly not by name. Busy days could mean very frustrated guests.

Midnight came and there was no problem, and the park remained busy until about 1:00 a.m., it then started to slow down.

That was a night I will never forget.

I (Ken) knew everything would be OK, unless someone decided to pull a stunt. I had been working a day shift and catching news coverage here and there throughout the day,

251

which included each time zone welcoming the New Year, since there were plenty of them doing that while it was still daytime for us. Places that hadn't bothered to reprogram systems for the "Y2K bug" weren't having any significant problems. Regardless, I was happy to have a day shift because NYE was always a very tough night for Custodial.

Annually on NYE, Disneyland would usually have fireworks at 9:00 p.m. to coincide with Midnight on the East Coast, where ABC's New Year's Eve broadcast was based. They'd cut to a live shot of Disneyland where everyone would appear to be celebrating the New Year at the same time as everyone in New York and Walt Disney World Resort. Then, there would be fireworks again at Midnight Pacific Time, preceded by the countdown.

After that, Custodial crews would spring into action with many of the same tactics used for parade and show cleanups (see Chapter 9). In addition to the usual mess of an extremely busy night, there were thousands of hats and horns all over the place and filling up trash cans. Clearing the crowds and getting the Hub clean would take about an hour. After the Midnight fireworks, many thousands of people would turn and try to head down Main Street to get out the exit. It was a wall of humanity, and as that mass of people receded from the Hub, we'd be there to get every straw, every popcorn box, every horn.

For 1999-2000, thousands of glow sticks also ended up as litter, including in the Rivers of America.

A lot of people in Night Crew would be brought in early to help sweep areas, and so there were several hours of overlap with day crew on NYE/NYD. I remember one New Year's Day I (Ken) opened Main Street at 4:00 a.m. after the NYE Closing Lead had been off at 4:00 a.m. We didn't see each other, though, due to how the timing worked on ending a shift and starting a shift. I was brought in so early so that we could be sure the park would be ready to reopen for the first day of that year.

Summer-Fall 1996 The Summer that Wouldn't Die

I (Ken) was there the year summer never ended.

Oh, sure, schools had gone back into session in August and September. The almanac said summer was ending in September. The birds of Disneyland, fat and happy, were all set to head back to the gym to work off the summer eats.

Disneyland cast members looked forward to recovering from working full-time and a lot of overtime, and many of them expected to make their usual transition to being full-time students and instructors. Some planned to work as few hours as they could get away with. Others planned to beg schedulers and coworkers for more hours to cover their bills.

You have to remember this was when Disneyland had a parking lot just south of its main entrance instead of another theme park. The "Resort" upgrade hadn't happened yet. There was no Downtown Disney on the West Coast, there was no Grand Californian.

But the crowds at Disneyland kept coming as though summer had kept going. The crowds kept coming... and coming. They were largely drawn by several new attractions, especially Indiana Jones, and stayed later to see the Main Street Electrical Parade before it "glowed away forever" after its much-hyped Farewell Season. It really was a ...*brilliant* (get it?) strategy. Why spend scores of millions of dollars on another new attraction when you could keep your park packed later at night by merely marketing the end of what was a summertime tradition?

The strategy worked - all too well.

It had been quite the summer. Anyone who wanted to be a live performer at Disneyland, or a stage technician, or anyone who was a fan of live Disney entertainment was in hog heaven. (Wait, no, that would be during the State Fair promotion back in the 1980s.) Just consider what Disneyland had that summer, **in addition to two nightly performances of the Main Street Electrical Parade:**

- Two daily performances of the Lion King Celebration along the same parade route. The film and the live performance based on it debuted in 1994, and so the popular Celebration was into its third and final year.
- Two or three nightly performances of the original Fantasmic! show, which had debuted only four years prior.
- A nightly performance of Fantasy in the Sky Fireworks. In those days, except for New Year's Eve, Disneyland only had such shows during the summer.
- Five daily performances of The Hunchback of Notre Dame Festival of Fools. With a set that wrapped around the audience, this crowd-participation show was very popular, drawing crowds to what had previously been a sleepy area. The film premiered at the start of that summer, so the show was new. If you saw it, you may have seen Eden Espinosa performing before she tried defying gravity.
- Five daily performances of The Spirit of Pocahontas at the Fantasyland Theatre. Like the film, the stage show had debuted at the start of the previous summer, so it was still relatively new.
- All of the smaller entertainment Disneyland is known for, from live nightly performances at the Tomorrowland Terrace and Carnation Plaza Gardens to the characters posing for pictures throughout the park, and everything between.

Add in the fact that the extremely popular "E Ticket" Indiana Jones Adventure: Temple of the Forbidden Eye had been open for only a little over a year, and Mickey's Toontown had expanded the footprint of the guest areas of the park for only three years.

These things all meant a lot of work for Disneyland Custodial.

Cleaning the Kingdom

As guests both rare and regular poured into the park to see all of the new attractions, shows, and bid farewell to the MSEP, the attendance count for 1996 swelled by about twenty-five percent, shattering park records. The *increase* in attendance alone was about equivalent to the *maximum attendance for an entire year* for all but the most successful theme or amusement parks.

The much-marketed ending date for the parade was pushed back to give the parade more performances and milk the popularity further. Park operating hours were extended. It was as though the summer had never ended.

Fortunately for me, I was heading for graduation; I had finished my university classes in the spring and was working on my thesis project (based on a certain Ray Bradbury book and the film Disney had made out of it). That meant I could work full time and overtime, and did. I had been "given a radio" (made Foreman) that summer, and this was quite a way to be broken in.

Little did I know, the woman who would be my bride had been hired and cast in the Plaza Inn. We would not meet in person for almost eight years, long after she ended her time as a cast member. But that's another story.

The final regular Disneyland performance of the Main Street Electrical parade was on November 25, 1996, thus ending a tradition that had started in June of 1972, before I was even a zygote. The parade had had some dark years, but ran every summer from 1985 - the year I first became an annual passholder - to 1996.

From the final guest performance, it was straight into the extremely popular holiday season, with the parade route filled with the popular Christmas Fantasy Parade, itself a 1994 replacement for the extensive and expensive Very Merry Christmas Parade. So once summer came in 1996, Disneyland didn't really have an "off season" the rest of the year.

The MSEP did run four more times (if I recall correctly) - during the two nights of that year's Disney Family Holiday

Party, an annual tradition for cast members and other Disney employees, and their families. My guest and I watched the very last Disneyland performance, the second performance on the second night, following the parade to where it exited the park from the Small World Mall.

The Disneyland MSEP was replaced for the summer of 1997 with Light Magic, but that's yet another story. The Disneyland parade was shipped to Walt Disney World to have a run in the Magic Kingdom. In the musical chairs scheme of things, Disney had sent the Electrical Parade that had run at the Magic Kingdom to Disneyland Paris many years before.

In July of 2001, Disney's California Adventure received Disney's Electrical Parade, which looked suspiciously similar to the parade that had "glowed away forever" from Disneyland and had that run at Walt Disney World.

That's the tale of the Summer That Never Ended, a year when cast members and the park they operated strained under the pressure of the increased demand, and rose to meet the challenge, flourishing in their performance. I can still recall scrambling to clean up the waiting area for the Jungle Cruise at the end of one particularly busy night, and hearing a radio call from one of our managers, Glenn, to all of the Foremen, saying that it looked like we had "pulled a rabbit out of a hat."

I keyed the radio to copy and said "Abracadabra".

Those were magical times, indeed. Magical enough to take summer all the way to the holidays.

Sometimes, things being especially busy for Disneyland Custodial wasn't a result of packed crowds or weather.

The Pirates Come Home

On June 28, 2003, Disneyland hosted a movie premiere for what would turn out be first of a wildly popular series of movies, "Pirates of the Caribbean: Curse of the Black Pearl".

Cleaning the Kingdom

A few days before the premiere, trucks showed up at night to unload huge bleachers. These were set up around the Rivers of America, facing Tom Sawyer Island. They went from the Pirates bridge almost to the Haunted Mansion. They were about thirty feet tall. It was an amazing sight to see.

In the morning as I (Lynn) was picking flower beds, I saw a helicopter fly from the backstage area behind Toontown, and it was carrying a huge screen. This was the screen that would be used for the movie showing that would take place that night.

Also, the parade route from Town Square to Frontierland was covered with red carpet.

Sweepers were continuously vacuuming the carpet throughout the day, so by the time the partygoers were ready to walk the red carpet it would be clean.

Guests started to line up in the Esplanade early that morning, and I'm sure some were there the night before too. Once the park opened that morning, the guests who wanted to wait alongside the red carpet could do so. They were lining up from 8:00 a.m. until about 6:00 p.m. when the event would start.

The guests weren't allowed in for the party and movie viewing; they were allowed to be there for the walking of the red carpet. How often could someone go and see their favorite stars and movie makers in-person and up close, especially standing inside Disneyland?

Custodial was on the ball.

Throughout that day, we were cleaning every nook and cranny on the Westside. I (Lynn) was Opening Lead in New Orleans/Critter Country and remember being taken away from my normal duty to clean and polish building fronts, pick flower beds, clean light fixtures at the direction of managers

Pretty much everything was looking really nice.

It was exciting to be a part of it, although I was due to go home before the screening would start, and from what we understand, most on-duty Disneyland cast members ended up being sequestered in the Festival Arena anyway.

257

Cleaning the Kingdom

Just as Lynn describes, I (Ken) felt there was an extraordinary air about the park that day. I had never seen the park as spotless and shiny as that day, and we strove to keep it that way before we handed it off to the people working in the evening.

The red carpet event was a thrill for fans. Many celebrities who weren't in the movie were also there, and announced. Everyone was waiting to see Johnny Depp. He was close to the end of the arrivals, and he took his time with as many guests as he could. From what I understand, he really appreciated his fans, and it showed because his security had to hurry him along because the movie was about to start.

As far as we know, the event was mostly flawless. The cast of Disneyland did learn much from this, and that was good because we hosted the same event for the next three movies in the series. We were happy that this movie was finally premiering as the attraction was ripe for adaptation thanks to the incredible work of the Imagineers who'd created it and the Facilities and Operations cast members who kept it in great shape for so many years. We were glad the movie was entertaining, was received well, and made a pile of money. The last thing we wanted to see is such a beloved attraction suffer a bad adaptation.

For the third movie I (Lynn) worked in the Esplanade that morning and remember coming on at 5:00 a.m. and seeing guests already lined up near our Area Locker, which was almost to Harbor Boulevard. The line eventually did make it to Harbor, and down past what was then the 15-minute parking area. Then, on the other side of the Esplanade near Downtown Disney, was another line that went to the ESPN Zone. Now *that* was a lot of people who all just wanted to get in to reserve their spot along the red carpet!

Cleaning the Kingdom

That's Hot

Disneyland Custodial could be counted on to steadily keep the park clean, day in and day out, and to prepare well for planned events. We also were on-the-spot for unplanned, unusual situations. One of these was cleaning up after a fire broke out in the northwestern area of the property, in a motel building that Disney had purchased in preparation for expansion. So this was a motel that had been on the east side of the old West Street.

The motel building was used for storage, and suffered a fire.

One of the Opening Leads that day was invited to extend his shift after doing his normal work that day so he could help with the cleanup. He ended up working a total of *19 hours* that day.

Conclusion

On slower days, we were constantly checking the time, waiting for that next break just to break the monotony.

On extremely busy days, we Leads might not even have taken our breaks (even though we were required to take them) and the day would zip by because we were just plugging away at our tasks, constantly going from one thing to another, helping guest after guest, cleaning one mess after another.

We might've squeezed in a break at our Area Locker, but that would often be a "working break" because our crew members would find us there and have questions or requests.

Some crowds were cleaner than others, but in general, more guests meant more trash. Our job was always picking up, even more on those busy days. If Disneyland knew about it ahead of time they could prepare better, by staffing more cast members. Sometimes there would be days the park was busier than had been predicted, and others it would be slower, especially if it was a rainy day. Either way, our Supervisors would scramble to adjust. Unexpectedly slow days were less of a problem for us hourlies than unexpectedly busy days, but the worst thing for us about the slower days would be not having enough to do, though we could usually find *something* to do.

Whatever the conditions, the men and women of Disneyland Custodial would adjust and tackle the tasks at hand, because "business is always picking up" and "nobody does it better".

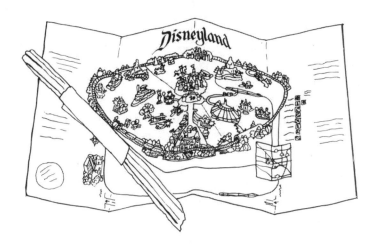

Chapter 11

Be Our Guest

What was it like to constantly interact with Disneyland guests?

Introduction

Every guest is a VIP. That's basic Disney University stuff. The guests were our customers, the reason Walt Disney built Disneyland in the first place. He figured if he built something he wanted, other people would like it, too. It's a living tribute to his two daughters and his grandchildren. For 60 years now, people have been able to enjoy the place with their grandparents, parents, children, and grandchildren, and of course their friends, dates, and another else with whom they like to spend time.

We met people from all over the world. That means they had different languages, cultures, traditions, expectations, and manners, and we were supposed to treat them all like they were King or Queen of the Magic Kingdom, whether they were people who were making their one and only visit of a lifetime, or regulars who'd visit more than once per week.

If a cast member was fluent in a language other than English, they could wear a pin indicating that. It was a big help.

Disneyland attracted such a diverse audience and much of that could even be seen in the guests who were serious enthusiasts. Whatever the socioeconomic status or demographic, we would see them. Almost any religious or political affiliation was represented. Some guests would want a private place to pray according to their religious tradition. Other guests would complain to us about theological implications of the Haunted Mansion. I (Ken) had an anthropologist complain to me about the word "primitive" appearing on a description of what could be found inside Tropical Imports.

Guests could be rude or weird, or nice and sweet. There were all sorts of people that would come to Disneyland, and we had tens of thousands of people in one place everyday, all mixed in with an enchanting setting that immersed the guest in what amounted to live theater with many improvised performances. This would mean we'd be involved in a wide range of situations in our guest interactions, something far more than what people usually experience handling customers at most entry-level retail jobs. We did have all of the typical customer service/service industry issues, but there were also things more specific to Disneyland.

While interacting with guests could be frustrating at times, more often it was a lot of fun. People were there to enjoy themselves and it was great to help them do that.

Cleaning the Kingdom

Our Disney University orientation and ongoing training told us that the Four Keys were Safety, Courtesy, Show, and Efficiency. We were taught to never point with one finger, but at least two or our whole hand. There was an acronym SERVICE, which, if we recall correctly, was:

Smile
Eye contact and body language
Respect and welcome
Value the magic
Initiate guest contact
Create service solutions
End with a thank you

"Valuing the magic" meant supporting, rather than detracting from "the show" whenever practical. A good example was that we shouldn't be chatting in front of guests about, the problems we were having with our car. Or, as another example, remembering that many guests, especially younger ones, believed the characters they were meeting in the park were *the* actual characters, and we shouldn't say something that would discourage this belief. One way I (Ken) would value the magic in my daily work as to do as little as possible to disrupt the experience at an attraction. If I needed to slip out a door in the portrait hallway of the Haunted Mansion, I tried to do so as inconspicuously as possible.

"Creating service solutions" could be as simple as offering a free replacement when a guest spilled their soft drink.

That was something we could do - replace things that were spilled or ruined or broken, for free. Guests were surprised and so appreciative of that. Just doing a little something made a big difference and could put their day back on track.

Even the most, how shall we put it, "lacking in motivation" Custodial cast members, would drop everything to help a guest. Guest service was reinforced *that* much.

263

Cleaning the Kingdom

When typical corporate thinking was brought in to Disneyland management and everything had to be documented, formalized, standardized, and named, this was called Total Guest Satisfaction

These days, Plaids are placed throughout the park, but in my time, if they weren't escorting someone, they'd be in City Hall, and later at the information board at the Hub, also. Sweepers were some of the most visible cast members throughout the park, and so guests would give us all sorts of feedback and ask us all sorts of questions. Most of the time, they wanted directions, show times, information about what was served at a restaurant or what was inside an attraction or where they could buy something in particular, or our personal recommendations. Our time was before the rise of the selfie, so we'd get asked to take pictures and we'd offer to take pictures before we could be asked. Some of us would photobomb, intentionally or not.

Being out and about, Sweepers would also see cast members from other Departments interacting with guests, especially the ride operators positioned at the entrance of the attractions. Although we'd get a lot of guest interaction, there were a few things I (Ken) was glad were *not* our responsibility:

- No guest could ever accuse us of shortchanging them when handling cash.
- We never hand to wonder if a woman was pregnant and ignoring (or unaware of) an attraction warning, or simply overweight.
- We didn't have to deal with guests who demanded their child still be allowed to ride even though they were short of the height requirement

No Ride For You!

We'd see parents get livid at the ride operator for not letting their under-height child through into a line or onto a ride.

Cleaning the Kingdom

One thing we did have to deal with that was attraction-based was when guests would show up at an attraction after closing and beg to be allowed on. Since one of our standard closeout tasks was making sure the waiting areas were clean, this was a frequent thing. The standard operating procedure at Disneyland was that the line for an attraction would be closed at park closing, which meant any guests already in line would be cycled through the attraction. This was a generous policy, but for some it wasn't enough. Sometimes the guests would get there long after the attraction had been cleared and was no longer operating.

We'd hear it all. "But this is my favorite attraction!" (Which is why you left it until the very end of the night?!?)

So every sweeper should have had this spiel memorized: *"Thank you for visiting. Disneyland's operating day has ended. This attraction is closed. It doesn't matter how far you've travelled, nor that this is your favorite attraction, nor what fatal diseases you claim to have. After operating for most of the last 16 hours, this attraction is now closed. Have a good night."*

Arthur

He just may have been the most beloved Disneyland guest ever. I (Ken) don't know of any other park regular who had *and still has* the status of Arthur Holmson in the hearts and minds of cast members. Veteran cast members loved him and passed down stories about him.

He shuffled along slowly with a cane, his diminished speed was the result of a stroke or two. He'd wear a red jacket, a checkered cap with his name embroidered on it by a park cast member, and would carry a bag with him that was surprisingly heavy given his age and physical condition.

Arthur would look around at the cast members, even the ones who were in the distance, wave to them, and greet them by name. If he didn't know your name by memory, it was most likely because you were new. "He's new," he'd remark to those in earshot. He would approach those he was familiar with and would say "Hi boy!", and would often ask (sometimes multiple times) "Are ya off dumorrow?" He'd often ask for other cast members by name, or would say, with distinction, "Where's Harrison? Heezoff!"

Treated like a cast member, if not royalty, he was apparently let into the park for free. Either that, or cast members would chip in and buy him an annual pass every year. He would show up at the dedicated Complimentary entrance turnstile, and in he would go.

He often spoke of Disneyland Park as his place of work. In fact, he was known for doing such things as regularly taking abandoned stroller tops back to Stroller Rental.

When the darkness of nighttime fell in the Summer, and The Main Street Electrical Parade would light up Main Street, U.S.A., Arthur would be there watching. The characters would all acknowledge him, and those that could call out to him would call to him by name.

The legends of his identity, why he was let into the park for free, and where else he'd hang out on a regular basis were plenty.

"He goes to the beach and talks the with surfers."

"He lived here before it was Disneyland Park."

"He helped Walt."

"He dove into the Rivers of America to save a kid from drowning."

"He has a car in the bag that he unfolds and drives home in."

In Arthur's day, there were a lot fewer annual passholders as the program was still unknown to most guests. Many of the park regulars who stood out as being different were looked at in a negative light by other passholders and by cast members. But not Arthur Holmson. We looked out for him. Security would make sure he was okay. He was one of the gang.

Cleaning the Kingdom

Whenever I saw Arthur in the park, I'd make it a point to say hello to him and see what he had to say. He was a fixture at the park, part of the culture. He was invited to certain cast member events and appeared in photos of a sort of cast member yearbook. In the mid-1980s a Custodial cast member drew a large cartoon of the park inhabited by caricatures of various Custodial cast members going about their daily work with their distinctive habits. It was framed and placed on the wall in what was then "Custodial Control", or the main office for Custodial. Sure enough, Arthur was depicted in the busy park, carrying a bag, wearing red, and saying, "Where's Bob? He's off! Hee hee!"

I first read about Arthur on Mouse Ears BBS, after which I kept my eyes out for him. (A "BBS" was a Bulletin Board Service, the predecessors to Internet Service Providers in which discussion forums were only open to those who dialed in directly to the BBS number.)

Sure enough, by keeping an eye out for him for a while, I met him.

Cast members would often drive Arthur home at the end of the day. I had the privilege of driving him home two or three times. I would pull my car as close to the Main Entrance ticket booths as possible while Arthur shuffled across the Red Carpet.

According to the legend, Anaheim police officers would also give Arthur rides home, and cast members told tales of being pulled over while driving Arthur home, only to have the police officer look in to the car, say "Oh, you're driving Arthur home. Go ahead." They weren't cited.

Arthur lived on Lemon, northeast of Disneyland Park, in a house that had a streetlight in front of it. He referred to his house as his "castle", which I suppose could be attributed to the old saying that "a man's home is his castle", but we knew it was a reference to his hangout.

I don't remember how I found out about Arthur's death. I might have read about first on Mouse Ears, or from the backstage notices that were posted everywhere.

Cleaning the Kingdom

I wasn't surprised, really, but I was saddened by the loss. This was in 1992. Fantasmic! was about to have its official world premiere and Mickey's Toontown was less than a year away from opening to the public, but Arthur's passing left a void.

Arthur was able to see Fantasmic! at least four times before he passed away at the age of 78. Sure, it wasn't as close and intimate as the Main Street Electrical Parade, but I'm sure he enjoyed it anyway. When Toontown finally opened, I couldn't help but imagine Arthur interacting with the characters, stepping on the talking manhole cover, and talking back to the mailbox.

An article appeared on the front page of the Metro section of the newspaper, complete with a photo of Arthur talking to an outdoor vendor in front of Sleeping Beauty Castle.

The service held for Arthur was jam-packed with Disneylanders, and even had Disneyland balloons. Unfortunately, I wasn't able to attend.

Arthur was a symbol of what the Disneyland culture had been, and his passing was like a sign that a new era was coming. In Arthur's time, Disneyland was still pretty much a theme park staffed by a large family of people who knew each other. The people who ran the park were almost all people who had come to work for the park as teenagers and stayed to rise through the ranks. It was easy for Arthur to know them and for them to know Arthur.

Many years after his passing, a lot of us chipped in and sponsored a brick on the Esplanade in honor of Arthur Holmson. Every day that I worked out there, I'd walk over those bricks to find C32 170. I'd pause to stare at it and remember. And smile.

Were These Even Guests?

I (Lynn) was working an off-season weekday evening shift when the park was closing at 8:00 p.m., and that meant

Cleaning the Kingdom

shops on Main Street would be open until 9:00 p.m. As Restroom Lead, my shift would have been 1:30 p.m. to 10 p.m. That also meant I carried a radio..

One thing that would come over the radio is called an ALL Call. That usually came from Security via their "Control" room, and it was transmitted to all Disneyland radio channels. At about 8:45 p.m. I heard the message come over the radio that the park was clear (of guests) to the Hub. These calls are made for several reasons, including so that people who want to drive vehicles through the onstage areas can start doing so, to make deliveries or get to something that needed to be fixed.

Around 9:30 p.m. I heard Control announce park was All Clear of guests. I was heading from the restrooms near the Alice in Wonderland attraction across the Hub and into Tomorrowland, so that I could get back to Custodial Central to turn in my radio and keys at the end of my shift.

On the walkway between Plaza Inn Restrooms, and Astro-Orbiter, I was approached by two women.

One was about 40 years old and the other was younger, maybe in her late teens. They both were dressed in Victorian dresses, with big hats, too. The younger one had a Mickey Mouse balloon. I remember looking closer at the balloon, because I hadn't seen one in that style in a long time. It was red, shaped as Mickey ears, and had a stamp on it that said "Disneyland".

In an English accent, the older woman asked me where they could find an eating establishment that was open.

I was a bit confused, because the park was closed, the park was clear, they were dressed not as a normal guests would be dressed, and I didn't recognize these as cast member or character costumes.

I told them the park was closed and I wasn't sure how they were missed by Security because the park was also cleared of all guests. It wasn't like they were inconspicuous. I "invited" them to start heading out towards the exit.

Cleaning the Kingdom

They said they were very sorry, and they started to walk in the direction of Main Street.

Right away, I looked behind me and there was a Security officer walking from the Matterhorn towards me. I yelled to him that he may need to escort these guests out of the park. I turned around to point them out to the officer, and the women were gone.

I'd literally turned my head for about 20 seconds, and yet they were totally gone. I told the officer about them, and he said he would check backstage, and I would check down Main Street. We got to Town Square and neither of us saw them.

I remarked to the Security Host that this was a weird situation, and I described them in more detail.

All he said was, "Well have a good night."

He probably thought I was tired, or playing a trick, or had inhaled too much of the cleansers we used. I almost forgot about it.

About three months later, I was backstage around a couple of other cast members who were talking about weird things they had heard or seen in the parks. One of them went on to tell me that she would hear two women, one sounding older and one sounding younger, talking in English accents in the Plaza Inn restrooms, but that it always happened after park closing. Then when she would check the restroom there would be no one there.

I had never shared my story with these other cast members before.

I was thinking those sounded like the same women I spoke to that one night.

That was eerie enough.

Then she went on to tell me that she also had seen two women in Victorian dresses, but never spoke to them.

I turned pale.

She asked me, "What's wrong?"

I told them my story and they said, "Wow, you spoke to the ghosts."

Cleaning the Kingdom

I don't have any beliefs in ghosts in the sense of them existing as the spirits of dead people and interacting with the living. But what happened that night certainly made me think more about them.

I have heard other stories from other cast members over the years, stories of weird things being seen or heard. Night Custodial staff told me some crazy stories, including of a woman in a white dress floating across the Rivers of America and a little boy running around in Roger Rabbit's CarToon Spin attraction. I have heard what sounded like feet running in the queue of that attraction at night, but it also could have been some of the mechanics they have in the queue.

I am sure most cast members have some sort of spooky story about working at Disneyland.

Not Going to Rest in This Restroom

Speaking of spooky stories, our friend Vince Mitchell tells of quite a crazy experience. This was about 1993, and Vince was in the back area behind Village Haus Restroom, and was with a Supervisor. They both went into the restroom through the back door, from the stock closet, and saw a guy lying on the ground in a stall. He was clearly dead, and that event alone could be traumatizing to most, but what happened five years later was just freaky.

After Vince had dealt with that dead guest, it was an unwritten rule that Vince would not work in that restroom anymore. It was emotionally too much for him, and he just couldn't go in there.

For this shift five years on, Vince was Restroom Lead on Eastside. He got a call that he would be watching over some trainees that were doing restrooms that night, and one of the restroom the trainees had was Village Haus. So he thought to himself that he could do this now, he could go in the restroom, it was time to face his fear. This time, he walked in through the front door of the restroom.

271

He walked over to where the stalls are and walked right up to the door of the stall where he found the corpse. He stared at the door for a bit, and as soon as he opened the stall door, the toilet fell off the wall and hit the floor, breaking into pieces, and water was splashing everywhere.

The next thing Vince remembers, he was at the Adventure/Frontier Area Locker, which is not close to where this took place.

He was freaked out, and to this day cannot go in that restroom or even walk by it.

Probably the Most Commonly Asked Question

Restrooms were the one thing I (Ken) would never joke with guests about. Whenever I could, I would try to lighten a guest's day with some humor, but when someone asked me where the nearest restroom was, I'd tell them as quickly as I could in a way that would also be clear, and even take them through the crowd myself to get them there quickly if need be. The last thing I wanted was someone having an accident, especially in my area!

A common follow-up question a guest would ask after getting an answer to "Where is the nearest restroom?" was "Is that the closest?"

Now why would we NOT tell them where the closest was?

Actually, sometimes, there was a closer restroom, but it would take a lot longer to get there. For example, if we were along the Rivers of America near the petrified tree, the nearest restroom as the crow flies (before West Nile Virus kills it) would be on Tom Sawyer Island. But the guest probably wouldn't want to swim there, or walk over and wait to take a raft to get there.

One sassy sweeper would react to "Is that the closest?" by cupping his hands and offering them to the guest. Not exactly a Disney University-approved response.

Cleaning the Kingdom

Criminals in the Kingdom

Most guests just wanted to have a good time. If they're keeping track of the money they're spending throughout the day and not having as good of a time as they'd hope, they may have felt like they were mugged. But there were a few guests who were there specifically to shoplift, or steal from other guests, or even steal cash from snack vendors.

Security Cast Members used to be very aggressive with people suspected of stealing, vandalizing, or assaulting someone. I (Ken) liked this. I felt protected, both as a guest and a cast member, and I thought it sent a strong message to discourage crime.

I (Ken) was sweeping near the Haunted Mansion when I saw a Security Host with an intense look, talking into his radio and weaving through the crowd. Like a lot of Security cast members in those days, he was in a costume themed to an area. Then I saw another Security Host behaving the same way.

Seemingly out of nowhere, a couple of other Security cast members joined those other two in surrounding a man who'd been heading out of Critter Country.

Everything seemed to stop and go silent as guests stopped chatting and turned to watch. The sounds of a struggle echoed as one Security Host put the guy into a chin lock as the others grabbed his arms and torso. Off he went, dragged backwards through Critter County and no doubt off to jail. Everyone else went back to what they'd been doing.

The suspect had forcibly taken cash from an Outdoor Vending cast member and had assaulted someone, and so a "999" call had been radioed, encouraging any available Security cast member to descend on him, which is what I had seen. It turned out he'd been carrying a large knife, too.

After a couple of negative news media portrayals, Security seemed to get kinder and gentler with guests who were suspected criminals.

Cleaning the Kingdom

Fight!!!

Yes, sometimes guests would get irritated with each other, even at the Happiest Place on Earth. Sweeper Bob Cobb saw two women fighting because one of the women accidentally hit the other with a stroller. Human nature, good and bad, exists inside the berm. Bob got between the two and calmed them down by distracting them. The whole thing ended fine after he intervened. Custodians not only picked up trash, we'd stop verbal and even physical fights. Getting involved was always a risk, though, and we were not trained nor encouraged to intervene. We were encouraged to call Security instead.

I (Lynn) witnessed a fight in the Small World line. It was the first year of the Small World Holiday and the line went all the way down the parade route to the Matterhorn area and onto the old loading dock for the former Motor Boat attraction. The location is now a small eating area.

The line was very long and I was on Lines that day. It was busy all over the park and I'm sure guests were getting frustrated. Someone cut into the line and a fight broke out. Before I could do anything, about it five Security Hosts came hurdling over the line ropes and into the line to stop the fight. The two men were taken backstage, and likely arrested, but definitely kicked out of the park.

Something I (Ken) figured is that if a Sweeper ever needed to act in self defense, it was good that we knew how to handle that broom stick and that metal pan so well. Better yet, with our knowledge of the place, removing ourselves from a situation in a way that a guest would likely not effectively follow us was a possibility. Fortunately, I never needed to defend myself from an aggressor.

Our buddy Vince did get involved, as happened one night just after park closing in Tomorrowland. He was dumping trash and was on his way back to the packer to dump his 8-liner cart, and was getting ready to go through the gate to go into the back area.

Cleaning the Kingdom

He heard someone asking for help, and it was a Security Host he knew, and this Security cast member knew that Vince had been learning martial arts for many years. The Security Host asked Vince to keep his eyes open, so he thought that was weird that he would ask him that, but Vince continued on his way to the back area to dump the trash into the packer.

He proceeded to head back onstage to take the trash equipment back to the office. He reached the vicinity of the former Rocket Jets when he heard the voice of his Security buddy: "Vince! Vince! Help him! Help him!"

His friend who was yelling that was struggling with a huge woman off to Vince's left. Vince looked to his right and saw a few Security officers struggling with a big guy who was hitting the officers with a cast on his arm. Vince charged the guy and hit him hard, and the guy went flying into the fence that was surrounding the Innoventions building. Vince then pinned the guy down.

All of a sudden, Vince felt a breeze go by and the big woman was running at him, and trying to get to Vince. The guy was telling the woman to get back.

At this time, Anaheim Police officers made it onstage and told Vince there was a police car backstage where he could take the guy. Vince took the opportunity to slam the guy down on the police car hood. He thought "When will I ever have a chance to do *that* again?"

His trash partner was frozen after watching the whole thing go down.

Unsurprisingly, the couple was on drugs and Vince had to write a report on the incident. Some of his friends in Security encouraged him to transfer and join them, but he declined, having other things in mind.

Altering the Altered Reality

Dealing with guests who were drugged up or were having psychotic breaks didn't happen every day for us, but every once in a while we'd have to deal with such a situation. Theme parks could be disorienting enough. Guests getting under the influence were just asking for trouble.

Sweeping through part of the Haunted Mansion line, I (Ken) reached the columns and steps, when I could tell something was wrong. The experienced ride operator looked on edge and he had held guests back from entering the foyer. The (SPOILER!) facade door had a sizable hole in the bottom half. That's when I noticed someone was hollering in the foyer. The ride operator was gazing into the distance to look for Security and First Aid nurses, who'd been summoned.

I took a peek into the room, and sure enough, there was someone who looked to perhaps be a guy in his late teens who was throwing himself around the room and yelling. He's kicked the hole in that exterior door and trying to crawl through it, but of course it was a facade and it wasn't possible for him to crawl through.

I encountered more guests who were suffering the effects of a mental illness that was impeding their dealing with reality than ones who were obviously having a bad trip, but then Day Custodial had little involvement with Grad Nites.

To clean the wall along the Rivers of America in New Orleans during a closeout, I put myself in the risky position of climbing onto the water side of the railing and making my way along the ledge. One slip, and I'd be in "the drink", along with my radio and whatever else I had on me. The park was clearing, but it hadn't been cleared to that point yet, and this woman approached me, talking. I soon realized she wasn't all there. I also realized she could push me into the water if she wanted. I called Control on the radio, and a Security Hostess with a gentle way about her came by and engaged the woman, much to my relief.

Cleaning the Kingdom

Little Girl Lost

While we did have plenty of negative experiences with some guests, there were plenty of opportunities to make a guest's day better or otherwise have a positive experience. One such way was reuniting lost children and lost parents.

I (Ken) really don't get why some parents get so hysterical. After all, half of all lost children are found, and half of those are still alive. Sorry - just wanted to see if you're paying attention (and to recycle a joke I used to use backstage.) Seriously, I know what it is like to be a lost child. I also now know what it is like to have your child lost in a crowded place. NOT FUN!!!

Fortunately, as far as we know, no child was ever lost permanently at Disneyland. You know why? The kidnappers change the kid's hair and clothes but always forget to change the shoes, and the parents always make it to where the camera monitors are so they can always notice their kid being carried through the exit because they always recognize the shoes! Again, I'm sorry; I couldn't help but poke fun at a bogus urban legend.

There was once one older kid who exited the park and boarded a shuttle and ended up on different shuttles all night. That's about as far as such a separation has ever gone.

If you're really worried about losing your child at Disneyland, consider getting them a disposable phone if they don't have a phone. Take a picture with your phone or tablet when you get there so you can see and show others exactly what your child looks like and is wearing. If the kids don't have a phone with your phone number, make sure they know your phone number. Kids can memorize those ten numbers at early ages.

Especially if a lost child was upset and crying, I (Lynn) would kneel down to their level and talk to them calmly. I would ask them some questions like their name and what their Mommy or Daddy looks like, and where he or she saw them last.

Cleaning the Kingdom

We carried stickers in our pouch, and could give the kids some to maybe get their mind off the problem for a minute while I would look around trying to find a parent who looked in distress.

Nine times out of ten, we'd reunite the child and parent before we could get the child to Lost Children near the Hub on Main Street. That means there were times we would make it all the way there (which is easier to do if you're already at the Hub).

The cast members in Lost Children were, as you might expect, very kind, patient, and reassuring. To a kid, they might look like Grandma. Unfortunately, there were times they might have looked, to a kid, like someone who just tried to cook Hansel and Gretel. I (Ken) was taking one boy there and he was already reluctant to go, and upset. As we neared the door, another child came running out, screaming, like he was fleeing a painful death. Through the doorway, we could see a woman who didn't have the friendliest expression on her face, It must have looked to the kid I was escorting that I was taking him to his doom.

One thing I (Ken) remembered from my Disney University trainer was to never *tell* the kid they were lost. We shouldn't let them hear that they're lost unless they have already stated they know they're lost. Sometimes, they didn't even realize they were lost or they weren't upset about it. It was much easier and more productive if they weren't upset, because we could get helpful information out of them. For example, we'd ask them what they want to be when they grow up. That was an important question, because we were desperate for ideas.

But seriously, management made it clear to us that if we picked a child up, we were on our own as far as liability. I usually didn't have any reason to pick the child up, but there were a couple of times where it was the right and effective thing to do.

Dealing with lost children or observing the children at Disneyland throwing tantrums or having trouble using the restroom because they're in the middle of potty training could reinforce someone who didn't want kids and tip the ambivalent to the "I don't want kids" category. The opposite could happen, too.

In November 2001, my first day back from taking a trip to Walt Disney World, I was in a fairly busy Tomorrowland when a Outdoor Vending cast member who was transporting a cart handed off a little lost girl to me.

She had her hair in little pair of tails, was wearing overalls, and was holding candy. She was calm and quiet, and the most adorable lost child I have ever dealt with. I crouched down to her level.

"Hi... my name is Ken," I said, pointing to my name tag. "What's your name?"

"Amanda. I can't find my Mommy."

"Okay, well we're going to find her, okay? How old are you Amanda?"

"I'm three."

"And what's your mommy's name?"

"Sarah"

"Okay. Let's go look for her..."

With most lost children, I'd take them by the hand due to a combination of their size and the crowd conditions. Amanda needed to be up higher so she could look for her mother and so that her mother could see her more easily, so I picked her up and carried her as we walked the area. As we said, nine times out of ten, a frantic parent will come running up to claim their child within seconds.

This time, however, we walked around for a little while, and then I decided to tell Lost Children I was on the way with her. As we made our way to Lost Children, Amanda pointed to places she had been with her "Mommy and Grandma".

She never lost her composure.

I was surprised to make it all the way to Lost Children with little Amanda. When we got there, there was nobody from her party waiting for her, and no other children. I handed her off to the hostess there, passing along the pertinent information. "Ken's going to go help find your Mommy," the hostess explained. I'm sure it wasn't long before mother and child were reunited. I had hoped to bump into her mother so that I could have seen that moment with my own eyes, and thank the mother for sharing Amanda with me for a few moments, and then Amanda would have been reunited with her mother without ever realizing that she herself was lost.

Suddenly, all of the doubts I had about wanting to be a Daddy were melted away. In 2007, my own little girl emerged into the world, and two years later, my little man-in-training was born.

When You've REALLY Lost a Relative

When the Ghost Host in the Haunted Mansion says there are 999 Happy Haunts there and (SPOILER!) there's room for a thousand, that's just part of the show. Some people, though, have apparently taken that as invitation to spread the cremated remains of their loved ones inside the attraction.

Unless you want your loved one swept up into a dust pan or vacuumed up - in either case, to be dumped in an industrial trash compactor - do not spread their cremated remains in the Haunted Mansion. That's all I have to say about that.

Making Friends

I (Ken) had been hearing about a residential Halloween display for years, called Hallowed Haunting Grounds. Mainly, I'd heard it had many of the same sorts of effects as the Haunted Mansion, but it was done at someone's home. I was interested in "home haunts" and when I was a teenager I did a very modest scene with props to give trick-or-treaters something to see.

Cleaning the Kingdom

More impressive were the make-up effects me and my school pal Francisco would apply to ourselves. I really got into that whole thing, but I had a friend who was much more into it than I was, and so when he invited me to go along to finally see the legendary HHG, I agreed.

It takes a lot to impress me when it comes to themed environments, especially when I've heard it talked up a lot.

I was very impressed. It was extremely well done, and it was in someone's *front yard*, and the front windows of their house. There was no indoor part to it. Visitors stayed outside.

I was not surprised when I saw a Disneyland annual passholder, Gary, who would stop to chat with me when he was visiting the park. This was exactly the sort of place I would expect to run into Disneyland enthusiasts. I knew this guy could appreciate this display as much as I did, and so I went on and on about what was so impressive about it, pointing to this and that.

Then Gary turned to me and asked, "Did you want to come inside?"

"Oh, this is YOUR place?!?" I'd never known that this guy would stop for friendly chats while I was working my shifts was the guy who had been in charge of this place I'd been hearing about for years.

He was especially appreciative of my compliments since he knew I hadn't been embellishing them to butter him up.

For the remainder of the years HHG materialized, I'd stop by one night each year to say hello and go inside for conversation and snacks. I even did little guest control here and there.

Not only was being nice to guests our job, but we never knew when a friendship would result.

There was one day I (Ken) was backsweeping the Indiana Jones Adventure line, and as I was nearing the temple entrance, I noticed someone standing off to the side of the line of guests, studying the Maraglyphs (the writing in the special font created for the attraction) and painstakingly entering them into a sketchbook. She was a girl, seemed to be early teens or younger, dressed up a bit like Dr. Jones himself.

I told her that if she wanted, I could save her a whole lot of time and provide her with the complete compilation of translated Maraglyphs, which had been provided to me by a frequent guest. She opted to have the compilation, and so the next day she met me as I was heading to the office to check in and I provided her with the information, and thus began a friendship that included me meeting her mother, and, eventually, when she was grown, me visiting them for a couple of weekend getaways in Oregon. She was a very creative and somewhat troubled person. As if the first meeting hadn't been a clue, she was obsessed with the Indiana Jones franchise, and that was just one of her fixations.

I was able to return her hospitality when she and her partner needed a place to stay for a night when visiting California.

Confusion is Easy

We knew the park like the back our hands, but it was easy for guests to become disoriented or to have their attention focused in one place when it should have been focused elsewhere. That's how I (Ken) was able to see a boy unloading from a Jungle Cruise boat slip between the boat and the dock, down into the water. Instantly reacting, a ride operator swing his arm down, grabbed the soaked boy, lifted him into the dock, and then walked him to CFA to dry off and, presumably, get new clothes courtesy of Disney.

Being in a crowded, unfamiliar place where your senses could sometimes be overwhelmed could prompt some to rely on the kindness of Custodial cast members. They might apologize for asking their question, but we would assure them it was no bother, no trouble to answer their questions. Often, it would allow us to pause for a minute to give our arms a rest.

Cleaning the Kingdom

Some guests would apologize for their difficulty with English. I'd point out to them they knew more English than I knew of any other language, and I understood English was a ridiculously hard language to learn. Just think of all of the people who have it as a first language and still don't get it right! If you're a good proofreader, you've probably found all sorts of errors in this very book. Am I rite oar what?

One lady asked me during the day what time Disneyland would be closing, and I told her it would be 12:00 a.m. - Midnight. She look confused.

"Midnight?"

"Yes," I said.

"Midnight?"

"Yes," I said again, not sure what the problem was.

"It will be dark!" she said.

I paused. "Yes, it will be dark." I paused again. "But we have lights."

She processed that for a second and it seemed to satisfy her.

One guy asked me how much it would cost to *exit* Disneyland.

I told him that if he just kept it between the two of us, I'd let him leave for free.

Those two conversations stick out in my memory because they were unusual conversations that were not with someone who was obviously having a break with reality. We would talk people in that situation, too, and those could certainly be unique conversations.

Especially after the Hungry Bear Restaurant was closed for the day, the Critter Country restrooms could be empty. I was doing my round in there one night when a woman slowly walked in. She didn't say a word. She must have seen the row of urinals, and must have seen me. I'm not the most feminine looking dude. But she kept walking, eventually made it to a stall, went inside to use it, and when she was done she slowly walked back out of the restroom, never having said a word. It wouldn't

283

have seemed so strange to me if there had been a line for the women's restroom, but I knew there wasn't.

Strike a Pose

While guests could be unintentionally amusing and entertaining, some did it deliberately. When I noticed a crowd forming around the "cigar store Indian" on Main Street, I peered over and saw that a fellow was posing motionless next to the figure. He was really good, and appeared to stay motionless for an extended period of time.

I quickly scanned the crowd to see if it was possible this was a setup to pick pockets, and didn't see anything that could appear to be that activity. This guy did a great job. To end his show, two friends of his carried him off into a store as if he was still a motionless figure.

Smoking

The guest smoking policy at Disneyland changed over the years. When I hired in, I (Ken) thought it was a good policy: no smoking inside, on attractions, or in waiting areas, where others were captive.

I was no fan of cigarette smoke, but I didn't begrudge someone their relief, even though cigarette butts were often another piece of litter and we'd occasionally get fires in our pans or even our trash cans because of still-smoldering cigarettes. Fortunately, people would also throw away drink cups that still had much liquid in them, and we could usually put out a fire by dousing it with a drink.

The policy was changed to restrict smoking to a handful of designated areas. Cleaning through those areas and cleaning out the ashtrays was an exercise in holding one's breath. This policy change also increased conflict. I'd get guests insisting I go stop someone from smoking who had clearly sought out a removed place to smoke so as not to bother others. One of those times, to make my point, I loudly sniffed the air and said, "I don't smell anything. Is it really bothering you?" I'd approach the smoking guest and softly tell them about our designated smoking areas.

Solicitation

Sometimes guests would ask us to do something illegal, unethical, or against Company policy.

While DCA was under construction, there was a preview center in the Esplanade, complete with a raised platform so guests who were willing to climb the stairs could get a look at the construction of Disney's newest theme park. I would go up there to get a look, and to make sure it was clean.

A man who I took to be from a country where petty bribes are common came up there and asked a couple of questions. Then he asked me if I could get him inside Disneyland if he put some money in my pocket. I politely declined.

Releasing Steam

Sometimes guests would get mad at us for the park being busy, or at least they wanted to vent to someone, and we were a target because we were there. Most the time I (Lynn) could take it, and then refer them to City Hall to file a complaint if there seemed to be no other way of pleasing them.

If it was reasonable, we were encouraged to diffuse the guest's gripe ourselves, perhaps in conjunction with other cast members nearby. But when all else failed, we referred them to City Hall because they could do more than we could to remedy the situation, if it was even possible. One thing anyone who has done customer service long enough knows is that some people just want to vent, and after they do, they'll be fine.

Cleaning the Kingdom

The Classics

Any sweeper who'd been around for more than a week had heard "You missed a spot!" more than enough times. A better thing to do is to team up with the Sweeper by asking, "How's business?"

The answer, of course, is "It's always picking up."

This set-up and response works a lot better than simply saying "I bet business is always picking up, huh?" If you said that to me (Ken) I'd just have to say, "Sometimes it really gets you down in the dumps, but I can always sweep someone off of their feet."

Since we wore nametags, I could expect "Where's Barbie?" Oh, that was *so* original. I hadn't heard that a bunch of times by the end of first grade.

Overheard

I (Ken) could never get enough of overhearing the exchanges that went like this:

Guest approaches an Attraction Host at an attraction that has gone 101.

Guest: "What's wrong?"

Attractions Host: "We're not operating right now due to technical difficulties. Please check back later."

Guest: "What happened?"

Attractions Host: "We have sensors that help keep the attraction running smoothly and safely, and sometimes there's a problem with a sensor, the attraction will be stopped by a computer program that monitors the sensors."

Guest (turning to a friend): "It broke."

Broke? I'd picture this giant fissure in the side of the attraction.

Cleaning the Kingdom

Out of Bounds

Guests sometimes went out of bounds. If we saw them walking around backstage we'd escort them back to the onstage area as soon as possible. Usually, they were looking for a restroom, and they were moving like it, too.

I (Ken) was deep into Critter Country near the exit of Splash Mountain, when I saw a teenaged girl standing up by the Drop 1 Runout of the attraction.

"Can I help you?" I called up.

"I got off the ride," she replied.

"Hold on," I said, and went to go get her. Got off the ride?!? Turns out she'd climbed out of her log just before Drop 1, which is by the snoring Brer Bear. There were no Attractions cast members out by that exit in those days. The Splash Mountain ride operators were aware that someone had climbed out of a log but they weren't exactly sure where she had gone until they caught up with us.

As apprehensive as I could get going on a new attraction that had heights or thrills to it, I would have been much more afraid of climbing out of an active ride vehicle. But that's just me.

Parades

Guests would line up early for parades, sometimes by hours depending on the parade. The Christmas parade was always a popular one, even after Very Merry Christmas Parade switched to the smaller Christmas Fantasy. A guest noticed there was quite a crowd on Main Street waiting and asked me how much longer until the parade. She wasn't expecting that it was still a bit of a wait before it would start.

"Jesus Christ!" she exclaimed.

"Yes, it *is* the Christmas parade, but He's not in it," I replied without hesitation.

Nobody ever fell for my favorite parade joke, until someone finally did.

"What are these people waiting for?" a mother asked.

"Direct from Spain, we'll be hosting the Running of the Bulls", I deadpanned.

She scrutinized the entertainment schedule, trying to find Running of the Bulls while her daughter tilted her head and said, "It's a joke, Mom."

The parade route runs through the east side of the Hub, immediately in front of Tomorrowland, but many guests wouldn't know that, and so when people started lining up for the parade and Guest Control hadn't yet put up ropes, there would always be people who thought they were grabbing a good spot as they sat on the curb on the west side of the Hub, by the Adventureland or Frontierland entrance. I'd try to catch them as early as possible to let them know where they needed to go to claim a good spot to watch the parade. One of those times, Ray Sidejas (the Top Jani) caught me and complimented my guest service. Lucky for me, he was always catching me doing something good, never when I was doing something like falling off the stone benches in front of the Castle as I picked flower beds in the morning and landing flat on my face.

Familiar Faces

As with Gary, who I (Ken) wrote about earlier in this chapter, there were guests who were frequent visitors and would stop the shoot the breeze. Some of them were friends I had made while an annual passholder or visiting the parks as a guest, others had become friends just because they liked to say "hi" to cast members

This was always welcome because it helped the day go by faster in a pleasant way, and we still looked like we were working. Actually, we usually were still working as most these guests would stroll along with us for a moment as we patrolled our areas. If someone who looked like management would get near us, these friends would ask something like "And where is the nearest restroom?" so as to appear to be a random guest rather than a friend.

Carlyn and Mark were a couple who'd stop by from time to time. I met them through a B.B.S. called Mouse House, which came after Mouse Ears. Mark was frequently mistaken for Francis Ford Coppola so people would sometimes ask me how I knew Mr. Coppola. Carlyn was a Registered Nurse and actually ended up working at CFA for a while.

In September of 1999, I saw notices backstage that Roland Barrett, an elderly, frequent park guest, had passed away. Roland and I would kid each other a lot as he stood in his cap and sweater watching the Disney princesses. He seemed to love nothing more than watch quietly as Ariel, Jasmine, and the others make the dreams of children come true.

The Distinctive Regulars

As some of you reading this are well aware, some Disneyland enthusiasts could be quite ...*intense*... about their devotion to Disneyland. We could identify with that!

And some guests who attended regularly, especially if they dressed or behaved distinctively, would get a reputation, or at least a nickname, among cast and other annual passholders alike. Katrina had a turbo-powered automatic wheelchair and it was a good idea to stand clear. Mr. Green Jeans was opinionated, but seemed to be a nice guy once I got past his gruff exterior. The "Prairie Family", so named because of the distinctive dresses worn by the girls (the boy wore home-made replicas of cast member costumes) adopted their nickname. I don't think Mr. Green Jeans got into any legal or in-the-media disputes with Disney, but the others did. Someone I know really well even was questioned by a private investigator hired by the Prairie Family.

Yes, guest interactions could be quite the experience!

A Changing Audience

Guests changed over the years. Some of that change was general of the culture, some of it was specific to Disney. A big change was the gigantic number of annual passholders, smartened up with too much behind-the-scenes knowledge as well as misinformation via fan media, entertainment news media, etc.

There was a time fans, critics, guests, cast members, and employees did not flock to social media to dish on the dirt, flaws, accidents, blunders, mistakes, failures, take-aways, backstage politics, cast member eatery price increases and portion decreases, rumors, upcoming projects, etc. Before I was a cast member, I'd first find out about a new ride when construction began, and even then it might be a long time before I got any idea of what the ride was going to be like. Sometimes, we had no idea until you actually rode it. I didn't have any idea if there had been cutbacks, or what better ideas had been tossed around before the lesser project was picked for construction.

Adolescence is starting earlier and ending later. Kids are exposed to so much more now than they ever used to be, and they're losing their fantasies and imaginary lives in one sense, but fantasizing even more in another sense. A girl may no longer believe she is meeting a real princess, but she may think she is one herself.

The cast must adapt to the audience somewhat.

How to Thank a Custodial Cast Member (or Any Cast Member)

First and foremost, have a great time, and tell them you're having a great time. If the park looks clean, tell them you noticed that.

Tipping cast members, other than restaurant servers, Bell Services, valets, and housekeeping is not encouraged. When we were there, cast members such as sweepers had to politely

Cleaning the Kingdom

decline a tip three times before we could accept it. Something you can do is note the name of the cast member and stop by City Hall to register a compliment, or do it through the official Disneyland website.

Conclusion

A smile and body language got us far. We learned to break down barriers, and not to react with anything but respect and helpfulness when we'd be surprised by a guest with a physical or mental condition we hadn't interacted with before.

I (Ken), in non-Disney job, held a dedication event (ribbon cutting, news media invited) for a project that was done in conjunction with a nonprofit. The head of that nonprofit had invited her parents to the event, and when we were wrapping up, the mother approached me and quietly thanked me. I was wondering what exactly she was thanking me for, then she went on to point out that her husband was suffering from dementia, and he had asked me essentially the same question over and over again, and I answered him respectfully, politely, and thoroughly each time, without a hint of irritation or impatience or dismissiveness or even pity.

Honestly, I didn't even realize he'd done this. Due to my training and experience with Disneyland Custodial, I took each question asked of me that day by anyone as a new question and an important one, as if I hadn't answered it thousands of times before.

There were many things like that we picked up over the year in our experience as Disneyland Custodial cast members. We could read a guest's body language. We would customize our approach to guests based on what we could discern about them.

When I hired in, most of our managers were people who'd either moved up to management directly from being hourly cast members in Custodial or had Disneyland Custodial experience at some point in their past. One manager that was

291

Cleaning the Kingdom

transferred in was a woman named Janet who'd come from the Hotel. On a quiet night in Frontierland she approached me and complimented me on the interaction I had just had with a guest. I didn't know what I had done that was so special. She described it to me. The guest was a woman who had a sleeping youngster resting his head on her shoulder, and she had asked a question as she approached me, What Janet had seen me do was deliberately maneuver around the woman so I could speak to the ear the kid *wasn't* sleeping next to, lean in, and quietly answer her question. I hadn't even thought about it. Practicing something over and over again really could make doing it automatic.

Walt Disney has often been quoted, especially to cast members, as having said that it takes people to make Disneyland what it is. Guests were part of that. Custodial cast members would deal with thousands of new people every day, and a few familiar faces.

Chapter 12

We Have Character

Who were the people who made Disneyland Custodial what it is?

Introduction

As with any workplace, especially with so many employees, there were people who were funny, a little "off", brilliant, annoying, high-strung, dull, or very odd. We witnessed all sorts of behaviors in coworkers, and surprised ourselves by some of our own behaviors.

There were so many cast members with diversity of backgrounds, education, lifestyles, age, and people who'd grown up in different parts of the country or world. Some came to work at Disneyland just for a job and some came to be a part of the magic that Disneyland promoted.

Cleaning the Kingdom

Yes, ladies and gentlemen, boys and girls, the folks described in this chapter are some of the people who worked at Disneyland.

Some of them were wonderful.

Some of them were odd.

Some of them could have handled things better.

Casting had to choose from the people who applied. In booming economic times, an entry-level theme park operations job isn't going to be the first choice of many people, so during those times, there can be some bad apples or people who just weren't cut out for Disneyland Custodial. There was a time when we couldn't believe the new hires we were getting. The economy was humming, people had the choice of where to work, and the Disneyland Resort was desperate to fill positions, especially due to expansion.

Most of the Disneyland Custodial staff was great, but all it took was a handful of outliers to really make things interesting, especially if managers were reluctant to get rid of anyone. There were times I (Ken) would tell new hires that if they showed up for work fairly regularly and didn't steal anything, they could probably keep this job as long as they'd like.

Being a Custodial cast member, like being any cast member, meant we worked with enough people that, statistically speaking, it shouldn't have been surprising when we'd lose someone to cancer, or a car accident, or even a murder, but it still hurt like crazy when it happened, and it is why certain sections of this chapter were not easy to write and may not be easy to read. As we were putting this book together, a Sweeper, Joey, was killed by a car while walking to work; another Custodial cast member, Christopher, died when his motorcycle crashed on the way to work; and someone we used to work with in the 1990s, Glenn, was crossing a street with his family after a Christmas event at church when his wife and his six year-old son were killed by a horrifically errant driver.

Cleaning the Kingdom

We were not immune to the tragedies of life, but we were also partakers of the joys of life as well. *That's life.*

We Were a Social Network

Most of us liked to talk. It was one of the reasons we were hired. I used to say that, before mobile phones, a couple of sweepers could share a peck in the Skyway restroom stock closet and five minutes later the person sweeping Critter Country would know about it.

Sweepers gained a reputation as flirts and players. We were certainly gossips. Of course this also meant that some sweepers seemed like mortal enemies.

When we were Leads, there were people we didn't look forward to having on our crew, but never felt like we didn't want to work alongside someone when we weren't Lead. We never felt like we had to avoid someone or couldn't stand to be around them. It's just a personality thing. As long as there were days I (Ken) could take a break where I could get away from everyone and read, I could work alongside anyone.

Making it Past the Filter

Disneyland, at least for Custodial and other Operations roles, had various levels of employment. There was:

Casual-Temporary or Casual-Seasonal (CT or CS) - This meant people were hired for the Summer, Holiday, or Spring Break season and were not accruing seniority or benefits. Ideally, they would perform well enough to be brought back for the next season, but Disneyland could simply not bring them back without giving any reason.

Casual Regular (CR) - After the end of the season, a CT or CS could apply to become a Casual Regular, which meant they would be "permanent" employees after passing a probation period of a few months. Ideally for Custodial, there'd be more people applying to be CR than available slots. They'd start accruing seniority and get certain benefits. Back then, they were expected to be available full-time for the on-seasons (Summer, Holidays, Spring Break), all day both weekend days, after a certain time in the evening on Fridays, and any holidays such as Monday holidays.

Regular Part-Time ("B") - This was the next step up, and these cast members were expected to be available any day of the year, and most of them in Custodial worked full-time year-round - don't like the words "part-time" fool you. Again, ideally for Custodial, there would be more people wanting to turn B than openings.

Regular Full-Time ("A") - This was the highest designation, the people with the most seniority.

Ideally, the bad apples wouldn't make it past the Casual Temporary status. However, there were times when things were so desperate people were being brought on directly as CRs, and kept past their probationary periods despite warnings from Leads and other rank-and-file sweepers that the people were lousy workers.

When I (Ken) hired in, people were around at least two years before they made Foreman. During our stressed times, however, people were getting their radios in as little as *three months*.

One man applied to Disneyland hoping to get a Management position. When he was told there were no openings at that time, he said he'd take whatever he could get and wait for an opening. So, naturally, they stuck him in Custodial. He was a good, reliable sweeper. He was one of those guys handed a radio very quickly, and he did make it to management. Some people grumbled about how quickly that happened, but I looked at it this way: better to have someone in management who worked in the trenches for a while than someone brought in from the outside with no experience as an hourly.

Cleaning the Kingdom

Unbelievable

One person I (Lynn) had working in my area with me now and then was this woman who had red frizzy hair that she'd sometimes put into cornrows. She claimed she had a car with a fish aquarium in it. No not just in it, but *built into* her car. She was not just playing around or trying to be funny, she was serious.

I asked "You're kidding right?"

She was serious, and very excited about it.

Another time this same person told me she had a horse, but lived in Garden Grove. If you're not familiar with Garden Grove, it isn't exactly equestrian territory.

I thought, *OK, I guess that could maybe be true.*

Then she told me she'd ride it to work. Yes, she was serious about this. She said she parked the horse at the Katella Cast Member parking lot (KCML).

I told her I'd never seen a horse in that parking lot.

She continued to insist she parked her horse there. I should have asked if I could see this horse, but I knew she couldn't be serious, but in her mind she was, as far as I could tell.

She also told me she was friends with Michael Jackson. This was back when he was still alive. After hearing the other stories she told, I caught on that she was going to say things that weren't true, and keep elaborating on them..

She managed to get banned from cleaning the Club 33 restrooms. She asked a high-up manager about their sexual orientation. She asked this as she was cleaning the restroom in there. Of course, this got back to our management and they realized they needed to keep her from working in Club 33 again.

We tend to think she wasn't trying to be funny and wasn't intentionally lying, but rather had a disorder.

Cleaning the Kingdom

The Rebel

One day while I (Lynn) was the lead in Tomorrowland, I had assigned a man to trash for the day. As we have explained, when doing trash we often push a 3-, 6-, or 8-liner cart through the area to dump the trash, then we'd push the cart back to the packer to empty each liner into it. Once we were done doing that, we'd rinse them out with water.

Well the packer for Tomorrowland, the place we'd dump the trash and wash out the liners, was right behind the gate in between Innoventions and Redd Rockett's Pizza Port. Just as this sweeper who was dumping trash brought back his liner cart, there was a CFA run, meaning nurses from First Aid were responding to someone who needed help; a potential medical emergency for a guest or cast member. These were, unfortunately, somewhat frequent given that scores of thousands of people were there. From heart attacks, to trip & falls, to fainting - people have health troubles at Disneyland just like anywhere else.

This particular time was not a life threatening emergency, but it still required CFA to respond. There are different ways to access different areas within the park faster. In this instance, going from CFA, which was on the south side of Plaza Inn Restaurant, to the person who needed help brought the response past our packer. As often is the case, Security cast members escorted the nurses to the scene.

A security officer parked his small SUV-type vehicle right in front of our packer. This particular sweeper who was on my crew got upset because parking the vehicle there impeded his work, so he got the water hose and sprayed the Security vehicle with water ...while the windows were rolled down.

I did not witness this, but was told later. He did end up in our Custodial office with Security, but wasn't fired. I think suspended, but I did have to write a statement although I did not witness the actual behavior. He was a generally nice guy.

Cleaning the Kingdom

(I, Ken, say he might have been a nice guy most of the time, but he had a short fuse and I would not have been the least bit surprised if I'd seen him on the news for shooting a place up. But back to Lynn...)

This same sweeper once found some cash and decided, rather than taking it to Lost & Found, that he'd stick it in the fingers of Walt Disney, as depicted in the Partners statue in the Hub.

Cave of Wonders

I (Lynn) was doing a shift as a Restroom Lead and a Custodial manager asked me to help him find a valve to shut off water to a restroom at Aladdin's Oasis. This was the venue that was between the Enchanted Tiki Room and the Jungle Cruise, in Adventureland. With most restrooms, the valves were easy to find, but not with some of the smaller restrooms. I didn't know where the valve was either, but we'd help our managers unless there was a darn good reason not to, and since he wanted me along to help, I did.

We searched in areas backstage behind where boat storage was for the Jungle Cruise, then we came to a staircase, neither one of us was familiar with yet.

At the last second, I realized where it went to: that was the Lion's Mouth at Aladdin's Oasis, where, by this time, storytelling aimed at younger kids was being performed. I warned my manager that we may not want to continue because we might interrupt a show.

He decided I was mistaken.

So, we emerged from the mouth of the lion right into the middle of the show. He walked right out onto the stage. Guests gave him funny looks. He waved and walked off. I thought it was hilarious because he had a suit on, and was not themed to the show whatsoever, but the performers tried to improvise by saying "Hello!"

Cleaning the Kingdom

Don't Make Me Mad as a Hatter

As Fantasyland Lead, I (Lynn) took a new sweeper out to area to show him what his portion of the area would be. After a brief description, and pointing out where the nearest restrooms for guests were, because that is the main question we get asked, I left him to work.

About 45 minutes later, I went to see how he was doing, and found him inside the fenced off area for the Tea Cups. The attraction was loading, but almost ready to go again. I looked closer and he was on his phone (a no-no) and leaning against a railing (another no-no).

The Attractions cast member asked if I was the Lead and told me she'd already asked him to get out of the way so they could start the attraction, but he told her to hang on!

I walked over to him and said, "You need to get off your phone now, and get out of this area".

He told *me* to hang on!

I then called a manager, but by the time the manager arrived, the crew member had left and went back to his job... sort of.

That day was his last as a cast member, and I had to write a statement. In some cases, it could take many write-ups and warnings before getting fired, but I think he either had some documented problems already, or his conversation with the manager didn't go well. Either way he was not a cast member any longer.

Sweeping Lines or Speaking Lines?

As Leads, we had the authority to assign out allotted crew members for the day as we saw fit. We'd generally try to give people the assignments they'd prefer, with respect to their strengths and weaknesses and seniority. We liked to make our crew happy, but our higher priority was the guest experience.

Cleaning the Kingdom

Sometimes we'd put someone on an assignment for their shift and they were not happy about it. I (Lynn) would always try to help with their requests, but many times their shift would fit the assignment, or I would want them in a certain section or on an assignment for a reason, such as their needed extra supervision or they have abilities that were best suited to that assignment. For example, stronger, more agile people were more effective at trash dumping than others. Someone who had an especially friendly and patient personality and good dexterity would be great at sweeping lines.

If someone was not happy with their assignment, they might just leave through CFA, claiming illness, provided they could afford to do so, but that was an extreme tactic. A more common tactic was simply to stiff as much as they could.

There was one guy, who I (Lynn) believe is still there as we write this, and he didn't like to sweep lines. While it wasn't a popular task with a lot of sweepers, I suspected his reason for him wanting an area and certain areas in particular was because he wanted to flirt with the female cast members in the stores. Yes, a lot of sweepers were quite the flirts, but the good ones did it while also keeping their areas spotless.

This guy's shift was always a shift perfect for Lines assignment, plus I knew if I put him in an area he would be slow, and not working as much as he should. I didn't want to have to constantly keep checking on him like a babysitter. He would get upset at me when I put him on Lines or Trash. I would have to go to management because he would refuse or if he did agree to sweep the lines he would not do a good job at them, on purpose, I assumed.

I even had another cast member threaten me, and got in my face because I put him on lines. I didn't understand some cast members didn't like sweeping lines. Ken and I both enjoyed them. One reason might have been that, by this time, unlike when Ken started, sweepers were held accountable on Lines more than simply by the visual check; by this time, the Lines assignment had a sheet of paper to fill out to document what they swept, the starting time, and the ending time. Of course they could've lied, but I do think some thought of it as a punishment. I actually thought there was some trust there, because it is harder to directly observe or to find within a few minutes someone sweeping lines, other than if they're standing in a shop or at a vending cart flirting.

The Boogie Man

There was a sweeper I (Lynn) had working for me often and he had a slight mental disability, but a super nice guy who I enjoyed on my crew. He enjoyed cleaning lines in New Orleans/Critter Country. I'm not making fun of his disability, but mentioning it helps paint this picture. It was during the second Holiday season with Holiday Haunted Mansion, which is when the Haunted Mansion gets redecorated and themed to the movie "The Nightmare Before Christmas". The year this happened, it was the debut of Oogie Boogie at the end of the attraction. This sweeper came up to me and asked if he could be taken off Lines because the Oogie Boogie guy scared him. Of course I did take him off Lines, but I pointed out to him that he couldn't see Oogie Boogie unless he rode the attraction, but a part of his mind he thought this character might come out after him. He was a nice guy and hardly ever complained - that is, unless you woke him up from a nap while he was on break.

By the way, sleeping during your shift, even on your break, was officially grounds for termination. With some people we let it slide, but in other cases it gave us the justification we needed to get rid of a bad apple.

What Do You Say to Your President?

Sweepers were notorious for being quick with a quip.
One night when Cynthia Harriss was President of the Resort, she and some friends were coming downstairs from Club 33. A Custodial cast member was also coming down the

stairs back into the New Orleans area. Cynthia said "Thank you for keeping the park clean, have a good evening, and good to see you".

The cast member's response was, "It is good to be seen."

One of Cynthia's friends looked back at the cast member and said "Hey good one".

The Horse

I (Ken) mention Harry Hemhauser a lot in this book. After my first day out of training in Vern Hoiland's area (which at the time was Small World/Matterhorn), I was right into Harry's area the next day, and that was my regular Summer season shift in 1990. It was 11:00 a.m. to 7:30 p.m. Harry's area was New Orleans/Critter County. I got an earlier shift in NO/CC the next Summer under Harry, and then the A Leads rotated and Harry was my Summer Opening Lead for every Summer right through 1996 in Adventure/Frontier. Harry would say he raised me from an embryo, complete with a tiny little pan & broom. I would counter that he'd planted the seed which became the petrified tree himself.

Harry was the longest continuously employed sweeper until he retired, which was after I left. He disliked being introduced to people that way because he was sensitive to what people thought of someone who would make a career out of sweeping. The way he told it, though, it used to be a middle class living, but with changes to Orange County and the country in general, and labor contracts at Disneyland, it wouldn't be that way for those who came after.

Earlier in Harry's sweeping days, his attempts at flirting with the ladies working in other Departments and getting a date were getting nowhere. Then he found out that oh-so-helpful (and false) word had spread that Harry was employed at the park under a prison release program.

Harry was into his second marriage when I worked with him, so he obviously overcame the reputation. He adapted that idea to use when anyone would tease him for being an older guy working as a Disneyland Sweeper. He'd sigh and say, "It's the only job I could get when I got out prison."

"You were in prison?" would be the response, usually from some young punk. "What for?"

Harry would grin and say, "Manslaughter. But I'll swear to my dying day those kids deserved every minute of it." I stole that one.

We'd used to find baby bottle nipples as we swept our areas, and Harry told me he'd once glued two of them to the female figure on the front of the Columbia and that they stayed there for days. I'm not sure I buy that one, but a story that was more believable was that before he was employed as a Disneyland Custodial cast member, he worked for Carnation at Plaza Gardens and that he got fired for frying a grasshopper or cricket and sticking it on a guest's burger.

"He said he wanted everything on his burger," was Harry's explanation.

Vern Hoiland

Vern is retired and we've interviewed Vern on our podcast. He was my (Ken's) Lead on my first shift out of training, and he was the person who told me not to look down at my feet, but to look forward, and any litter would catch my eye. It was great advice. He was another he might have been second to Harry in seniority.

For some time in the 1980s, Vern was promoted to being a Supervisor (salaried) but he reverted back to his Lead shifts as an hourly, which paid more when all was said and done.

The Snowman

This guy, another senior "A" Lead, was quite the storyteller. It didn't matter if we'd known him for years or he

Cleaning the Kingdom

had just met us, he'd have an entertaining story to tell and whether or not it was true, it was captivating. He often carried around pictures (actual wallet pictures... things we used to have before smart phones) that would correspond to his tale. He'd tell you some of his stories, but then you'd know too much. Some of those stories involved opponents in war.

It must have been an experience being with him in a battle.

Equal Pay For Equal Work

The details of who was getting what hourly rate could get complicated. It was all supposed to be based on hire date, seniority, and whatever premiums applied to particular assignments and shifts. A woman we worked with discovered that other sweepers who were supposed to have the same pay rate as her were somehow receiving a few more cents per hour than her. We never heard if there was anyone other than her who was left out. Since it was figured out that she was not being shortchanged, but that others were being overpaid, she was told that if she brought the matter to the attention to those who could correct the discrepancy, she would not get the increased pay rate. Rather, everyone who was getting the slightly higher rate would be knocked down to the lower rate.

She went ahead and made noise anyway.

Sure enough, her pay rate stayed the same and the other sweepers had their pray rate lowered accordingly.

Right or wrong, how popular do you think she was after doing that?

Sexual Harassment is a Serious Matter

I (Ken) attended sexual harassment training in the old Custodial Central conference room. A feisty woman, Sue Ellen, who was into the grandmother level of life, was part of the same

305

Cleaning the Kingdom

training session and before we even got in there she was
cracking jokes.

She was the kind of woman you wouldn't harass, not
because she would have turned you into Human Resources, but
because she would have cut you down to size so quickly you
wouldn't know what hit you. Her attitude on the matter was
"Bring it on!"

The instructor for the training brought along a coworker
because she heard we could be difficult.

When she informed us that we weren't allowed to
engage in sex at work, she reminded us that there were cameras
in many places that we might not even realized (fat chance - we
scrutinized every inch of that place) and that the people in her
Department had to watch those videos.

My hand shot up.

She gave me a nod.

With a straight face, I asked, "Are there any openings in
your Department?"

That was NOT my last day.

One of the important things I learned in that training
was that I had to report sexual harassment even if it didn't
involve people in Custodial

I'm sure glad I didn't have that training session earlier.

Why? Well, because while I was working in
Frontierland, I'd chat with this friendly Ride Operator who
reminded me of Suzanne Somers' character from "Three's
Company" (Look it up, youngsters.) She was frequently kept at
the initial height check at the entrance to the Big Thunder
Mountain line, away from actually operating the attraction. She
confided in me that one of her Supervisors was asking her out
and it was making her uncomfortable and she didn't want to go
out with him but wasn't sure what to do.

I gave the best advice I had. I told her he'd keep
persisting unless she was direct, blunt, and made it clear she
was not going to go out with him. Being "too busy" or evasive or

trying to hint was not going to work.
She was thankful for my advice.
She went out with him.
She married him.
Last I saw them, they'd had two kids together.
And to think, if I had already had that training, I would have reported that guy before they'd ever had their first date.

A Minor Problem

Disneyland used to have many other companies with employees working at Disneyland, and those companies had their own hiring practices. As for Disneyland itself, the minimum age to be a cast member fluctuated. Sometimes applicants had to be 18 to be considered, sometimes 16 and 17 year-olds could work for Disney.

I (Ken) not long after turning 17.

In Custodial, when I started, our schedules were printed on paper and posted by day. The whole week was displayed on the wall. For example, you could look at the Monday sheet at the Main Street part and see what names were in which slots. You could hunt for your name, and if you found it, you could see who else would be working in that area. It was easy for me to find my name because minors had their names in brackets, (like this).

I was in my family home, enjoying a summer day.

And then a call came in to the house. It was Dispatch, They wanted to know where I was. I thought I had the day off. I hadn't seen my name on the schedule. They were expecting me. They asked me if I wanted to come in late. I thought about it for a moment. I was sitting in South Pasadena. That was about a 45-minute drive to Disneyland, if there was no traffic. With traffic, it was about, oh, 60 hours or so. And that was just the drive.

So that was the one and only time I got a "No Show".

I couldn't figure out how I had missed my name on the schedule. I figured I hadn't looked hard because it had been seven days or so since I'd had a day off. The schedules worked, for the most part, on calendar weeks. So, technically, someone could have Sunday and Monday off one week, work Monday-Saturday, and then work Sunday through Thursday the new week, and thus work ten days straight, and not get overtime.

Sometime after that, the morning Lead in my area asked me if I wanted to extend my shift and work overtime. I agreed. The closing lead came on and realized I was too young to legally work overtime, and sent me home. Why had I been offered OT in the first place?

Finally, on my first New Year's Eve, I was scheduled a late shift. The park was open until 2:00 a.m., so we could work quite late. Except... I was still a minor, and the Supervisors realized this, and I wasn't allowed to work past 12:30 a.m. So I ended up having a short shift and my walking time was 12:15 a.m. I had to work just late enough to work through the countdown and fireworks to welcome the New Year, and then I was free to drive home with all the drunks on the road, and the ones who weren't drunk and in cars on the road.

I finally realized why I had No Showed, why I had been wrongly offered overtime, and why I had been scheduled for a shift that was too late: The brackets had, for some reason, disappeared from my name on the schedules, and I hadn't noticed.

On Point

There was a longtime sweeper named Ed who was so reliable you could set your watch to him. He worked the same area for all of his shifts, took his breaks at the same time, and wouldn't take extra time on his breaks. Trying to get him to deviate from this was asking for trouble. I was backstage taking a break at the Area Locker one day when I heard Ed telling Vern Hoiland to leave him alone.

I asked Vern, "What did you do to him?"

Vern said all he did was ask Ed how he was doing, and

Ed didn't like that.

I got along just fine with Ed, because he was so dependable and I didn't try to interact with him any more than he initiated. One time, I was surprised when he asked me about a book I was reading on break. I told him that if I could make a living reading books, that would be a great career.

He replied, "Well, you could always be a critic."

That's about as much as we ever spoke to each other. When I was his Lead, I'd give him the area he wanted (Adventure, in those years) and the breaks he wanted. I knew what they were, wrote them on the schedule, and that was that. He did his job and never caused me any trouble. The one accommodation is that he did not adjust his coverage per the crowds. The boundaries of his coverage of Adventure did not change.

I (Lynn) also got along with Ed, he was a nice guy, did what you asked of him most or the time and he was always in the area when he was supposed to be. He didn't talk too much, but one day he asked me, "Where did we get all of these idiots on our crew?" I replied with "I have no idea."

We heard Ed had a Ph.D. People might scoff at the idea of a Custodian having an advanced degree, but he wouldn't have been the only one. Most people would be surprised at the educational backgrounds of some sweepers as well as their financial assets, in part because, sometimes, people took the job because of layoffs after many years in their chosen professions, and they ended up staying on board at Disneyland.

Ed used to be more communicative and was a Lead at one point. My favorite story about him was that he was showing a new hire his area on Main Street when a manager (probably from another department) interjected that it looked bad for them to be "just standing there together talking". Ed turned to the manager and said, in his firm, deep voice, "If you'll pardon me, this fellow is new. I need to show him his area. In a moment I'll be done, and then we can all go along our merry [EXPLETIVE DELETED] way!"

Eventually, Ed appeared to be suffering some physical condition that was making it increasingly difficult for him to sweep, and so his days of sweeping Adventureland came to an end.

Being a Sweeper was a job that made certain demands on us physically, mentally, and emotionally. The onset or progression of certain diseases or conditions found in the general population could limit or remove a person's ability to continue to carry the pan & broom, literally and figuratively. It would be nice if everyone could retire on their own terms, at a time of their choosing, and do so with sound mind and body, but life is such that some of our brothers and sisters of the jani knights didn't end their sweeping days that way.

The Incredibly Shrinking Man

Ron was an older guy and morbidly obese. We couldn't believe we were saddled with this guy, who couldn't possibly be up to snuff physically. There were times he was taken away by paramedics.

Still, he was friendly.

Ron got surgery and slimmed down. He became one of our best workers, and he was also able to take on another job going around selling people on the same weight loss surgery he'd undergone.

Brian

A man by the name of Brian taught me a lot about people with intellectual disabilities. He'd been active in the Special Olympics, and his mother had apparently done a lot of work for the organization. As a result, he had pictures of himself with various celebrities that he'd show us. Physically, he looked no different than anyone else. He was friendly and did his job well.

Cleaning the Kingdom

It was interesting to see how his mind worked. He would start conversations with us and would continue the same conversation throughout the day, so if we hadn't seen each other for an hour, he'd pick up where we'd left off. It sometimes took me a moment to remember where we'd been in the conversation.

He was good at silent segues or connections. For example, one holiday season I asked him if he was taking any days off. He told me "No, my brother's in town." It took me a bit of thinking to remember that he didn't get along well with his brother, and so he was working as much as he could so as to be around his brother as little as possible. Brian confirmed I got it right. He also had a great sense of humor.

Which Twin Was I - The Evil One or the Good One?

In the next chapter, we'll address a favorite pastime by some of us, which was doing impersonations.

There was one person I (Ken) "impersonated" without even trying. He'd been a Busser and then a manager. John bordered on being a salaried assistant manager and hourly a couple of times. I thought it was kind of a raw deal for him to be bounced back and forth. Finally, he got solid footing as a manager and hit his stride.

We were both white guys with glasses and thick brown hair, in a similar style and I guess there must have been other similarities, too.

Before I realized that people were mistaking us for each other, I was getting confused as people were attempting to continue conversations with me that they'd started with him. It was very strange when someone approached me and started talking about something as if I knew exactly what they were talking about when I had no clue what they were referencing, and they clearly expected me to know.

Cleaning the Kingdom

A less disconcerting result of the mistaken identity was when someone would ask, "Weren't you just here wearing a tie?"

Finally we were both aware of what was going on, and we had a good laugh about it. There were times the managers and Leads on duty would have an outdoor, stand-up meeting in front of Custodial Central when it was behind Casa Mexicana, and the others present told us not to stand next to each other because it threw them off.

His Name Was Walt

Widening the Disney Look to allow for certain mustaches opened up employment as a Disneyland Cast Member to more people, which was the whole point.

Walter was a guy who not only had the same first name as Walt Disney, but the same mustache. His mustache, like his hair, was silver by the time he hired on with us. He enjoyed pointing out that he had the name and mustache of our great founder.

Sadly, Walter collapsed and died in front of his fellow sweepers while in the breakroom attached to the Storybookland Canal Boat storage. This happened shortly before we started to get AEDs placed around the park. I have no way of knowing if an AED could have saved Walter, but the timing sticks out in my mind.

His widow wrote a lovely, appreciated note to Custodial because he died in a place he liked to be, after being able to work there for a while and make magical memories for guests..

Eric

Over and over again, people said they'd remember his smile. Eric did have a great smile. Behind it, though, there must have been some pain. I'd never had any problems with him at all or noticed anything off. What I (Ken) had heard, and of course I wasn't there nor did I see any evidence one way or another, was that Eric and some other sweepers, including his Lead, were suspended and facing possible termination over the allegation that they were consuming alcohol backstage while they were on-duty. The allegation isn't important, other than to point out that it is not that anyone broke or stole anything, or harmed a guest. This is not to excuse what happened, if indeed it did happen. It would have been a violation of policy. In the wake of getting suspended, Eric took his own life. This hit us hard.

Something that stands out strongly in my memory was how management and our schedulers responded to this. Since Disneyland is open every day, Disneyland Custodial needs to be staffed every day. How would it be possible for the many Custodial cast members who wanted to attend services for Eric to do so? The answer came in giving people split shifts (practically unheard of for Sweeping), moving their shifts earlier or later, and having managers get into Custodial whites and do the sweeping themselves, including some managers who were not in Custodial. It was a remarkable gesture, and my respect for all of those managers rose even higher.

Helmuth

Helmuth was a longtime Sweeper whose father was a performer at the Indian Village in Disneyland, which was replaced by Bear Country (now it's Critter Country). Helmuth had a string of "No Shows", which was highly unusual, before Custodial was informed that he'd passed. From what I heard, it wasn't clear whether his death was accidental or intentional, but it appeared to be self-caused. Either way, he was too young to go.

The best story I have of Helmuth involves someone else being on his case and trying to bust him.

We had our own pans, with our names on them.

This person who was trying to bust Helmuth found Helmuth's pan & broom set aside backstage, with no Helmuth in sight, even though it wasn't time for his break. So this person stood by that pan & broom for a while, just waiting to lay into Helmuth when he returned from wherever he was goofing off. He waited. And waited. He was irritated at Helmuth for leaving his coverage area for so long, but satisfied that he'd finally caught Helmuth in the act.

Lo and behold, Helmuth came around the corner from the onstage area, sweeping with another pan & broom set, also with his name on that pan. He must have been pleased with himself for leaving that other set as a decoy, because it had worked like a charm.

A Brave Woman

Cancer is scary enough. Cancer plus pregnancy is a recipe for agony.

Soledad, who went by Christina, opted to put cancer treatments on hold and carry her pregnancy with her third child as long as it took to give the baby boy a healthy start in life. He was delivered early so as to allow her to resume fighting the cancer, but as much of a fighter as she was, it took her before the age of 30 in 2008.

Victims of Two Extremely Disturbing Murders

Is that fair enough warning?

U.S. Army Sergeant Maribel Ramos was 36 years old when she was murdered by her pathetic roommate who apparently wanted her but couldn't have her. Her body was found in May 2013. She'd served in Iraq and was about to get her degree from California State University, Fullerton, when she disappeared.

Cleaning the Kingdom

Maribel had worked with us at Disneyland Custodial years before.

The murderer was sentenced to fifteen-years-to-life.

Neal Williams worked on the DCA Custodial team. He and his wife had two sons, Devon and Ian. In August of 2007, his wife made a lousy attempt to cover up the fact that she callously smothered Devon (age 7) and Ian (age 3) as they slept in their beds and then brutally, viciously hacked Neal to death with a samurai sword, stabbing and slashing him over 90 times. She'd tried to frame Neal but didn't do a stellar job of planning or handling questions from law enforcement. Her defense attorney tried to throw Neal and her parents under the bus. The prosecution argued it was a planned murder with the motivation of her being free of her responsibilities and able to carry on with an old flame.

Neither of us worked with Neal, but those who did said he was nice, a hard worker, and respectful. He loved to read and was known to do so on his breaks. He lit up when he'd talk about his kids.

The murderer, someone one of Neal's coworkers said was the most evil person she knew, was sentenced to death.

Conclusion

It was painful to include some the things we did in this chapter. Although we worked in the Happiest Place on Earth, we were not immune to the sad things about life. It was the job of every Custodial cast member to put those things aside, keep a chin up, and help make magic for the guests.

We also had all of the office or workplace politics stuff found anywhere else (especially when it comes to punching a clock, schedules, hourly pay), but there were also things more specific to Disneyland. Rarely, there would be apples so bad, we were better off having a hole in the schedule than to have that person on our crew.

Cleaning the Kingdom

But there were also a lot of great people. There were hard workers and people with great personalities we could trade jokes with all day.

You just never know who that person is who is sweeping up popcorn.

Chapter 13

Whistle While You Work

So what did we do to keep ourselves entertained while cleaning the Kingdom?

Introduction

Well, sometimes, things were so busy we didn't need to do anything but try to keep up. See Chapter 10 to read more about that. Even on those busy days, we needed to lighten the mood from time to time. On slower days, it's how we kept each other from falling asleep.

When we'd spend 8-12 hours per day, 4-7 days per week cleaning and dealing with difficult guests and managers from other Departments, there were different things we'd do to keep ourselves entertained or blow off steam, and since Custodial could be a combination of a pseudo-paramilitary operation, office culture *a la* "Dilbert", and an entry-level service job full of students, layoff refugees, and retirees, it would get interesting.

Let's get something straight. There were many times when our jobs could be very difficult. There was much to get done while in Custodial, and it not only *seemed* like the work never stopped, it truly didn't because even when the park closed, it was going to be back open before too long. Some of us made time to have fun. It seems like most of the people who didn't, didn't last.

Some of our hijinks, pranks, and games were things that weren't expressly forbidden, at least not until someone later decided to order an end to them. Even if not clearly forbidden, they might not have been the kind of thing that was encouraged. Others may have violated written rules that were rarely enforced. And others didn't break the rules at all.

How does one handle a guy who, on a hot day, fills a liner with water and jumps in to cool off? Would anyone notice the bags of Sani Sorb Bits we tossed into the moving baskets of parts over the guests in the old Star Tours line? Nobody, except someone in a helicopter, was going to see the Custodian sunning himself on the roof of Mission to Mars, because there were walls all around him.

A lot of things changed over the years that made some of these things impossible to do. Things became more locked up, more monitored, more regulated.

A Disney University slogan for cast members was "We work while others play." But sometimes, we played, too. In a few ways we were officially encouraged to play. In recent years, sweepers have been known to do "broom art" using water and their broom to draw characters on park walkways. When the merchandise team starting coming up with a glut of different pins, Custodial cast members were encouraged to wear lanyards and trade pins, following a set of rules. Some sweepers were also set up with helmets and rollerblades for pre-parade work.

Some ways we'd amuse ourselves which didn't last long, like when one Custodial cast member decided throwing water balloons around backstage on hot summer days was a good idea. Some of the ideas were not only to entertain the sweepers, but to enhance guest interaction. Such was the case when some sweepers learned magic tricks they could do with items they carried in their sidepack. Kids and adults alike got a kick out of custodians taking a moment to entertain them with a trick.

When The Guests Are Away the Jani Will Play

In the early days of Disneyland up into the 1980s, Disneyland was not open every day of the year, as it is now. For example, there was a time when it was closed on Monday and Tuesdays. It made sense to do much of the maintenance and heavy cleaning on those days. Longtime Day Sweeping Foreman Vern Hoiland remembers hosing off the Castle and building fronts while on a manlift. Now, that is something Night Custodial does. With the park being open every day, and with generally increased attendance, it is more difficult than ever to keep the park clean. In the past, it was a regular thing for cast members to see the park without guests in the daytime, but during our time, that would be an extremely rare sight and it would look strange to us.

Having the park clear of guests and having daylight allowed not only for certain work tasks to be done, but allowed for some play, too. Vern recalls Custodial cast members would find time to have fun on these days by playing broom hockey on the Tomorrowland Terrace dance floor. They would find a ball, and use their own brooms, and they even had teams and competitions. It was a perfect area for this because the entrances to the dancefloor to stage left and right would be the goals.

Although we arrived on the scene long after Disneyland became a 365-day-per-year operation, I (Ken) got a little taste of what it was like with the guests all gone with Utility shifts, but they weren't really daylight shifts. In the traditionally slow seasons, meaning the times other than Summer, two weeks for Spring Break, two weeks for Christmas and New Year, and the week of Thanksgiving, when the park closed at 6 p.m. (which it often did Monday through Thursday, provided it wasn't a holiday) and there was no private party or Grad Nite, a crew of us would be brought on in the evenings to handle details, like cleaning lighting fixtures. All of the overnight activity wasn't happening yet, so not only were there no guests, there were few other cast members. This really allowed us to examine all of the details of the park without having to stop to handle some other responsibility, and since we were working with each other (whereas most of our normal routines involved working separately), the jokes and gossip could fly.

Onstage While Onstage

If the performers in Entertainment knew us and knew they could count on us, they might occasionally interact with us as part of their show. Bob Cobb, during his time as a Sweeper, had fun with the characters and was part of their little show one time. Bob was doing his normal sweeping routine and came upon the Mad Hatter and Alice. They were performing a small show for some guests. The character incorporated Bob into their show by having him tap tap sweep, tap tap sweep. This, when put together, would sound like the song "We will Rock You" by the rock group Queen. The characters got the guests involved and after it was over they received applause and Bob took a bow with the characters.

Resistance is Futile

After Ken quit but I (Lynn) was still around, there was a system that went into place for cast members in most operations departments and that was a clock-in system. Yes, we already had a clock-in system to clock in at the start of our shift and clock out at the end of the shift, and yes, we already had to check in at Custodial Central before starting our shift.

This system made it so we had to not only clock in at Harbor Point, then at Custodial Central, but also into this specific system. Then, for lunches, which were unpaid, we had to clock out and then back in.

I was talking to a friend who was a cast member with me at the time and he jokingly said that we should call the computer system Landru, a "Star Trek" reference. For those of you who don't know what Landru was, it was a machine that ruled a planet for thousands of years, controlling the attitude and behavior of people telepathically. There was, however, an underground resistance to Landru.

So we started to call our new system Landru. It caught on. I would even say over the radio "I'm going Code 7 [taking lunch] after I clock out of Landru."

The office would just respond by saying "10-4"

Eventually, a manager asked me what I was talking about I told him, he kind of laughed.

Then things got even more carried away.

My friend had stickers made up with an image of the guy who played Landru on the television series, and his name. We put these stickers near some of the computers. Some people would ask what it was and others just accepted it.

One day we found a clip of the Landru episode of "Star Trek" and put it on a DVD and played it on repeat in Custodial Central, displaying on overhead screens. I don't think the people in charge knew who was responsible for this, and it stayed on for almost two hours before someone took it out. It still cracks me up.

We figured instead of getting mad about this new system we would have fun with it. There was no harm. I am not sure if they still call that system Landru, but I am sure a few still remember him.

I Could Have Been Dipped For This

I (Lynn) was working in Toontown one summer, and some guest left a dirty diaper all rolled up on a bench. I put the diaper in my pan and walked backstage. When I got back there, I flipped the diaper out of my pan and hit it with my broom, and it got stuck in the hills of Toontown. So if you were standing on stage looking at Minnie's House it would be to the right of her house and on the big green hills. I didn't *try* to make it up there, but somehow I managed to do just that. When I went back onstage later, you could see the diaper from the guest areas. I think it stayed up there the rest of the summer too.

Working Toontown in the summer was tough. It was probably the hottest place in Disneyland Park, and can become very crowded on a busy day. There is a stock closet in the Post Office in downtown part of Toontown. On the outside of the door, it looks like the door would just be for show, but it is a working door to get access to an interior that is mostly used for Night Custodial to store their cleaning supplies. It was normally kept cool, because it also housed the electronics for the interactive play elements in that building. There was a ladder inside there and I was able climb to the second floor of that building and look out. It was a place for me to just step away from the crowds for a few minutes and cool down. I would also use some of the supplies, which could be convenient if I had a spill or needed something closer than going all the way back to our locker, which was back behind Minnie's House.

Cleaning the Kingdom

They Did Take A Dip

Tomorrowland went through changes during our time there. A good chunk of the land was overhauled in 1998, but before that, things could get slow there. The Carousel Theater was there, off-limits to guests since America Sings closed in 1988 (this is the building that would later become Innoventions). Mission to Mars likewise closed to guests, eventually, and the Space Place restaurant, which is, as of this writing, serving as seating for Pizza Port and a waiting area for Space Mountain, was also closed. Tomorrowland was also close to our clothes lockers.

Thus, Tomorrowland was a setting for much goofing off. Some sweepers who were on trash duty (emptying the trash cans in the area) in Tomorrowland would get their round done as fast as they could. Ideally, when people assigned to "trash" did that, they could then do some other tasks to help out before having to do another round. But these particular guys would take the Monorail over to the Disneyland Hotel and go swimming, then get back on a Monorail and back to work. This was before the Resort expansion when the Monorail pulled right up to the Hotel and the pool was nearby. They would use the towels left out by guests. I'm not sure if they ever got caught, but it was risky. It was an effective way to cool off in the summer, to be sure.

There was another sweeper known to go swimming and "fishing" in the Submarine Voyage lagoon, and this was while it was still an operating attraction, although he probably didn't do the deeds during operating hours. Sweepers usually shared their personal equipment lockers for their pans and brooms, and his locker mate would open the locker to find a prop fish.

Speaking of the Submarine Voyage and taking a dip...

Exploring every space was something some sweepers seemed determined to do. Usually, a sweeper, especially a Lead, could do this without getting caught or there being any trouble.

But every once in a while, something would go wrong. One such instance was when a Lead was working the Small World/ Matterhorn area and decided to go someplace he'd never gone before, which was on the catwalks inside the Submarine Voyage show building. Through a back door near where the parades would step off, he entered the show building, which had a low ceiling, and was filled with water under the catwalks.

The Submarine Voyage had been closed years before, and the attraction was left intact.

The Lead made his way along a catwalk, just a bit above the water. He came to a barrier that necessitated that he climb over to continue, which he did. Then he thought he should end the adventure and get back to his area. As he was climbing back over the barrier, he knocked his radio loose and it bounced off the catwalk and into the water, where it promptly and quickly sank!

The Lead returned with a long picker to try to retrieve the radio, but it was no use.

He had no practical option other than to tell the Assistant Manager on duty, meaning his Supervisor, what had happened. Saying he'd simply misplaced his radio would've made him look way too careless.

That is how that Lead got his only written reprimand. He wasn't fired, he wasn't ordered to pay, he didn't even "lose his radio" (lose standing as a Lead), although he had *literally* lost his radio. He must have had some goodwill built up, or something. But he realized that one of the problems with being where he was is that if he'd injured himself or something like an earthquake or terrorist attack had happened (this was post 9/11), he could have easily been trapped in there for a long time with nobody having any idea where we was.

Speaking of Radios

When we had Lead shifts, we had to carry a radio. Sometimes we wanted to have fun, or we were just plain tired of

Cleaning the Kingdom

the radio and some of the calls we would get, and that would influence how we used the radio.

I (Lynn) remember Ken and I were eating lunch together down at the Westside Diner (previously the D.E.C., previously The Pit), which was below New Orleans Square. Mind you, we announced over the radio when we were starting our unpaid lunch. I was New Orleans Lead that day and received a call from a manager that there was a banana peel near the train station. I said "10-4 ", figuring someone on my crew would take care of it.

The manager later called again saying that it was still there. He could have just bent over and picked it up himself.

I had called in my lunch, so he must have known, or maybe he forgot.

I finally had to leave from my lunch to run upstairs to get it, and of course by the time I got there, someone else had taken care of it.

And thus was born a running joke with Ken. We would say to each other on the radio "Hey, you have a banana peel over here".

I (Lynn) was Lead in New Orleans one day and I was short on people, because of crew members calling in sick. To try to help out the areas that are short on people, the managers would shift cast members around, and some people were "Undistributed" on the schedule so that they could be sent out as reinforcements. Well we had a cast member with the last name Head.

Can you tell where this is going?

The dispatch clerk called me on the radio and said "Lynn in about ten minutes you will be getting Head."

I laughed and said "10-4".

Playing around on the radio was a favorite, but we had to be careful because our radio channels were subject to FCC jurisdiction and if they were being abused, could be taken away. Officially, we were supposed to keep our transmissions on the Custodial Channel as terse as practical. If we had more than a

Cleaning the Kingdom

sentence to say, or thought we might be starting a dialogue, we'd either ask the person we radioed to switch to the chat channel along with us, or we'd simply ask them for a phone number or tell them the number they should call to reach us.

There were also times when someone would accidentally key their radio, sometimes for minutes, without knowing it. Perhaps they were leaning against something and it was holding down the button. We'd listen closely to see if anything juicy was said.

If we wanted to say something that we wanted everyone to hear except for one Lead in particular, we'd ask that Lead to switch to the chat channel (where they were expecting to "meet" us), and then we'd quickly tell everyone else what we wanted to say. That was a risky and rarely used tactic, though.

One Lead didn't have the best English. He probably knows more languages than the both of us combined, but his English wasn't the best. He could communicate, but sometimes it was hard to understand him. He was a great guy and friend, but we did get a kick out of how he'd pronounce things.

I (Lynn) was Men's West, which meant I was the Men's Restroom Lead on the Westside of the park, and this cast member was Men's East. Sometimes Men's East and West would meetup to discuss any changes or problems. I needed to meet up with him, and called him on the radio to ask him where he was. So I called and asked him "What is your twenty?" which means I was asking for his location.

His response was hilarious. He says, "I right here". As if that helped! What's more, he'd pronounce it as "I rye ear". Even when he'd give a location, he'd say "I rye ear by Plaza Inn." But he didn't even give a location this time.

I responded to his vague answer with "10-4. Where is 'right here'?"

His response? "Rye ear!"

I said "10-4. I will be right there". I had no idea where "right here" was, but that became the joking way to respond to someone when they asked where we were: "I rye ear."

Cleaning the Kingdom

Long before we were doing that, every once in a while Leads would radio each other and ask, "What's your twenty?" ("Where are you?") The other person would respond, and that was it.

About ten minutes later, the second person, who'd been standing around for those ten minutes, would radio to the first and ask, "Are you going to 87 [meet] me?"

To which the first person would respond, "No, I just wanted to know your twenty."

Other times, we'd give a location that no longer existed, like "87 me at the House of the Future." The other person knew full well the House of the Future was long gone; it was just a way of having fun.

Petra was a Lead who was the object of much radio fun, and I (Ken) think it started when she was one of the nighttime Parade Leads, which meant she was dealing with many other Leads throughout the evening. The official way to end a radio conversation was "10-4" or "Custodial Adventureland copies." If we were being informal, we might say "Thank you" or even "Thank you, Petra." With Petra, every Custodian with a radio would join in so that after one legitimately ended a conservation with "Thank you, Petra" the rest of us would all chime in one after another, with "Thank you, Petra.". So all you'd hear for two minutes was "Thank you, Petra" from different voices. I'm not sure why this started. Maybe it was because it would make Petra laugh, or because people thought she was cute. She once caught up to me when I was talking with a frequent guest who was a friend of mine and had once been a Westside ride operator himself. After we talked and she walked off, my Anglo buddy turned to me and he didn't even have to say anything. I recalled he had a thing for Latinas and I chuckled, realizing he had been hoping I would draw that conversation with Petra out as long as possible.

Something similar to the long string of "Thank you, Petra" transmissions would happen when someone would botch their radio call or ask a dumb question over the radio, or had just transmitted something embarrassing, unaware their radio had been keyed or said something we were very happy to hear (like "Can you please send Joe Stiff to the office." [probably to get disciplined]) We'd all chime in with a long succession:

"Adventureland copies."

"New Orleans copies."

"Red Leader copies."

When I was a closing Lead for that time period, it almost was like there was a comedy radio show taking place as I was going about my work. The trick was to not upset our managers, or Control, or the FCC.

There were certain actors, mostly lodged in our minds from 1980s television, whose names we'd try to slip in anywhere we could. The radio call "10-9" meant "Please repeat", but we found that saying "Ted Knight" worked, too. It was legitimate to call another Lead and ask them if they had a certain cast member in their area. Nobody seemed to catch it when I asked Ralph if he had Conrad Bain in his area. Ralph told me "Negative. He's hanging out with Willis." Whenever there was a sign-up sheet in the office, Conrad Bain was likely to write his name down. Look up "Diff'rent Strokes", kids.

Yes, it was silly and juvenile, but it was still a way to have fun.

When someone radioed us to clean up a drink spill, it was legitimate to ask if the drink had been a diet soda or not, because diet would not get sticky and thus was easier to clean up. Sometimes the guest who'd spilled the drink was still there and could tell the person who'd initiated the call what was in the cup. Other times, the reply might come back, "I don't know. I haven't been down to taste it." Due to these legitimate transmissions, we'd play around with other calls, too:

"Adventureland, you have an ice cream spill in the Aladdin's Oasis waiting area."

"10-4. What flavor?"

Cleaning the Kingdom

Flirting and the Sights to See

Sweepers often exercised their freedom of movement to check out an attractive guest for as long as they could, and of course, sweepers could start conversations under all sorts of pretexts, even just, "How are you enjoying your stay with us?" It wasn't just with guests, either. Sweepers were notorious flirts with cast members from the attractions, stores, restaurants, and yes, even the ones working at those mess-generating vending carts. Unsurprisingly, there were also some intradepartmental romances, too, and sometimes marriages resulted. There were many cast members married to other cast members.

While I (Ken) was all for a good romance, there were times Leads needed to pry someone on the crew away and get them back to work. If they were backstage, I could do it like this:

"Pardon me," I'd say as I approached "Joe" and the lady with whom he was talking. "Joe, your boyfriend called. He said you need to pick up some eggs and milk on your way home, OK? Sorry to interrupt, but I just had to tell you before I forgot."

There was an instance when I wanted to help a guy on my crew out, because he'd been doing a good job and it was his actual break, so I approached and said:

"Sorry to interrupt. Joe, I just wanted to let you know I thought what you did for that elderly lady was very sweet and kind. Thanks for going out of your way to help her. You're a good man, sir."

Joe didn't catch on. Confused, he simply asked, "Huh?"

The lady he was trying to pick up caught on to what I was attempting, and started to laugh. "He's trying to help you out," she told Joe.

The Art of Stiffing

There were folks who'd elevate stiffing to an art form.

If they needed an excuse to get backstage, they'd toss their pro towels in a can and then they "needed" more so they would go back to the Area Locker to do that.

"Needing" to use a restroom (which we did backstage) was a great excuse.

If someone wanted a longer time out of their area, they could intentionally spill something on their costume and they'd need to go get a costume change.

It wasn't hard to see if someone was standing around backstage *not* working, so stiffs might find a secluded place to hide.

There were probably many, many more tactics to stiffing, but we don't know them because we weren't stiffs.

Going Magellan

Exploring every inch of the property we could was often an adventure. As someone (Ken) who was interested in the physical aspects of the park both as an enthusiast and a student of theme park design, what might be of no interest to others could intensely fascinate me. Other than getting to see things we'd never seen before and go places we hadn't gone before, the goal was to never do anything that would hinder the Show at the moment or later. We were to do no harm.

I had scrutinized the technical drawings of Splash Mountain, ridden the attraction many hundreds of times, and had been evacuated off the attraction many times, but getting to explore the attraction at my own pace when it was closed for refurbishment was something I just had to do, and I was glad I did.

Vince Mitchell, myself, and a couple of other sweepers took advantage of the time after regular park hours ended and before Grad Nite started to put on some hard hats and explore the Matterhorn. I did (and do) have a phobia about "outside" heights. I seem to be fine in buildings and airplanes, but I'm not so good standing near a cliff. I knew I was going to be nervous at

Cleaning the Kingdom

the top of the Matterhorn but I was not going to pass up my chance to get there.

Up an elevator, up some stairs, and then to a ladder, we made it. We were at the top of the Matterhorn. Yes, I was nervous, but yes, it was a great view, and I'm glad we did that.

And yes, there was a basketball "half court" inside the attraction, if a hoop and a mark on the floor count as a half court.

Flipping Out

In break rooms throughout the Resort there were televisions. There was someone who put on soap operas every day in break room on the east side of Main Street. A friend of mine (Lynn's) got sick of it, so he brought a universal remote control from home and programmed it one day to that television.

We would be sitting in there on break while the soaps were on, and from under the table he would change the channel.

Some would look around to see how that happened, because everyone else was used to physically going to the television in order to change the channel.

Someone would get up and put it back to the soap opera.

Sometimes, he'd just be walking by the room and he'd change the channel without being in there.

Inside every grown man is a boy who likes to come out and play sometimes.

Pranked

I (Lynn) was Adventureland Lead, and after the park closed we were all out picking through flower beds for trash, and sweeping any remaining litter from the area. This short woman on the crew who was always joking around took the liner out of the metal trash can and then hid inside the trash can.

Someone else on the crew went over to that can to stick some trash inside.

The woman inside grabbed the other crew member's hand. The unsuspecting mark of the prank took a big jump back. The prankster emerged and ran off.

Jason was put in the middle of two of the most senior Leads, Vern and Harry. Vern told Jason to go to Harry's area to borrow a skyhook from him. When Jason reached Harry and asked to borrow a skyhook, Harry wanted to know who was requesting it. Jason told him it was Vern.

Harry angrily snapped that Vern could never borrow a skyhook from him again, not after bending the last one he borrowed. He sent Jason back to his own area, and therefore back to Vern.

Vern demanded to know why Jason had returned without a skyhook. When Jason told him what Harry had said, Vern was upset and demanded action. He marched Jason to Custodial Central to have the poor guy write a statement that was going to get Harry, the most senior of Sweepers, in trouble.

Mary, a senior manager for Custodial, looked over the statement and had Vern and Jason stay while she brought in Harry. She solemnly looked at the young man and the two seasoned veterans.

"This is very, very serious, gentlemen." She recounted the accusations contained in the statement - destruction of property, strife within the Department, disparaging comments flying back and forth. Jason didn't want to be there. Then she said Jason needed to fix one little detail. It was a small detail, but very important. He'd neglected to date the statement. She handed it back to Jason, who started to write the date:

April 1,...

And that's when Jason realized what was going on.

The statement was posted up in the office.

We don't stock skyhooks at Disneyland.

Cleaning the Kingdom

Pranks could be as simple as having the Stores cast members who embroidered hats put a couple of sweepers' names on some pro towels. Those two sweepers could then convince newer sweepers that they were supposed to get their own set of monogrammed pro towels, and there was something wrong if they hadn't.

There was also a prank that was best to play on Supervisors who were known to be high strung.

We used to mix some of the cleansers ourselves, from concentrate, into opaque spray bottles with squeeze triggers. There was a cage by Custodial Central with empty bottles, and there were containers of concentrated cleansers, and we were to follow the dilution instructions and put the right amount of water in the spray bottle and the right amount of the concentrated cleanser, and then, if it was a new bottle, write with a marker what was in the bottle and where it belonged (Tomorrowland, for example).

A Custodial cast member would approach a Supervisor with a bottle and say something like, "I don't think these are being mixed at the right ratio." After unscrewing the nozzle, the hourly would say, "I can tell by the taste", and would start chugging.

If played right, the Supervisor would start to freak out and urge the hourly to get to a restroom to vomit.

The prank was possible because some of those cleansers could look an awful lot like Kool Aid..

A Welcome to the Club

Speaking of pranks, I (Ken) had my first area Lead shift in Tomorrowland. It was typical of Leads to be nervous and frazzled during their first as such, especially if the park was busy. I was getting one call after another.

Then Men's East (Restrooms) called and asked me to 87 him by the restrooms back by the Autopia. I moved swiftly to meet him there, thinking there might have been something that needed to be swept up or a problem with someone on my crew. When I reached him, Eddie Ramos knew his work was done and he told me I'd fallen for what I had known was coming, but had slipped my mind in the hustle and bustle of covering Tomorrowland. I turned around and hurried back to the Tomorrowland Area Locker, which in those days was behind The Center, meaning it was between Space Mountain and Main Street.

Sure enough, as I slipped into the backstage area, I could see other Leads scattering in different directions.

They had completely emptied the Area Locker of all of its contents and hidden them. The spray bottles, the spray cans, the pushbrooms, the mop handles, the mop heads, the packages of pro towels, the bags of Sani Sorb Bits, the rolls of trash bags - it was all removed.

Instead of irritation, I felt a sense of acceptance. It was an initiation ritual that I had known about for years, and since I had been a cast member for six years before making Lead, I was glad to be so welcomed. I yelled my thanks to the fleeing pranksters.

This initiation ritual stopped being *carried* out when a certain someone who shall remain nameless, but whose surname sounded like a fast food company founder, expressed concern that it was going to happen to her.

Going to Breakfast

There were Closing Leads and a few others who got into the habit of following up their shifts that ended at 1:30 a.m. with a breakfast together at a Denny's across the street from the park. Thus, the night could carry on another couple of hours. I (Ken) think I joined in on that a grand total of one time, partly because I started seeing a Ride Operator who also worked closing shifts, and we'd go to the IHOP instead. Considering how many years I was a cast member, I dated very few cast members, and while my wife had been a cast member, that's not how we met.

Typically in the Summer season or any night the park closed at Midnight, 1:30 a.m. would be the end time for the latest Day Custodial shifts, which always included Leads. However, during the one and only season of Light Magic, the nighttime "streetacular" that replaced the Main Street Electrical Parade, the confetti cleanup would continue so late that some people we're working until at least 2:00 a.m.

The Best Cleanup Calls

Once in a while, someone would ask to clean up a conference room where some sort of meeting or party had taken place, and there would be leftover food or desserts. We were always happy to "clean" that up!

Wait Watchers

There was a lot to like about working mostly outdoors and getting to move around a lot.

When I (Ken) reached a point in my life where I decided I needed to lose weight but didn't think I had the time, money, or interest to join a gym or get workout equipment for my apartment, I decided I could find enough exercise voluntarily throughout my shifts. And you know what? It worked. By being very strict about what I ate and deciding to dress and move around in a way I thought would help me lose weight, I did. Did I need to move as much as I did to do my job effectively? No. But nor was I in any way neglecting my work.

Like so many others, I eventually put the weight back on, and then some!

Impersonations

Doing impersonations of fellow Custodial cast members and celebrities, or even impersonating a fellow jani impersonating a celebrity, became such a favorite activity for a while that I (Ken) had shifts where the majority of conversation I had with some of the other people on the crew was through impersonation.

I was praised for my impersonation skills, but nobody was better than Johnny D. He might have been the instigator of the whole thing in the first place. He was so good, I'd request his Ken Pellman impersonation and we'd have a good laugh over it.

Nobody was a better audience than a young man named Jeremiah. He'd make requests and then he'd laugh so hard at our performances, he'd literally beg for mercy. I told him I wanted to clone him and do a stand up act with an audience full of his clones.

Indiana Jones and the Sweeper of Doom

There's no other place I (Ken) would ham it up more than inside the Indiana Jones Adventure, which had an extensive, highly themed queue. There were three of us assigned to it during the day for our regular Summer 1996 shifts - Francisco and Connie were the two others. Two of us would be scheduled together while the third had his or her days off or worked somewhere else. The attraction had opened in March 1995 so it was still the big new "gotta do" thing for guests.

We described the responsibilities of this assignment in Chapter 7. One of the responsibilities involve backsweeping the line, which I enjoyed doing.

I would play along like I was cleaning the Temple of the Forbidden Eye, rather than sweeping through an attraction at a theme park. I used my putty knife to check the movement of the blocks forming the pillars as if I was concerned about them shifting., I told people I was looking for a snake that had gotten away (some people exiting told me they'd see it!) and, if I was in the room with the collapsing ceiling when someone triggered the effect, I would "push" the ceiling back up with my broom handle. I'd answer questions in-character, if possible.

We had a radio in Indy, so Custodial Central, Custodial Adventureland, or a manager could reach us, and so we could hear if the attraction went 101, because we might need to do a cleanup of hydraulic fluid. This allowed me extensive practice with the radio, which proved to be timely because later in that Summer season I was made Lead.

The Disney Gallery

When it was above the Pirates of the Caribbean entrance, the Disney Gallery straddled the Custodial areas of Adventure/Frontier and New Orleans/Critter County and was technically the responsibility of the latter. Whichever of those two areas I (Ken) was working, I'd still climb the steps of the Gallery to make sure everything was great there and see if I'd bump into any guests or Gallery cast members I knew.

It was one of the best places to hang out in Disneyland because of the people who were there, the artwork and merchandise, and the fact that it has been designed to be an apartment for the Disney family.

As of this writing, the space is occupied by the Dream Suite, which amounts to an exclusive hotel room.

The exhibits were often populated by things we couldn't find anywhere else - art director models for attractions, concept paintings, sculptures, etc.

Some of the merchandise sold there over the years was exclusive to the Gallery and just the kind of thing to make collectors open their wallets and gladly shell out hard earned cash.

Cast members staffing the Gallery were often friendly, experienced, and very knowledgeable about Disney artwork, history, and trivia. The atmosphere and these cast members, in turn, attracted guests who were enthusiasts of various things Disney.

I'd loved the Gallery from the moment I first walked in as a guest, so it was a nice place to sweep through as a cast member.

I imagined what it would have been like for Walt Disney to host parties there (he died before he could use the space), or to wake up in the morning and look outside to see the guests enjoying Tom Sawyer Island. Parts of the Swiss Family Robinson Treehouse were at the same level and nearby, and I could imagine Walt's face catching the attention of some kid as he glanced over while climbing the steps in the tree.

It would have been very easy for Walt to walk over to Club 33 from the apartment, or to walk downstairs and backstage to a car and head off to the studio in Burbank without being mobbed by guests.

The Disney Gallery also attracted a special kind of crowd, both cast member and guest. The Store Operations cast members who worked in the Gallery regularly were usually an excellent bunch.

One fellow won a slot in Walt Disney Imagineering's first Sorcerer's Apprentice talent search program and went to work for Imagineering. Julia Onder became a Disneyland Ambassador for the park's 40th Anniversary celebration. Beverly B. and Anne S. would often be working together - Beverly being a very experienced cast member who had seen a lot at the park, and Anne being a young lady whose status as unmarried attracted many a man to the register, trying to think of a good question to ask to start a conversation.

I also found a level of friendship with Bev C. (who would later staff the animation-themed shop in California Adventure) and Michelle E. If I recall correctly, Nathan E., who volunteered to DJ my wedding reception, used to work there, too. I even remember when Stacia Martin worked in the Gallery. Stacia was (and is) one of those people I thought of as the very model of a

Cleaning the Kingdom

Disney cast member. It was like she came right off of a Disney live-action movie screen (like "The Happiest Millionaire, if it had been released in the 1980s) and right into the park.

It was always nice to walk around the Gallery and take a look at the pieces, even if they were familiar and I'd seen them many times before, or check for new merchandise. Witnessing the reactions of other guests discovering the place for the first time was a real treat, and often would lead to fun conversations and new friendships.

I would work through the Gallery as often as I could. The bathrooms - not accessible to guests - needed to be checked, the trash needed to be emptied, the Gallery needed general sweeping from time to time, and there were the rare instances of something getting spilled or stuck on the floor. The steps needed to be mopped after a rain or if liquid was spilled on them.

Bev B. had worked in New Orleans Square stores since 1967. Having worked in the classic One of a Kind shop until switching to the Disney Gallery when it opened in 1987, she had been in places where she developed relationships with Disneyana collectors, Disney artists, and Imagineers.

Sometimes to the consternation of her fellow cast members and the benefit of the guests, Bev would become engrossed in conversations with some of her regular guests. And if guests were not in the room, she'd chat with the likes of me.

It was always great to take a moment to pass through the Gallery before descending the stairs back into the busy area.

What Is Real, What Isn't?

Guests weren't always sure what was real or natural and what was an Imagineering illusion or Entertainment performance.

If there was lightning visible in the distant sky, we could say to reacting guests, "It looks like real lightning, doesn't it?"

"It's Disney lightning?" they'd ask.

Wildlife

The cats of Disneyland have been getting more famous, and everyone knows the place has lot of ducks. There have also been possums, mice (duh!), rats, yetis, crawfish, turtles, birds of prey, crows, and many other birds.

Sure, the bird droppings could be a problem. I (Ken) used to wonder who was spilling paint in the area early in the morning, but then I realized it was from a bird of prey.

Watching the animals, especially watching the birds eat up spilled popcorn, was a nice diversion.

I would try to be nice to the animals whenever possible. One opportunity came when a mother duck was trying to get many very, very young ducklings from the decorative fountain by the train station in New Orleans Square to the Rivers of America, and it was a busy day. I managed to clear a path for them through the crowds and keep kids from chasing the ducklings. Finally, they made it to the raft dock and started jumping into the water.

Fun Ways of Working That Are No Longer Allowed

We used to not only ride around without seat belts, but we'd pack into the back of pickups and ride around the back area that way, especially if we were on an Events or Utility assignments. I (Ken) was sitting alone in the back of a pickup as we drove through the back of house.

Out of nowhere, I was airborne, a few feet above the bed. The truck stopped as I landed back in the bed. The driver called out to me to see if I was OK. The driver had forgotten, or had claimed to anyway, about the speed bump.

One of the things the Parade crew would do is clean back areas. Usually, this was done with pushbrooms and pan & brooms, but sometimes we'd break out the same large, industrial, gas-powered vacuums we used in post-parade cleanups. There was a road that barely fit in the space between the park and Harbor Boulevard, called Schumaker Road. It had a lot of leaves on it this particular day, and some litter, especially against the wall retaining the berm. To clean it, our Lead drove the pickup, another person was on the passenger side with a leafblower to blow the debris into the road, and we sat on the lowered gate of the pickup, dragging two vacuums behind the pickup. It was very effective. Our Lead was pleased and bought us soft drinks at the Inn Between.

This is yet another thing would get someone fired now.

Messing With Minds

Messing with the minds of new hires was a lot of fun.

If I (Ken) was at the Area Locker and anyone else from my crew was around, and Custodial trainees were being brought by, I'd tell my crew member, under my breath, to play along.

Then the shouting would begin. "YOU TOOK AN EXTRA FIVE MINUTES ON YOUR BREAK?!? THAT IS NOT ACCEPTABLE!!!"

"I'm sorry! I'm sorry! It won't happen again. Please forgive me," my crew member would plead.

"IT HAD BETTER NOT HAPPEN AGAIN, OR INTO THE PACKER YOU'LL GO!!!"

If a new hire was unfamiliar with the Area or with their assignment, the office would radio us to meet the person back at the Area Locker.

I'd take the opportunity to hide my name tag, and then I'd arrive at the Locker, looking around nervously.

"Hey, have you seen the Lead?" I'd ask the new hire.

"No," he or she would say.

"Have you ever worked with this guy before?"

"No," again.

"Aw, man, he's a real tough one. Really tough. Very mean. You'd better watch it with that guy." I'd go on and on describing myself as some power-hungry jerk.

The new hire might mumble something.

That's when I'd turn my back to them, make my name tag visible, and turn around to introduce myself.

Conclusion

On one hand, cleaning for your money sounds mundane or undesirable. But *what* and *where* were we cleaning? We were bringing a sparkle, a shine to magnificent works of art that were designed to delight millions of people, to bring them reassurance.

With many jobs, things are about as fun and enjoyable as you make them. The subculture of Disneyland Custodial, the larger culture of Disneyland Cast Memberhood, and the unparalleled setting in which we were working gave people with the right attitude virtually limitless possibilities to decide to enjoy their employment.

Chapter 14

Eyewitness to History

What was it like being a Disneyland Custodial Cast Member on some important dates in history?

Introduction

For thirty years now, Disneyland, with very few exceptions, has been scheduled to be open every single day. Election Day. Christmas Day. Even "Weird Al" Yankovic's birthday. And so, cast members have been on-property when

343

significant events have been happening in the world, both triumphal and tragic.

Then there have been special days in Disney history, too. While every day at Disneyland can be an exciting day, some are more exciting than others. And while Disneyland is the Happiest Place on Earth, there are days Earth is not such a happy place in general.

Before the proliferation of mobile phones and social media, Disneyland cast members were still connected to the outside word by landline telephones and many televisions spread throughout the backstage areas, and even more radios. Plus, Security kept in contact with City of Anaheim authorities. Word about anything significant would spread through the cast like a wildfire spreads through the foothills during Santa Ana winds.

9-11-2001

The most significant event from an American perspective that has happened in our generation (so far, anyway) happened on September 11, 2001. I think we all know what happened that morning, and don't need to explain, but for all of us we can remember where we were and what we were doing that day. I (Lynn) was supposed to be working Restrooms from 11 a.m. to 5 p.m.

As I watched from the comfort of my home all the tragic events unfold on television, many Day crew Custodians were already at work, like Vern Hoiland, who was a Lead on the Esplanade that day. As he watched the events unfold on a television in Custodial Central, surrounded by others, the word spread that it may be possible the West Coast could be targeted next. None of us knew the scope of this thing yet. The second airliner's impact cleared any doubt: this was a coordinated event, but how big was it going to be? Then, of course, word came about the Pentagon being hit, so this was not confined to New York. *What else will be hit?* we all wondered.

Cleaning the Kingdom

     Disneyland, being a popular, world-famous patriotic symbol of American culture and history would have to be a tempting target. Upper management decided to close all the Disney theme parks in the U.S. I (Lynn) was called by our office and given the option to come in to work or stay home with pay - a highly unusual offer. It isn't so unusual to be called and offered the day off *without pay* due to something like extreme weather, but to be proactively offered, on-the-spot, the choice to stay home and still get paid was remarkable.

     I decided to stay home. It was a tough day as an American, to witness all that we had that morning, and I wanted to be with my family.

     For some, going to work was their way of dealing with it. If I had gone in, I probably would have been assigned to Utility.

     Vern, being out in the Esplanade, witnessed Security shutting the gates to the Esplanade, which was an extremely rare sight, especially in daylight. Guests could not enter the Esplanade, and therefore Downtown Disney, from Harbor Boulevard. As such, Vern saw guests being turned away, some upset and others understanding the need for the parks to be closed. The hotel guests were able to stay and were taken care of. One of our fellow Sweepers by the name of Bill had been visiting the newly expanded Tokyo Disney Resort and was supposed to fly home that day, but was stuck in Japan.

     It was something at the time none of us could believe. We all felt very bad for the families that were directly affected by this horrible act, and we were hurt, upset, and confused because our country had been attacked. Disneyland was closed for the rest of that day.

     On September 12, 2001 Disneyland reopened, and it was a very slow day in the parks. DCA was only seven months old. That day I (Lynn) returned back to work, and it felt somber. We were told that if we needed to talk there would be counselors around backstage to talk, or if we just needed to step off stage for a moment, that was OK to do. We were also told to try to put on a happy face; that the show must still go on, and guests may be at Disneyland to escape the real world and the news, so we were to not talk about the incidents on stage unless asked by a guest.

That following Friday, Sept 14, 2001, there was a special ceremony in Town Square on Main Street. I (Lynn) was on Restrooms that day and had the Main Street restroom split. At 12 Noon I happened to be working in the City Hall restroom. I walked out on the porch area to watch the ceremony.

There was a full minute of silence.

It was one of the quietest times I had ever heard it at Disneyland.

All the music in the areas was turned off, all the attractions, and stores were shut down temporarily, and all the cast members were invited to the ceremony.

There were thousands of guests and cast members.

Then, we all sang God Bless America. There was not a dry eye around. It was one moment I will never forget and one I remember every time I go up on that porch at City Hall.

For one Sweeper, Bob Cobb, there was a deeper connection.

Bob worked for American Airlines as a mechanic full-time at LAX. Disneyland Custodial was his part-time job. On September 9, 2001, Bob was one of the mechanics who inspected what would be Flight 77. The planes were normally good for three days after a full inspection. Two days later, that plane was deliberately flown into the Pentagon in Washington D.C.

In the following weeks, Disneyland began extra security precautions.

As cast members entering the Katella Cast Member Parking Lot, we not only had to have our parking sticker on our car but show our ID as well. Then, getting on the shuttle, we had to show our ID. The shuttle used to drive right up to Harbor Pointe, which is where we'd walk through a security checkpoint to get backstage. After these events, the shuttles dropped us off on the Esplanade. Then, we'd enter Harbor Pointe by scanning our ID and showing a Security cast member.

For guests, temporary tents were set up outside in the Esplanade, a set of tents on the eastern side and some on the western side. Guests now had to open their purses, backpacks and more to get past these tents. Once through the tents, guests could go between DCA and Disneyland without going through bag checks again.

Many other precautions were undertaken after 9-11 at Disneyland Resort.

Disneyland History

We witnessed much Disney history during our years in Sweeping.

Gone Too Soon

I (Ken) was working on the evening of Sunday, April 3, 1994. Word spread among the cast that one of our corporate leaders had been killed in an accident. There weren't many more details than that, not even word about who exactly it was. For those of us who paid attention to the corporation as a whole, who cared about the future of the company, who wanted careers with the company and were investing in the company, there was the added concern beyond the basic human sympathy over a tragedy.

As it turned out, it was our President and Chief Operating Officer, Frank Wells, who for nearly ten years, had, along with Chairman & CEO Michael Eisner, transformed the corporation after helping to save it from corporate raiders.

It was a huge blow to the company, which had been on a roll with a renaissance in Feature Animation and new projects in the theme parks.

A memorial was held at corporate headquarters, the Walt Disney Studios in Burbank, but Disneyland cast members were invited to watch a live feed on a screen at the Opera House on Main Street (home of the Lincoln show). I watched there, and was glad I did. It was a moving ceremony.

Disney's California Adventure

Perhaps the biggest Disneyland event that took place during our time was the opening of Disney's California Adventure. This was the park built on the old Disneyland parking lot in front of Disneyland Park.

I (Lynn) remember when I was hired in,1998, cast members were already parking at the Katella Lot, then were shuttled in. Construction began in 1998, and October of that year a preview center was set up in what is now the Esplanade area. There was a big wall with windows to look in at the construction, and a tower with stairs you could climb to look over the construction area. The preview center had a temporary feel, being inside tents. It had concept art inside. Since we were to sweep through the preview center as part of covering that area, we got to see it over and over again if we worked there.

The anticipation was amazing, and the buzz was that this park would be better than Disneyland.

I remember that during this time, the Main Gate restrooms to the left of the Disneyland entrance were being refurbished, along with that whole building that housed lockers, and guest services, and a small shop. In the meantime there were temporary restrooms set up in what looked like double wide trailers in the Main Gate area. That lasted for maybe six to eight months.

The Resort was growing from one theme park and two acquired hotels to two theme parks, adding a Disney-designed hotel, and adding Downtown Disney to tie it all together.

We were given cast member preview tickets, and had to choose a day to go out of a series of available preview dates. My wife and I (Lynn) stayed at the Disneyland Hotel the night before our preview, just to make our first time visit to what we had thought would be this amazing park. This was about a week before opening to the public.

We were optimistic during our visit as we walked around this brand new park, but as the rainy day went on, it became more and more a of disappointment. Yes, there were some great things, but we felt they were outweighed by an attempt to keep the park relatively cheap to build.

The day before DCA was to open to the public, Disneyland closed early and guests were allowed to queue up in Disneyland overnight to be the first into DCA. I (Lynn) didn't work very late that night because I was due to open Tomorrowland that next day. I do remember the excitement as the guests were stationed around the Hub to stay the night.

I came in the next morning, February 8, at 5:00 a.m. The guests who had stayed that previous night were still there, as they had been all night while I had slept in my comfy warm bed. The guests looked tired

Later in the morning the guests were ushered out of Disneyland and into the Esplanade.

There was then a big opening ceremony, with many stars, and Disney Legends. I remember while working in Tomorrowland and hearing the fireworks, and watching it on Cast TV, which was a channel piped in to most breakroom televisions.

Although all the attention was focused on DCA, the projection was that not only would DCA get slammed with guests, Disneyland would also see huge crowds. Those predictions never came to be.

DCA did not see big crowds, and at Disneyland, it was a pretty slow day. We actually let cast members go home early if they chose to. It was a disappointment to many, and I think either word had got out from the previews that it was not as exciting as predicted, or guests wanted to stay away to avoid the crowds, since the previews had been crowded and large crowds had been predicted for the grand opening.

Cleaning the Kingdom

DCA certainly did have birth pains and growing pains, but has subsequently been reconfigured, renovated, and expanded with some great elements.

Golden Anniversary

Another event that happened while I (Lynn) was working at Disneyland was the 50th anniversary celebration of Disneyland's opening. This took place in 2005 and part of 2006.

In the years leading up to the celebration, Disneyland had been in bad shape. Some of the buildings needed attention, there had been a couple of tragic accidents, and some of the attractions needed some overdue maintenance. Even the Castle's colors were fading.

Matt Ouimet was brought in from being President of the Disney Cruise Lines to become President of Disneyland Resort. Along with him came Greg Emmer, who hired into Disneyland in 1968 and worked the Matterhorn Bobsleds, then went on into management, and before coming to Disneyland, was at Walt Disney World. He became the Vice President of Disneyland. Those two led a major restoration of Disneyland and sought to get cast member morale back up in time for the 50th Anniversary.

As the months got closer to the 50th, the park looked beautiful. There was a media day set aside to kick off the 50th celebration on May 4, 2005. Disneyland was closed for a special media preview event. Most of the event took place at night, but during the day we were cleaning everything we could. The place looked awesome.

The 50th celebration kicked off on May 5, 2005. With this celebration came many new offerings.

A new fireworks show called "Remember... Dreams Come True" was one of them. This was an amazing fireworks show that featured music or sound effects from every land in Disneyland, and the biggest display of fireworks we had seen at Disneyland

We also received a new parade: "Parade of Dreams".

All the opening day attractions had one ride vehicle painted gold.

We also received new name tags that were gold with the year we started at Disneyland printed on them.

There were many more offerings that went with this celebration, but on July 17, 2005 was the big ceremony. This day, a stage was set up in front of the Castle. Many stars, Disney Legends, dignitaries and more were on-hand for this huge celebration. I (Lynn) remember I was on parade crew that day, and as the event took place, we were set up, and prepared to cleanup after the event was over. We stood off to the right of the castle. Golden Mickey ears had been given out to guests that day and I (Lynn) remember seeing a sea of gold all the way down Main Street.

It was an amazing sight.

As soon as the event ended, we jumped in there to clean up. We started at the Hub and worked our way down Main Street to Town Square.

It was crazy; there were so many guests it was hard to move. I couldn't see if there was trash on the ground or not, but we managed to make our way through. I think we even went back up towards the Castle to do it twice.

That year was a busy year at the Resort and went off very well. It was fun and exciting to be there during this historical event.

40th Anniversary ...and Others

1995 was a big year for Disneyland. The Indiana Jones Adventure opened that year, and the 40th Anniversary was celebrated, including with a big ceremony at the Castle and a "Time Castle" being buried. I (Ken) strongly suspect the castle prop itself was not buried, even though that was the impression given, but the items themselves were probably placed in another container and buried. Maybe I'm wrong. Maybe the

351

castle was, indeed buried. I'll go in twenty years and see for myself.

I was there with thousands of other cast members as we took a group picture on Main Street. I am one of those dots in the crowd. We had fun doing that.

Later, I watched the ceremony at Sleeping Beauty Castle, where it was good to see various Disney VIPs. On days like that, if you knew who to look for and kept your eyes open, you'd see many Disney-famous people.

My wife and I were there ten years later as guests to celebrate the 50th Anniversary. We were put in a line that snaked through DCA before heading to towards Disneyland Park, with cast members lined up to welcome all of us.

I had made a point of being at the kickoff for the 35th Anniversary in January 1990, before I was a cast member. Then there were festivities on July 17, 1990, when I was a new hire. It's hard to believe the Resort is now celebrating its 60th Anniversary.

Conclusion

Life continued to happen as we worked our shifts at Disneyland, and some of it happened in front of us. Other things were happening elsewhere, but we could see it on television backstage, and even when it was horribly distressing, like when I (Ken) was watching the Columbine High School mass murder spree on television during my lunch, we still went back onstage and did what we could to give guests a clean, carefree, uplifting experience.

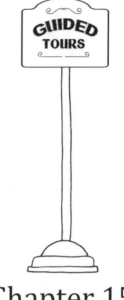

Chapter 15

Rubbing Elbows

Who might we see at Disneyland?

Introduction

Disneyland is a playground for all, including the rich & famous. Being about an hour away from Hollywood (well, about three-to-thirteen hours in traffic) means many household names from showbiz can drop in to the Happiest Place on Earth on a whim. Some come for work, such as taping a television special in the park or making an appearance at the Anaheim

Cleaning the Kingdom

Convention Center, and manage to slip away for some fun.

There was a night I (Ken) was sitting, as a guest, on the balcony in what was then the Disney Gallery (currently the Dream Suite) above Pirates of the Caribbean, overlooking the Rivers of America. I was waiting for Fantasy in the Sky fireworks, the long-running classic aerial pyrotechnics display, before the advent of Fantasmic!. After Fantasmic! premiered and became a huge success and that balcony become a high-demand spot, it would be turned into a premium viewing-and-dessert experience, and of course still later the Gallery was replaced with the Dream Suite. But this was a night back when it was first-come, first-serve FREE viewing of the fireworks. It was a more simple time.

I was sitting next to a man who was using a wheelchair and very obviously living with muscular dystrophy, and his friend who would push him, and the three of us were chatting as we passed the time waiting for the fireworks. It didn't take long in such situations for people to discern that I was a Disneyland enthusiast who also happened to be a cast member. These two men seemed especially interested in hearing about celebrities visiting Disneyland, as many people are, but more on that later.

A place like Disneyland always attracts people with a very wide diversity in their backgrounds, and some of those people happen to be celebrities. At Disneyland everyone is to be treated like they are special. "Every guest is a VIP." But sometimes, some are more special than others.

Celebrities were not automatically treated differently. If they attract a crowd, Security might step in to protect them. Many celebrities paid to be escorted by a Plaid, who would be a Guest Relations Cast Member, who were the ones who performed as Tour Guides. There was more than one reason to hire a Plaid. The Plaid could be the "bad guy" in keeping fans from harassing the celebrity, the Plaid could answer their questions and impart trivia, and the Plaid could get them past waiting areas where they might be mobbed or have to wait a long time for an attraction. Seeing a Plaid walking with people but not as in the typical Tour Guide role is a good tip-off that at least one person in the group is famous.

Some celebrities did what they can to enjoy Disneyland in the same manner as the average Joe. When a sweeper encountered Ron Howard waiting in line at It's a Small World, the sweeper told him there were ways he could avoid the wait. Howard's response, with his children in tow, as that he and his family shouldn't get to jump ahead of everyone else just because of what he did for a living.

Celebrities have been coming to Disneyland since the July 17, 1955 invitation-only televised "opening" of the park. Actually, they were probably there before that, too, for Walt & Lillian's wedding anniversary party and probably with Walt trying to get some to invest, open concessions, or purchase surrounding property. That televised show was hosted by Bob Cummings, Art Linkletter, and someone by the name of Ronald Reagan, and many celebrities were attending with their families, such as Frank Sinatra, Jerry Lewis, and Sammy Davis Jr. Disneyland was baptized with celebrities, and for many Americans, it had been born on television, and Walt Disney was a celebrity as a result.

Most celebrities visiting Disneyland just wanted to enjoy the place and, usually, have a good time with their family. Sometimes, we'd get an "official" heads up that they were going to be there, as it would be noted on Roll Call (information) sheets posted in Custodial Central. Other times, the only tip-off came from word of mouth, as this was before everyone was testing or using Twitter.

We were not to call attention to them. We were to treat them like any other guest - warmly and politely. Like any other cast members, sweepers were not to approach celebrities as fans or ask for an autograph or picture, but some cast members did it anyway. I (Ken) remember pulling aside someone on my crew after they'd obtained an autograph and told them it was not cool to do that. Some people are willing to risk a job doing janitorial work to get a signature from a celebrity they like. I understand that. For us, the authors of this book, the larger concern was making sure our guest, whether a celebrity or not, was having a great time. Like any other guest, we were to wait for them to approach us, or, if we saw they needed some help, we could approach them. Since many celebrities opted to pay for a Plaid to take them around the park, we saw many celebrities but interacted with few.

There were two times celebrities were guaranteed to be at Disneyland that happen every year. The Candlelight Ceremony, a beautiful annual holiday tradition, was performed on a Saturday and a Sunday in early December and celebrities were narrators, telling the story of the birth of Jesus Christ between performances of associated Christmas songs. The other time was for taping of holiday specials featuring parades and new attractions at Walt Disney World and Disneyland. Famous singers would record video performances that would be played on the holiday television specials as if they were live.

Then there have been events that happen less often, such as Disneyland anniversary events for milestone anniversaries. This was how I (Ken) saw people like Fess Parker (Davy Crockett himself!) and Randy Travis, who sang a birthday song to Disneyland.

Then there were events that only happened once or twice, like the Blast to the Past 1950s-themed overlay to the park, where I watched people like Chubby Checker perform live.

The rise of hand-held social networking and the TMZ/paparazzi business meant celebrity visits to Disneyland might become trending subjects before they've been there even a couple of hours. While I'm sure Disneyland enjoys the publicity, and sometimes the celebrities agree to pose for Disneyland photographers, others probably find it more difficult to simply enjoy a day at Disneyland.

Cleaning the Kingdom

Before They Were Famous

Many people who've worked in Disneyland Custodial have gone on professional positions elsewhere. We're all over the place.

One example of a Disneyland Custodian who made it is John Lasseter. Before he was a movie director at Pixar, before he worked for Disney Animation, before he was a Jungle Cruise skipper, he was helping to keep Disneyland clean. Now, he's a Chief Creative Officer for the Company. Not bad!

Not in His Pajamas

Some celebrities were well-known to be frequent visitors. Hugh Hefner had been. It might seem strange to some people that Hefner, who made his fortune on airbrush female nudity, would be fond of a place built on childlike innocence, but it made sense to me (Ken) as both Hefner and Disney were in the entertainment business and thrived on being a strong leading brand in their genres, and both sold fantasy.

I remember Hefner, when he was married to Kimberly Conrad, being escorted around the park by a Plaid. Their son was riding in a stroller. I couldn't help but think that the Plaid (Guest Relations cast members were generally very attractive) was thinking either "I can't believe I have to escort this pig around" or, conversely "Ooh, maybe he'll discover me?"

Once his marriage to Conrad was over, Hefner was visiting frequently with multiple platinum-haired women together, including those who became the stars of "The Girls Next Door". I've never been to the Playboy Mansion, but sometimes on television it is depicted almost like a decidedly adult take on theme park-style fantasy settings.

This is as good of a place as any to mention that we had a fellow Sweeper who was in culinary training. He ended up leaving Disneyland Custodial to work in the kitchen at the Playboy Mansion. I remember seeing him on television in that setting. He later returned to work for the Disneyland Resort in a culinary capacity. It turns out he didn't think the compensation at the Mansion was high enough. And that's when heterosexual men everywhere shouted "You're being paid in access!!!" But I digress.

The King of Pop

Even before he became Captain Eo, Michael Jackson was well-known to be a huge Disneyland fan and frequent visitor. Sometimes, he'd come in disguise, but sometimes he wouldn't. If he was recognized, which he was sure to be if he wasn't in disguise, he'd be mobbed.

One incident I (Lynn) remember clearly happened when I was not yet in Custodial, but in Foods. I worked at the Plaza Pavilion in 1992 as a Busser. The Plaza Pavilion is where the Jolly Holiday Bakery is today. The park had closed, and I was sweeping around the tables outside. I heard a group of people walking very fast as I looked up there was a group of what looked like security officers in suits around a person, and that person was Michael Jackson. It all happened so fast I just thought, "Wow!" I was a fan of his growing up in the 80's.

One Sweeper who had a much closer encounter with Michael Jackson was a cast member named Vince. It was in 1994. Vince was on Limited Work, which is what you do when you are hurt and can't perform your normal job, as the physical activity accommodates your injury. That day, Vince was passing out paychecks backstage behind Main Street. Back then, you could pick up your paper paycheck on pay day, which was Thursdays. Vince's role that day had him wearing a suit. He had heard from other cast members that Michael Jackson was walking on Main Street. Too curious to pass up the opportunity, he wanted to go check it out. He went onstage and saw what looked like dozens of Security cast members in suits. He walked right through them, and next thing he knew he was standing right next to Michael Jackson!

Vince said "hello" to him, asked him how his day was going, and told him to have a nice day. Then, Vince simply left. When Vince went backstage, some cast members asked him what was going on, and he said, "Oh, nothing." It's amazing what you can do if you're dressed right.

Another time that Jackson was being mobbed, he was there for a multi-day visit, with a boy who I (Ken) believe later was involved in abuse allegations against Jackson. I was working, minding my own business by sweeping the Small World area, and I got caught up in the mob as Jackson and his young guest made his way to and from the attraction. Suits and Security were trying to protect Jackson and his friend. I was jostled and pushed and found myself pressed towards the gloved one. I would have been pressed against him - if Craig Smith, Director of Theme Park Operations, hadn't been sandwiched between us!

Elizabeth Taylor

Described as a first by a Disneyland spokesperson at the time, Elizabeth Taylor had a private party on Thursday, February 27, 1992 to celebrate her 60th Birthday. About a thousand people attended and the party was based in Fantasyland and there was a fireworks show, while Disneyland was only doing fireworks during the Summer season and on New Year's Eve in those days.

A thousand people may sound like a lot of people, but at a place like Disneyland, it is a tiny number. On that day of the week, for that time of the year, Disneyland would typically be open for general admission from 10:00 a.m. to 6:00 p.m. with an attendance of 10,000-15,000 people. Thus, private parties could be held in the evening. Most famous people celebrating at the Resort will simply take a group around during regular operating hours. Private parties, if not a Disney event, are usually purchased by a large business or other organization.

Cleaning the Kingdom

Taylor was a friend of Michael Jackson's, who must have had some influence over her decision to have her 60th Birthday Party as a private event at Disneyland. Indeed, just a few months before, Taylor was married to her eighth husband, Larry Fortensky, at Jackson's Neverland Ranch, which itself took inspiration from Disneyland.

Usually, guests there during normal operating hours were allowed to trickle out at their own pace. If closing time was 6:00 p.m., the lines for attractions would be cut off at that time, allowing anyone already in line to experience the attraction, and the shops and restaurants would all be shuttered, except for those on Main Street. Security cast members would start at the extremities of the park and move towards Main Street as they made sure the areas behind them were clear of guests. Sometimes, if the guests were exiting too slowly, guests for a private party would be let in at the other end of the entrance turnstiles and ropes would divide the two different crowds so the party guests wouldn't mix with the still-leaving day guests. Well, in situations like this party, daytime guests were strongly encouraged not to linger. Security wanted to make sure the park was cleared and cleared relatively quickly.

Some Sweepers were hand-picked to work the event, including to pass out towels in the restrooms.

Disneyland Security did an awesome job of keeping out party crashers, including uninvited paparazzi. Invitations had a special security code. Disney asked the Federal Aviation Administration to keep the airspace restricted during the four-hour event, as airspace intrusions had been an issue during the recent nuptials. Instead, Disney provided video of the event to eager television stations to use in the news and entertainment programming.

Cast members wore wristbands in addition to having their regular ID. Disneyland cast members were assigned to accompany approved media from all over the world, members of which were wearing special bracelets.

Cleaning the Kingdom

A lot of people younger than us might wonder why there was so much fuss, but Taylor had been a child star whose stardom only grew as she beautifully aged into adulthood and through the decades of remaining in the spotlight throughout her life. Having been a star of movies and television as well as the tabloids, and raising awareness of what was one of the biggest causes of the time - fighting HIV/AIDS - having her birthday party at Disneyland, so soon after marrying a man a couple of decades younger, was a combination made in tabloid editor heaven.

The Birthday Girl was escorted by a horse-drawn white carriage. Others were transported in vintage cars. Trumpeters announced arrivals.

Barry Manilow acted as Master of Ceremonies and sang to Taylor.

We can only imagine what the bill for that party must have been.

Disney characters and other cast members mingled with party going celebrities. Mickey and Minnie were happy to see the likes of David Geffen, Jackie Cooper, Alice Faye, Ann Blyth, Robert Stack, Carrie Fisher, Michael York, Tom Selleck, Shirley Maclaine, Carl Bernstein, Dennis Hopper, Stevie Wonder, Melissa Manchester, Jon Voight, Henry Winkler, David Bowie, Cheryl Tiegs, Gregory Peck, Delta Burke, Gerald McRaney, Dionne Warwick, Joni Mitchell, Rod McKuen, Geena Davis, Eva Marie Saint, Dennis Christopher, Nolan Miller, Nicholas Roeg, John Forsythe, Linda Gray, Roddy McDowall, Marvin Davis, Rick Dees, Barry Diller, Waldo Fernandez, Sandy Callin, newspaper columnist Liz Smith, Jack Haley Jr., Earl Holliman, Tab Hunter, C. Thomas Howell, Carole Bayer Sager, Elton John, Eva Marie Saint, Jeffrey Hayden, Brian Keith, Brenda Vaccaro, Esther Williams, Jane Withers, Gladys Knight, Alan Ladd Jr., Cindy Crawford, and Richard Gere. Well, maybe not Gere.

Taylor called it the best birthday party she'd ever had.

Getting Footloose

I (Lynn) was in the Plaza Inn restrooms cleaning the sink.

I heard a voice ask me "How's it going?"

I looked up and it was singer-songwriter-guitarist Kenny Loggins. He was there that day for Disneyland's 45th anniversary and had just performed at a stage that was set up in Town Square. He seemed like a nice guy.

In the Nic of Time

Both of us have had close encounters with Nicholas Cage. Lynn's encounter was inside the Frontierland candy shop, which is now a pin store, next to the Shooting Gallery. Lynn was inside there sweeping up all the jelly beans that had fallen all over the floor, because there were these jelly bean dispensers in the store that were set up in a way that spills were common. He heard a voice asking the cast member behind the counter for some fudge. Lynn recognized that voice; it was Nicolas Cage, and his then-wife Lisa Marie Presley. It was odd that they both had white makeup on their faces. It probably wasn't the best disguise. Ken's encounter was while working around the Indiana Jones attraction and realizing the guest walking in front of him, accompanying a child, was Cage.

From the Squared Circle

What was opened as The Pond and later became the Honda Center was on World Wrestling Entertainment's circuit of venues, and some of the professional wrestling superstars would slip in for visits. I (Ken) saw Mick Foley on two different occasions, one of which he was walking around Frontierland alone with a handful of backdoor passes. Possibly a frugal man, Foley did not want to pay for a Plaid, and it appeared like fans were not impeding his enjoyment of the park. This was probably in 1999. The other time, I saw him backstage with his family.

Messing With Ego

Dustin Diamond, best known for portraying Screech in the television series "Saved By the Bell", was a frequent visitor.

During a parade clean up, a sweeper politely asked if Diamond could step to the side, off of a large piece of trash.

Diamond, perhaps jokingly, pulled out "Do you know who I am?"

The sweeper pretended not to know, at least long enough to yank Diamond's chain: "No, no I don't."

Diamond: "Do you know 'Saved By the Bell?'"

Sweeper: (pauses) "Oh, sure. You mean that *kids* show, right?" (pauses) "I'm just messing with you."

Do You Believe In Miracles?

For many years, the Children's Miracle Network Telethon was hosted by Disneyland, based at the Small World Meadows Amphitheater, better known by the name of the experience that was hosted there, Videopolis. This charity was about hospital care for children, and it was founded by the Osmond family, John Schneider, Mick Shannon, and Joe Lake. Marie Osmond, Schneider, and Merlin Olsen used to host the national portions of the telethon. Every year, they could be seen backstage at the facility. Osmond would later make regular appearances at the park in connection with selling her dolls.

Olsen and his wife had been in childbirth classes with my (Ken's) parents. I wanted to approach him with this tidbit and make him feel really old, but since we weren't supposed to approach celebrities unless they clearly needed assistance and I figured the guy was busy enough dealing with an around-the-clock television telethon broadcast, I didn't even try.

Cleaning the Kingdom

Visits From Royals

Royals, like anyone else, enjoy visits to the Magic Kingdom. Of course, their visits necessitate special protocols, especially if they are a head of government.

I (Ken) saw Sarah Ferguson, Duchess of York, twice. The first time was while she was married to Prince Andrew and second time was after their divorce. Not surprisingly, her entourage and the accompanying Disneyland staff was much reduced the second time.

Presidents and Vice Presidents

Politicians have also enjoyed this quintessentially American institution, sometimes before they were in their highest office (like Barack Obama, who visited as a child), sometimes during, and sometimes after. There's a picture of Jimmy Carter jogging through Frontierland in 1982. Truman, Eisenhower, Kennedy, and Ford all visited as adults. I (Ken) recall the visit of George H.W. Bush visited as Vice President and during his successful campaign for President. It was in September 1988, so I wasn't a sweeper yet, but I was an annual passholder. He was there for an organized event along with longtime Los Angeles Mayor Tom Bradley and California Governor George Deukmejian.

No Presidents are more associated with Disneyland than Ronald Reagan and Richard Nixon.

Reagan, as we noted, was a co-host of the television coverage the Disneyland invitation-only opening party, now cited by Disney as opening day. He also returned as California Governor and then post-Presidency in January 1990 to kick off the Disneyland 35th Anniversary celebration. I (Ken) still wasn't working there, but I was there and saw the President.

Nixon, while Vice-President, helped open the 1959 expansion that included the Submarine Voyage, Matterhorn Bobsleds, and Monorail. He was apparently very fond of

Disneyland, having visited in the opening year and at least twice in the 1960s.

To Be Clear

There was one time where I (Ken) witnessed issues with paparazzi. I remember growing up watching John Travolta on "Welcome Back Kotter", "Grease", and "Saturday Night Fever" so he was one of the first celebrities I had any concept of being a celebrity.

After years of experience as a sweeper and being so familiar with Disneyland, we'd quickly notice anything out of place. While working in New Orleans, I noticed a photographer, obviously a professional photojournalist, scrambling for a photo. His stare was riveted to Tom Sawyer Island. So I noticed Travolta, carrying his son Jett, and moving towards the raft to return to the mainland. It looked like Travolta and the entourage were trying avoid the photographer and so they changed direction and went towards another part of the island where there was an alternate dock.

I was sad to see someone scrambling to keep their kid from being photographed in a place where they had brought their child to have a good time. I understand the photographer was trying to make a living, and that Travolta and his son were in a place with thousands of other people, many of whom had cameras, but it somehow just seemed *wrong*. But whether Travolta or the photographer was to ask where the nearest restroom was, it would be our job to direct them to it.

Thomas Kinkade

We both saw Thomas Kinkade painting Sleeping Beauty Castle. Well, he wasn't painting *on* the castle but making a painting *of* the castle, for the park's 50th Anniversary. There he was, on Main Street, USA, with a small work area designated by ropes, painting away.

Cleaning the Kingdom

You never really know who or what you're going to see at Disneyland.

When Lynn Had Trouble Holding Back

I (Lynn) am a big U2 fan. I also happen to play drums. On a slow day in 2005, I was sweeping the Hub. I was planning on going to the U2 concert at the Pond (now the Honda Center), the next night.

It was a slow day.

I look up and see a few Plaids walking with the drummer from U2, Larry Mullen Jr.

I normally am not star-struck, but being a big U2 fan since I was in junior high school, I have to admit I was that time.

I didn't say anything, but I sure *wanted* to.

Pirates

Much media and many celebrities were brought to Disneyland for the world premiere of "Pirates of the Caribbean: The Curse of the Black Pearl" on Saturday, June 28, 2003. This was the first movie of the series, and Main Street, USA was turned into a giant red carpet to lead celebrities to New Orleans Square, where a giant raised viewing area had been constructed facing a giant screen on Tom Sawyer Island.

Celebrities made their way down the red carpet while the park was open to guests, some who could manage to line the area and catch a glimpse.

I (Ken) had never seen the park as thoroughly clean as it was that day. Lynn and I were working opening shifts and we kept the place spotless.

The Marrying Man

Sometimes, we could tell someone was famous even if we didn't recognize them, even if they didn't have an entourage or swarming fans. We could tell just by how they looked and behaved.

Such was the case one day when I (Ken) was working the Esplanade, and emerging from the Mickey & Friends tram area was a woman who had the looks of a model, both in physical appearance and accessories. She was wearing sunglasses and ridiculous heels, especially since she was wrangling some young children.

Then I noticed a man who was also wearing sunglasses and had good looks, as he caught up to the woman and children.

I still couldn't place either of them, so I turned to another sweeper and asked them who it was. This was something I frequently had to do if I wanted my curiosity satisfied.

The other sweeper recognized the man as Lorenzo Lamas.

Based on when this was and a couple of other clues, my guess is that the woman was Playboy Playmate and centerfold Shauna Sand, Lamas' fourth wife and mother to three of his daughters.

And the Rest

I (Lynn) have seen many others over the years, mostly just walking by. I have seen Cher, Kobe Bryant, Sylvester Stallone, Johnny Depp, Orlando Bloom, Cal Ripken Jr., Tommy Lasorda, Kelly Ripa, Regis Philbin, and many others. At times it seemed like a daily thing, if you knew where to look.

I (Ken) likewise saw many other celebrities, mostly just in passing, such as George Lucas, Carrie Fisher, Tom Hanks Robin Williams, Yeardley Smith, Luke Perry, Jennie Garth, George Wendt, Danny Bonaduce, and Gilbert Gottfried. Brad Garrett and family were being escorted by a Plaid and I saw them standing around the Tiki Room exit. Garrett's a little hard to miss. Tommy Lasorda wasn't living far from Disneyland and that's probably why Lynn saw him and I saw him twice. M.C.

Hammer was walking out of Toontown with a child on his chest in one of those baby carriers. That sight stuck out to me because I was used to seeing him dancing. It was great to see Bob Hope, who was there to turn on the Christmas lights for the season.

I was sweeping in Tomorrowland near a guest who was seated on a bench. He offered a greeting and that's when I recognized him as bombastic local sitting Congressman Bob Dornan. "Aren't you..." He was. In front of Pirates of the Caribbean, I interacted with another local conservative rabble-rouser, Wally George and his daughter (his youngest, who was still a child, not Rebecca De Mornay.)

Disney-Famous

Everyone has their own interests and hobbies. Depending on whether a sweeper was a sports fan, a porn connoisseur, or followed Wall Street, they'd get excited about seeing someone most of us wouldn't recognize.

As for me (Ken), I always got a kick out of seeing someone who'd excelled within the company by which we were employed, such as executives or Imagineers. We might see them at events geared towards news media, such as anniversary celebrations or attraction debuts, or even working on a project. If we were lucky, we'd catch them enjoying the park as guests. I was generally more excited to see "Disney-famous" people than celebrities, probably because I grew up in a neighborhood that was frequently used for location shooting for movies and television and would see child actors walking the hallways of my high school.

I very much enjoyed artist signings at the old Disney Gallery, when it was above Pirates of the Caribbean. A cast member discount sure came in handy, and with the signings in the earlier years, there were fewer restrictions and, it seemed, less hassle. This is how I was able to meet people like Colin Campbell, Claude Coats, Rolly Crump - Disney Legends.

Cleaning the Kingdom

Bob Gurr was a Disney Legend who could be seen at events such as the opening of the new Autopia (2000) or simply walking around Disneyland like anyone else, as if he hadn't been involved in the design of just about anything that moved in the park.

Whether it was a Disney Gallery event or another special event, meeting Legends Marc and Alice Davis made this enthusiast happy.

When I hired in, Jack Lindquist and Ron Dominguez were still around and in charge. Jack was the first President of Disneyland (depending on the source, C.V. Wood might have claimed that title back when the park originated). Jack had long been a major mover and shaker for Disneyland, but Disney had been short on executive titles until the 1984 arrival of Michael Eisner and Frank Wells, two outsiders, to helm to corporation. So Jack was the first President of Disneyland because the title was created in 1990 and he was appointed to it. Ron Dominguez was a member of one of the families who'd owned, and lived on, the property on which Disneyland was built. He and his family moved off the property literally as the park was starting to take shape around them, and was hired to be a cast member just before the park opened, stayed with the company, rose up in the ranks. So nobody's Disneyland roots go back further than Ron's.

The first time I met Marty Sklar, who was President of Walt Disney Imagineering at the time, was at the Splash Mountain grand opening in 1989, which was before I got my job. I bumped into him again when I was working and walking through the Adventureland restroom. It was a busy restroom and I offered to take him to a backstage restroom but he declined. He probably thought I was weird. And well, I *was.* I am.

I was fortunate to be able to talk on a personal level with Van France multiple times, and also met Dick Nunis many times. Van made it a point to tell me how important Custodial was.

One day I was working in Adventureland when I saw a familiar face checking color swatches. It was John Hench! *John*

Cleaning the Kingdom

Hench!!! Here was the guy who'd worked on Fantasia and other Animation achievements, painted official portraits of Mickey Mouse, received an Oscar for his special effects on"20,000 Leagues Under the Sea" and went on to be one of the greatest Imagineers ever. I relished opportunities to say "hello" to people like John and thank them for their contributions to the media and theme park experiences I've enjoyed, and the knowledge they shared about design. John was known to visit Disneyland as a guest and encourage other designers to do so to get the perspective of their customers.

Someone who could have benefitted more from exercising that tactic was CEO and Chairman of the Board Michael Eisner, although it might have been hard to pull off. He's a tall man, after all. He never surprised us with his presence. His visits were known about ahead of time. We were always painting the roses red when we knew he'd be around. There was one day I knew he was in the park working on something. The office radioed me and asked me to call. That always means special instructions. This time, I was told to go into Michael Eisner's trailer, which was parked by the old Administration building, and make sure it was clean. And that I did. He had a tray covered in slices of fruits and vegetables. This was after his heart trouble and surgery, and so this spread made a lot of sense.

Because of working at Disneyland, I met a Walt Disney Feature Animation background artist, Tom Woodington, at a company party. He contributed to features such as "Beauty and the Beast", "Aladdin", "The Lion King", "Pocahontas", "The Hunchback of Notre Dame", "Hercules", "Tarzan", "Fantasia 2000", "The Emperor's New Groove", "Brother Bear", and "Home on the Range". We were able to talk about the company and get perspective from each other. He was kind enough to invite me to visit him at work, which I did. If I recall correctly, he was working on "Tarzan" at the time. So there I was, getting to walk the halls of the distinctive Feature Animation building with one of the artists, and he'd point out the various producers as we saw them, asking, "Are you a big enough geek to know who that is?" Tom left this world too soon due to health issues.

Also because of working at Disneyland, I was able to go along on a working visit with Bruce Gordon and his design team who were trying to figure out how they were going to renovate Tomorrowland. This was in the very early 1990s, and the project was turned over multiple times until finally being done in 1998 (see Appendix I for more on that). I'd see Bruce Gordon from time to time as he was doing work at the Resort.

Bruce, along with David Mumford, acted like unofficial historians for Disneyland and Imagineering and were some of the most well-known Imagineers to Disney enthusiasts due to their presentations at fan events and their work on some treasured books. Like Tom Woodington, both men were taken from us too soon, but seeing Mumford or Gordon at Disneyland had always been nice and I'm thankful for those memories.

Disney Legend Tony Baxter, who I'd met during my obsessive tracking of the construction of Splash Mountain, was also someone I might see during my shift, either working, or because he was visiting the park for fun, since he was still an enthusiast after all of those years of it being his job.

Being a cast member also meant being able to see special presentations like that of the Sherman Brothers (See Chapter 2). But I also interacted with Richard Sherman and his wife as they were visiting as guests one Friday evening. I was working in Adventure/Frontier, not far from the Pirates of the Caribbean along the Rivers of America, when I saw them walking together through the crowd. I just wanted to wave and say "hi", as I'd seen presentations by the Sherman brothers (Richard and Robert) before and taken pictures with them, and felt no need to delay them with my sycophant babbling. But the Shermans stopped, smiled, shook my hand, and formally introduced themselves to me. I'd never met the Mrs., before, and she seemed really nice.

We talked about dinner options, as they were trying to figure out where to eat. I was thinking *You wrote some of the most well-known Disney songs of all time...the least Disney could do for you is host you at Club 33!*

We parted ways, with me thanking Richard again for all of the great songs I like to listen to. What better place than Disneyland Park to run into someone like that? Richard and his brother had written songs for iconic attractions long operating in that park and most cast members probably didn't recognize Richard as he strolled around. Who knows? Maybe that's the way he liked it?

With most executives at the Resort or the larger Company, encounters were few and far between. When Michael Eisner was CEO of The Walt Disney Company, I (Lynn) would sometimes hear when he was coming to the park, or that he was there, but I wouldn't see him up close. It could be obvious when he was coming because we'd have to "paint the roses red", so to speak. One night, I was walking from Haunted Mansion to New Orleans restroom, and I saw a group coming my way. It was Michael Eisner and some others. Michael was something like 6'6" so he was hard to miss. He clearly saw me coming, since this was almost park closing time and I was the only one in the walkway coming his way. I thought he might look at me and at least say "Hi." Nope. As soon as he got close to me he looked down, and kept walking. I didn't take it too personally, but I thought, "You could at least greet your cast members." Oh well.

Another time, I (Lynn), was Opening Lead in New Orleans. The area was not left in the best shape by the closing crew that previous night. The flower beds were awful as they had much trash in them. I was going around with my picker and bucket trying to get them in shape for the day.

The new President of the Resort, Matt Ouimet, who had been living at the Resort for about two weeks because he was newly moving to southern California, would be seen in the parks often. He walked up to me and asked me if I would be ready for the park to open.

I responded "Sure, but I'm not sure how great it will look over here."

"Why is that?" he asked.

I went on to tell him what a terrible job the closing crew did the night before.

He said "OK, let's try to get it moving to have it looking nice for the guests." So he *actually picked out some of the trash with me.*

I thought it was very nice of him, and that he actually cared.

I guess it got back to my managers and they were not happy about it. I didn't get in trouble but, I was told to not share our Department problems with the President of the Resort. I didn't get that because I was just being honest. Maybe I was too honest?

Matt was a great president and went on to really get the park looking nice for the 50th Anniversary. He was always seen out talking with the cast members and watching the parks.

I (Ken) can vouch for that. In those days, on weekends, Lynn was opening New Orleans/Critter Country, and I was opening Adventure/Frontier. I'd see Matt come through there before the park opened, taking a close look around. After things started getting better under his leadership, I made a point of telling him so. He was very humble about it and gave credit to everyone else.

As of this writing, Matt heads up another theme park company, which owns Knott's Berry Farm, and he's been doing great things for them.

Back to the Balcony

On that evening, waiting on the balcony of the Disney Gallery for Fantasy in the Sky fireworks and chatting with these men so eager to hear about celebrities, I noted that while we were there, over in Tomorrowland was a live show hosted by a local disc jockey going by the name Hollywood Hamilton, who did a weekly show from Tomorrowland Terrace that often featured celebrities. I was able to see Will Smith there as I

Cleaning the Kingdom

worked, during his Fresh Prince days and before his superstardom in major motion pictures.

On this particular night, I noted, comedian Sam Kinison was appearing with Hollywood Hamilton. The men said something to each other about my remark that I didn't quite catch. We shook hands and parted ways after the fireworks. Within a few days, I saw those two men on a local television talk show. Turns out the reason they were in Disneyland is that they *worked with Sam Kinison*. They went by "Doug and Dave" and Doug incorporated his muscular dystrophy into his comedy routines.

Not long after I saw them on television, they ran into me again. This time I was working at the Main Gate and they were leaving the park. They seemed as excited to see me as I was to see them. I told them I had no idea what they did for a living when I was talking with them. And thus started a friendship. I'd sign them into Disneyland, and they invited me to premiere of a 30-minute movie in which they starred, essentially as themselves. Unfortunately, Sam Kinison was killed by a drunk driver not longer after I began my friendship with Doug and Dave; surprisingly, that drunk driver was not himself! I'd see and hear Doug and Dave making appearances in various Howard Stern productions. After Doug passed, Dave and I continued to stay in contact. I remember when Dave was excited to tell me that he was working at the theater Disney owned, El Capitan, as a Disney cast member. Dave took pride in infusing his sensibilities as an entertainer into his role as essentially an operations cast member. When Custodial sent sweepers to assist operation at El Capitan (See Chapter 16), Dave would tell them he knew me.

We could meet anyone and everyone while working as a sweeper at Disneyland. As Harry Hemhauser, then the longest-employed sweeper, used to tell us, odds are we'd probably told a serial killer where the nearest restroom was. Harry always had an interesting perspective. And he's met Walt while working. That's a little hard to beat.

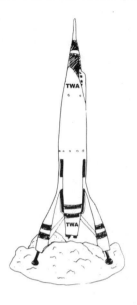

Chapter 16

Missions and Colonizations

Did you know that the Disneyland Resort is not the only place Disneyland Custodial cleans?

Introduction

Being part of the World Famous Disneyland Custodial Team, we sometimes had the opportunity to work outside of the Resort. This was not a regular occurrence, but there were times when we in Custodial took our procedures and high standards to places outside of Disneyland. It might be for a movie premiere, a parade, a show, or helping with the community. Wherever we went, the cleanliness and guest service followed.

Can You Sweep With All the Colors of the Wind?

One of the events retired longtime Sweeping Lead Vern Hoiland remembers fondly was the premiere of the animated feature "Pocahontas" in Central Park, New York City. Vern and other Disneyland Custodians went to be a part of the setup and cleanup for the movie premiere.

Walt Disney Feature Animation was on a roll with increasing success during what is now called a renaissance. "Beauty and the Beast" was topped with "Aladdin" and then "The Lion King" was wildly successful at the box office and in music and merchandise sales, along with all of the other ways the Company was capitalizing on its new intellectual property.

The powers that were decided was that the way to keep the party going was to make the premieres of the animated features big public spectacles in and of themselves, rather than simply having a bunch of celebrities walking into a movie theater on a red carpet.

In June of 1995 Disney went to Central Park, where "Pocahontas", would be shown on three 92-foot screens. It was the largest movie premiere in history, and had a live performance by Vanessa Williams. And, of course, Disney CEO Michael Eisner was there.

When the Disneyland Custodial detachment first arrived days before the event, the park was not up to Disney standards by any means. There were homeless people living in the restrooms, and those restrooms were just plain disgusting and Graffiti was plentiful.

The Disneyland Custodial crew cleaned the restrooms and the area where the premiere would take place. Later, they were told it was the cleanest it had ever looked and the City of New York wanted them to stay longer!

Cleaning the Kingdom

Tickets to sit on the lawn were free to the public, as long as people called a phone number to claim their tickets. Disney personnel estimated that 100,000 people showed up.

When it was all over with, the people were gone and left behind was tons of trash. There were huge piles of trash to clean up. It took Custodial days to eliminate the mess before they finished and came home.

Disneyland Custodial also participated in other movie premieres, including "The Hunchback of Notre Dame" in New Orleans at the Superdome. That was in June 1996.

The following June, Disneyland returned to New York for the premiere of "Hercules". This allowed Disney to call attention to the New Amsterdam Theatre, which had just been reopened after being renovated under a long-term lease. This premiere involved a very familiar thing to Disneyland Custodial: The Main Street Electrical Parade, which had recently ended its run at Disneyland in an unpredictably popular final season. A special Hercules unit was added to the parade just for this event.

Most of the lights on Broadway were turned off for the parade route.

Disney stopped sending Custodial and everyone else involved to odd locations for animated feature premieres in 1999 after the folks were sent out to a jungle for the premiere of "Tarzan" disappeared, and never to be heard from again. Go ahead and prove us wrong, if you don't believe us.

Celebrities, Sailors and Sweepers

For the extremely big-budget live action feature "Pearl Harbor", Disney really went over the top. This premiere took place on the carrier *John C. Stennis* in Pearl Harbor, Hawaii.

The ship traveled from San Diego to Hawaii with 2,500 sailors on board. Thousands of people, including the stars of the movie, watched the movie on the enormous deck of the ship on May 21, 2001. Four Disneyland Custodial Leads were sent: one each from Night Custodial and Day Custodial from each of the two theme parks. Two of them traveled on the ship from San Diego, and two flew to Hawaii. Not a bad memory for a humble jani!

El Capitan

The Company owned and operated this venue on Hollywood Boulevard, literally across the street from the famed Chinese Theater (the original one, not the one that used to have the giant sorcerer's hat structure in front of it). Especially before the Disneyland Resort got an AMC at Downtown Disney in 2001, it was the go-to place for special screenings of Disney movies along with pre-movie entertainment and related experiences, such as exhibits and interactive play areas.

If you are unfamiliar with southern California geography, Hollywood is part of the City of Los Angeles and without traffic, it was about a 40 minute drive, almost entirely on freeways, from the Disneyland Resort, which is in an entirely different county. But there's always traffic. With traffic, it was just shy of about a three day journey.

As long as they had their shots and U.S. passports, Custodial cast members could be selected to be sent to El Capitan to help keep the venue clean.

It's where Disney-owned ABC's late night talk show *Jimmy Kimmel Live!* is recorded, so it can be broadcast, uh, later, not live.

Everything's Coming Up Roses

Disney had a long history with the Tournament of Roses and what is usually called "the Rose Parade." The parade takes place in Pasadena (not the one in Texas) on New Year's Day most years, and on January 2nd if New Year's Day is a Sunday. That's a very, very busy time at Disneyland (see Chapter 10). And yet, Disneyland Custodial still sent sweepers in 2005.

Cleaning the Kingdom

As part of promoting the Disneyland 50th Anniversary, Disney had a float in that year's parade called "The Happiest Celebration on Earth." An unprecedented two-and-a-half minute kickoff show with Disneyland Resort cast members was performed in front of the float before that float led the parade. Mickey Mouse was also the Grand Marshall. Because this kickoff show involved confetti, Disneyland Custodial was there to clean up.

Rollin' Down the Highway

Disneyland Custodial adopted, for cleaning, a landscaped section of the 57 Freeway, officially California State Route 57, which runs through Anaheim. I (Ken) drove that freeway many times on my way to and from my shifts at Disneyland, but I never once pulled over to pick up a single piece of litter. Shh... don't tell anyone.

Colonization

With Disneyland being the original Disney theme park, Disneyland Custodial was called upon to help new Disney theme parks set up their Custodial teams.

Your authors were not quite hired when Walt Disney World was being built, I (Ken) was around when Disneyland Custodial's 'Top Jani", Ray Sidejas, was in France helping to get what is now called Disneyland Paris opened. Another manager, Jeff, helped out with Hong Kong Disneyland.

The biggest colonization for Disneyland Custodial during our time was Disney's California Adventure, now known as Disney California Adventure (see the difference?) Since this was going to be the second theme park at the Disneyland Resort, nobody would have to move their residence, permanently or temporarily, to help out.

Mike Sweeney, who would later become the third manager to oversee Disneyland Custodial, was actively involved in design issues as they related to Custodial, such as where the restrooms would be and how they'd be configured, and various operational issues as they related to Custodial.

In general, the two parks would be staffed by two separate teams. It wasn't like someone could expect to be sweeping in Paradise Pier one day and Tomorrowland the next. In fact, after the new park did open, when I (Ken) was working in the Esplanade, I got groused at for going through the DCA entrance to clean up something that was just past the turnstiles.

As with other Departments, before DCA opened, those of us in Custodial were given the choice of moving to DCA or staying at Disneyland.

We were assigned an appointment time to meet with managers to discuss and decide what we wanted to do. The appointments were set up according to seniority, so that the most senior cast members would get to choose first. It might have been nice if people with a certain level of seniority would've been able to "vote off the island" some people with lower seniority to make them leave Disneyland, but that wasn't how it worked.

Since this was being done by seniority, when it was our turn, the managers could tell us what our seniority would be if we moved to DCA, and based on who had already asked to move, what our seniority would be if we stayed at Disneyland. This expansion was creating many opportunities for cast members.

In my (Lynn) case it would have been easier to rise up in seniority faster if I chose DCA, because at that point I had only been in Custodial for about two years. I was unsure of what I could expect. What if DCA was a flop and my hours were cut? When you're paid by the hour, these things are very important.

I decided to stay at Disneyland and I am glad I made that choice. I still moved up in seniority, and started getting more Lead shifts, too.

As for me (Ken), I didn't agonize over it. I had recently been hired into a professional position outside the berm and working at Disneyland had shifted from being my main source of income to being my second job, a part-time involvement that was more of a hobby. What was more important to me, aside from enjoying the perks of being a Custodial cast member as explained in Chapter 2, was having a foot in the door because I still was seeking a professional position with Disney.

Plus, my heart was with the original Disney theme park.

I had been wary of DCA ever since I first heard the concept after the previous concept for a second theme park had been scrapped. It seemed like a weak concept to me, and when I first heard it, I thought it might be possible for it to be good if the execution was exceptional. However, as we saw finalized plans and the park started to take shape, my reservations were not abated.

We'd get asked by guests about the construction, and as a loyal cast member, I did my best to sell DCA and demonstrate enthusiasm on my part to get the guests interested and even excited, but most reactions were tepid at best.

I was genuinely pleased that the Resort expansion was taking place, that there was going to be a great new Disney-built hotel, and that there would be Downtown Disney and a second theme park, even if the actual park didn't appear to be compelling to me. It was also great to see that Anaheim's Resort District upgrades were making the surrounding area a lot better.

But I stayed put with Disneyland, as did our most senior Day Custodial cast members, who had little to gain from moving to DCA. The most senior hourly to make the move was a man by the name of Tom, who became the Harry Hemhauser of DCA in terms of being the most senior sweeper.

· Another person to make the switch was my pal Dale, a very enthusiastic and conscientious cast member. As a Lead, he was stickler and if you stiffed him he'd be on your case like white on a Sweeper costume. However, it wasn't long before Dale found that DCA was not to his liking, and he switched back

i

to Disneyland. Custodial leadership at DCA was disappointed, but we were happy to have Dale back at Disneyland.

The experienced sweepers who made the move to DCA had to school new hires on the ways of Disney. Casting appeared to be having some challenges filling openings not only in Custodial, but other Departments as well, since there were literally thousands of new hourly positions created by this expansion of the Resort. There was many people who were brought aboard and didn't last long. When the first-year of overcrowding didn't happen, and then when 9-11 hit tourism and the economy, it wasn't as much of a problem. More people needed jobs, after all.

For a while, the Custodial Central office in the old Administration Building served as such for both parks. That made the place very busy as clerks working Dispatch sat side by side and handled everything for both parks. On the plus side, we would see our friends who'd made the move, if only for a few minutes at the start or end of our shifts. Since our time as cast members ended, A separate Custodial Central was established for DCA, more conveniently located for those working in that park.

Today, when you visit DCA, you'll see the same level of Custodial excellence you'll find in Disneyland. Also, the park itself is a much better experience than it was when it opened, thanks to the hard work of not only cast members, but Imagineers and executives like the late Steve Jobs. It took a lot of work and a lot of money, but now there is much more to like about DCA.

Conclusion

Disneyland Custodial gained a reputation for being at the top of its game. As such, it has been asked to help in other places, giving cast members a chance to travel for work. When Euro Disneyland opened (that's Disneyland Paris, for you youngsters), it was said that sun never set on Imagineering. But what was said of Imagineering was also true for Operations, including Custodial. Whatever hour it is where you are right now, there's a "Disney Sweeper" keeping things clean and helping guests.

Cleaning the Kingdom

Chapter 17

The Empire Strikes Back

Sometimes, being world famous for successfully doing your job isn't enough.

The title of this chapter refers to the company contracted to take over some of Disneyland Custodial responsibilities.

There was a time when Disneyland Custodial consisted of a trinity: Night Custodial, Day Custodial Bussing, and Day Custodial Sweeping.

This trinity was responsible for keeping everything at Disneyland clean; everything bordered by Ball Road on the north, Harbor Boulevard on the east, Katella Avenue on the south, and West Street on and the west. There were a few motels and other businesses in the southeast corner of that rectangle and also around the northwest corner, but other than that, Disneyland Custodial handled it. The Disneyland Hotel, across West Street, was not owned or operated by Disneyland until the late 1980s.

Disneyland Custodial cleaned the parking lot. Disneyland Custodial cleaned the offices backstage. Disneyland Custodial cleaned every toilet on-property. Disneyland Custodial kept the onstage and backstage areas clean.

Night Custodial would do the heavy cleaning: hosing down walkways, doing windows, brassing King Arthur Carousel poles, vacuuming and waxing floors.

Bussing would keep the seating areas of the restaurants clean, and do Events cleaning with Sweeping. (A few restaurants had their own staff bussing).

Sweeping would keep the attractions, landscaped areas, walkways shops, and restrooms clean and do Events cleaning with Bussing.

Then things started to change.

Team Disney Anaheim, a new administration building, was built after the demolition of the Global Van Lines building, and a company called Empire was contracted to clean TDA. Outside contractors took on more of the backstage areas, including many of the backstage restrooms. Even the nighttime cleaning of Innoventions was given to outside contractors.

Innoventions was an especially touchy subject, since Day Custodial Sweeping was expected to respond to calls from Innoventions during operating hours.

With the Resort expansion came new parking areas, and the responsibility for those areas, especially overnight cleaning, being handled by contractors.

Cleaning the Kingdom

Bussing was ripped away from Custodial and taken over by Foods.

The goal of Bussing, as part of Custodial, was to keep restaurants clean. But when it was made part of the restaurant operations, it became part of a system in which the restaurant management was rewarded for bringing in profits. I (Ken) have nothing against profits, but the concerns we had as Custodians was that Bussing wouldn't get the support it needed, because they didn't directly generate revenue.

There was at least one study of the remaining Disneyland Custodial, and rumors that Custodial would be further torn apart by reverting only Night Custodial back to Facilities, and/or splitting up Day Custodial (which was Sweeping, no more Bussing by then) and assigning sweepers to managers in various locations of the park.

One of the most vocal people in expressing their concerns about these notions was Harry Hemhauser, who was the longest-employed sweeper at that time, the guy with the most seniority. Harry, Vern Hoiland, and I (Ken) had a meeting with Cynthia Harriss, who, if not the President of the Disneyland Resort at that point, was Executive Vice President. She met with us in the Disneyland Custodial conference room in the old Custodial Central, behind Casa Mexicana. Cynthia was very friendly and didn't seem the least bit condescending. She appeared to actively listen to what we had to say.

Harry and Vern were both articulate fellows, certainly not dullards or unconcerned about the world around them, as some people might picture career janitors. That no doubt helped.

One of the things we did was express our support for Ray Sidejas, Manager over Disneyland Custodial.

We truly had a sense of ownership and took pride in keeping Disneyland clean. Taking Bussing away from Custodial and giving contractors work that would have otherwise gone to Custodial Cast Members diminished that sense of ownership. For example, some sweepers would be less likely to clear some trash off of a table in break area if the responsibility for cleaning that location had been transferred to an outside company.

Fortunately, Day and Night Custodial remained together and based out of Custodial Central. Ray Sidejas remained at the top, and later lead Custodial at DCA.

Chapter 18

Apart of the Magic

How does one go from being "A Part of the Magic" to being "Apart of the Magic"? How do you leave a job like Disneyland Custodial?

Introduction

Well, sometimes you do it kicking and screaming. Literally. We had people make their last appearance as cast members while having psychotic episodes, even running down Harbor Boulevard in the middle of the night. We had people whose time with us has ended with a trip to a mental health facility.

That's not how we left.

Nor were we escorted out after accumulating far too many attendance points. Points were things you *didn't* want. The system was ridiculously lenient, and there were times it wasn't even enforced, at least for some people. Points accumulated for things like calling in sick, calling in "transportation", being late, and no-showing. Points would be removed after twelve months. Depending on their status (A, B, CR), a cast member had to stay under a certain number of points for the previous three months, six months, and twelve months. Sometimes, managers would grant an instant ADO or allow a shift change so that someone could avoid accumulating too many points.

Of course, people would use calling in sick to basically take a short vacation. Someone could call in sick for multiple shifts in a row and not accumulate more points, although after several shifts missed, a doctor's note was required. People with Casual status did not get sick pay, but for cast members who did get sick pay, it really was like taking a vacation.

The trick was not to take so much time off as to screw yourself over when you were actually sick.

Discipline was progressive. First came a verbal warning, then a written reprimand, then a three-day suspension, a five-day suspension, and then termination. Like points, discipline would drop off after a year, so if one had a verbal over a year ago, it was back to getting a verbal the next time.

It really was a lenient system, but it was also a very common way for Custodial cast members to lose their jobs. I (Ken) told new hires that if they showed up fairly regularly and didn't steal anything or assault anyone, they'd likely have a job for as long as they wanted it.

Hall of Shame

As with other workplaces, sometimes rules were convenient ways to get rid of problem employees. We had one

Cleaning the Kingdom

guy who got quite the reputation in his short time with us as a lousy worker and doing boneheaded things. One time, as his female Lead was leaning over the railing along the River to get something, he stuck his hand down the back of her pants. When she righted herself and asked him what the deal was, he claimed to be protecting her from falling into the River. She, who was fond of the fairer sex, quipped, "You might not get this, but you're the first man to have his hand down my pants in a long time!"

One day, notorious stickler Harry Hemhauser was standing at the Dispatch desk and the clerk took a call from this guy who began with something like this:

"Hey, I was just calling to make sure my buddy clocked out for me at the right time last night."

Giving someone else your ID to clock out for you was grounds for termination. Harry wasn't about to let that chance pass. He called our management's attention to the matter and the guy was vanquished.

Sleeping, even on break, was a big no-no. People did it, but being caught was grounds for termination, and some people were terminated that way.

As described in this book, when Indiana Jones Adventure opened, Sweeping had cast members dedicated to the attraction. It wasn't long before some of them figured out there was a little hidden space between the restrooms that they cleaned; the restrooms that were primarily for cast members but also available to guests who were in urgent need. There was a pipe chase between the restrooms, but past the pipe chase was a simple space. These individual sweepers made it a place to rest or even nap. It was discovered and a camera was put in place to catch the errant cast members, and those cast members did notice the camera. Nobody was fired, but they were rotated out of the assignment and that gave other sweepers the opportunity to have Indy shifts.

391

Word would spread when one of the bad apples would get terminated. Sometimes we'd shake the hand of the manager who got it done and thank them. Not only did the bad apples create more work for the rest of us, but they were a risk to the reputation of Disneyland Custodial, especially if they behaved problematically with guests.

Why Lynn Left

I decided to leave Disneyland and Southern California altogether. I had been at Disneyland for nine years in Custodial.

My wife was expecting, and we were living in a small one bedroom apartment. We tried to find a place to buy, even a condo. At that time prices were outrageous (and still are by my standards), so we had to figure out what to do.

Should we rent a bigger place?

Should we just try and make it work in our small apartment?

My wife had family in St. George, Utah, and we used to visit them every now and then. We really enjoyed how beautiful it was, how quiet, how safe it seemed, and the prices to buy a house were much more affordable.

I applied for a few jobs just to see if anything happened. We also prayed about the situation, because we wanted to be sure this was the right thing to do.

I got an interview and got a job.

We bought a house, and moved here in July 2007. Our son was only 6 weeks old at the time.

I had to quit Disneyland.

I really did enjoy the job. Yes, I complained at times, but who doesn't complain about something at their job?

It was such a fun place to work, and I had many friends I had made over the years. The experience I had gained was something that can't be learned at any other job. I still miss it today, which is partly why I started the podcast The Sweep Spot.

I think many people leave, for whatever reason, and find after they are gone, they miss it. It was like no other job. The attachment is inexplicable. I miss the music, the atmosphere, the memories, seeing others enjoy themselves, the importance I felt when cleaning the park, the nice weather, the discounts, getting to go to the park as often as I wanted, and my friends.

Who knows? Maybe I will end up back there, but I'm not planning on it.

When Ken Left

This is what I wrote in June 2015 when I left. Ray Sidejas printed it, posted it at the entrance of Custodial Central, and gave me a special pin.

* * * * *

When I came to work at Disneyland in June of 1990, it was called just Disneyland, not a "Park" or a "Resort." I was just 17. Casting was located where Cast Health is now, but it would have a stint near the Big A before it would move back on-property. I got my driver's license primarily to drive to work at Disneyland, that summer before my Senior year of high school. I was such a fan of Disney that I had passed up working at the park for Spring Break so that I could go on a family trip to Walt Disney World.

A lot has changed at Disneyland since that June, and in some cases, the more they change, the more they get back to the way they were before. I was here to see these things come and go: Performance Excellence and Empowerment Evolution, Afternoon Avenue, the Toy Story Funhouse, Light Magic, Rocket Rods, Festival of Fools, Chip & Dale's Acorn Crawl, Aladdin's Oasis Restaurant, plenty of parades and shows, Cosmic Waves, The Mighty Ducks, the Anaheim Angels and countless Cast Members (some more than once!). Paul Pressler came, and

after vowing to make THIS the Employer of Choice, he left for
The Gap.

In 1990, it cost guests $27.50 - which is $40.90 in
today's dollars - to get in the gate. We had Supervisors, not
Assistant Managers. We clocked in at Harbor House using actual
paper timecards, and then we took them to Custodial 'Control'
with us. The office was by train storage for Big Thunder
Mountain, which, by the way, had no gates in the loading area.
We might eat at the D.E.C. Leads typically started two hours
before the park opened, the park often stayed open until 1am on
Summer nights, and closed at 6pm most Monday-Thursdays in
the off-season, allowing for private parties at night. We
returned to pick up our time card at the end of our shift using
our 15 minute walk time, during which we'd put away our pan
& broom, also change into our street clothes at our personal
locker, and, if we were doing as trained, we'd go to Costuming,
across from Space Mountain in the Administration Building (it
wasn't 'Old' back then), and do a one-for-one exchange of
costume pieces - which were all white and didn't include a
"sidepack" - so that we could return to our personal locker to
put the pieces away until our next shift. If we got lazy, we'd wait
to exchange costumes until the next day before our shifts.
Taking any of the costume pieces past Harbor House - unless
you had a pass to dump the cans in the parking lot - was
grounds for termination, and typically did result in termination.
We'd stick the time card in the time clock for the punch, and
leave the card there at Harbor House, only clocking out at our
actual off time or later. Once a week, we had to stop somewhere
to pick up our paycheck. Maybe we'd stop to shop at Company
D, which was in a mobile room across from Harbor House next
to the mobile room that housed my first costume locker.

Most of us drove to work, and after we'd clocked out,
we'd make our way across the (5? 6? 7-way?) intersection-
from-hell to our car, which could be as close as where K-Lot
shuttles currently load, or as far away as where the Hyperion

Theater sits. Maybe we'd go across the street to Acapulco for a bite or drink.

A lot of people were brought on board as Casual Temporary, and they could only make Casual Regular if they were promising. They wouldn't make it past CR probation unless they were reliable and effective or very good and pretending to be. We also had annual written evaluations, delivered via a meeting with a manager.

Pin trading was done by guests only, and usually not here. Splash Mountain was a year old. We had Arthur Holmson and Mr. Green Jeans to keep us company; much more slurry and no pavers; attractions with gender-specific roles; Keel Boats; a Country Bear Theater; Big Thunder Ranch & BBQ; the Peoplemover; the Skyway; the Submarine Voyage; CircleVision 360; two floors of games at the Starcade, which was staffed by Cast Members, not contractors staffed by moonlighting sweepers; Mission to Mars; Captain Eo; a Motor Boat Cruise; a Fantasyland Autopia; The Main Street Electrical Parade; and the Tahitian Terrace. We did not have mustaches; a Pooh ride; McDonald's fry stands; cotton candy; Aladdin's Oasis; the State of California regulating our rides; lock out/tag out requirements or ride access control; Innoventions; Toontown; FastPass; FastTrack; HISTA; Buzz Lightyear; Indy; Fantasmic; sweepers moonlighting as pushy photo takers; a parking structure; TDA; Downtown Disney; the Paradise Pier Hotel; Grand Californian Hotel; or California Adventure. There were about six places in the park for a guest to get a burger, instead of three, and the shops and restaurants were open longer hours - mostly park hours. We were celebrating 35 Years of Magic with a huge parade with show stops and a giant, rigged slot machine - giving out one (and ONLY one) Geo car a day - right where the Walt Disney statue currently stands. Security was hardcore, would eject and prosecute criminals, and would even keep people with offensive attire out of the park.

We could operate packers without a key. Women usually didn't dump trash, and the guys who did had to use

Cleaning the Kingdom

either an 8-liner cart or a 2-wheel cart, and had no dolly. We didn't have sorting, we didn't even have recycling cans in the area.

Bussers were part of Custodial (though separate from Sweeping) and actually kept their own domains clean. In fact, events crews were roughly half Sweepers and half Bussers, and both Sweepers and Bussers were pulled to parade cleanups. Day Sweeping did things like polishing plaques and drinking fountains and wiping down cans as part of our opening procedures, and we actually swept out cans and picked beds as part of our closeout. Bad closeouts were rare and grounds for being chewed out. Nobody carried pickers unless they were picking beds, and yet the park stayed clean anyway. It helped that ride ops kept people from taking food into attractions. We handled all Custodial activities on property - not steady contractors. It was almost unheard of to make Lead in less than two years, and there was no "Custodial Adventureland" or "Custodial New Orleans"; they were "J27" and "J28".

Disney was headed by Michael Eisner AND Frank Wells, Jeffrey Katzenberg ran the Disney Studios, we didn't own ABC or a Cruise Line, "EuroDisneyland" was under construction, "The Little Mermaid" was new, "Beauty and the Beast" had not been released, and "Aladdin", "The Lion King", and everything that followed was still far off.

My first shift out of training was a day shift with Vern in Small World/Matterhorn. My next shift, and the rest of my Summer shifts through 1996 were in Harry Hemhauser's area – (33H and then 33F), I had the 11-7:30 shift my first Summer, which usually meant sweeping lines (Splash, Mansion, Train). Wouldn't you know it? My final shift is a day shift in Small World/Matterhorn. I knew I had been here for a long time when Ed P started talking with me. Then there were the Roll Calls when I'd look around the room and I was the person who had been a Cast Member the longest, and that's including the managers. I'll always have the fond memories of the people and the events that have made this an adventure, including the rare

Cleaning the Kingdom

times when I'd get into a little trouble. As with any place, there are some of you I'd rather not have had to deal with, but you are very rare indeed and most of you probably don't read anyway.

I'll remember how easy it was to quickly get from point A to point B before most of the doors in this place were locked with locks for which we didn't have keys; quiet Westside nights; being the Adventureland closing Lead with Joanne M being the Fantasmic Lead and making cookies and Kool-Aid; being at the top of the Matterhorn; degreasing the Space Mountain track; being in the Very Merry Christmas Parade; seeing the capsized keel boat, last performances of "Captain Eo" and "America the Beautiful", and taking the last Submarine Voyage ride; taking breaks (all legit, of course) in out-of-the-way nooks, because you can only deal with so many people for so long, especially when you are trying to read; messin' with the heads of new hires; how I made Lead because of the Armory 8 Rebellion; being hazed during my first area Lead shift, and why new Leads are not hazed anymore; the Skyhook Incident; the Dog Days of Summer; everyone who had a radio thanking Petra; my week on limited work; walking the track of Indy; watching the fireworks from behind the pilot house of the Mark Twain; riding around in the back of the pickup trucks - and once getting launched into the air due to a speed bump. I've been treated like a moron degenerate simply for being a sweeper. I've seen countless celebrities. I've found love and romance here, even proposing to my wife at the Snow White Grotto wishing well. I've seen people trying to make a family in a family park - right there in the Haunted Mansion. I remember when Francisco A. and I were rewarded for helping a ride operator run into Indy while it was operating to retrieve a guest's backpack. I remember when management did everything they could to allow as many of us as possible to attend the funeral of young Eric A after he took his own life. I remember when Custodial had a newsletter called "No Dust Required". I remember using dust, Envy, Micro Mist, Blast It, pro towels made from dead trees. I remember official Custodial parties off-site that I never attended.

Cleaning the Kingdom

Yes, it has been quite the experience being here from 6/24/1990 to 6/26/2005. I've spent a lot of my life wearing whites, and now I must move on because I can't work five days a week in the Summer, only Friday-Sunday as I have since 5/2000. But I will be around, as old Janii never die, they just become annual passholders or have friends sign them in. If you see me either around the Resort or out "beyond the berm", please feel free to say hi.

Thanks to the management folks who stick up for Custodial, the individual sweepers, and everything that made Disneyland great to begin with; and thanks to everyone who worked hard with me. A special thanks to Mary Cobb, The King, Craig N, Mel, and any scheduler or clerk who ever accommodated me and made my life easier.

I'll continue to be a Public Information Officer for the County of Los Angeles Department of Public Works, and continue to contribute to LaughingPlace.com.

I'll be spending my newfound free time sleeping in; enjoying the company of my beautiful, dear, sweet, intelligent wife - Helloooooooooo, nurse!; going places on weekends; spending my holidays with my family; and doing a million other things I haven't had time to do while working 70 hours a week, including every weekend.

As a wise man once said, "Without you, trash happens!" Is this the Happiest Place on Earth? It is if you make it that way. Strive to keep Walt's dream alive, even if those around you don't or obstruct your way. You're not just cleaning up, you are making magic. The people of this world want that old time Disney Magic, so give them as much as you can. Make sure I'll still have a great place to bring my yet-to-be-conceived kids. There is a wonderful, historical legacy here at Disneyland Custodial. Be worthy of carrying on that legacy, and carry it with all of your might. You've been a lovely audience. Thank you and goodnight.

Cleaning the Kingdom

* * * * *

The Armory 8 Rebellion to which I referred in that message is how I became a Lead. I had told management I was interested in being a Lead, but hadn't been given a radio. Then a Lead had been busted for something like calling in sick when it was obvious by his whereabouts that he wasn't. A party was held by him or in his honor and a bunch of Leads called in sick to attend the party as kind of a protest. Their loss of their radio was my gain, and the gain of others. I became Lead during the Summer season of 1996.

I (Ken) had three distinct phases of my time as a Disneyland Cast Member:

1. Dependent/Student - from June 1990 through May 1996.
2. Establishing Myself/Full-Time Devotion - from June 1996 through April 2000. Other than the Summer/Holiday/Spring Breach seasons, this was the only phase I worked full-time.
3. It's a Hobby - from May 2000 through June 2005.

Throughout those phases, I was looking to make a career with the Company, especially in show writing and design, and that is what I studied in school. In the spring of 1996 I interned with Landmark Entertainment Group. There was a Thursday that spring in which I got up in the morning, worked on the last project for a class all day and night in Orange County, not sleeping, drove Friday morning to North Hollywood to intern for Landmark Entertainment Group, then after my day there, struggled to stay awake in horrendous traffic to get to my

Cleaning the Kingdom

Friday evening shift at Disneyland. By the time I'd made it home and got into bed, it had been a 42-hour day for me.

I got my university degree, started working full-time for Custodial under the "B" classification, and looked to find a career position as I did freelance writing. There were a few possible opportunities with theme park design companies that didn't result in an offer.

At the end of the 1990s, I interviewed with Walt Disney Imagineering. The recruiter promptly left and then layoffs ensued. I needed a job that could pay me enough to live my modest lifestyle and save for the future, and working full-time plus overtime as a Disneyland Custodial Lead wasn't cutting it.

I took a new full-time salaried job in May of 2000, sure that I'd be forced to quit Disneyland. If you would have told me I'd still be at Disneyland through June of 2005, I would not have believed it. But management and the schedulers worked with me. Since I could work Friday-Sunday and any actual holidays year-round, that's what they allowed me to do. The two exceptions were the Spring Break and Year-end Holidays, which were both two weeks. They had to schedule me, and I had to call in sick for some of those shifts. I kept my attendance good enough that this wouldn't be a problem for me.

As long as I was accommodated, I stayed, because I enjoyed being there and the other perks. I'd take ERs and ADOs when offered because working seven days a week got a little draining. Mary Cobb knew she could count on me to ER, so she'd literally come through the area and tell me when I was leaving, rather than asking me when I wanted to ER.

Building on my professional experience with my new job, I tried to get a public relations or Cast Communications job at TDA, but that didn't happen. When word came down that all of us would have to work full-time in the Summer season of 2005, I had to finally call it a day.

I was very happy to be able to make it through my honeymoon in December 2004 as a Cast Member, because I took my bride to Walt Disney World for a week (she had never been, but was a huge Disney fan – especially of Snow White) and then we went on a Disney Cruise – a first cruise for both of us – for a whole week. Fun stuff. Fattening stuff.

Time Moves On

Two years after I (Ken) quit, Disneyland was ready to accommodate people like me again, as I was told by a Manager. While I would have enjoyed being an active part of that team again, it wasn't worth giving up my weekends, especially being a husband and a new father. Some of my contemporaries who'd been in the same boat did return and didn't last long.

As with any job, one needs to change with the times and adapt, or it is time to leave. From what we understand, some things have changed, and many haven't.

I (Lynn) am guessing about 2006 we got a new clock system. While we'd always had to clock in as we arrived for our shift and clock out at the end of our shift, this was different and was used as proof of taking our lunches and when we took them. We had to clock in outside the office upstairs on a counter that used to be used for Costuming. Computers were set up everywhere for us to use in the Areas. There was a computer back at New Orleans Area Locker that was in a cart type thing. For Adventureland we had to go upstairs to the breakroom. For Fantasyland, we used the computer the Attractions cast member also used inside their little closet by our Area Locker. So on, and so forth.

For Esplanade, it was the worst. We had to go through Harbor Pointe, which required a scan in and showing our ID to Security, then walk over to Harbor Pointe on the inside and use that computer. We had to clock in and out for lunches, but not breaks.

One of the drawbacks was that we had to use the computer that was in our Area. So, if we were by the Tiki Room entrance and wanted to zip across the Hub for lunch at the Inn Between, we had to go back to the Bengal Barbecue, go backstage, go upstairs, and use that computer, then hurry down stairs, through Adventureland, and over to the Inn Between. We might be delayed by guests, a spill, or whatever else, and while we were at that moment officially not being paid, were we going to ignore the need? We were supposed to you had to notify the Office so they could change our time in the computer.

That's just one example, and might sound like a small change, but many small changes add up to changing the overall work environment.

Exiting the Berm

Nobody, especially not a teenager, goes to work and hourly job in Operations at Disneyland, especially Custodial, hoping it will be their career - even if they're Disneyland enthusiasts. They do it because they need to get a job to enter the workforce, or were downsized, or hoping to get their foot into the door at the Company, or need some income or benefits, or because they're retired and need something to do.

Some people were surprised to find themselves staying longer than they thought they would; some pleasantly so, some not so much.

There were many reasons to want to stay. The perks, the stability and job security, and the benefits could be something difficult to find elsewhere.

There were also many reasons to want to leave. Some moved on to their planned career they were striving to enter, having worked at Disneyland while in college.

Some relocated for personal reasons. Some found another job they aren't excited about, but pays more, and some get fired.

I (Lynn) know many people who were just working at Disneyland until they finished school then, moved on to another job, and some stayed with Disneyland as a second job. Disneyland was a great place to work while in college. We learned so many skills that weren't specific to actual custodial work. We developed communication and interpersonal skills, decision making, patience, manners, discipline, and learned about cultural differences. It was also an interesting talking point on a resume.

There were those who didn't leave on their own terms, whether it was health issues, death, or firing.

As we already noted, poor attendance got people fired. We all needed days off every now and then, and sometimes we weren't able to ask for them weeks in advance or they were granted. Everyone had their reasons, but as long as it wasn't a habit, it wasn't a problem.

Another way to get fired was not following a safety rule. Safety was number one at Disneyland. I am not talking about just forgetting to put gloves on while working restrooms. I'm talking about major safety issues, such as walking through an attraction while it is running.

Stealing got people fired. Believe it or not, yes, some cast members did steal, whether it was money, merchandise, custodial supplies, or food. Even something in a trash can was still considered Company property. I remember having to get permission from a Manager to take home cardboard boxes. Leaving the property, our bags would be quickly checked.

Plenty of Custodial Cast Members would quit and come back to work with us again months or years later. Our buddy Vince did two separate stints as a Custodial cast member, but when the second one ended he didn't give notice at least two weeks in advance, which earns a "No Rehire" status. Giving two weeks notice was very important. A fellow Sweeper named Ralph would called me (Ken) "Two Weeks" for about five years, since he expected I'd quit.

One of the reasons I (Ken) applied to work at Disneyland even though I didn't live close is that I wanted to gain practical knowledge of the operation and design of Disneyland, and get a foot in the door of the Company. Being a Sweeper was great for the first part, but maybe not so much for the second. Although I wasn't one of them, there were Custodial cast members who became Managers in Custodial or elsewhere in Operations, or landed a position in Facilities, or in Team Disney Anaheim, the Studios, or Imagineering.

When working in Custodial became my hobby instead of my survival, I enjoyed it all the more. The fact that I willingly gave up my weekly three-day weekends to stay on board said something about the upside to being a cast member. I still have dreams in which I'm working in Disneyland Custodial again, or I've been summoned back, but I can't get past Security because I remember I had to hand over my ID to Mike Hart when I quit. I'd kept my Disneyland ID on my person at virtually all times for fifteen years.

I also remember that I'd tossed my pan (metal, of course!) into the Rivers of America, in keeping with tradition.

I (Lynn) think we could both say it was the best job we have had in terms of the fun involved in the actual work.

Every once in a while, while working, we'd hear the distinctive Custodial whistle, turn and scan the crowd, and it might be someone we used to work with, or someone who left long before we came aboard who had a few questions about who was still around. Either way, there was this feeling of brotherhood. The bonds continue. A few years ago, tired of only seeing each other at funerals, a Custodial Reunion was conducted, put together entirely by volunteers, independent of the Company. It was a huge turnout. Annual reunions have followed.

Being "Apart of the Magic" doesn't have to mean being apart from those with whom we formed friendships.

Appendix 1

The Magic Mishandled and Restored

As shocking as this may be, not everything was always done right at Disneyland.

As far as I (Ken) can tell, Disneyland has always had excellent marketing and public relations. Sometimes, things haven't lived up to the high expectations created by such great enticement.

Overview

Here's a very brief, and perhaps too simplistic overview of how things went wrong for Disneyland during our time there, and how things came back. EuroDisneyland (now Disneyland

Paris) opened in 1992 with one beautiful theme park and far too many hotel rooms for a place that is easy to access from Paris, which already had many hotel rooms. Financial difficulties resulted. The old guard of Disneyland who'd been around from the beginning, retired. The leadership of Disney Stores, which had grown rapidly (too much, it later turned out) was put in charge of Disneyland in preparation for Resort expansion. The Company's President & Chief Operating Officer Frank Wells, who'd been a very effective partner for Chairman & CEO Michael Eisner for ten years died unexpectedly in an accident. The dot-com boom took off, and institutional investors were demanding unrealistic growth. Lowering costs and increasing revenue "enough" from a mature business like Disneyland Park was extremely difficult. Ambitious Resort expansion plans were scrapped for something that ended up not being appealing enough. All of this happened in front of the ever-watching cynical eyes of the new class of online critics, who focused on what they perceived to be the negative.

So, some things got bad.

But then there was new corporate leadership, and new leadership at Disneyland. Disneyland Park was fixed up for the 50th Anniversary. When the Company acquired Pixar, it got Steve Jobs and John Lasseter, among others, who were interested in raising quality at the Resort. DCA was overhauled and expanded. The Company got its footing in what I call enthusiast relations.

Was everything horrible before? No. Is everything great now? No. But in my (Ken's) opinion, certain things were mishandled, but subsequently things were restored as much as they could be.

If you want more detail, keep reading.

The economy was booming in the mid-1990s, in part due to Internet features being newly accessed by the public. Help Wanted signs were everywhere. More retail businesses were open around the clock. This meant Disneyland Casting went from having its pick of an abundance of applicants to scrambling to find people who'd be passable as cast members. Finding, and keeping, a quality cast was apparently difficult.

Then there was the retirement of the old guard of Disneyland, including President Jack Lindquist. Jack was replaced by Paul Pressler. Paul had just been growing The Disney Store explosively. Subsequently, that part of the corporation ran into all kinds of trouble and had to shutter stores and the division was sold off to be operated by another company. But what's really important was that Paul expanded it enough that Disney Chairman and CEO Michael Eisner figured Paul was the man to steer Disneyland from being a park and hotel to being a Resort (second theme park, additional hotel(s), and retail/dining/entertainment space).

As corporate ladder-climbers are prone to do, Paul brought along people he knew to replace or subjugate the old guard.

Paul had his mandate from Michael, now untempered by Frank Wells, Michael had his mandate from Wall Street, meaning institutional investors who wanted short-term gains and demanded consistently high growth at that. Remember, these were the days where people thought "dot com" companies were going to turn them into millionaires and billionaires.

Although made a villain by many, Paul Pressler did not strike me as a bad guy. He was brought in to the Resort to do a job, and he did it. That job was expanding it to the Resort, and trying to maximize the returns from a built-out, old part of the company.

Some of the challenges for Disneyland in this era included:
- Maintenance wasn't keeping aging elements at the level some guests and cast members expected
- Struggling to hire and retain cast members who were good fits for Disneyland

- Changes in leadership and processes of the Company's design arm
- Disney enthusiasts forming online communities and networks where they could scrutinize and criticize Company offerings, policies, and management in ways not possible before.

Some of the unfortunate coinciding events included:
- A couple of fatal accidents
- Some things looking shabby when they weren't supposed to
- The expensive streetacular Light Magic lasting just one Summer season after replacing the beloved Main Street Electrical Parade
- A long-awaited, overdue overhaul of Tomorrowland that wasn't strong enough
- A second theme park that fell short of expectations

Light Magic

After starting in the 1970s, the Main Street Electrical parade was changed and expanded until it became mostly set in its look and its float roster, staying pretty much the same into the 1990s. The Walt Disney World Resort Magic Kingdom had received a new nighttime parade, called SpectroMagic, and so the obvious question was bandied about - would Disneyland Park get an overhaul to the MSEP or would it get a new experience? Surely, the same old MSEP couldn't just continue on.

A plan was finally put in place. The MSEP at Disneyland Park would be promoted as having a "farewell season" 1996, while promoting that a new experience, Light Magic, would be premiering in 1997. Disneyland cast members wore name tags touting 1996 as the farewell season for the MSEP. There were even fiber-optic signs placed at the park exits touting that Light Magic was coming in 1997, so that as people left after seeing the

Cleaning the Kingdom

MSEP for what they thought would be the last time, they could be inspired to look forward to the new show. And yes, cast members would be given Light Magic name tags in 1997.

Surely, with the new golden age of Disney Feature Animation and the advancements of technology, a magical new experience could be created featuring the rich assortment of new characters and settings, and using the latest in special effects. Instead of dwarves working away on a twinkle-light mine to the Baroque Hoedown, we could look forward to Ariel, Belle, Aladdin, Simba, and all of their friends frolicking in a potpourri of fog, projections, lasers, fiber optics, and so forth, all with catchy, endearing new theme music incorporating familiar portions of the newer hit songs. It was sure to be a big hit, right?

Right?

Well, the guests got projections, fiber optics, lots of Mylar confetti, and new music. But whatever Light Magic was, it was not quite what they expected.

The MSEP, promoted as a classic that was "glowing away" forever, kept record crowds, driven by new rides such as Indiana Jones, later in day, especially the rapidly growing number of annual passholders. In fact, just the increase in attendance over the yearly average was more than all but the select top theme parks in the world see as their total attendance in a year. The parade's public run was extended beyond the already longer-than-seasonal extension, into November. The final performances were during the Disney Family Holiday parties (for Cast Members, employees, and family) in December. The park's operating hours were extended for the duration of the parade's run. The third busiest day in park history up until then was recorded during this time.

From a marketing and financial standpoint, things were going extremely well. Simply advertising that a parade that had existed for decades was going away was enough to piggy-back on other recent additions such as the Lion King Celebration and the Indiana Jones Adventure to pack the crowds into the park. Disney was even able to sell the little lights from the parade in gussied-up boxes. Everything was going great for Disneyland management, led by former Disney Stores head, Paul Pressler.

Then, Light Magic "premiered" during an annual passholder party. At the time, then-Disneyland Resort President Paul Pressler was referring to annual passholders as "our most important guests" who were "a part of our Disney family."

The MSEP was a tough act to follow. Throw in the mix that much of the vocal element of the online Disney fan community was growing ever more hostile towards Paul Pressler and the Entertainment Department's status within the hierarchy of priorities and the resulting alterations to the park for their projects. Finally, the show (and yes, it was a show that traveled down the parade route with set stops, not a traditional parade) was not quite ready for prime time when it was premiered for the annual passholders at a fateful special party.

It would be a legendary night in park history.

Some of the most influential passholders in the crowd gave the show a thumbs-down. Some of the passholders went straight back to the shops to return the special show-related merchandise, and some went to City Hall to complain and ask for a refund. Word hit websites and discussion forums, and the bad word-of-mouth spread like wildfire. Disney even aired radio commercials featuring clips of guests talking about how much they liked Light Magic in an effort to counter the negative talk.

Understandably, Disneyland management cooled to the idea of subsequent special parties just for annual passholders.

Whether or not the show was a good one or not, that fact is that it appeared for just one season.

Here's a description of the show.

There is a brief moment of narration, and then previously unknown fairies - apparently an effort to capitalize on the enduring popularity of Tinkerbell, but considered scary-looking to some - emerge to the sounds of "Little April Shower". After that, a blast of the horn awakens the traditional Disney characters, who join the party in their pajamas. They are welcomed with "Be Our Guest". All of the music during this portion of the show is strictly instrumental, and the clogging on the part of the fairies is reminiscent of a hit stage show of those days - Riverdance.

The pixies show the Disney characters their pixie dust, which leads to more recognizable Disney music, until the arrival of rain threatens to put a damper on everything. This is when projection screens rise on the float, on which animated images are presented, accompanied by a medley of classic Disney songs, starting and ending with "When You Wish Upon a Star."

Live action shots of kids you don't know, smiling and looking up for some reason (supposedly to the stars), take over after that, to the strains of the show theme again ("Dream our dreams..."). The screens go back to where they came from. Suddenly, the show starts imitating the Ewok village celebration from the original version of "Return of the Jedi", building up to...

A fairly long sample of the Baroque Hoedown, thereby reminding everyone of what Light Magic replaced... no doubt meant as a tribute. Audience members (kids) are picked to help throw "pixie dust" at the crescendo, and Mylar confetti comes raining down on everything. This takes us back to the show's theme music, with the pixies attempting to use sign language in their choreography.

Light Magic is also the show for which the entire "Small World Mall" area was changed from a wide, flat slurried expanse to a terraced area with light towers. So, Light Magic physically changed the park as well as the relationship of the frequently-visiting online-active annual passholders with Disneyland management.

A small demonstration of an effect used in Light Magic was seen by cast members as a bit of a teaser about the show long before it debuted, and that demonstration was very impressive. Unfortunately, it didn't translate to the show itself and a wider audience.

The Mylar confetti was a lot of work for Custodial, too. It seemed like it was showing up in flower beds long after it had ceased to be used.

Tomorrowland

Sure, there was some scary science fiction, but In the 1950s and 1960s, there was much optimism in thinking about the future, too, and the 1967 overhaul of Tomorrowland benefitted both from Disney's successful presence at the 1964 World's Fair and planning for what became Walt Disney World Resort.

Time marched on, and another overhaul of Tomorrowland was needed. The world had changed, however. Disney had opened EPCOT Center in 1982, with Future World taking a serious look at the future. Outside of EPCOT Center, there was more negativity about the future.

There was an overhaul of Tomorrowland planned for 1992, then it was delayed and scrapped. Different overall approaches were considered. Then, it finally started to happen and was due to premiere in 1998. When people thought of the future in 1996 and 1997, they'd think of the annual Consumer Electronics Show or the World Wide Web. This posed a challenge.

Disneyland enthusiasts awaited an all-new exciting ride-through attraction that would use the building at the Peoplemover track, rumored to be something like the Test Track attraction at Epcot. Unfortunately, there had been many problems with Test Track, and if rumors are to be believed, the Company was relying on a sponsor for the new attraction, and that deal fell apart. Further rumors describe other corporate politics causing problems for the overhaul of Tomorrowland as well.

On May 22, 1998 the new Tomorrowland, and Rocket Rods, debuted. The ride itself was on the old Peoplemover track. The former CircleVision preshow area contained queue switchbacks among former Tomorrowland ride vehicles, including part of a Mark III Monorail. The vehicles were painted to resemble technical drawings. The circular theater had also been retained for queue switchbacks, although on the screens was a loop that consisted partly of sped-up film footage.

Continuing along through what used to be the CircleVision exit, guests would make their way down a dark, newly constructed staircase (or nearby elevator), and a newly constructed tunnel that would take them under the surface of Tomorrowland so that they could reemerge in the former Peoplemover loading structure.

Rocket Rods was presented as a futuristic mode of transport that might someday also make stops in other places around Anaheim. However, the attraction, which was opened without a sponsor, was plagued with operational, maintenance, and artistic problems and went into "hiatus" in September 2000, never to return.

The old CircleVision building was renovated into Buzz Lightyear Astro Blasters, which opened March 10, 2005.

The interior of Space Mountain was completely rebuilt, with the exact same track layout as it had since 1977, and it reopened in 2005.

In addition to Rocket Rods, a couple of the other attractions of the 1998 Tomorrowland are gone now, with Innoventions closing as we were putting this book together and Honey, I Shrunk the Audience going away a few years back.

DCA

Here's something I wrote at the end of 2001, which was DCA's opening year:

The Disneyland Resort finally blossomed and became much more or a resort than ever before. The entire feel of the area is so much different than it was before all of the construction began. With the surrounding area looking better, a beautiful new hotel in the heart of the Resort, a hot shopping, dining, & entertainment pedestrian mall that ties everything together, the weakest part of the expansion, ironically, seems to be the new theme park itself.

Some folks love Disney's California Adventure park, and the previews were packed. The problem for Disney is that there are too many people, from Average Joe Tourist, California Jane Local, Annual Passholder Tom, Cast Member Susie, to Imagineer John who think the new park is either way below Disney standards or just not attractive enough, especially at the same price as Disneyland Park. The mainstream news media has documented these sentiments, the crowds have been below expectations (September didn't help, either), and Disney has changed admission guidelines and offered special deals in response.

Here's what I wrote in November 2003 with some more perspective:

Disney's earlier ambitious plans for southern California had been scaled back and replaced with a park unlike any other Disney had built. Indiana Jones Adventure had been the last major ride-through "E" ticket attraction built at the Resort as Disney looked towards opening a whole new park.

When presented with the concept and some of the details of Disney's California Adventure park, some park enthusiasts were unimpressed. Some changed their minds once the park was open; others felt like their reservations were confirmed. Those satisfied with the plans for the new park compared it to the size and offerings of Disneyland Park, though Disneyland Park was the really the first park of its nature and opened in 1955, an entirely different era than 2001, when Disney had established experience and reputation in opening six previous major theme parks.

Attendance for the park was slow after it opened to the general public. The company officially cited weather, a bad economy, and, later, terrorist fears as the reasons for the attendance numbers. Some company insiders and enthusiasts, however, blasted the park for the attraction mix and even for the basic concept. Two prominent operating participants pulled out of the park, and it became the butt of two unnecessary, stinging jabs in the popular nationally televised prime-time series The Simpsons, the only theme park to be hammered by name - twice, no less. One of the occurrences was even repeated ad nauseam all week as a teaser for the episode. This was a sign that it was more than just nutty Disney fans who thought the park left something to be desired. The perception of the general public was that it wasn't up to par.

Accidents

Here's something I wrote in November 2003:

On Christmas Eve 1998, Disneyland Park's safety record received an unprecedented stain. For over forty-three years, no Disneyland park attraction had killed anyone known to be properly behaving, but that record came to an end with an accident that would prove fatal and would seriously injure two others and psychologically scar dozens of park guests and cast members who witnessed the accident and its aftermath. It was an easily preventable accident that some blamed on changes in operating procedures, some blamed on changes in maintenance procedures, and still others blamed on a combination of both. There were probably a few people that maintained it was an unavoidable freak accident - the case never went to trial, so the underlying cause is a matter of opinion.

The fact is, though, that this was the first time a Disneyland Park guest had been killed while simply minding their own business. Based on the Anaheim police reports, the State of California report, and the Resorts own admissions, this past [2003] September's accident on Big Thunder Mountain appears to be the second case in less than five years in which a guest died under such circumstances.

Restoration

Here is yet more I wrote in November 2003:

* * * * *

Paul Pressler, who in late 1998 had been promoted from the Disneyland Resort to oversee Walt Disney Parks and Resorts, left to be CEO at The Gap, his position-hopping finally paying off with a top spot. Of course, his departure led to the departure of many others, some of whom joined him at The Gap. Jay Rasulo, from Disneyland Paris, assumed Paul's role. Cynthia Harriss, who seemed to embrace the role of Disneyland President, left (or was removed, depending on who you believe) abruptly in October after rumors she'd be following her longtime boss, Paul, out the door that had persisted ever since he left.

Some enthusiasts and old-school insiders have been encouraged by her replacement - Matt Ouimet, and his VP, Greg Emmer. The Disneyland Resort may be entering a new era, but then again everyone ultimately still answers to Michael Eisner, who has a reputation for micromanaging and demanding significant growth. Disneyland Park is older and established, and needs renewal of an aging infrastructure.

* * * * *

Matt Ouimet and Greg Emmer proved to be great for Disneyland. It also helped on the corporate level that Bob Iger became CEO, and then when Disney bought Pixar, Steve Jobs and John Lasseter got involved.

Under Matt, things started getting repaired and restored at Disneyland again. Morale improved. He would literally walk the parks and talk with cast members, and take a close look at things. Greg did likewise.

As a result, the park got into great shape for its 50th Anniversary celebration.

Matt moved on in July 2006. In less than three years, he'd made a big difference. He eventually ended up at the top of Cedar Fair, which owns Cedar Point and Knott's Berry Farm theme parks, where he is doing some great things.

DCA has been expanded and almost completely overhauled. Attractions like Radiator Springs Racers and World of Color, and settings like Buena Vista Street have improved the quality of the park experience by leaps and bounds.

Reminiscent of 2005, in 2015, the Disneyland 60th Anniversary "Diamond Celebration" has seen Disneyland tidied up, classic attractions "plussed" (enhanced), and new nighttime shows that will last much longer than Light Magic.

Like many long established companies with intense enthusiasts, the Disneyland initially had trouble adapting to influences magnified by emerging communications made possible through Internet and smart phone technologies. Fortunately, Disneyland, along with the Company as a whole, has somewhat channeled strong enthusiasm through D23 and has made great use of social media.

Does Any of It Matter?

While it is more obvious that we need to work, it is no less true that we also need to play. I'm certain that leisure, recreation, relaxation, and entertainment help us to recharge, help us to cope, and help motivate us, allowing us to be more effective in our professions and our lives.

So, yes, Disney does matter.

That's why we care. That's why some of us are so demanding and have high expectations when it comes to what the Company produces. We think it is important, that it is worth something, that it means something, and we want to see it stay that way. We want to be able to share the wonder, share the memories, share the magic that we felt years ago with our parents, years from now with our own grandchildren.

Like many things, Disney culture is cyclical. Just as it has been a better investment at some times than other times, the productions of the Company have been better at some times than at others. There are glorious mountaintops, and then there are shadowy valleys, and sometimes there are just plain ol' plains. You can argue specifics all day and night until your muscles atrophy and you have destroyed what little social life you had (and some people do), but I don't think the general idea is something that can be denied.

What should enthusiasts do when they think the Company has fallen into a slump? Should they moan and groan all over the social network, day in and day out?

Criticism can be healthy. It can even be productive. Careful evaluation and analysis is good. We should, however, never forsake balance. We need to remember why we even care in the first place, stop and smell the roses (or, the simulated candy aroma on Main Street, U.S.A.), and escape by enjoying the parts of Disney culture for which we have high regard.

None of it would last if people weren't cleaning it, so as always, Custodial deserves thanks.

Finally, I leave you with this question: "Is there such thing as Disney magic?" and my response:

Dear Mr. Pellman-I am 8 years old. Some of my little friends say there is no Disney Magic. Papa says `If you hear in on The Sweep Spot, it must be true.' I had been looking all over social media for an answer, and I saw that some people say Disney is evil, others say Disney was once good and is now bad, and still others say Disney is just a business and exists only to make money. They all agree that there is no such thing as Disney Magic, and some of those people work for Disney! Please tell me the truth- is there Disney Magic? -Virginia O'Malley, 95 West One-Hundred Fifteenth Street.

Cleaning the Kingdom

Virginia, your little friends are wrong. Those naysayers in cyberspace are wrong - even those that work for Disney. They have been affected by the skepticism of a skeptical age, and the cynicism of a cynical world. They do not believe except they see, or sometimes, even if they do see. They live only for money and stimulation of their senses. They think that nothing can be which is not comprehensible by their little minds, held in their hands, or filling their stomachs. All minds, Virginia, whether they be adult's or children's, are little. In this great universe of ours people are like mere insects, ants, in our intellect, as compared with the boundless world about us, as measured by the intelligence capable of grasping the whole of truth and knowledge.

Your friends are caught up in a rush to lose their childlike innocence, which is something very precious indeed and to be cherished.

Yes, Virginia, there is Disney Magic. It exists as certainly as love and generosity and devotion exist, and you know that they abound and give to your life its highest beauty and joy. Alas! how dreary would be The Sweep Spot if there were no Disney Magic! It would be as dreary as if there were no Virginias. There would be no childlike faith then, no poetry, no romance to make tolerable this existence. We should have no enjoyment, except in sense and sight. The eternal light with which childhood fills the world would be extinguished.

Not believe in Disney Magic! You might as well not believe in Santa Claus! You might get your papa to hire men to audit The Walt Disney Company (and there are plenty of people who would like to!), but even if they did not see Disney Magic, what would that prove? Nobody can bottle Disney Magic, but that is no sign that there is no Disney Magic. The most real things in the world are those that neither children nor adults can prove exist, but can only experience.

You find and look over the floor plans for The Haunted Mansion, and see how everything works, but that still doesn't mean it isn't haunted. You can see how animated characters are created, but it doesn't mean they aren't real.

Virginia, Disney Magic is the serendipitous and synergistic convergence of so many different things, that it is very hard to explain. And when something is hard to explain, some people say it isn't there. But they are wrong.

Disney Magic is real. Disney Magic is more than just clever marketing. Disney Magic is more than just the side effects of too much sugar from a churro & lemon quench beverage followed by a ride on the Mad Tea Party. It is more than just your own wishes and desires playing tricks on your mind. It is something more than the hard work of thousands of very talented people originally led by charismatic visionary from Midwestern America.

Disney Magic is there when a little girl wants to learn to read because Belle likes to read. It is there when a nervous man proposes marriage to an overjoyed lady in front of a fairy-tale castle. It is there when man who is usually wearing a three-piece suit in a busy office with "Vice-President" on the door is simply "Grampa" for a day, wearing shorts, embroidered mouse ears, and a smile from ear to ear as he cruises aboard a paddlewheel riverboat

Disney Magic is there when a boy dreams of soaring through the clouds on a magic carpet, racing Aladdin, and when a girl screams with delight as she meets a cowgirl named Jessie. It is there when a child no longer fears monsters under his bed because he knows they are just doing their job. It is there when a series of drawings makes people of all ages laugh, cry, and cheer - together. The Magic is there when people from all over the world meet each other while enjoying entertainment, food, and shopping among a collection of classical architecture from many different nations, gathered in central Florida.

From colorful fireworks in the sky, to floats made from a thousand points of light depicting fantasy settings, to a nightly display of Mickey's imagination, Disney Magic abounds.

Cleaning the Kingdom

It is in the beautiful songs that play in your head because of the Disney experiences you have had - songs about love, romance, hope, faith, joy, dreams, and fun.

Virginia, Walt Disney was not the first, nor the last, to tell the story of Peter Pan. However, Disney Magic is why James T. Kirk can say "Second star to the right, and straight on 'til morning," and everyone knows what he is talking about.

Disney Magic is what distinguishes Disney from so many other things. People talk about "Disney movies", but they do not talk about "Paramount movies", or "Warner movies". Universal Studios is now part of a company called Comcast. Warner Brothers is part of a company called TimeWarner. Paramount is part of a company called Viacom. Columbia and TriStar are part of Sony. MGM, a name that once meant grand things, is now alive thanks only to a man by the name of Bond, James Bond. Disney, however, still exists - as The Walt Disney Company, no less. Disney Magic a big reason why.

It is an intangible something extra that makes Disneyland Park and other places a special experience.

It doesn't blanket everything The Walt Disney Company does, but it is present here and there, alive and well around the world thanks to those who work hard to cultivate it, and those who assist by believing in it. Yes, The Walt Disney Company is indeed a business, and it is there to make money, and some of the people there make some bad decisions. However, the company makes money best by supplying us with good doses of Disney Magic. Every company exists to make money - but every company does it by providing goods or services. There are few things better to provide than Disney Magic.

And just like there will always be villains or at least antagonists, there will always be people anywhere you go who will make bad decisions. Still, they haven't destroyed Disney Magic. It still lives.

No Disney Magic! Thank Goodness it lives, and it may live forever. A thousand years from now, Virginia, nay, ten times ten thousand years from now, it may continue to make glad the heart of children of all ages. Humanity would be blessed.

Yes, Virginia, there is such thing as Disney Magic. It only works if you let it, and works best if you believe strongly in it. Believe, Virginia.

Sincerely,
Ken

Appendix 2

How to be Safe

Did you hear about that tragic accident at your local theme park?

Are theme parks death traps? Are they run by callous people who care little about public safety? Has the push for bigger thrills gone too far?

Did you know that **you** are the one with the most control over your own safety in a theme park?

Some of the anecdotes contained in this book depict risky behavior. However, anyone who has been through

Cleaning the Kingdom

Orientation at Disney University knows that the first priority is Safety. I suppose a cynic might say the first priority is actually *profit*, because if it was really safety, the Resort wouldn't have been built in the first place. Well, perhaps. What was there before? It was farmland. There are accidents on farms. What would likely be there if not the Resort? Maybe an industrial area, maybe office buildings, maybe shopping centers, or maybe housing developments. Those places all have accidents, too.

The fact is, safety is a very high priority at the Resort. During any given busy day, there can be scores of thousands of guests and thousands of cast members on-property. There are live animals, countless automobiles, and large, heavy, complicated systems of moving parts including pieces of machinery operating for upwards of sixteen hours straight. And yet, serious injuries are rare, and deaths are very rare.

You are taking certain risks when visiting the Resort. Yes, you are. But it could be a lot less risky than many other activities you might have done instead. While we were working on this book, there was a Measles outbreak tied to Disneyland and it made a lot of news. Frankly, we're surprised this hasn't happened more often. It could happen any place where a high number of people pass through the same structures or congregate. Disneyland just happened to draw the short straw this time.

Since the attacks of 9-11, Disneyland adopted "bag check" procedures. At first, these took place in front of each of the two theme parks, but were quickly relocated to the western and eastern areas guests encounter before they reach the booths to purchase admission. That way, guests can move from one theme park to the other without having to go through the bag check process again. If the addition of DCA had been after the 9-11 attacks, no doubt the bag check processes would have been incorporated into the design of the Esplanade. As of this writing, the set-up still resembles a temporary one. While these bag checks may screen out or discourage some of the mentally ill from bringing in certain contraband, the real value is reassurance for people who don't really think these matters through. If someone who has at least half their wits about them really wants to bring in contraband, the bag check isn't going to stop them. Is that worrisome? Not really. Disneyland operated for forty-six years without these bag checks, and acts of terror were, thankfully, not a problem. Then again, many more people were flying on airliners for much longer and they could bring boxcutters on-board, and there wasn't a problem as a result of that. Until there was.

Statistically, your risks aren't from those with nefarious intentions. They are from inattentiveness, risky behavior, or mechanical failure.

Common sense goes a long way to help in at least two of those factors.

When working in Custodial or any job, it takes common sense to succeed. When I (Lynn) first became lead a friend told me you just need to use common sense and you will be a fine lead. Well that also goes for when it comes to safety.

Yes I am sure we have all done things that were not safe while working at Disneyland, but again use common sense. For instance, you're not going to go running through an attraction when it is running, or at least anywhere near the track, right? Well, most don't anyway.

There used to be days when if there was time, the Lead would let us walk through an attraction after closing time. I (Lynn) remember walking through Haunted Mansion after the park closed and collecting change on the track area. There's a slot in the flooring for the Omnimover (Doombuggy) system to flow through the attraction. Half of us would walk on each side of the slot, collect the change, and see who came up with the most at the end. Then we would throw the money in a waterway where change was collected, then donated to a certain organization depending on which well, or water passage it was.

It is my (Ken's) opinion that it took over 43 years of operation before there was a guest killed at Disneyland who did absolutely nothing to bring about his own death. Then, less than five years after that first instance, there was a second one.

The first one was to bring on new safety measures. Add in high Worker's Compensation costs, and the pursuit of safety was pushed over the top, in the opinion of some.

The Future of Theme Park Warning Signs?

You walk through your favorite theme park ride and you notice some changes. There are small signs everywhere that catch your eye.

Do not climb this tree.
Caution: Ground hard.
Warning: Curb!
Danger: Ramming person in front of you repeatedly with stroller may result in altercations.
Smoking Area - Notice warning on cigarette packaging.
The churro cart you pass has a sign that says:
Failing to chew food properly before swallowing may result in choking.
Finally, reach the entrance to your favorite ride and you notice a big sign in at least a dozen languages, Braille, an audio recording of the text in two dozen languages, and a cast member interpreting the sign into American Sign Language. The text of the sign, in English, reads:

>>>DANGER - WARNING - CAUTION<<<

In this attraction, the normal conditions of physics are still in effect, including, but not limited to, inertia, entropy, and gravity.

This ride is a high-speed turbulent, bumpy potential death machine that may shake you like a rag doll with sharp drops, sudden turns, spins, and inversions, and also features heights, darkness, cutesy music, extremely loud noises, special effects, hard walls, hard flooring, moving parts, flashing and strobing lights, potential allergens, and a shop filled with cheaply made but overpriced trinkets at the end.

Here's a list of all of the people who have developed injuries or have died while or within ten years of riding this attraction, even if this attraction couldn't possibly have been a contributing factor.

Please keep your hands, arms, feet, legs, and any other part of your body or belongings inside the vehicle, and remain seated with your behind firmly planted in the seat at all times until you are told to disembark by a certified state official presenting you with a court order. Do not hold your breath, hyperventilate, or jerk your head in a violent manner. Continue to breathe normally. If you have an asthma attack, please use your inhaler. Do not ride if intoxicated or under the influence of any controlled or illegal substances, have heart, neck, or back conditions, suffer from motion sickness, are pregnant, or have any other preexisting conditions that could be aggravated by this attraction.

Supervise your children (gee, what a concept). Should anything happen to you, during or after your experience on this attraction:

1. It will immediately be publicized to the entire park, as well as all news media outlets, who will be given unrestricted access to film you, any medical procedures being administered to you, and complete, unfettered access to our facilities.
2. Your personal lawyer and spokesperson will be immediately notified. If you do not already retain the services of such people, and can't afford them, a lawyer and a spokesperson will be appointed to you at no cost to you.

Registered nurses and surgeons are standing by in our fully equipped, on-site emergency medical facility to attend to you.

Cleaning the Kingdom

By order of the U.S. Department of Amusement Park Safety, prepare to be strapped in with a seatbelt, belts around your legs, and belts around your arms. You will be further secured with a lap bar and confined in a cage.

A Federal officer will verify that you are properly wearing the required helmet, kneepads, elbow pads, safety goggles, and flame-retardant suit.

Please have your medical records and complete medical history ready, a long with the report regarding your complete physical, including CAT, ready to present to the host and hostess to verify that you are able to experience this attraction.

Okay, so I was being a tad silly. But there is over-coverage by major media outlets on injuries, both major and minor, sustained at theme parks.

It goes back to Christmas Eve, 1998 when a freak accident took place at the dock in Frontierland in Disneyland Park, where the Mark Twain and the Columbia pick up and unload passengers. A rope pulled an eight pound metal cleat from the side of the Columbia, a replica of an early American sailing ship. The result was that one male guest received fatal head injuries, his wife received serious head injuries, and a Disneyland cast member received serious injuries to her leg and foot. Other guests and cast members suffered emotionally, including sweepers who were some of the first cast members to respond.

This accident was arguably the darkest moment in the history of the Disneyland Resort.

Ever since then, theme park accidents and injuries have received increased attention in the news media, whether or not they are mainly the fault of the guest. Even some small injuries that could have happened walking down a public street have made it to major newspapers.

Changes at the Parks

Changes were made at Disney parks meant to increase safety, or perhaps just maintain it in a world increasingly filled with careless, inattentive people and focused news media scrutiny. Disney parks have seen the addition of what I call "idiot gates" and black and yellow warning striping in loading/unloading areas. Generic signs apparently telling you to hold hands, remain seated, supervise children, and not to dance have appeared everywhere.

Then there are changes done in response to actual accidents.

For almost seven years, Roger Rabbit's Car Toon Spin treated tens of millions of people to fun without a problem. One night in September of 2000, a little boy "fell" out and was, tragically, severely injured. The ride was closed long enough that children were conceived and born before it was open again, because of state involvement. When it was reopened, the ride vehicles were heavily modified. It doesn't matter that, as far as I can tell, someone who was sitting down couldn't fall out of the vehicle the way it was before. Someone deemed the changes as necessary for protection of the guests.

And yet, on some attractions, there is little or no restraint to protect people from themselves. There's really nothing stopping anyone from leaping off back of the Mark Twain into the paddlewheel, leaping off of Tarzan's Treehouse, or getting out of the ride vehicles on Pirates of the Caribbean, It's a Small World, Haunted Mansion, or Splash Mountain. What's to stop someone from leaving their Matterhorn bobsled behind and diving from the side of the mountain?

Theme Parks Are Very Safe

Even before these changes, theme parks were very safe.

Accidents aren't increasing...you're just hearing about them more. Considering the ratio of accidental deaths and serious injuries to the number of visits per year to permanent amusement parks, and you realize that you are in far more danger traveling to and from the park than you are at the park. Take Disneyland Park, for instance. It sees 15 million visits a year, which averages out to around 341,000 people a day visiting. This isn't including the staff. For that many people in an area that is less than 100 acres, you're talking about very few accidents. It is one of the safest places on the planet.

Visiting a theme park is one of the safest of all leisure activities. Sports, rock or pop music concerts, dating - all are more risky than attending a theme park.

Theme park owners want you to make return visits, and they want you to tell everyone else what a great time you had, so they will visit, too. They certainly don't want you to be injured for life, telling everyone what happened to you and where, and they definitely don't want fatalities on their hands.

In addition to negative publicity, accidents also result in almost guaranteed lawsuits, liability issues, insurance costs, attraction downtime, clean up costs, etc.

So, if only from a purely profit-minded standpoint, theme park owners have an interest in the safety of their guests. They thoroughly test and regularly inspect their attractions, and put them through regular maintenance.

Aside from the profit motive and any state theme park regulation, other forms of regulation, such as building codes, are in effect. (Walt Disney World, it should be noted, is not subject to most of the county building codes, and instead has its own.) Also, any accident resulting in a fatality is already under the jurisdiction of the county coroner. It isn't as if theme parks aren't regulated, even if a state government does not have specific regulation of theme parks.

Safety is the top priority at Disney parks. Anyone who has been through the first day of Disney University orientation knows that. Cast members are trained to focus on safety, regardless of what their particular job is.

Cleaning the Kingdom

Disney theme parks are staffed with registered nurses and emergency medical response teams, and guests are surrounded by other people. If a guest was to have a heart attack, he would likely receive attention faster if he was at a theme park than if he was at home.

Furthermore, in addition to accidents on attractions, Disney parks also have prepared for disasters. You could be safer at a theme park than in your own home!

Still, accidents and injuries do happen at amusement parks, due to a number of factors.

What Causes Accidents and Injuries

By far, the most common factor is intentional guest misconduct, such as entering restricted areas, climbing on things, horseplay, standing up on a ride when riders are supposed to be seated, getting out of attraction vehicles, reaching out of the vehicle, or otherwise reckless behavior.

Also, assaults can and do happen in theme parks.

Guests can also cause accidents and injuries through a temporary lapse in judgment, inattentiveness, confusion, failing to heed directions, and ignoring warnings. Disneyland Park's Indiana Jones Adventure is rough and bumpy. The warning signs clearly indicate this, yet people have ridden it and then complained about those very things. People who can't handle being bounced around a little shouldn't ride it.

Operator error can cause accidents. People aren't perfect. At a major theme park, the staff is dealing with tens of thousands of people, many of which do not understand their language, interacting with complicated machinery with moving parts, and live animals. Most problems, however, are not caused by operator error.

Mechanical failure can cause accidents. Failure can occur due to shoddy parts, shoddy installation, lax maintenance, or by freak accident. Things wear out, or don't always function as they should. Very few theme park accidents are the result of mechanical failure.

However, there are usually several layers of safety that prevent injuries even if something goes wrong.

From what I understand, the fatal Disneyland Columbia accident involved the breakdown of several layers of safety, any one of which could have prevented the accident. Thankfully, procedures were revised to prevent that sort of accident from ever happening again.

What Can Be Done to Keep Your Theme Park Visits Safe

Let me make it clear that I do not consider myself a safety expert, nor am I writing on behalf of Disney or the theme park industry in general. I'm offering these observations based on experience. Consider these tips from one theme park fan to another.

Park Management

The only way the management of a theme park can guarantee that no one will ever get hurt at a park is to close it.

Seriously, are there things that theme parks can do to increase safety? Yes.

First, park security needs to be empowered and encouraged to throw out violent people. *Guests who assault other guests or cast members should never be rewarded for their behavior.* They shouldn't be treated as wronged customers who are expressing their frustration when they've crossed that line. They should be thrown out at the very least, and perhaps banned and persecuted as well.

Park security also needs to be empowered and encouraged to throw out otherwise destructive or negligent guests. When the choice comes down to ticking off a person with problematic behavior, or inconveniencing or compromising the safety of a majority of the park guests, the choice should be clear.

Theme parks also need to be sure they are attracting, hiring, properly training, and retaining competent maintenance personnel and operators. As painful as it might seem in the short term, this will probably require paying higher wages and treating employees well.

Mostly, though, the power rests with the park guest.

Guests

What can you do?

Plan ahead. Find out what kinds of attractions await you. Does anyone in your group have any conditions that you need to keep in mind? Do they have dietary or medication needs that will need to be taken care of during your visit?

Peer pressure works wonders. Disapproval of dangerous behavior discourages it. This is especially true of those who are in your group. However, if individuals or an entire group that you're not with are being hostile, reckless, or disruptive, don't play cop. Stay aware, keep clear, and make sure the proper people are informed. There's a difference between speaking up to a rude person on behalf of an employee who isn't allowed to (or in the absence of an employee) and sticking your nose where it really doesn't belong, or where it could get broken.

Parental supervision works wonders. Make sure your child is prepared:

Tell your child to do as told, and to follow what you do. Make it clear to them that when they're on a ride, they need to follow the rules and remain seated until asked to disembark. They shouldn't move to leave until you do.

Determine if an attraction is suitable for your child's temperament, size, and experience level.

Do not force your child to ride something to ride something they are afraid of. They can become irrational and hysterical, even jumping out of moving vehicles. Do not lie to the child to get them to ride. Most will grow out of their fears naturally, but forcing them into what amounts to a traumatic experience where they have no control is not the way to go, and lying to them about how "scary" something is will only diminish their trust in you.

If you are already riding an attraction and your child starts to panic, do not jump off. Seemingly harmless parts of attractions can actually be dangerous.

Observe the height restrictions and warning signs. Do not argue with, berate, insult, plead with, or try to circumvent a park host or hostess who is enforcing safety guidelines. Those guidelines are in place to protect you and your child. Neither you nor your child is an exception to the rules. The park employee is not getting paid enough to put up with such nonsense, and such behavior on your part exposes you as a bad parent and a jerk in general.

Self control works wonders:

Know your limits. Over-exertion, heat stroke, exhaustion, dehydration, lack of sleep - these are all things to look out for. Also, some people are better than others at handling rougher or more thrilling rides.

Customer demand works wonders. If you notice something that needs attention, let park management know while you are there, and follow up after your visit with an e-mail, letter, or call.

Pay attention to warning signs, observe restrictions on who should ride an attraction, and listen to directions from park workers. Take all of these things seriously. Ask questions if you do not understand something - explain your concerns.

Observe the equipment and physical condition of the facility. If it looks run down and isn't supposed to, don't ride.

Observe the operators. Are they attentive? Do they seem competent?

Remain seated until asked to disembark. Keep every part of you and your belongings in the boundaries of the vehicle.

Cleaning the Kingdom

For the love of all that's decent, do not touch, splash, or drink flume or "river" water. Rides where you are supposed to get wet have treated water, but you still shouldn't drink it, and splashing it involves putting your hand where it should not be anyway.

Listen to the operators, and do what they say, unless they are clearly confused. They know the machinery much better than you do.

In the extremely unlikely event that you are present when something goes wrong, *don't interfere.* No matter how good your intentions are, you can make things worse if you don't understand what you are doing. Follow directions instead.

Do not allow your children to climb or stand on something that isn't specifically intended for that purpose. I've seen the results of such behavior, and it ain't pretty.

Don't go anywhere you clearly aren't supposed to, or through doors marked "Employees Only", "Authorized Personnel Only", or anything similar. Do not go through doors marked "Emergency Exit" unless there is an actual emergency or you are directed to do so by a park employee. A ride breaking down is not an emergency.

Some other things you might not be thinking about when it comes to theme park safety, but should be considered anyway:

Wear sunblock. The last thing you want on your vacation is a horrible sunburn.

Theme park shows and rides are often very loud. You may want to carry hearing protection.

Wear comfortable clothing, including comfortable shoes. You're going to be walking all day. Be careful about long hair and wearing clothes that are too baggy.

Drink lots of fluids - water, first and foremost. Anything with caffeine will contribute to dehydration. Drinking too much alcohol, especially on a hot day, is not good at a theme park.

Eat healthy meals. Do not try to save money by eating too little. You are going to be working your body hard while

Cleaning the Kingdom

having all of that fun, and you need nutrients, strength, and energy. You might want to carry something like snack bars with you. If you do carry actual food with you, be mindful of spoilage so that you don't get food poisoning. Don't overeat while enjoying those themed restaurants. Don't let your kids overdo the sweets.

Wash your hands before eating anything, and after any visit to the restroom. This sounds like common sense, but plenty of guys visit the restroom and never wash their hands - just so that you know, ladies. Furthermore, just putting your hands on railing is probably exposing you to germs.

Getting back to actual ride accidents...

I believe "rider responsibility" laws can actually help reduce theme park accidents and should be supported if theme parks are going to be regulated specifically by states. Without them, people may feel free to be more reckless, assuming that it is the park's responsibility to protect them from their own gross negligence and that, even if they are injured, it will mean they'll be financially set for life. Unfortunately, their stupidity can also result in others, like you, getting injured.

There are hundreds of millions of annual park visits, and the serious injuries are so few that you're in more danger traveling to and from the theme park than you are once you are

It is my sincere wish that nobody, especially a child, be seriously injured or killed when they are supposed to be having a great time. Remember - theme parks are very safe. Disney in particular has an excellent record. But you aren't immortal, even when visiting The Happiest Place on Earth. Use common sense and pay attention, and you're almost guaranteed to never have a problem.

Disneyland Custodial has an important role in safety. Every cast member does, to be sure, but without Disneyland Custodial the park would quickly become an unsanitary place. So Disneyland Custodial does deserve much credit for Disneyland Safety.

Afterword

If your favorite theme park is clean, thank a custodian.

Being in Custodial involved much more than picking up trash, as you have seen in this book. The great men and women who work hard to help make Disneyland clean and safe come from so many different backgrounds with different goals in life, but for those four-to-ten hours every day, they have the same goal and that is one that has been the same for the past 60 years.

Disneyland Custodial is one of the proudest Departments with such a great worldwide reputation for cleanliness.

Yes, it is hard work, but at the end of the day it can be very rewarding.

Walt Disney wanted Disneyland to be a place that was different than the other amusement and theme parks; he wanted a place for families to have fun together in a safe and clean environment. We think that goal, with extremely rare exceptions, has been met day in and day out.

Once someone comes to work for Disneyland, they never see it the same way again. It is impossible. The curtain has been pulled back, and if they want the magic, they need to find it in a different way. It is still there, even if they see things with a different perspective than before. No matter how cynical, no matter how upset, no matter how much they complain, whine, shake their heads, and declare that the park is going down the tubes, most cast members have a certain pride in Disneyland Park, a certain fondness and nostalgia about it, and will do their best to keep the magic alive for the guest, the Kings and Queens of the Magic Kingdom.

Cleaning the Kingdom

Sometimes a cast member can lose sight that for people from all over the world, this is a special place. They don't know about the cast member's trials and tribulations, and they shouldn't. A cast member isn't Jane Smith from Orange with a house payment and a car that is in the shop. She's Cast Member Jane at Disneyland, the one who makes the guest's day brighter and solves any difficulties they may be having in an otherwise magical, memorable experience.

No matter how much someone has read up on it, no matter how many backstage pictures someone has seen or how many times they've actually been backstage, no matter how many friends a person has who are cast members, no matter how many times one has read fascinating books like this one, they just don't have the experience that actually working in the trenches gives a person.

There are slow times, tedious times, scary times, fun times, fast times, frustrating times, easy times, and magical moments. There is no other place like it, and being a Disneyland Custodial cast member is a unique experience.

If you want to thank a Disneyland Custodian, do so when you see them. It was encouraging when guests let us know they appreciated what we were doing and marveled at how clean the park was. Another way to thank them is by giving a compliment at City Hall or through the official website. General compliments about the park cleanliness are great, and if you want to thank individual Custodial cast members, remember their name and where and when you saw them, and what they did that caught your attention.

There is so much more that could be written about cleaning the Kingdom. We realize that this book is mostly our perspective and we were two Disneyland Day Custodial Sweepers who worked there for less than a third of the park's history. Other Sweepers have additional things to say, and Bussing and Night Custodial cast members have worthwhile perspectives, as do the counterpart Custodial cast members in DCA. We look forward to their stories, whether we get the privilege of writing them into a book or someone else gets to do that.

If you want to share your stories, or if you want to reach us for any reason, just head for the second star to the right, and straight on 'til morning. Or, find us at www.TheSweepSpot.com

Kindly gather your belongings and watch your head and step. Thank you for joining us. Have a magical day.

Glossary
How to Speak "Jani"

We used these standard radio codes frequently:

10-4 - You know this one, right? It's "Gotcha".

10-7 - "On lunch". We never said it this way. We'd say it as "Code 7".

10-9 - "Please repeat".

10-19 - The office, or Custodial Central.

10-20 - "What's your location?" Like 10-7, we'd never say it this way. Instead, we'd ask, "What's your 20?"

10-21 - "Call on the phone", as is "10-21 10-19" or "10-21 4123"

10-22 - Cancel

10-23 - Stand by

10-87 - "Meet". This would be said as "10-87" or as "87", as in "87 me at the House of the Future."

101 - The attraction is down and not operating.

102 - The attraction is down because of a serious problem.

103 - The attraction is down because of a very serious problem.

104 - The attraction is operating.

105 - The attraction is operating with reduced capacity.

106 - The attraction is back to operating with full capacity.

415 - Disturbance or fight. We'd indicated if it was verbal or physical.

Cleaning the Kingdom

904 - Fire

5150 - Mentally ill

Medical Cleanup - Blood or semen.

Code 1 - First Aid cast members requested for a minor injury or illness.

Code 2 - First Aid cast members and paramedics needed.

Code 3 - Person is dead or likely dying.

Code 4 - Situation under control.

Code H - Human Code H

Code U - Urine. May be horse, human, or whatever, since urine is pretty much urine from a Custodial perspective.

Code V - Vomit

Custodial One – Call sign of the supervising manager for the shift. Later, the park was split so a manager would be assigned to Eastside or Westside for the shift so we'd get a call from "Custodial East One".

C-27, formerly J-27 - The different Lead assignments had different numbers as call signs. C-13 was a Parade Lead. C-27 was Adventure/Frontier Lead. Formerly, it was "J" for Janitorial, then later "C" for Custodial. Then the numbers were dropped and it became "Custodial ___". Custodial Adventureland, Custodial Men's West (for Restrooms), etc.

Cleaning the Kingdom

Some of these terms were used by cast members in general, not just Custodial

A - As in, "She's an A": Someone who had the status of Regular Full-Time. Even when most of us were moved from place to place outside of our Summer Season assignments, "A"s typically stayed in the same place, with the same days off, and the same shift, except for extra days and such, until they requested a move.

ADO - Authorized Day Off. These would usually have to be requested two weeks or more in advance, before the schedules were posted. They could be granted by a manager on-demand for someone who was trying to avoid calling in "sick" or "dependent" or some similar thing.

Area - 1) A division of the park assigned to a Lead. **2)** A smaller division of a Lead's area assigned to a sweeper. **3)** Onstage, as in "He's in the area."

Area Dump – Dumping the area trash cans, as opposed to a "bullet dump".

Area Locker - A supply closet, usually mobile but rarely moved, that served as the base of Sweeping operations for a Land (Area). Some had a picnic bench & table adjacent.

Attendance - Usually used in reference to being disciplined, as in "I've been suspended for attendance." Can also refer to the projected or actual attendance at the park that day, as in "Attendance is 60K."

Attractions Host - Ride Operator or Ride Op.

B - As in, "He's a B": Someone who had the status of Regular Part-Time (Despite the designation, many "B"s worked full-time year-round, and did have benefits as permanent employees.)

Backstage - Area where guests are generally not allowed.

Backsweeping - Going against the flow of guests when sweeping a line.

Bags - Bags of Sani Sorb Bits, which were used to clean up a Code V. "I had a three-bagger today."

Ball Gate - The Security gate off of Ball Road leading to either the Team Disney Center or the northern backstage area.

Berm - Literally, the raised formation encircling the park on which the Disneyland Railroad traveled. This feature helped keep out many visual intrusions that would otherwise interfere with the settings of the various lands. The term came to be used as a symbol, as in "I'm looking for employment outside The Berm."

Boats - Cleaning boats at Pirates of the Caribbean when the park closes before midnight. "I need you to help me with boats tonight."

Breaker - A person assigned to cover the breaks of others, usually in the area.

Broom - Hand-held brooms usually used with pans. "Broom" would never refer to a pushbroom.

Bullet - A bagged trash can.

Busser - A cast member who cleaned tables and the general grounds around a restaurant / eating area.

Call - Contact via radio. This is not to be confused with calling someone on a park phone ("10-21"). We'd get calls to "10-21 10-19" or to 87 someone on our crew at the Area Locker or to clean up a Code V at an attraction exit.

Call-in - When someone calls in to say they won't be in.

Can - Trash Can

Cart - Could be 3 liner cart, 6 liner cart, 8 liner cart.

Cast Member - Someone who works at A Disney owned property.

CFA - Central First Aid

Closeout - Doing all the tasks required before going home if you're there at night.

Company - The Walt Disney Company.

Control - Security's radio base that would issue All Calls, which were calls to all radios, which would be done at park opening, park closing, when guests were cleared to the Hub and then cleared out of the park entirely. All Calls would also be made when parades started, when attractions went 101 and when they went 104, and for paramedic runs.

Costume - Uniform

Costume locker - Lockers for our costumes, and street clothes when working.

CR - Casual Regular

CS or CT - Casual Seasonal or Casual Temporary

Custodial - Includes Day and Night and formerly Bussing.

Custodian - Official name for the cast members who clean the park.

Custodial Bussing - There was a time when bussing was under Custodial. You either were a Sweeper Custodian or Bussing Custodian.

Custodial Central - The title for the main Custodial offices, a.k.a. "The Office" or "10-19". Was called "Custodial Control" for many years.

DCA - Disney's California Adventure, later Disney California Adventure (don't ask us the difference). This is the second theme park built at the Disneyland Resort and has a separate admission gate than Disneyland Park, and generally keeps a different set of cast members.

Disneyland - Since this entire book is about the Disneyland Resort, when we write "Disneyland" we mean the original theme park.

Disney University - Initial orientation.

D.O.B. - As far as we knew, this meant "dump out back", a place in the northern backstage area with a raised platform enabling hauls of trash to be unloaded into parked trucks.

Down - When an attraction is supposed to be running, but isn't.

ER - Early Release. Leaving a shift early. We'd only get paid for hours worked, so sometimes ERs were offered by management to save money, especially if attendance was under projections and/or everyone on the schedule showed up. Sometimes a sweeper would plead for an ER.

Extend - The opposite of ER.

Flower Beds - Landscaped areas, whether or not there were actually any flowers in them. Part of covering a sweeping area keeping the flower beds clean. When a sweeper is told to "do beds", it meant to pick through the landscaped areas for any trash. This was a standard task of a close-out.

Foreman - Interchangeable with Lead

Hole - Can refer to an unfilled shift in the planned schedule or the result of someone calling in, no showing, or being pulled. "I have two holes out here."

General Sweep - A basic sweep through a line or area.

Graveyard - a.k.a. Night Custodial, Third Shift

Guest Control - Cast members responsible for controlling the guests behind roped areas for a parade, show or other events. Or sometimes directing guests to a certain space or area. Most of these shifts were filled by Attractions Hosts but cast members from other Departments could fill these shifts as well, as did some Custodial Hosts/Hostesses on some occasions.

Harbor House/Harbor Pointe - Where we would go through security to gain access backstage off of Harbor Blvd. via shuttles. In earlier years, it was where our paper time cards were for clocking in and out.

Honeybucket - Usually a lidded, bagged trash can backstage where horse droppings were dumped, but a mobile honeybucket was used in certain parades.

Hub - The Central Plaza. In later usage, could refer to an online cast member information source.

Jani - A Custodial cast member. Ray Sidejas, the second person to run Disneyland Custodial, had a license plate that read "TOP JANI"

Janitorial - An earlier name for Custodial, from whence we get "jani". The thinking shifted over the years from the set of Departments being grouped under Facilities and thus having Department numbers that were of that series (Disneyland Day Custodial Sweeping was #749) to being part of Operations. Thus, it became Custodial Guest Services as we had "custody" of the areas, and our role was much more than just cleaning.

Lead / Foreman - An hourly cast member responsible for an area and cast members within that area. During our time there were many female Leads and "Foreman" might be used of them, too.

Lead Pet - Same concept as teacher's pet.

Lifer - A cast member who is destined stay the rest of their career.

Line - Queue

Locker - Area supply closet and meeting place, also the more conventional meaning.

Logs - Cleaning logs at Splash Mountain when the park closes before midnight. "I need you to help me with logs tonight." Or, a hardbound book kept in Area Lockers with blank pages for notes written by Leads.

Medical - Being off of work due to medical/health issues. "He's still out on medical."

No Rehire - "I got a 'no rehire'." A designation Disney management makes on someone's file that will prevent them from being re-hired later or by another department.

No Show - Failed to show up without (enough) warning.

Office - Custodial Central. "He went to the office to talk with Marci."

Onstage – Guest areas.

Open, Opening - As in, opening up the area.

Packer - Industrial sized trash compactor, often with pungent liquid pouring from a corner.

Pan & broom locker - A locker assigned to each cast member to store their assigned pan and broom. Most of us shared one with another cast member. Later, larger group lockers were added near Area Lockers.

The Park - Disneyland Park

Peon - An hourly person or shift other than a Lead; the people working with the Lead. "I had peon shift today, but tomorrow I will be Lead."

Picker - Used to pick up trash out of flower beds, flower planters, and little nooks and crannies.

Pipe chase - The space, usually dark and narrow, where the plumbing pipes attach to the toilets and urinals in the restrooms.

Pixie Dust - Sometimes referring to the granulated substance used to clean up a Code V or other liquids.

Cleaning the Kingdom

Plaid - Guest Relations cast members, who worked as Tour Guides, escorts, and staffed City Hall. So named because of their costume.

Pre-parade - May consist of sweeping, mopping, or collecting bigger trash items from the guest prior to the start of the parade.

Pro towels - The paper towels folded up we kept in our pouch, and before we had pouches, in a back pocket.

Points - Attendance points. These were negative things, not good things. Cast Members who accumulated too many points would be disciplined progressively: verbal, written, three-day suspension, five-day suspension, and termination.

Post-parade - Cleaning by sweeping, gathering big trash items, or using vacuums, etc. After the parade has ended.

Pulled - When you are reassigned. Usually, it is to restrooms. "You're being pulled. Go to the office."

Pushbroom - Never say "broom" if you mean pushbroom.

Queue - Line

Radio - A multi-channel walkie-talkie that allowed Leads and select others to communicate with on-duty Supervisors, the office, Security/Control, each other, and other Departments. Paramedic runs would be announced to everyone with a radio, as would parade step-offs, park opening, and park closing. If someone was stripped of their Lead status, they would be said to have "lost their radio".

Ripped - When an area or restroom is messy. "The Thunder line was ripped because we had no lines person".

Roll-call - A meeting held early in a shift in which managers discuss with the Leads what's going on that day, and Leads can discuss concerns they have.

Sani Sorb Bits – a.k.a. "Dust", "Barf Dust", or "Pixie Dust"; product used for cleaning up a Code V or a few other cleanups.

448

Cleaning the Kingdom

Shift Change - To change shifts with another cast member. It might be to a new time, day or off.

Show, Good Show, Bad Show - Our role as a cast member was that we were part of a show, the Disneyland experience is that show. Good show is when you're performing as instructed, attractions, restrooms, stores running up to Disney standards, therefore things look and sound great, bad show could mean you or an attraction, restroom, etc. does not look up to Disney standards.

Sidepack – A pouch attached to a Sweeper's belt.

Sorting – Picking bottles and a few cans out of trash taken backstage.

Split - Your assigned restrooms.

Stiff - Verb: to be lazy, to neglect one's responsibilities; Noun: Someone who is lazy or neglects their responsibilities.

Stock - Supplies, such as paper towels and cleanser.

Stock Closet - Usually for restrooms, where supplies were kept.

Stomp Board - Wooden, then later plastic square board with a handle used for light compacting of trash onstage while doing an Area Dump.

Suit - A Supervisor/Manager, although the dress code did switch to somewhat business casual.

Supervisor - Any Assistant Manager or Manager. Other than perhaps to get our annual review, all managers were our supervisors, because of the varying shifts.

Sweeper - A Day Custodial Sweeping cast member; a Custodial cast member who was not a Busser.

Sweeping - The Day Custodial Department, also the activity.

Terminate, Terminated - Fire, fired.

Third Shift/Night Crew/Night Custodial - Custodial members who worked after park hours to prepare park for the next day.

Two Weeks - As in, "I put in my two weeks." Notice of quitting.

Up - When an attraction is running. "Splash is back up."

Utility - Any work outside of the usual operating coverage. For example, scrubbing building fronts would be Utility.

Verbal - A verbal warning for a type of discipline.

Walk, Walk time - Leaving at the end of your shift and the time allotted to do it. "Go put this away, and then walk."

Written - A written reprimand, which was more serious or the next step after a Verbal reprimand. "I can't call in. I've got a written.

About the Authors

PLEASE NOTE: Nothing contained in this book may be construed to be in any way representative of our employers nor to be the opinion of our employers. This book is solely the responsibility of the authors, who produced this work independently of any employment.

Lynn Barron

I grew up in Lakewood, California, which is about 20 miles from Disneyland. I remember going to Disneyland with my Mom and Dad for the first time when I was about 5. Then over the years went with summer camps, friends and family. When I got to high school I was in marching band and we had the opportunity to march down the parade route at Disneyland. Then my jr. and senior year of high school I had an annual pass. This was before everyone had a pass. It was rare to have a friend who had one, but my friend Jon and I did and we had a blast. Then in 1991 I hired into Disneyland and worked in foods, part time at the Plaza Inn and Plaza Pavilion until 1993. I was an annual pass holder again from 1995 until 1998, and the reason I stopped being a pass holder in 1998 was, because I hired into Disneyland again and this time into Custodial. So I started in August 1998 , and glad I went into custodial because it gave me a chance to work everywhere in the park and I met some great people while I was there including my good friend and co author of this book, Ken. I quit Disneyland in 2007 and had my son Luke with my wonderful, beautiful, wife Erin. That is when we moved to Utah. I noticed that I missed Disneyland. I loved working there and like any job it had its struggles, but I actually missed the place Disneyland. I decided to start listening to Disneyland podcasts. This gave me the opportunity to stay in tune with the place I missed. One of the first podcasts I found was WEDWay Radio. After listening to their show for a year or so I started thinking about starting my own podcast. I knew I loved history and especially Disneyland history, but I wanted to incorporate my stories and experience working there too, and that is The Sweep Spot. My first choice for a co host was Ken. At the time he couldn't commit to it, but he did come on the show as a guest frequently over the next few years until in 2013 he was able to commit and is still with me today as my co host of The Sweep Spot podcast. It is then we could talk more often about doing a book on Disneyland custodial and our experiences. I remember Ken and I talking about this book when we were working together at Disneyland. So as of now the podcast has been going strong now since 2011, and has been an amazing time. Just from the podcast I have had a chance to meet and interview some amazing people including Bob Gurr, Rolly Crump, Tony Baxter, and some great people from other Disney related podcasts, authors, other former cast members.

Going to Disneyland as a child, then in high school, then as a passholder, and working there all have their own experiences, and memories, but nothing beats going there with your own child. Now our family tries to go to Disneyland at least once a year. It is such a joy seeing my son Luke experience things for the first time, that I have so much of my own memories doing. I now understand even more why Disneyland is so different, because it is for the whole family, and started out that way. Disneyland is still special to me, because of all those amazing memories, and this is why I co wrote this book with Ken. It has been such a great experience to write a book. Going through interviews with people I worked with, to doing research, to trying to remember all the events that happened while I worked there. The hardest part was to find the time to write, but thanks to my amazing wife Erin and my son Luke for having so much patience with me during this time has been a blessing. I hope everyone who reads this book can learn at least one thing about Disneyland they didn't know, and that it will showcase the amazing role that Custodial plays at The Disneyland Resort.

Today Lynn lives in St. George, Utah with his wife, son, and 3 dogs. Currently working at a middle school doing custodial work. While playing drums at church and teaching drums, and running The Sweep Spot podcast. he can be found on twitter @lynnsweepspot and email at thesweepspot@gmail.com

Ken Pellman

Ken Pellman resides with his stunningly beautiful & patient wife, their two strong-willed kids, & their elderly-but-feisty dog in sleepy, little-known Anaheim, where he hears the Disneyland fireworks every night and often sees them, too. Frequent trips to Disneyland during his childhood became much more frequent when his parents bought annual passports for the entire family in 1985, planning for the kids to get their fill of Disneyland during that year & be done with it. Instead, Ken became interested in the history of Disneyland, theme park design, & collecting Disneyana, and obsessed with the construction of the original Splash Mountain.

Soon after becoming an Original Splashtranaut, Ken joined the world of online Disney enthusiasm, becoming active on Mouse Ears BBS (and later Mickey's Kingdom BBS and Mouse House BBS), later moving on to active participation in Usenet groups focused on Disneyland and being around to witness the launch of LaughingPlace.com, urging the owners to create discussion forums on the website in the days before mainstream social networking. Ken subsequently had his columns and media reviews featured at LaughingPlace.com.

Ken became a Disneyland Cast Member in June 1990, joining the world-famous Disneyland Day Custodial Sweeping team, where eventually he met and became good friends with Lynn Barron. In June 2005, after fifteen years and two days as a Cast Member, Ken became "apart of the magic" and returned to being a Disneyland annual passport holder.

Today, Ken has over 15 years of experience as a Public Information Officer and freelances as a writer, editor, and voice talent, and of course he also co-hosts The Sweep Spot. He can be followed on Twitter @Kenversations and e-mailed at kenversations@flash.net.

Acknowledgements

Lynn

I would like to thank the following people who either helped with this book, our podcast (The Sweep Spot), I worked with, or supported me in life. My good friend and Co Author Ken Pellman who I couldn't have done this book without, has always been there for me when we worked together and to this day, My Wife Erin Barron which we had great memories going to Disneyland many times as pass holders, and now as a family and thank you for your support and patience during this book writing process and dealing with my Disneyland obsession, and my son Luke Barron the smartest, sweetest kid I know, my Mother In Law Anna for watching Luke, My Mother Jo ann, who always supported me with whatever I did, My Father Woodrow Barron Jr. who seemed to never give up, and was a good man, my sister Keri, My Grandad Woodrow Barron Sr. who loved books and wrote himself and think he would be proud of me, Phil Covey, David Smith my friend and our publisher, Russell Flores for advice and help with podcast, Anakaren Aguirre, Dennis Watcher, Bob Cobb, Vince Mitchell, Rob Goodale, Brett Filbrun, Vern Hoiland, Disneyland custodians past and present, Walt Disney, Nate Parrish, Matt Parrish , Daniel Hale, Tommy Allison, John Van Winkle , Randy Crane, Ray Hedgpeth, Billy Morton, Dale Smoot, Greg Kobziff, Jen Rice, Ernest Blair, Tommy Townsend, Jeff Baham, Aaron Robbins, Jason Calhoun, Doug Barnes, Kyle Crocker, Leon Green, Sam Gennawey, Micechat , Marci, Chris Strodder, David Koenig, Bob Gurr, Rolly Crump, Jeff Heimbuch, Chris Strodder, Tony Baxter, Mike Larsen, my custodial trainers Brian and Petra, Lorenzo, Christina, Jessie, my friends who I went to Disneyland with as kids George Molina, Scott Williamson, Jon Hines, the listeners of The Sweep Spot, and my Lord Jesus Christ for who made all this possible.

Ken

I've wanted to write this book for a long time. I don't think it would have happened without the nagging of Lynn, so I thank him for his nagging and for being my partner in crime. Thanks to everyone who has ever assisted Disneyland Custodial in fulfilling its mission, especially those of you who contributed to this book. Thanks to all the guests and cast members who made being a jani fun. Thanks to Mike Sweeney, Mary Cobb, Marci Childress, John Borders, Vern Hoiland, Harry Hemhauser for your support of me as a jani and for your inspiration. Thanks to my parents, Bill and Barbara, and to Lydia Larson, and Skip Nicholson for your instruction in English and for everything else, and thanks to Lydia again for sticking up for me when I was a third grader. Thanks to Adam Bezark, Dave Cobb, Andy Megowan, Rick West, Doobie & Rebekah Moseley, John Frost, Jeanne Granucci, Donna Guyovich, Ida Ramos, and Kurt Floren for believing in me and opening doors for me. Thank you to our publisher David Smith, Rolly Crump, Tommy Allison, and Russell Flores for your help with this book and the podcast. Thanks to my fellow Splashtranauts Jesse Prince, David Prince, James Uwins, and Bob Barber. Thanks to Frank Nosalek, Marcy Dyment, Pam Dahl, Doug Bady and Dave Lerman, Dale Smoot, Jeremiah LeCompte, Mike Vaughn and the entire "Friday night" group, Sean Kilian, Craig Arbour, Marina Janofsky, True Beck, Tony Baxter, Bruce Gordon, David Mumford, and John Stone. Thank you to Shannon for sharing childhood trips to Disneyland with me and being my best friend as long as you lived, thank you to my siblings Kim, Vicki, and Chris for everything, and thanks to Kori, Keelie, and Kyle, all my extended family whether you're family by birth or marriage, and most of all Jesus for your love.

Recommended Reading and Listening

David Koenig
Mouse Tales: A Behind-The-Ears Look at Disneyland

More Mouse Tales: A Closer Peek Backstage at Disneyland

Mouse Under Glass: Secrets of Disney Animation and Theme Parks

Realityland: True-Life Adventures at Walt Disney World

Jeff Baham – Mousetalgia Podcast
The Unauthorized Story of Walt Disney's Haunted Mansion

Nate Parrish – WEDWay Radio Podcast

Russell Flores
Seen, Un-Seen Disneyland: What You See at Disneyland, But Never See

More Seen, Un-Seen Disneyland: An Un-Official, Unauthorized Look at What You See at Disneyland, but Never Really See

Rolly Crump
Its Kind of a Cute Story by Rolly, told by Jeff Heimbuch

Lynn Barron and Ken Pellman - The Sweep Spot Podcast

Cleaning the Kingdom

Synergy Books Publishing is a full-service publisher and distributor.

Read these other fine books by Synergy Books Publishing

In the Shadow of the Matterhorn
By David W. Smith
Never-before published stories of working at
Disneyland. In addition, learn what it was like
growing up right down the street from Walt
Disney's first "Magic Kingdom." Amazing stories
About life, love, and laughter at Disneyland.

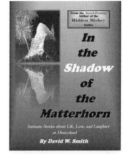

Hidden Mickey 5: Chasing New Frontiers
By David W. Smith
Mystery, treasure hunt, love story: Hidden Mickey 5
blends adventure with the lure of discovery while
at Disneyland! This final stand-alone novel of the
Hidden Mickey series takes readers to secret
locations inside Disneyland, (that really do exist!),
while following cast member Blain Walters and
international singing sensation, Malaysia Hosner
when they stumble on a 40-year-old mystery.

Seen, Un-Seen Disneyland
By Russell D. Flores
A beautifully photographed, this full-color book of so
many things that people who visit Disneyland see,
but never notice is a must-have for any Disney fan!
The intimate photographed details are meaningful
and have either historic or interesting significance.
Discover amazing facts about Disneyland and Walt
Disney!

Synergy-books.com

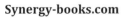

459